Shojo Beat

Komomo Confiserie

Volume 1

Story & Art by Maki Minami

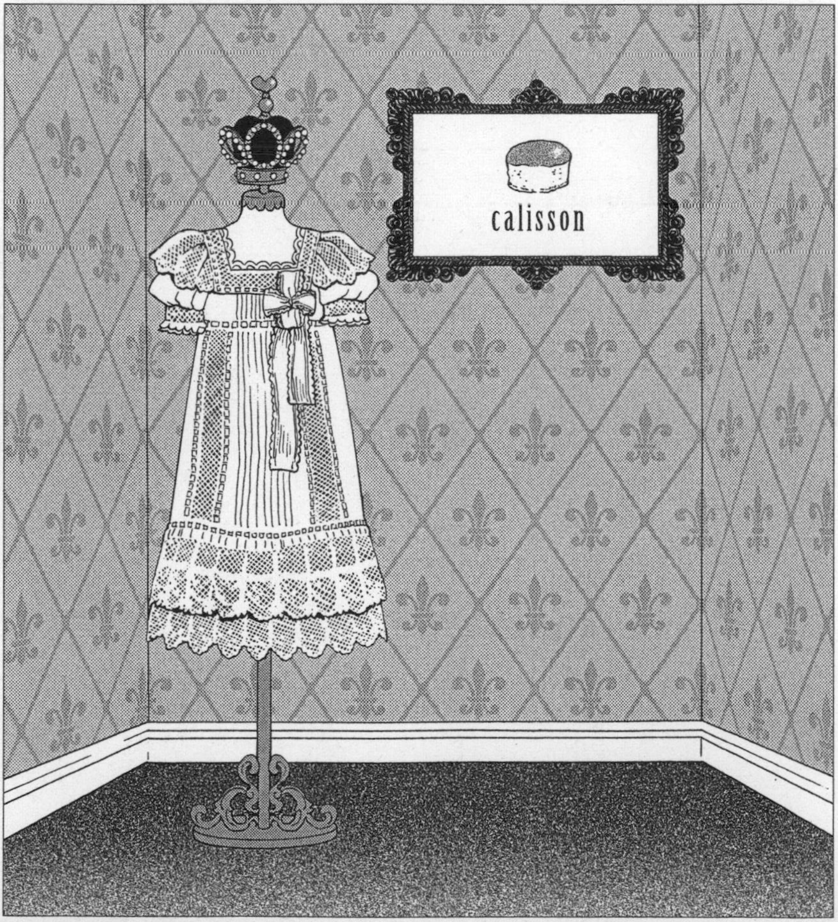
calisson

Komomo Confiserie

CONTENTS

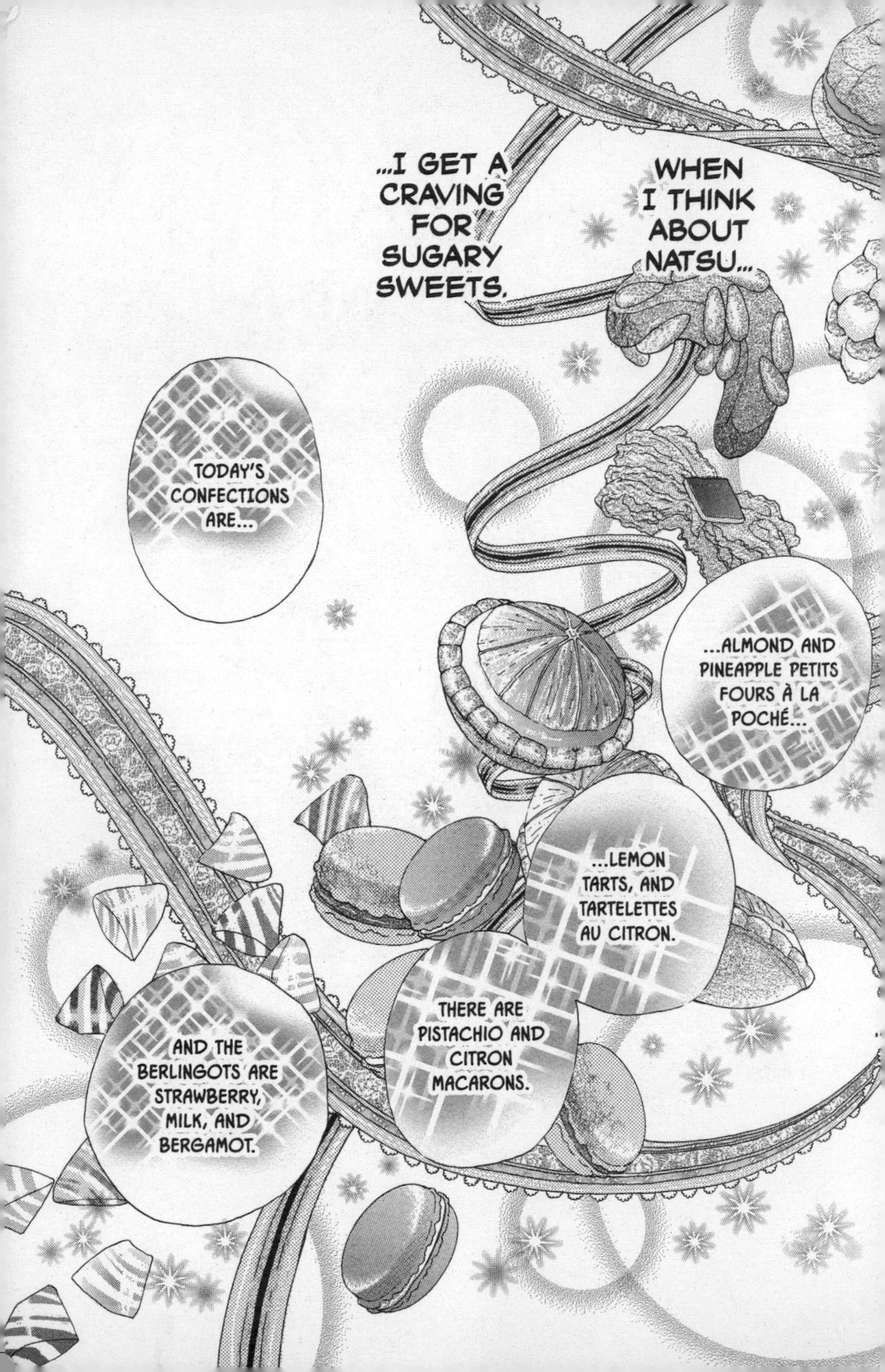
WHEN I THINK ABOUT NATSU...
...I GET A CRAVING FOR SUGARY SWEETS.
TODAY'S CONFECTIONS ARE...
...ALMOND AND PINEAPPLE PETITS FOURS À LA POCHÉ...
...LEMON TARTS, AND TARTELETTES AU CITRON.
THERE ARE PISTACHIO AND CITRON MACARONS.
AND THE BERLINGOTS ARE STRAWBERRY, MILK, AND BERGAMOT.

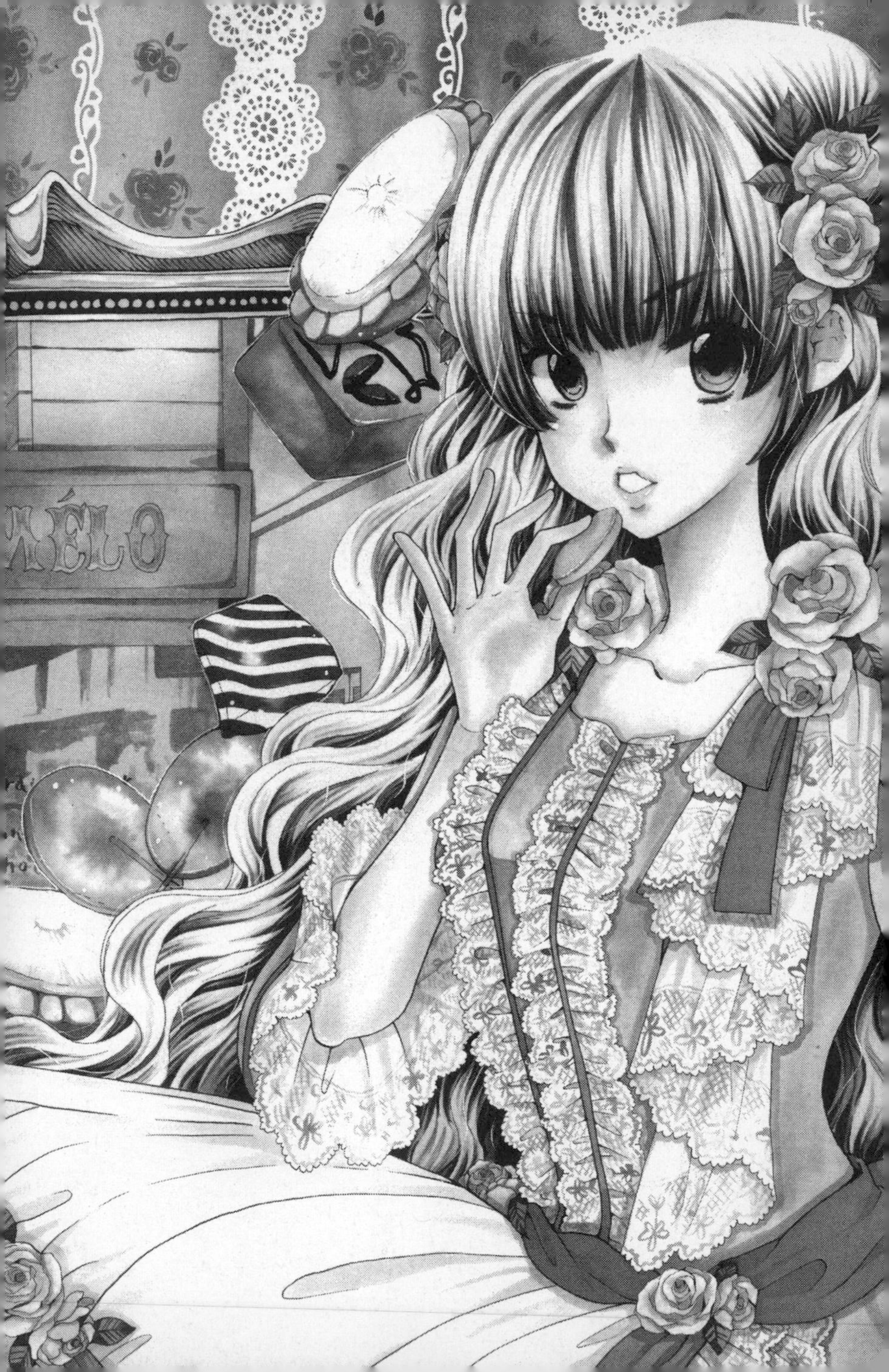

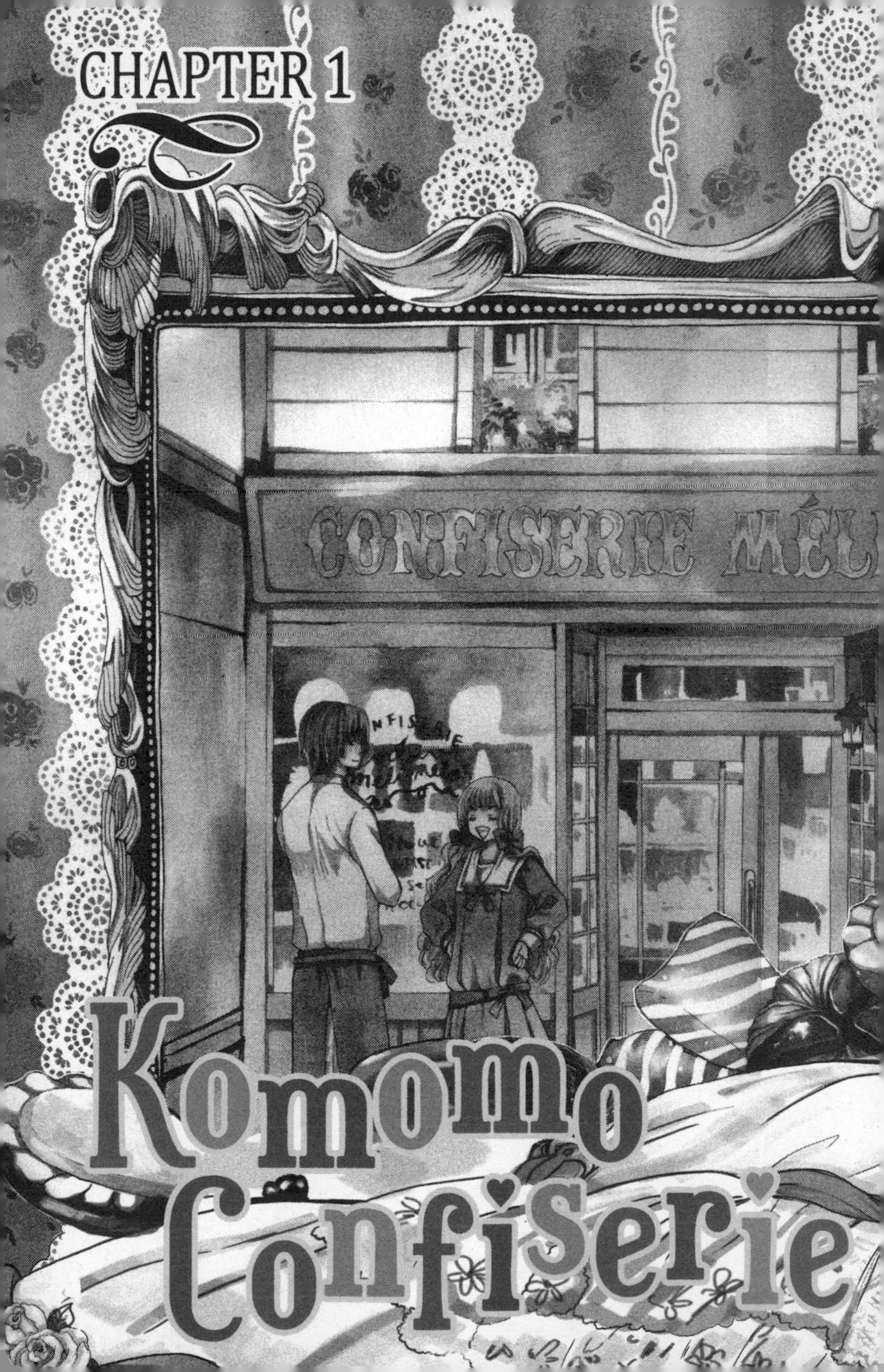
CHAPTER 1
Komomo Confiserie
CONFISERIE

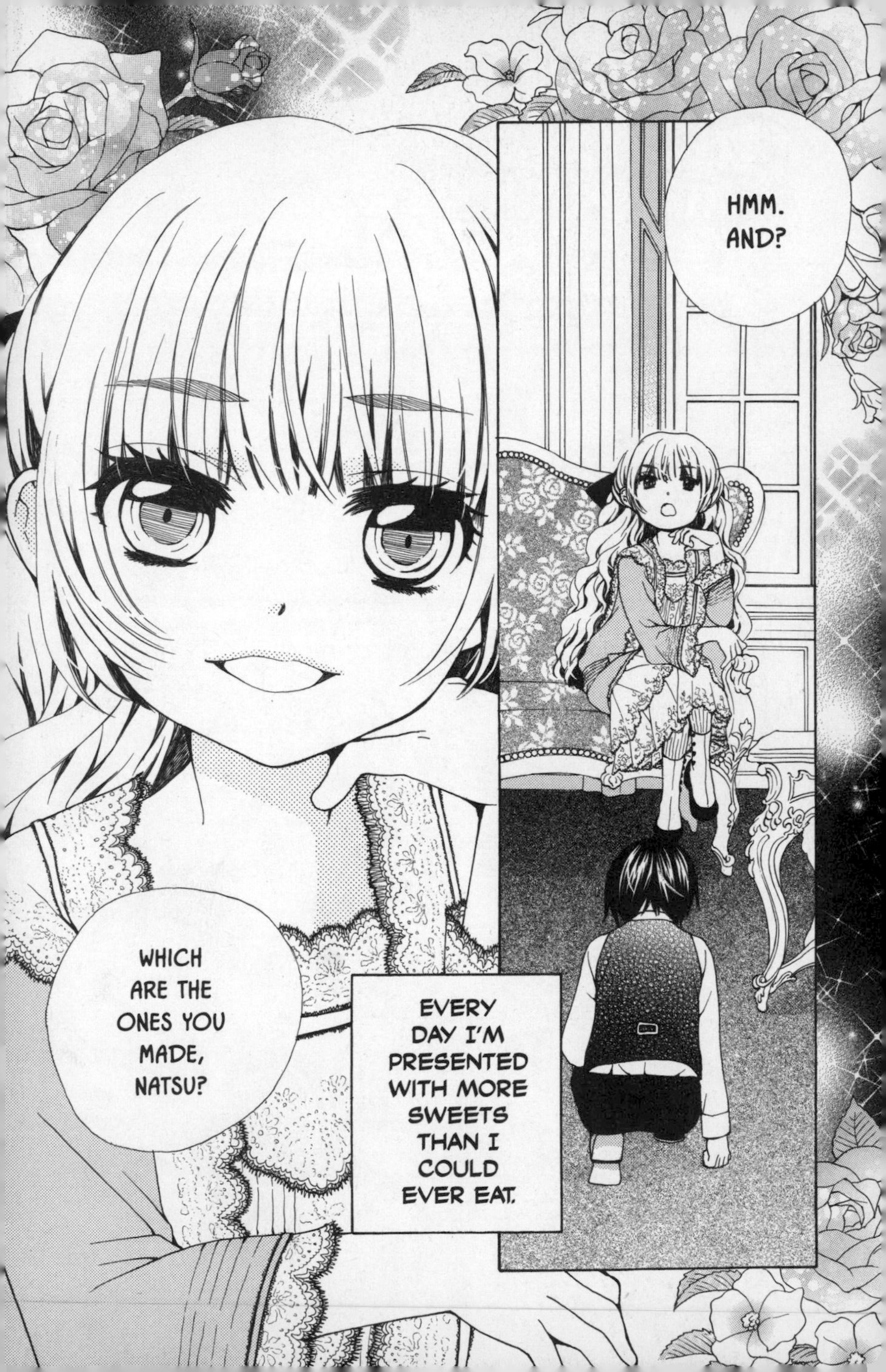
HMM. AND?
EVERY DAY I'M PRESENTED WITH MORE SWEETS THAN I COULD EVER EAT.
WHICH ARE THE ONES YOU MADE, NATSU?

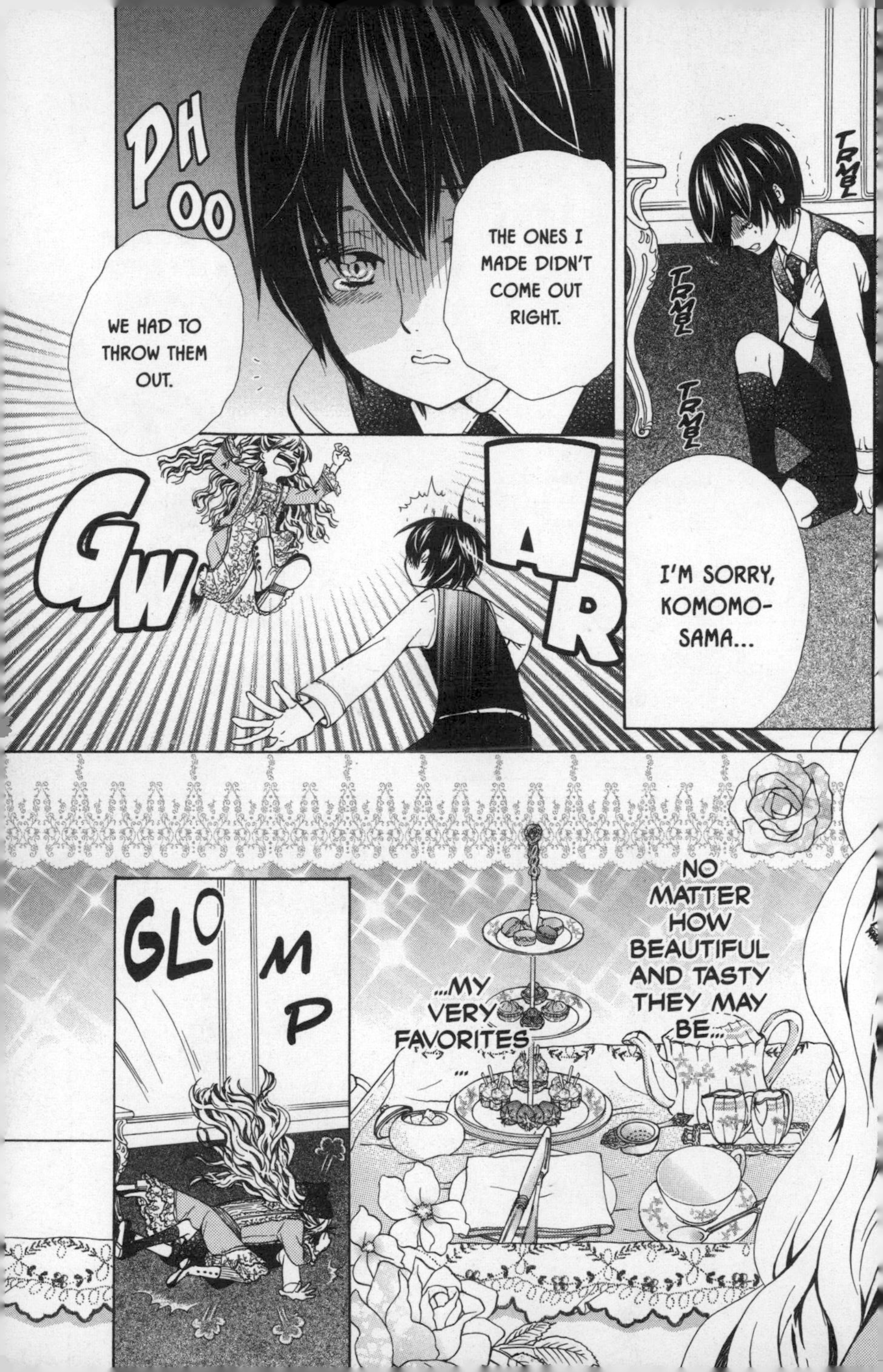
TRMBL
TRMBL
TRMBL
I'M SORRY, KOMOMO-SAMA...
PHOO
THE ONES I MADE DIDN'T COME OUT RIGHT.
WE HAD TO THROW THEM OUT.
GWAR
NO MATTER HOW BEAUTIFUL AND TASTY THEY MAY BE...
...MY VERY FAVORITES ...
GLOMP

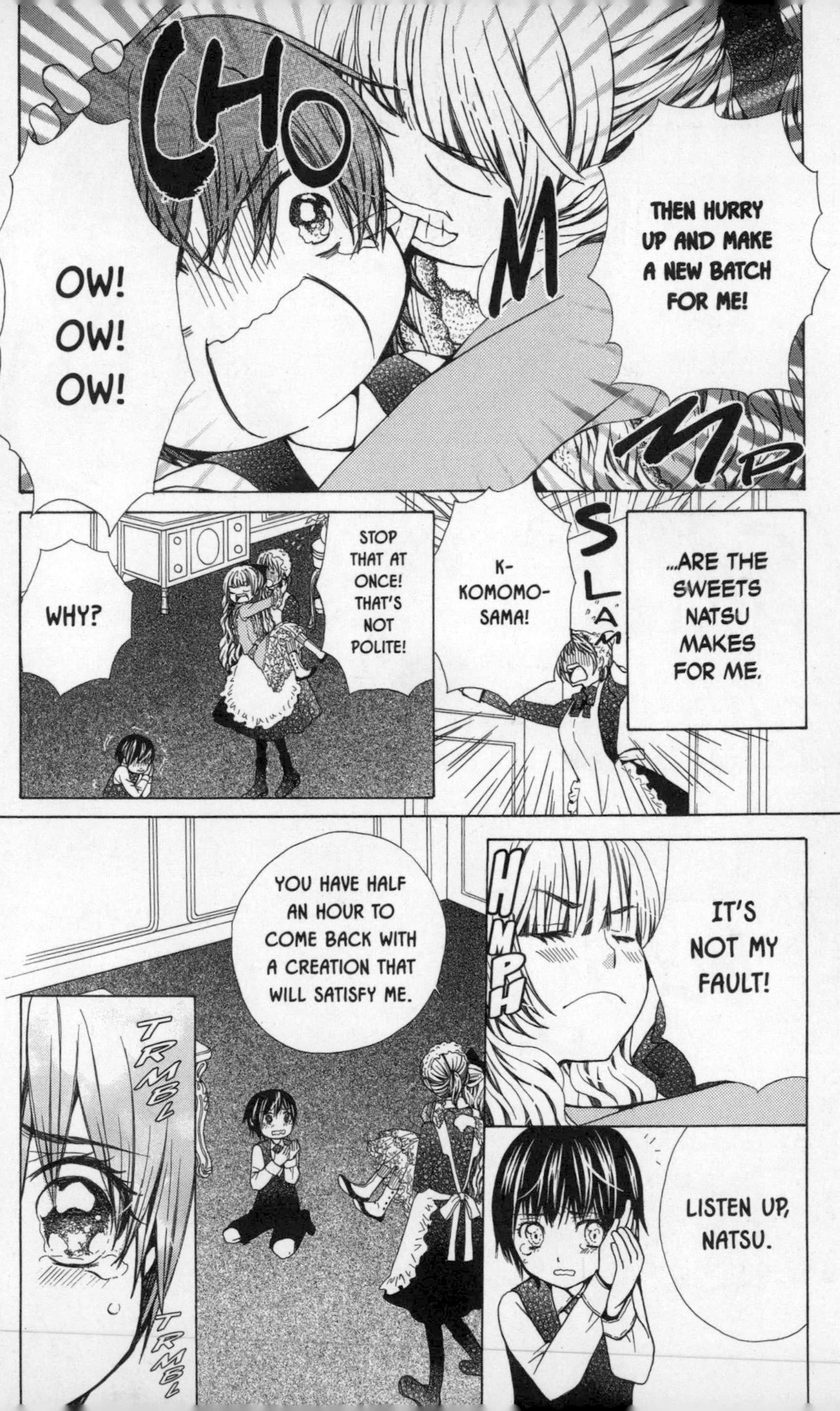
THEN HURRY UP AND MAKE A NEW BATCH FOR ME!
CHOMP
OW! OW! OW!
...ARE THE SWEETS NATSU MAKES FOR ME.
SLAM
K-KOMOMO-SAMA!
STOP THAT AT ONCE! THAT'S NOT POLITE!
WHY?
IT'S NOT MY FAULT!
HMPH
LISTEN UP, NATSU.
YOU HAVE HALF AN HOUR TO COME BACK WITH A CREATION THAT WILL SATISFY ME.
TRMBL
TRMBL

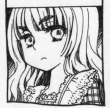

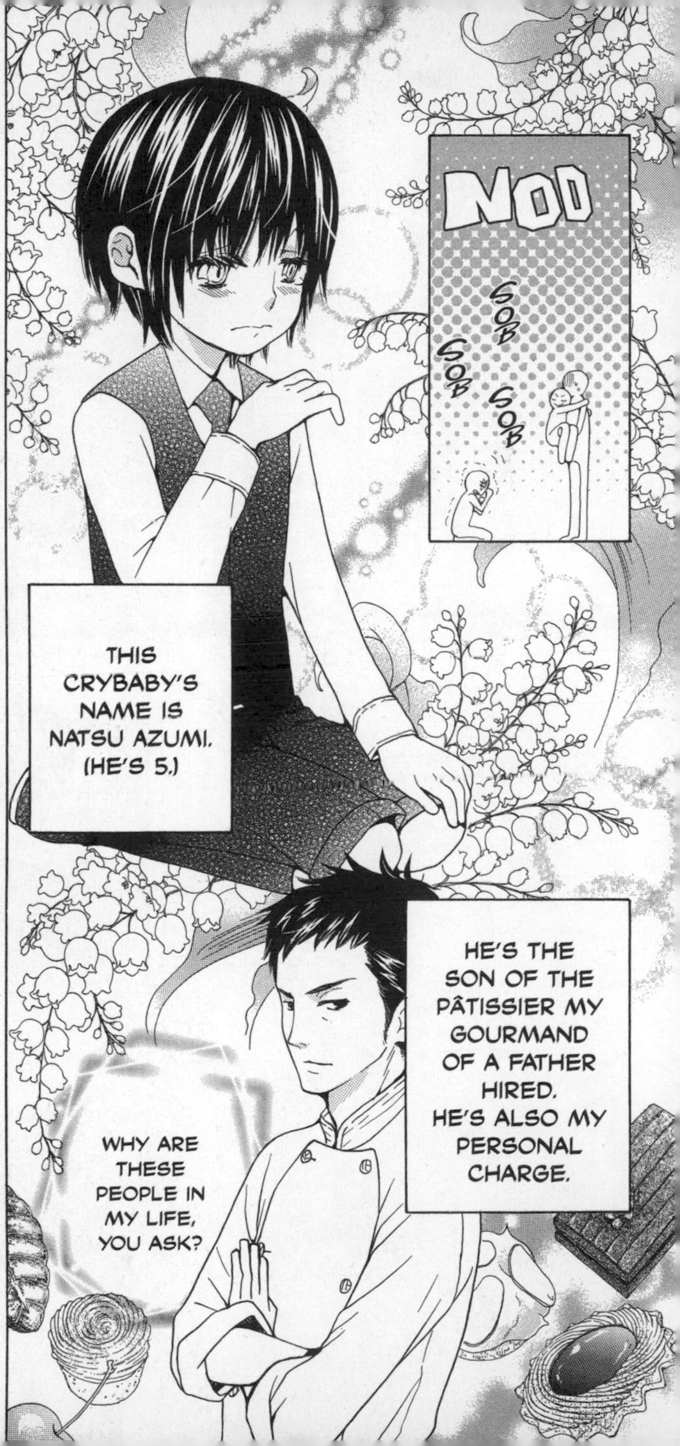
NOD
SOB SOB
SOB SOB
THIS CRYBABY'S NAME IS NATSU AZUMI. (HE'S 5.)
HE'S THE SON OF THE PÂTISSIER MY GOURMAND OF A FATHER HIRED. HE'S ALSO MY PERSONAL CHARGE.
WHY ARE THESE PEOPLE IN MY LIFE, YOU ASK?

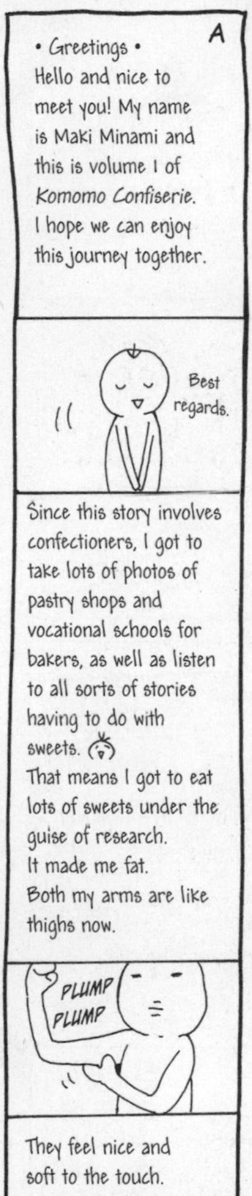
A
• Greetings •
Hello and nice to meet you! My name is Maki Minami and this is volume 1 of *Komomo Confiserie*. I hope we can enjoy this journey together.
Best regards.
Since this story involves confectioners, I got to take lots of photos of pastry shops and vocational schools for bakers, as well as listen to all sorts of stories having to do with sweets.
That means I got to eat lots of sweets under the guise of research.
It made me fat.
Both my arms are like thighs now.
PLUMP PLUMP
They feel nice and soft to the touch.

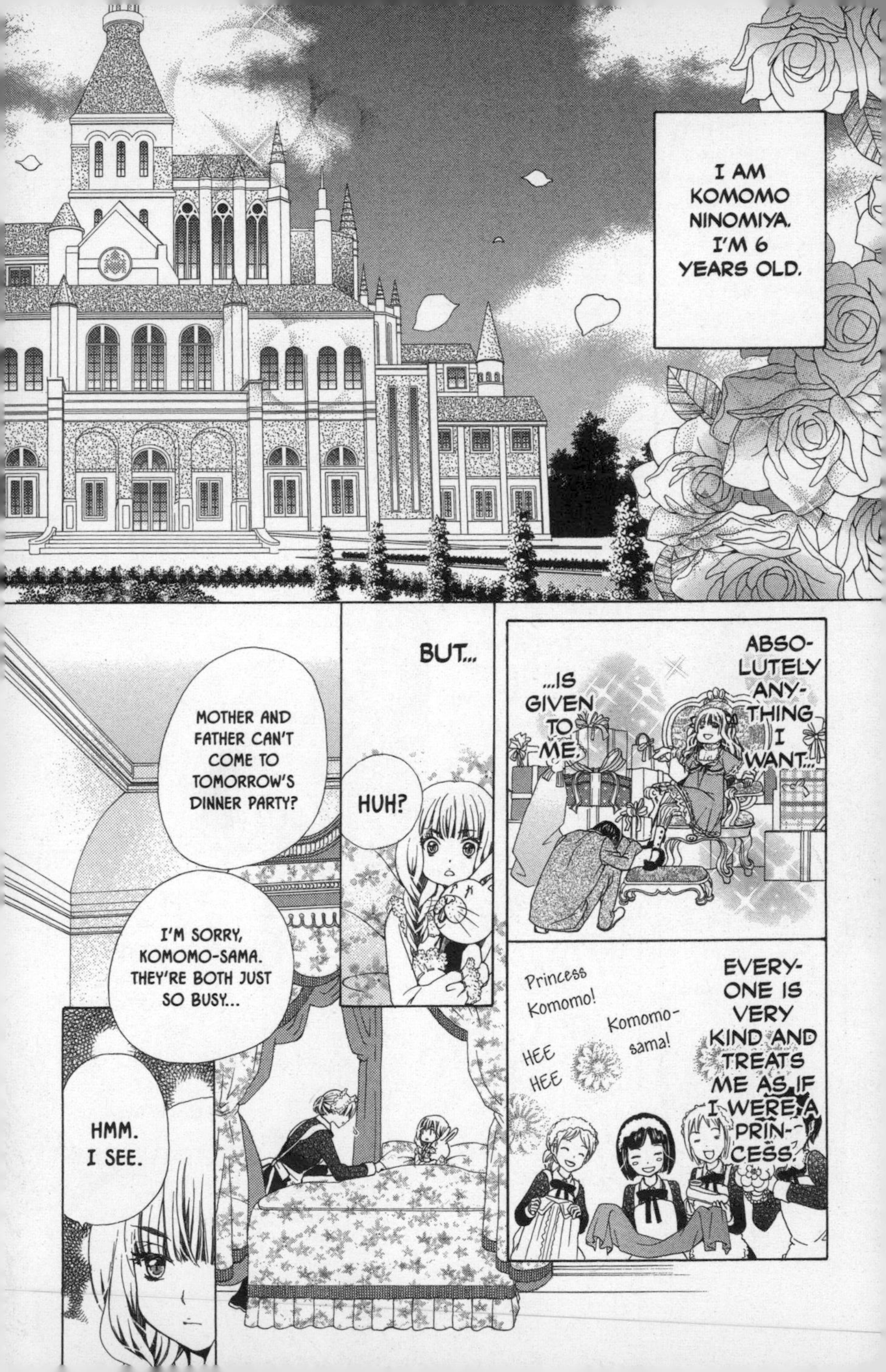
I AM KOMOMO NINOMIYA. I'M 6 YEARS OLD.
ABSOLUTELY ANYTHING I WANT...
...IS GIVEN TO ME.
EVERYONE IS VERY KIND AND TREATS ME AS IF I WERE A PRINCESS.
Komomo-sama!
Princess Komomo!
HEE HEE
BUT...
HUH?
MOTHER AND FATHER CAN'T COME TO TOMORROW'S DINNER PARTY?
I'M SORRY, KOMOMO-SAMA. THEY'RE BOTH JUST SO BUSY...
HMM. I SEE.

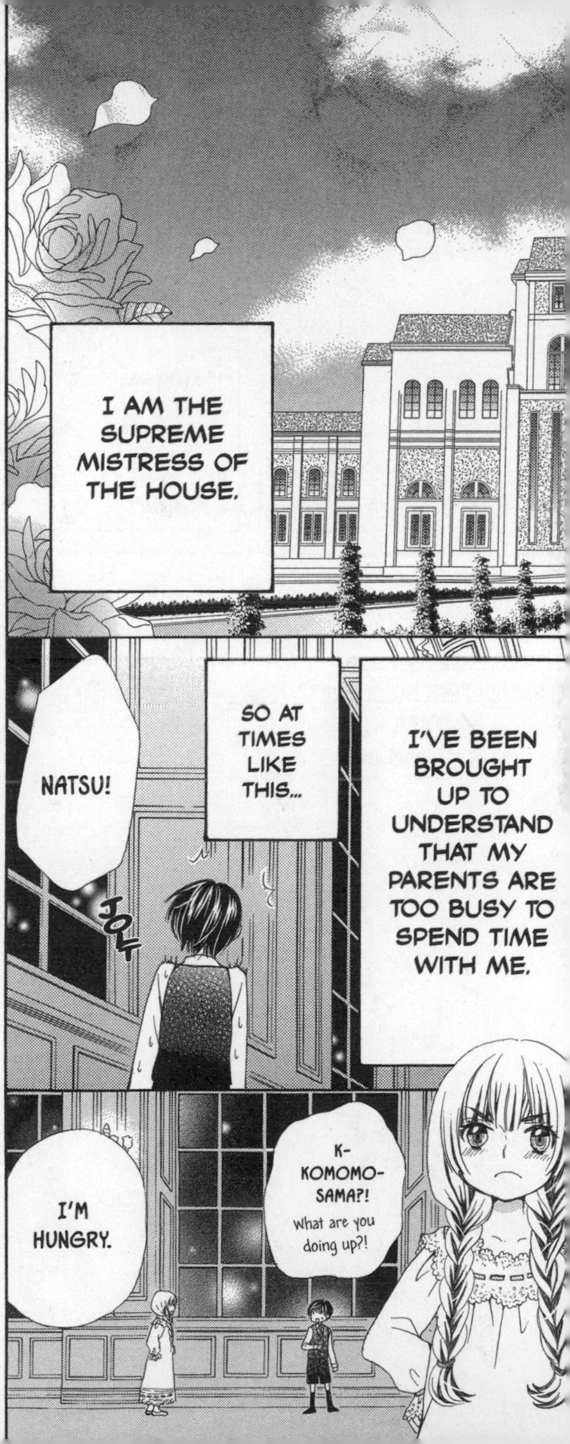
I AM THE SUPREME MISTRESS OF THE HOUSE.
I'VE BEEN BROUGHT UP TO UNDERSTAND THAT MY PARENTS ARE TOO BUSY TO SPEND TIME WITH ME.
SO AT TIMES LIKE THIS...
NATSU!
JOLT
K-KOMOMO-SAMA?! What are you doing up?!
I'M HUNGRY.

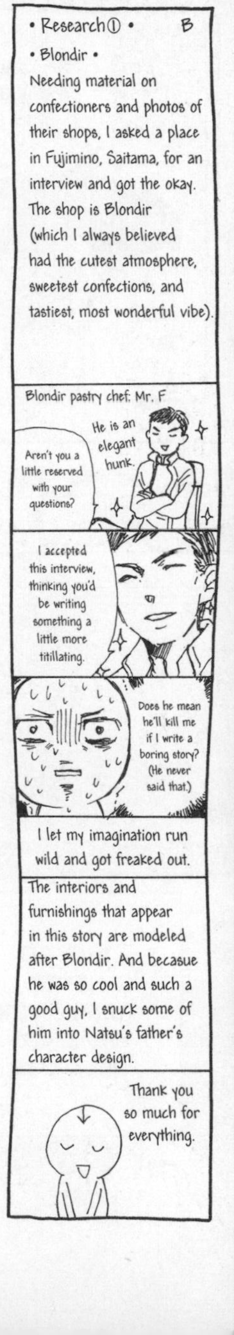
• Research① •
B
• Blondir •
Needing material on confectioners and photos of their shops, I asked a place in Fujimino, Saitama, for an interview and got the okay. The shop is Blondir (which I always believed had the cutest atmosphere, sweetest confections, and tastiest, most wonderful vibe).
Blondir pastry chef: Mr. F
He is an elegant hunk.
Aren't you a little reserved with your questions?
I accepted this interview, thinking you'd be writing something a little more titillating.
Does he mean he'll kill me if I write a boring story? (He never said that.)
I let my imagination run wild and got freaked out.
The interiors and furnishings that appear in this story are modeled after Blondir. And becasue he was so cool and such a good guy, I snuck some of him into Natsu's father's character design.
Thank you so much for everything.

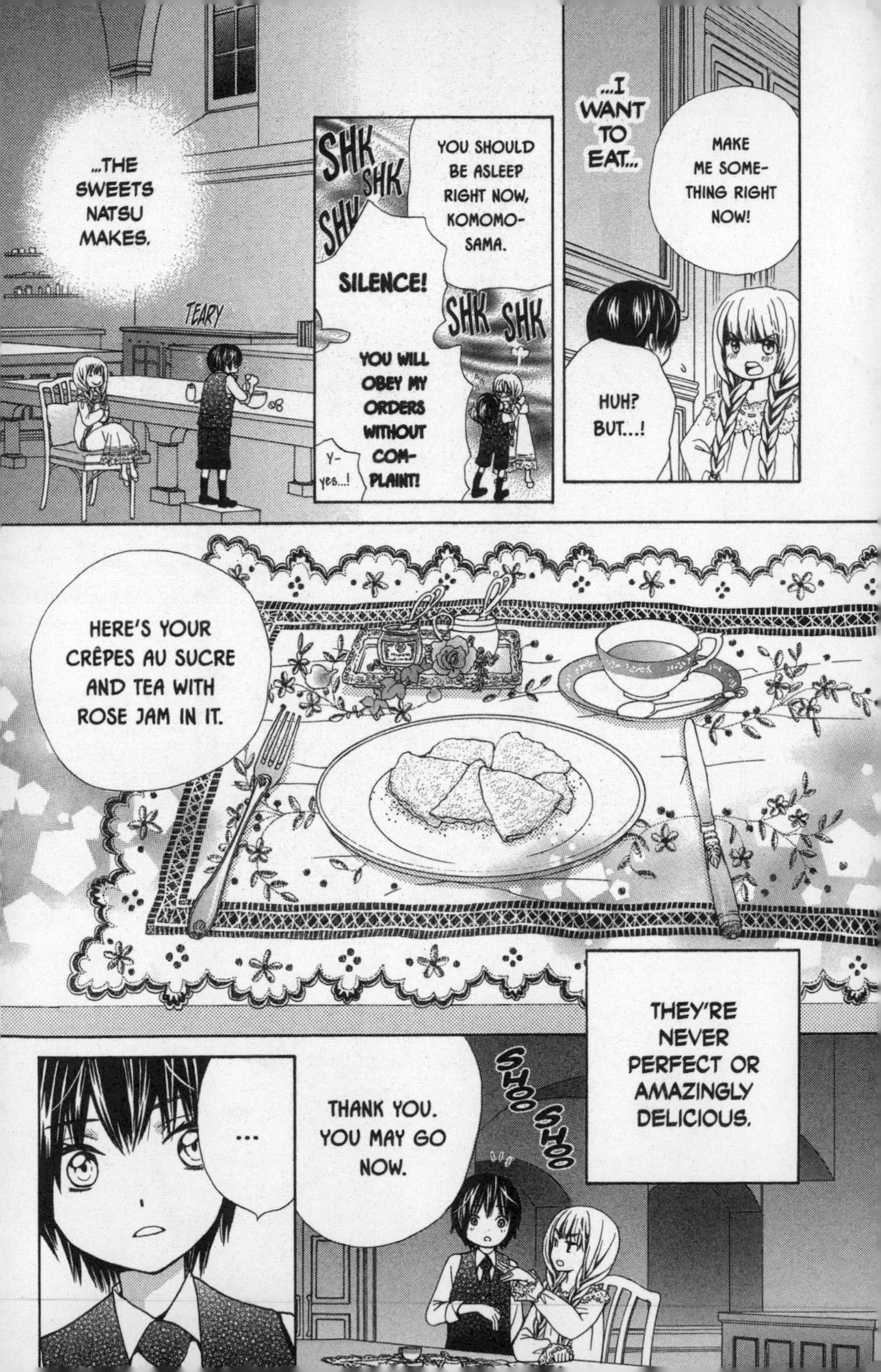
MAKE ME SOME-THING RIGHT NOW!
...I WANT TO EAT...
HUH? BUT...!
YOU SHOULD BE ASLEEP RIGHT NOW, KOMOMO-SAMA.
SHK SHK SHK
SILENCE!
SHK SHK
YOU WILL OBEY MY ORDERS WITHOUT COM-PLAINT!
Y-yes...!
...THE SWEETS NATSU MAKES.
TEARY
HERE'S YOUR CRÊPES AU SUCRE AND TEA WITH ROSE JAM IN IT.
THEY'RE NEVER PERFECT OR AMAZINGLY DELICIOUS.
SHOO SHOO
THANK YOU. YOU MAY GO NOW.
...

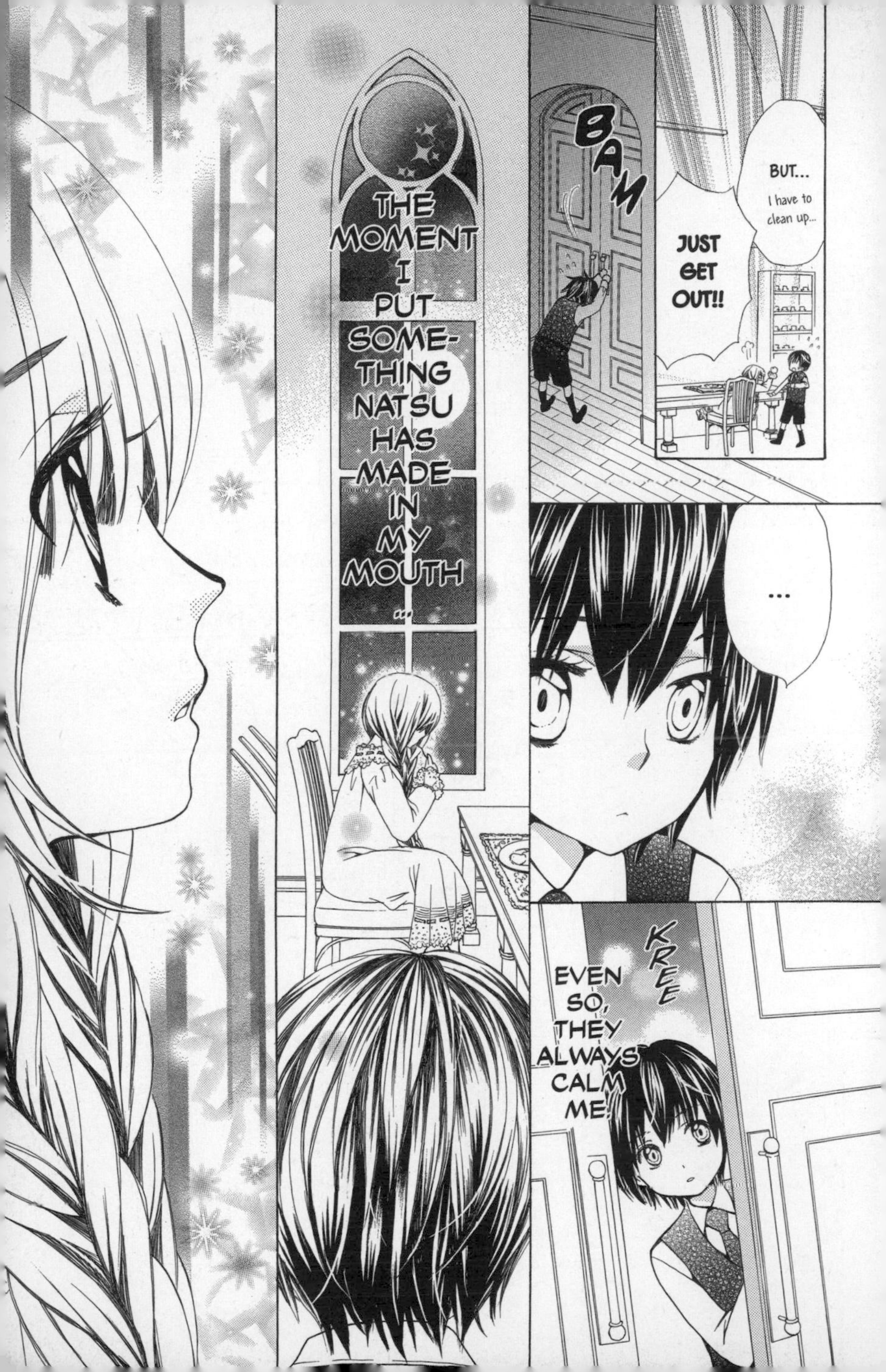
BUT...
I have to clean up...
JUST GET OUT!!
BAM
...
KREE
EVEN SO, THEY ALWAYS CALM ME.
THE MOMENT I PUT SOMETHING NATSU HAS MADE IN MY MOUTH...

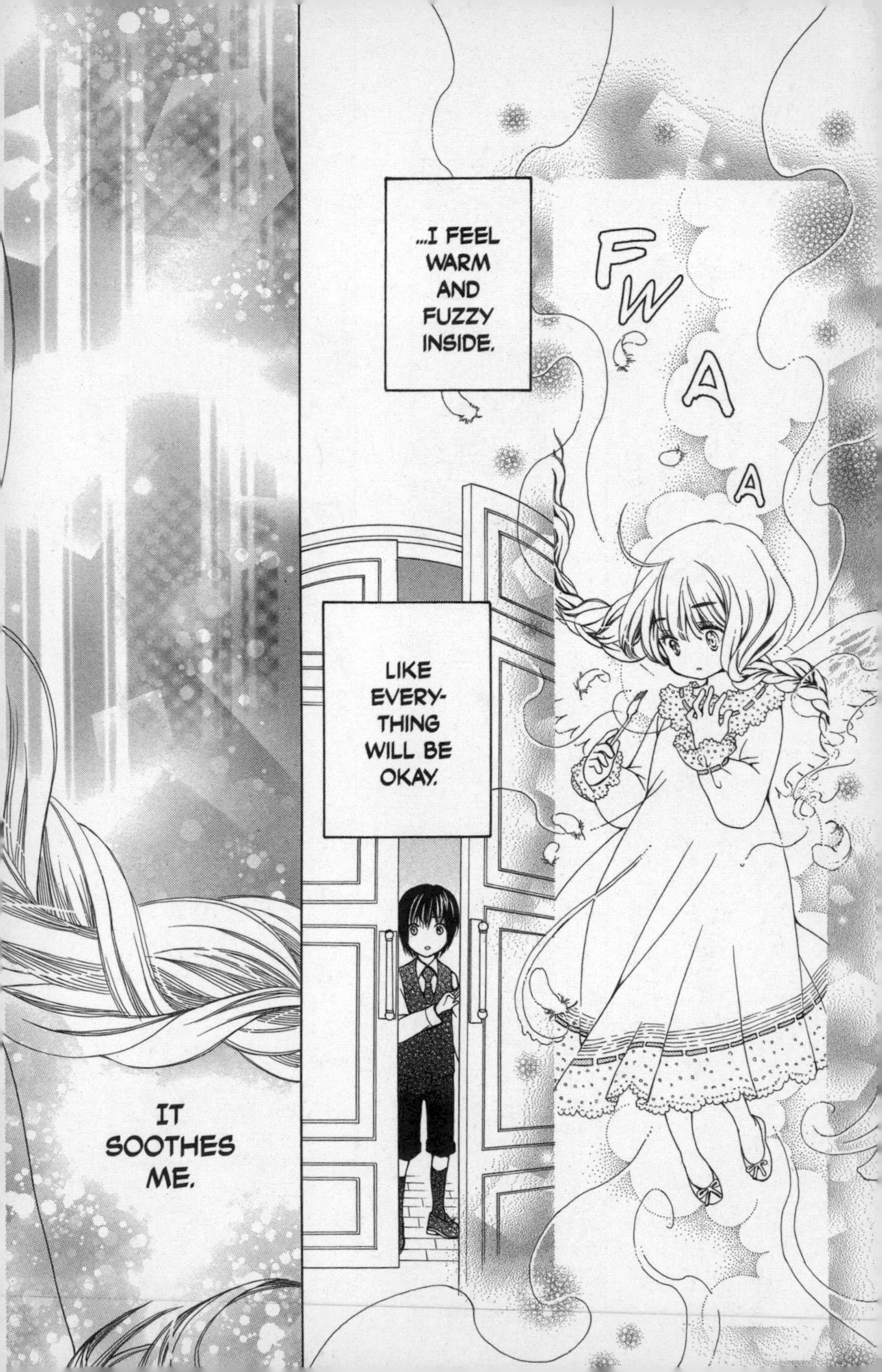
FWAA
...I FEEL WARM AND FUZZY INSIDE.
LIKE EVERY-THING WILL BE OKAY.
IT SOOTHES ME.

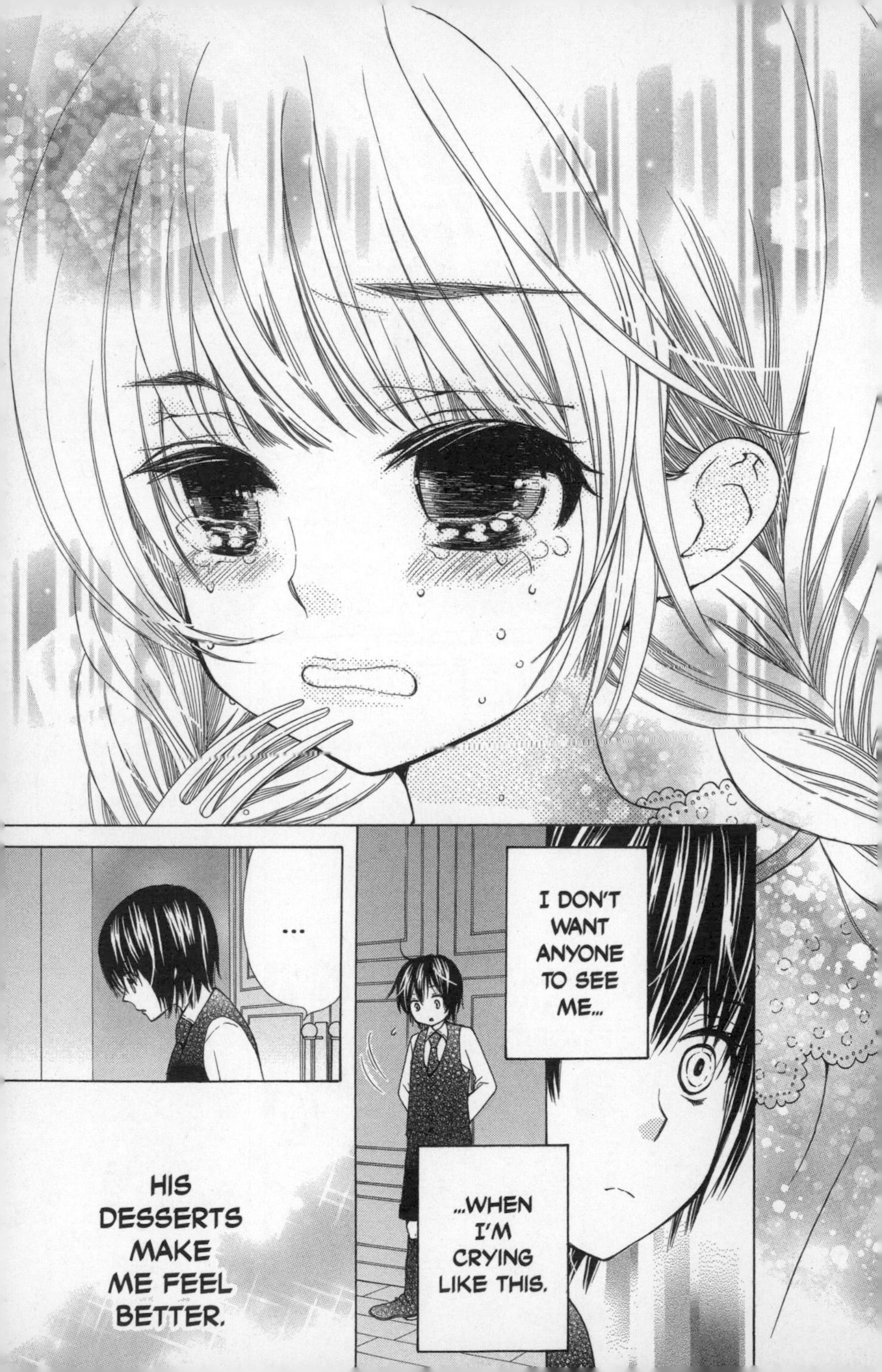
I DON'T WANT ANYONE TO SEE ME...
...WHEN I'M CRYING LIKE THIS.
...
HIS DESSERTS MAKE ME FEEL BETTER.

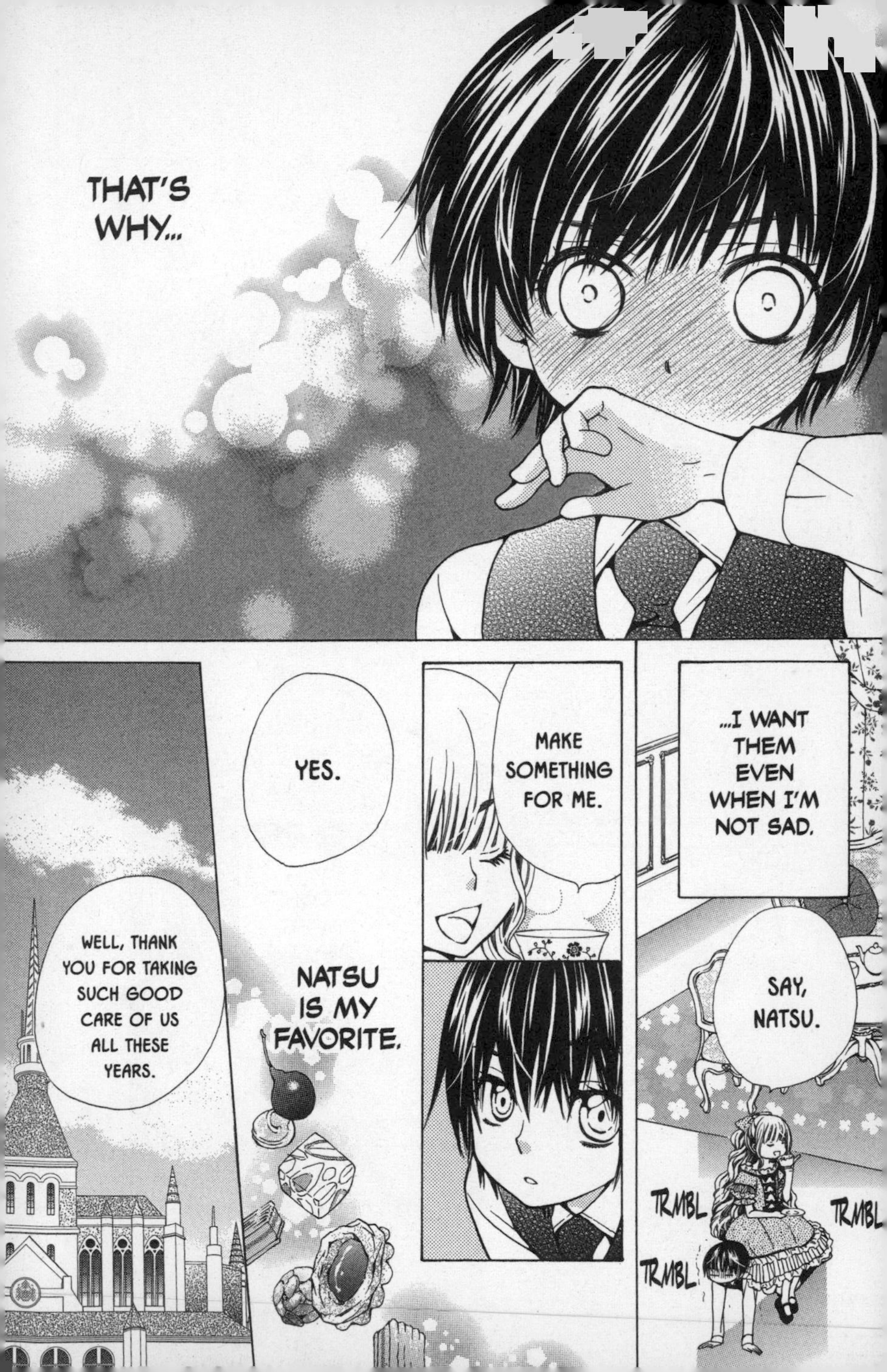

THAT'S WHY...
...I WANT THEM EVEN WHEN I'M NOT SAD.
SAY, NATSU.
TRMBL
TRMBL
TRMBL
MAKE SOMETHING FOR ME.
YES.
NATSU IS MY FAVORITE.
WELL, THANK YOU FOR TAKING SUCH GOOD CARE OF US ALL THESE YEARS.

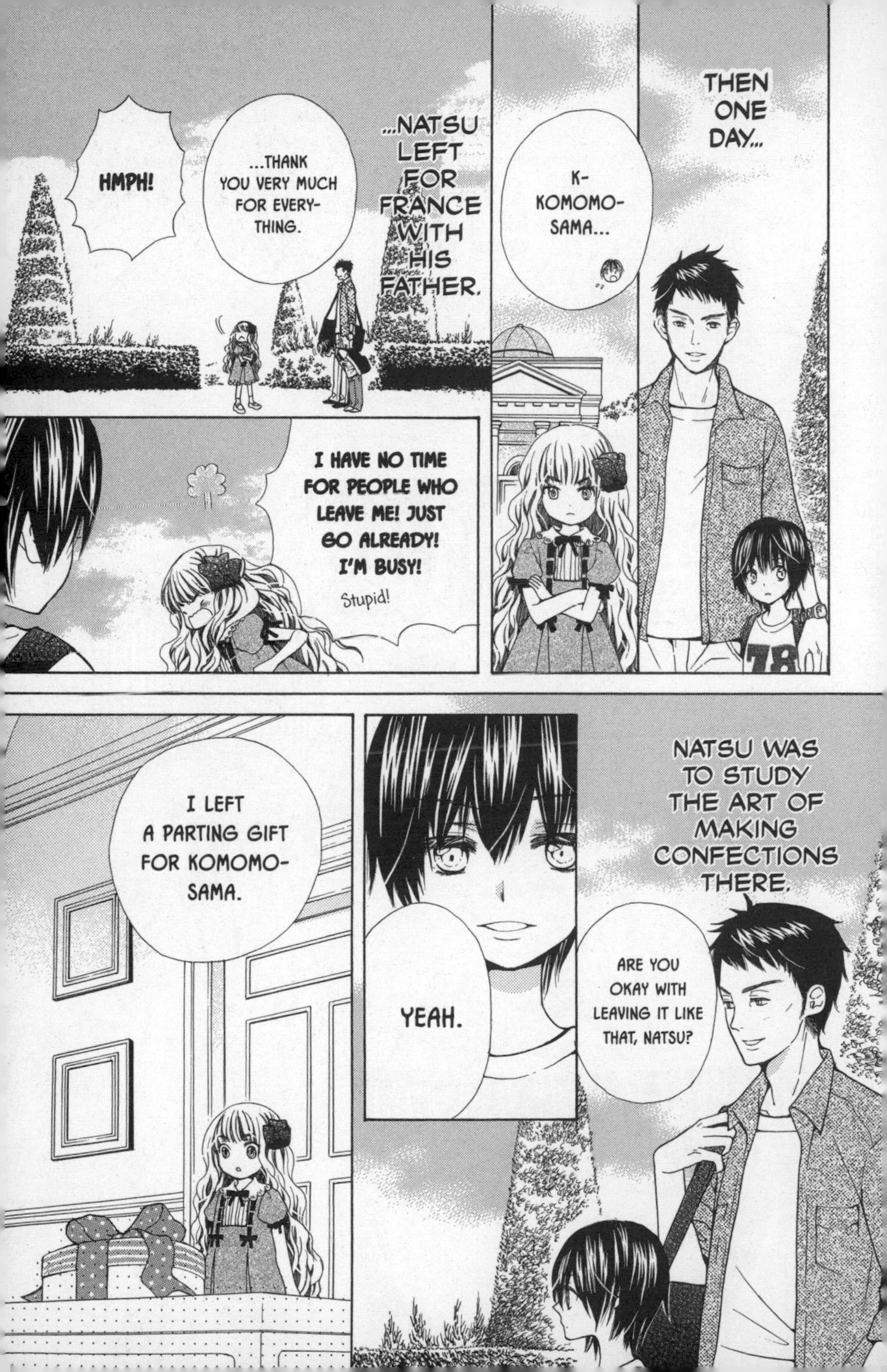
THEN ONE DAY...
K-KOMOMO-SAMA...
...NATSU LEFT FOR FRANCE WITH HIS FATHER.
...THANK YOU VERY MUCH FOR EVERYTHING.
HMPH!
I HAVE NO TIME FOR PEOPLE WHO LEAVE ME! JUST GO ALREADY! I'M BUSY!
Stupid!
NATSU WAS TO STUDY THE ART OF MAKING CONFECTIONS THERE.
ARE YOU OKAY WITH LEAVING IT LIKE THAT, NATSU?
YEAH.
I LEFT A PARTING GIFT FOR KOMOMO-SAMA.

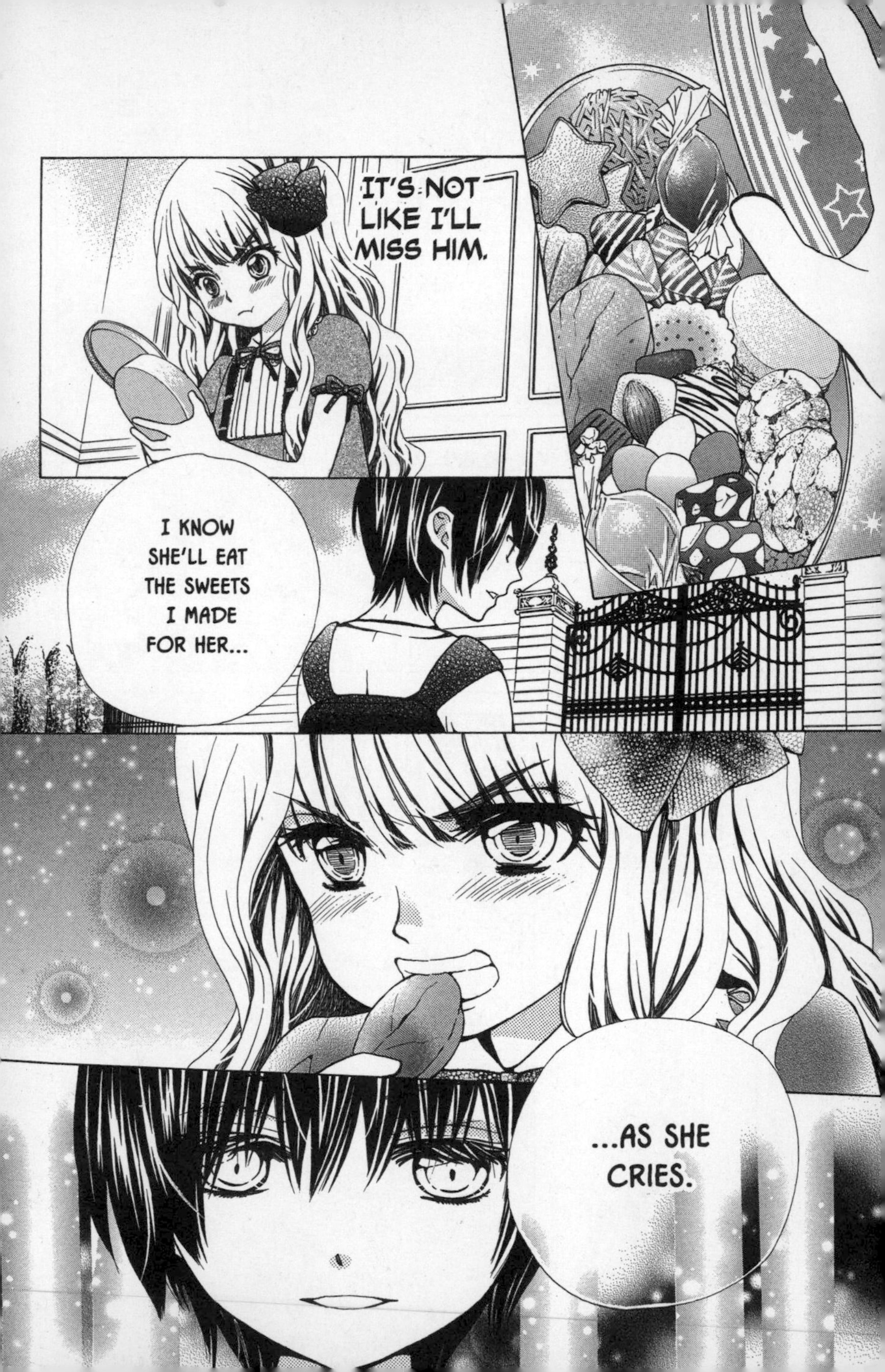
IT'S NOT LIKE I'LL MISS HIM.
I KNOW SHE'LL EAT THE SWEETS I MADE FOR HER...
...AS SHE CRIES.

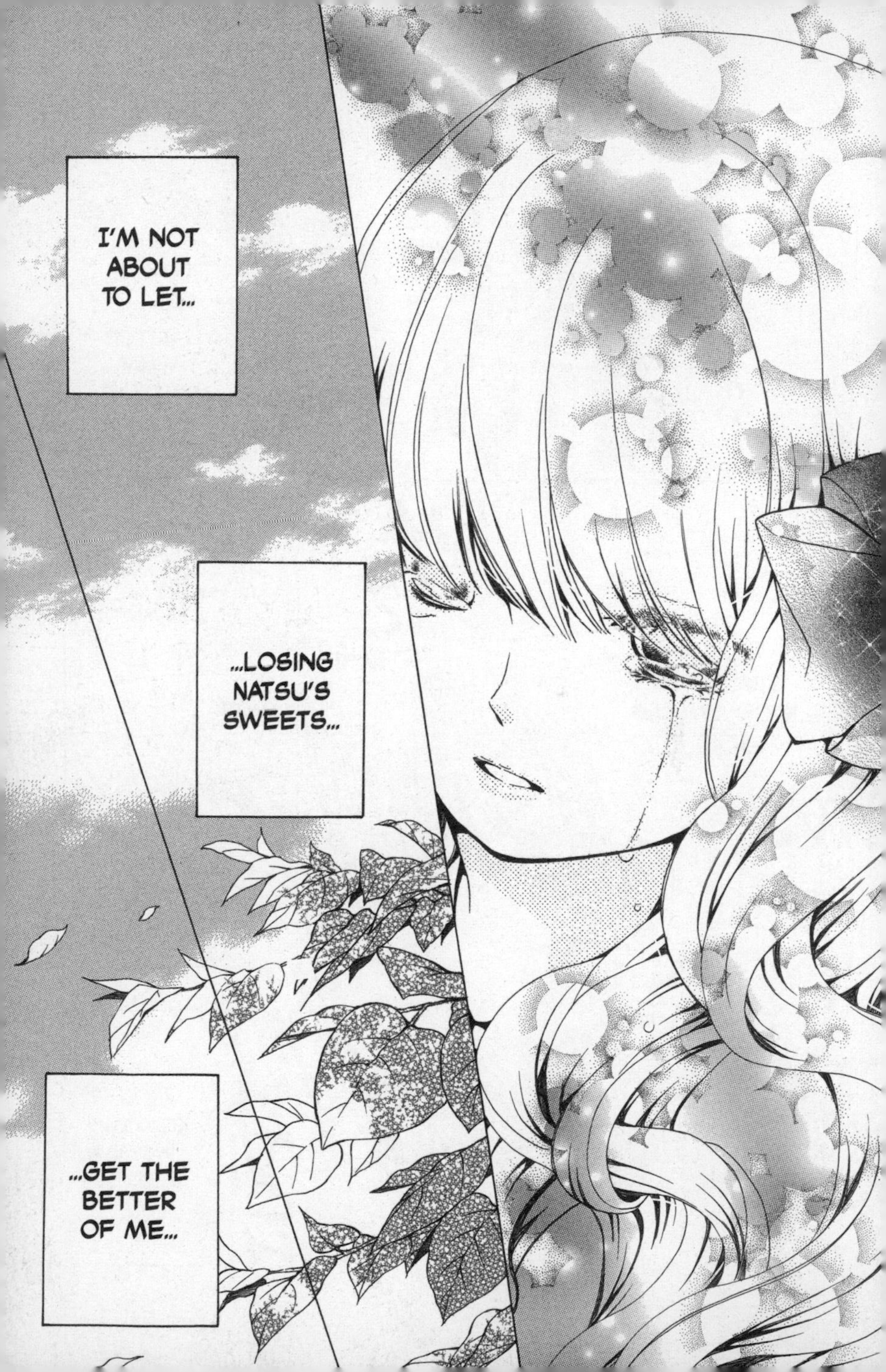
I'M NOT ABOUT TO LET...
...LOSING NATSU'S SWEETS...
...GET THE BETTER OF ME...

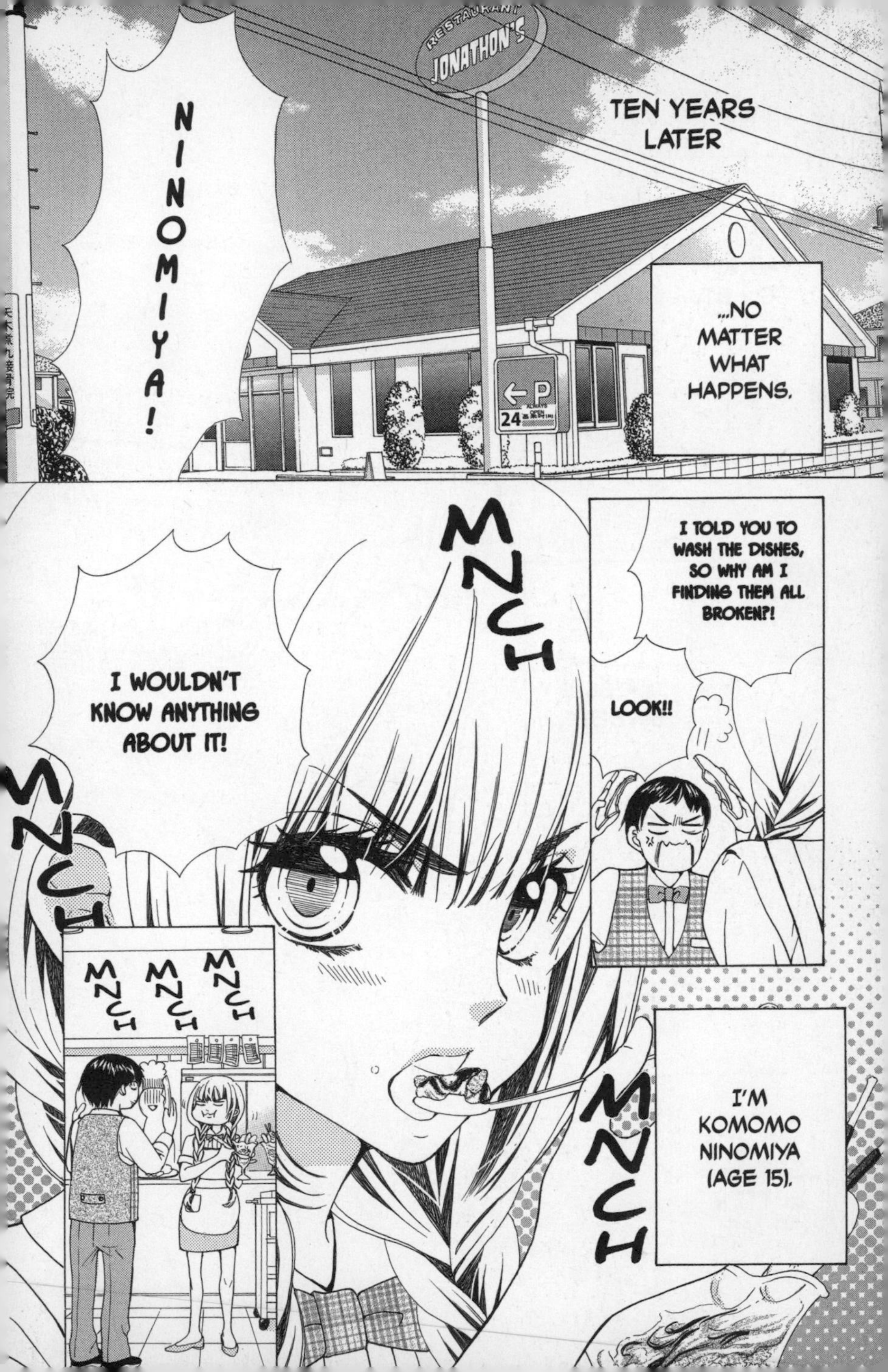
RESTAURANT
JONATHON'S
...NO MATTER WHAT HAPPENS.
TEN YEARS LATER
NINOMIYA!
I TOLD YOU TO WASH THE DISHES, SO WHY AM I FINDING THEM ALL BROKEN?!
LOOK!!
MNCH
I WOULDN'T KNOW ANYTHING ABOUT IT!
MNCH
I'M KOMOMO NINOMIYA (AGE 15).
MNCH
MNCH
MNCH
MNCH

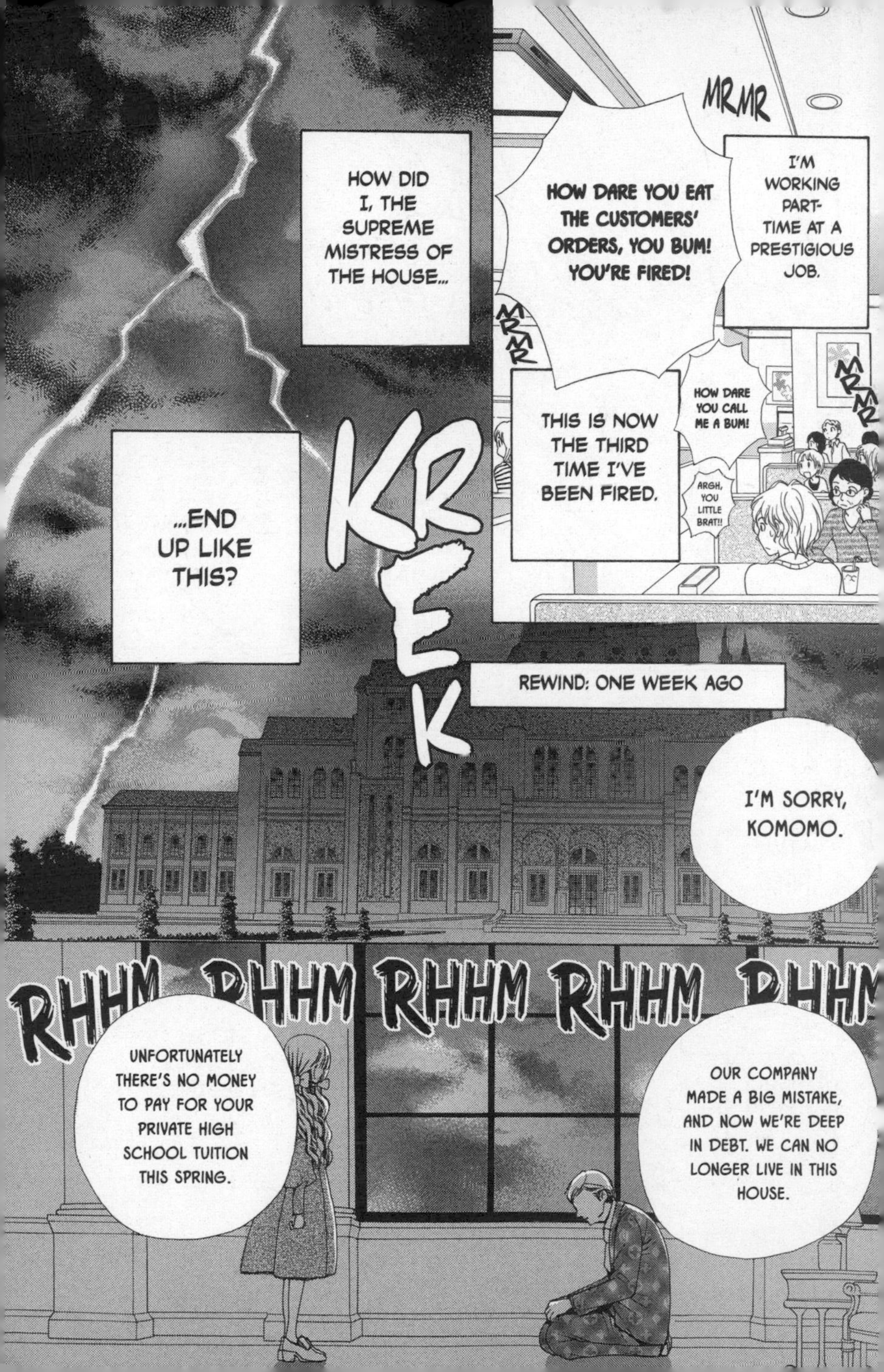
MRMR
I'M WORKING PART-TIME AT A PRESTIGIOUS JOB.
HOW DARE YOU EAT THE CUSTOMERS' ORDERS, YOU BUM! YOU'RE FIRED!
MRMR
HOW DARE YOU CALL ME A BUM!
ARGH, YOU LITTLE BRAT!!
THIS IS NOW THE THIRD TIME I'VE BEEN FIRED.
MRMR
HOW DID I, THE SUPREME MISTRESS OF THE HOUSE...
...END UP LIKE THIS?
KREK
REWIND: ONE WEEK AGO
I'M SORRY, KOMOMO.
RHHM RHHM RHHM RHHM RHHM
OUR COMPANY MADE A BIG MISTAKE, AND NOW WE'RE DEEP IN DEBT. WE CAN NO LONGER LIVE IN THIS HOUSE.
UNFORTUNATELY THERE'S NO MONEY TO PAY FOR YOUR PRIVATE HIGH SCHOOL TUITION THIS SPRING.

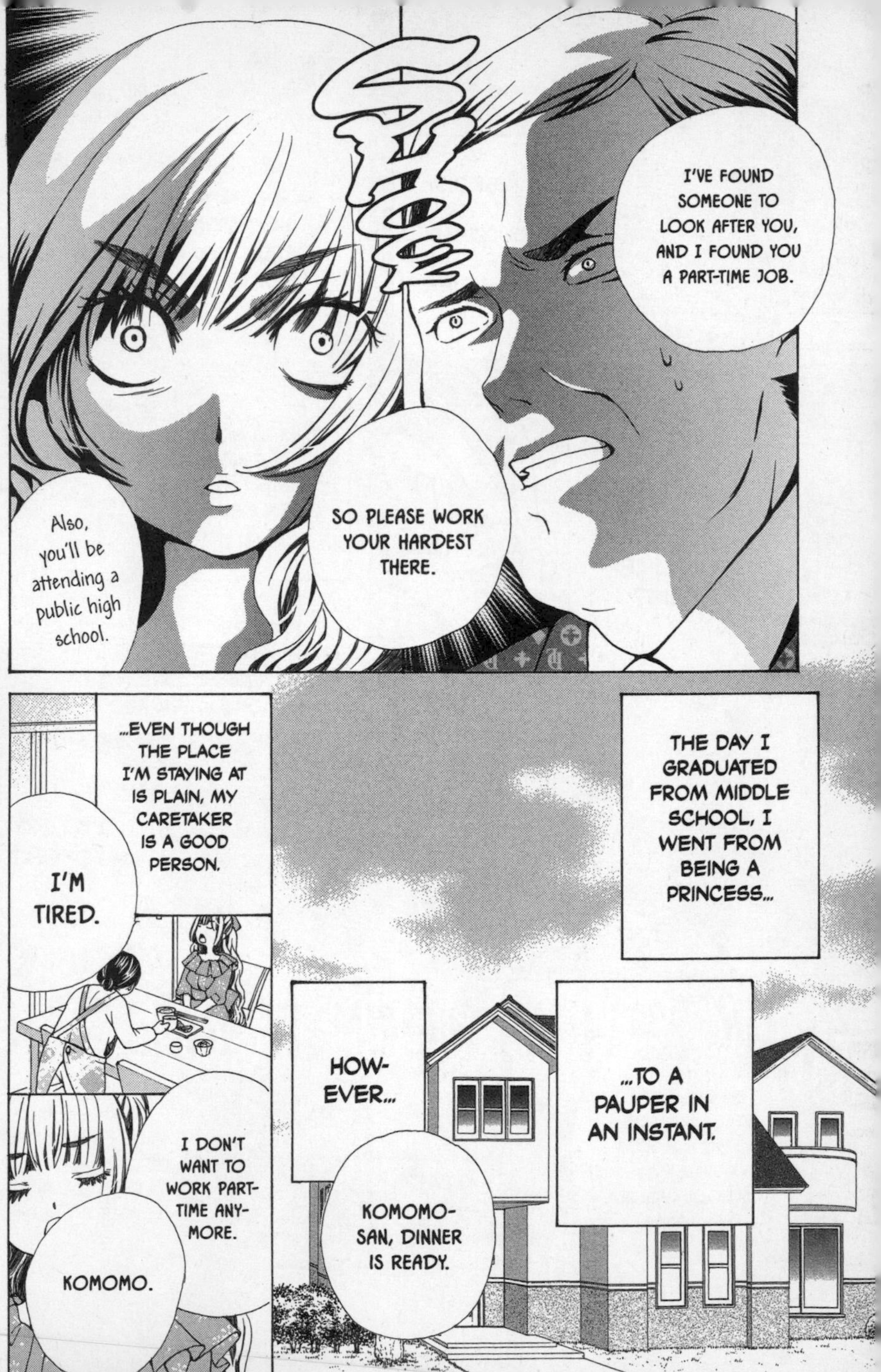
I'VE FOUND SOMEONE TO LOOK AFTER YOU, AND I FOUND YOU A PART-TIME JOB.
SO PLEASE WORK YOUR HARDEST THERE.
Also, you'll be attending a public high school.
THE DAY I GRADUATED FROM MIDDLE SCHOOL, I WENT FROM BEING A PRINCESS...
...TO A PAUPER IN AN INSTANT.
HOW-EVER...
KOMOMO-SAN, DINNER IS READY.
...EVEN THOUGH THE PLACE I'M STAYING AT IS PLAIN, MY CARETAKER IS A GOOD PERSON.
I'M TIRED.
I DON'T WANT TO WORK PART-TIME ANYMORE.
KOMOMO.

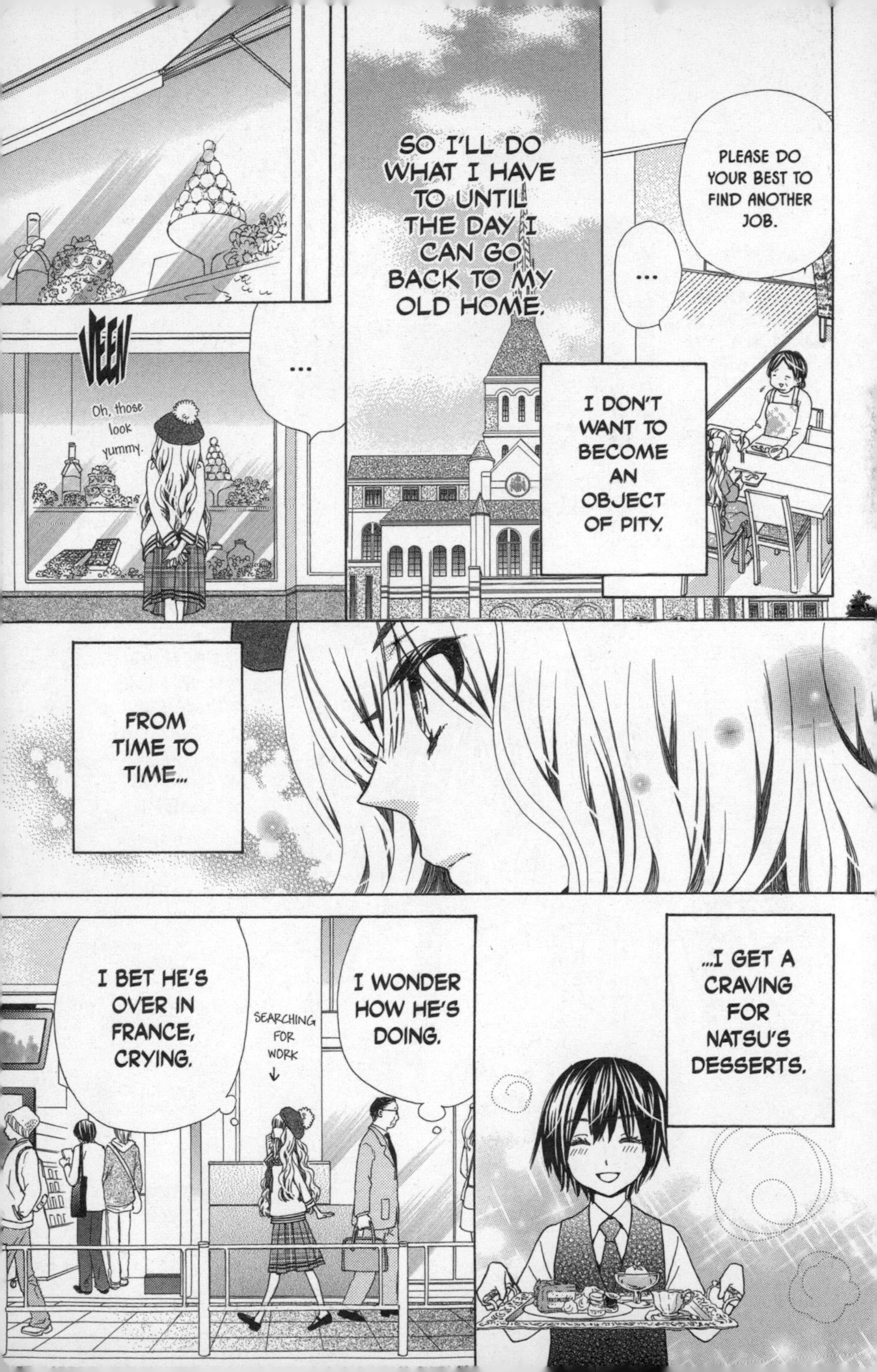
PLEASE DO YOUR BEST TO FIND ANOTHER JOB.
...
I DON'T WANT TO BECOME AN OBJECT OF PITY.
SO I'LL DO WHAT I HAVE TO UNTIL THE DAY I CAN GO BACK TO MY OLD HOME.
VEEN
Oh, those look yummy.
...
FROM TIME TO TIME...
...I GET A CRAVING FOR NATSU'S DESSERTS.
I WONDER HOW HE'S DOING.
SEARCHING FOR WORK
I BET HE'S OVER IN FRANCE, CRYING.

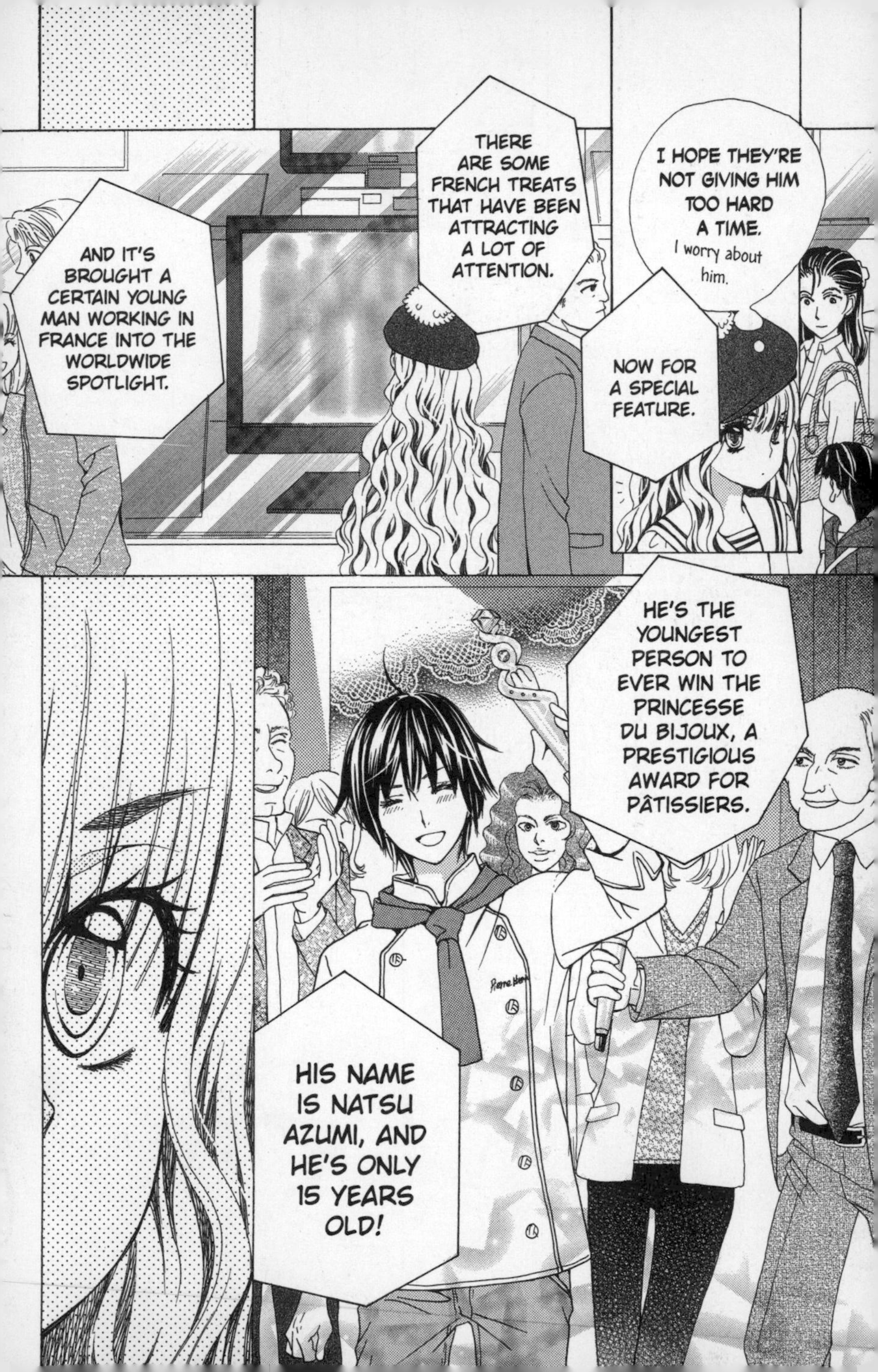
I HOPE THEY'RE NOT GIVING HIM TOO HARD A TIME.
I worry about him.
NOW FOR A SPECIAL FEATURE.
THERE ARE SOME FRENCH TREATS THAT HAVE BEEN ATTRACTING A LOT OF ATTENTION.
AND IT'S BROUGHT A CERTAIN YOUNG MAN WORKING IN FRANCE INTO THE WORLDWIDE SPOTLIGHT.
HE'S THE YOUNGEST PERSON TO EVER WIN THE PRINCESSE DU BIJOUX, A PRESTIGIOUS AWARD FOR PÂTISSIERS.
HIS NAME IS NATSU AZUMI, AND HE'S ONLY 15 YEARS OLD!

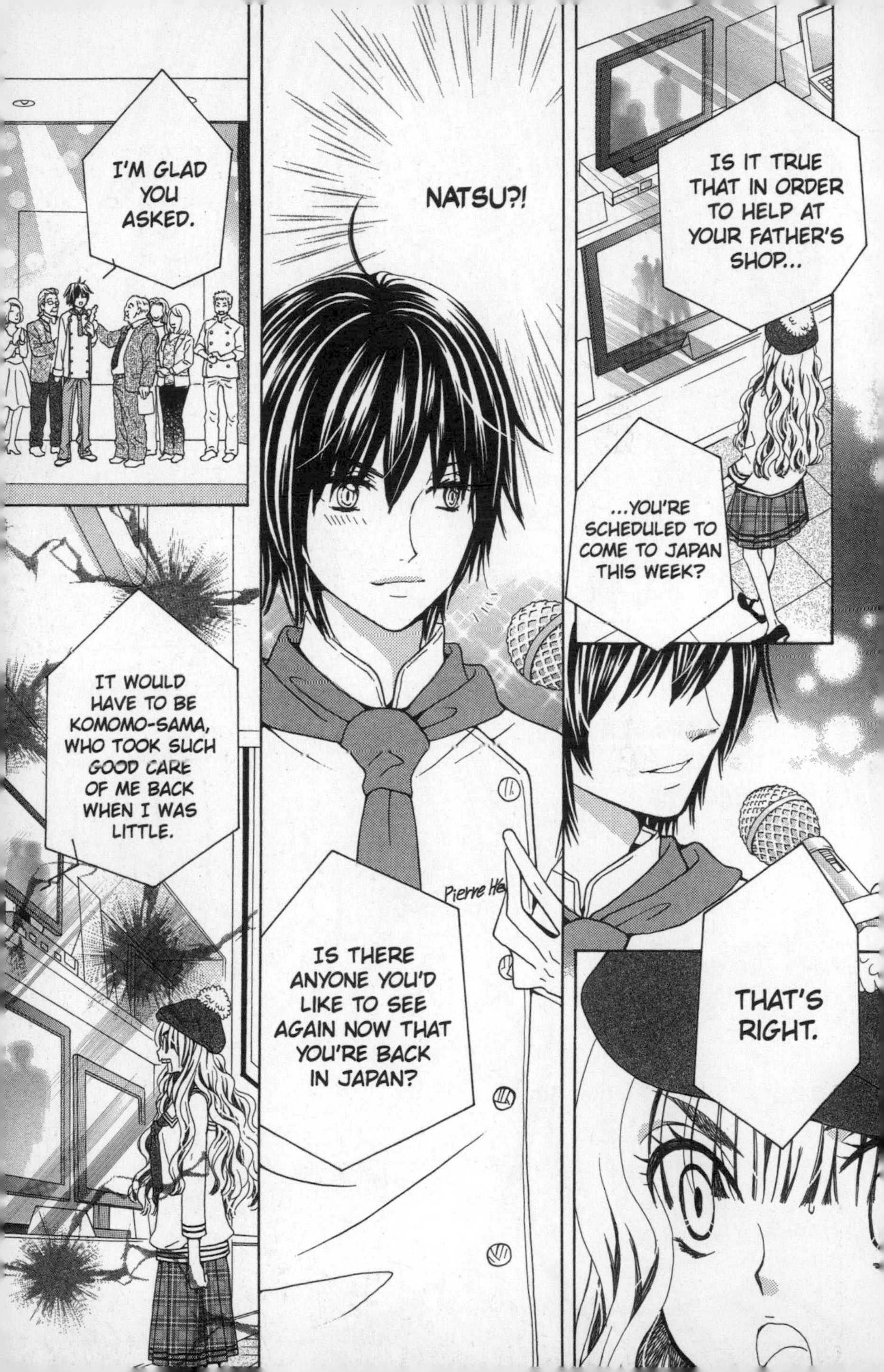
IS IT TRUE THAT IN ORDER TO HELP AT YOUR FATHER'S SHOP...
...YOU'RE SCHEDULED TO COME TO JAPAN THIS WEEK?
THAT'S RIGHT.
NATSU?!
IS THERE ANYONE YOU'D LIKE TO SEE AGAIN NOW THAT YOU'RE BACK IN JAPAN?
I'M GLAD YOU ASKED.
IT WOULD HAVE TO BE KOMOMO-SAMA, WHO TOOK SUCH GOOD CARE OF ME BACK WHEN I WAS LITTLE.

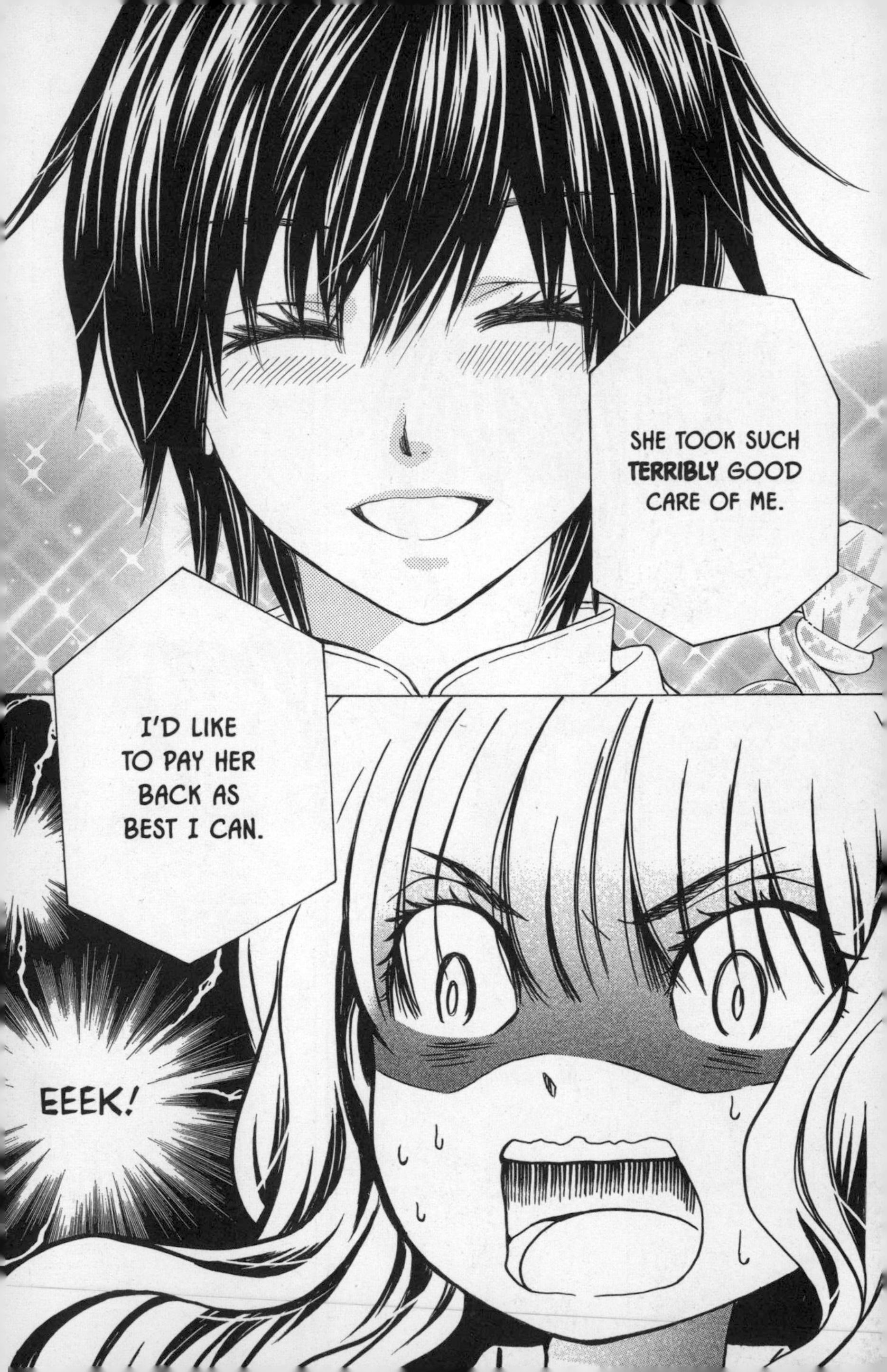
SHE TOOK SUCH TERRIBLY GOOD CARE OF ME.
I'D LIKE TO PAY HER BACK AS BEST I CAN.
EEEK!

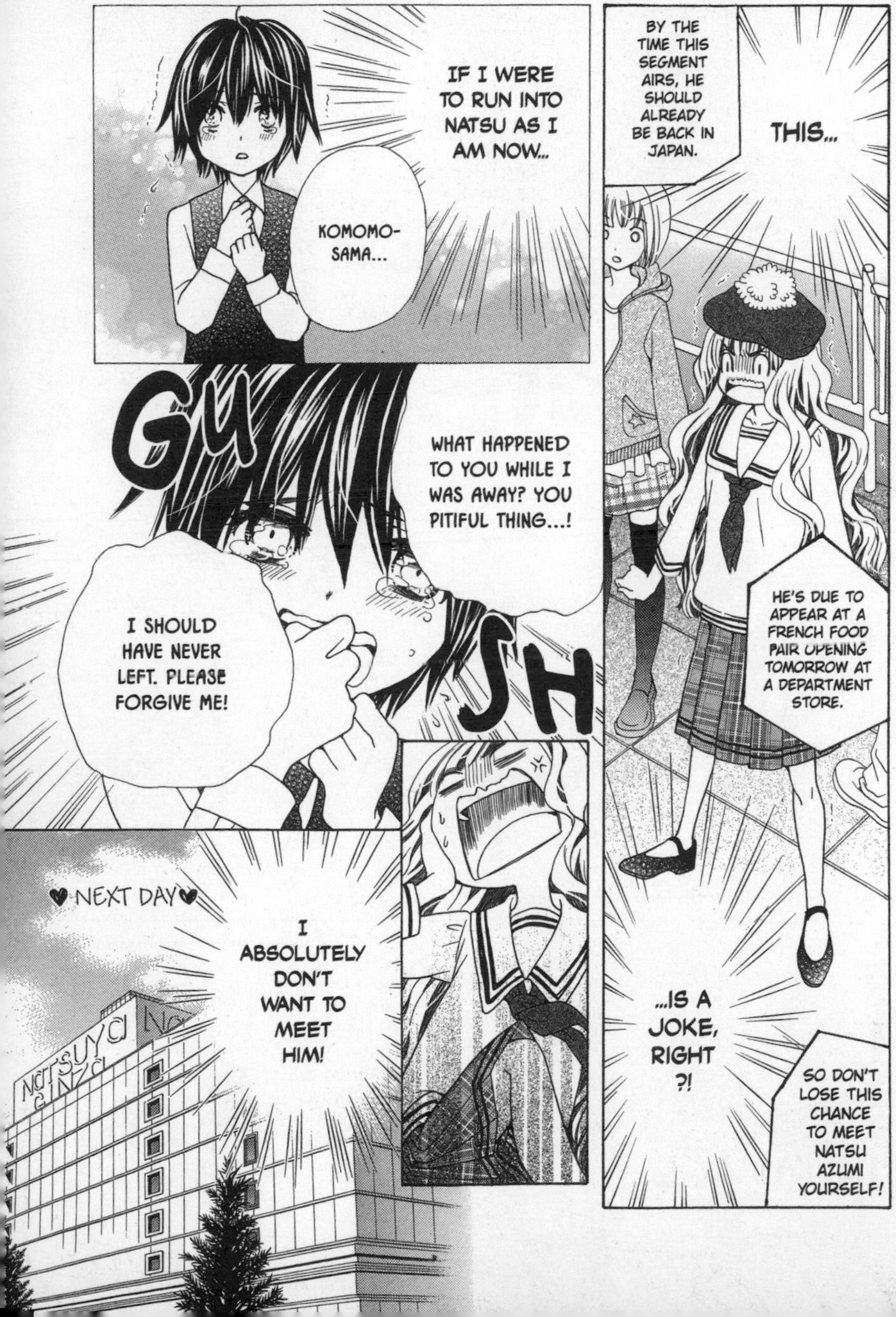
BY THE TIME THIS SEGMENT AIRS, HE SHOULD ALREADY BE BACK IN JAPAN.
THIS...
HE'S DUE TO APPEAR AT A FRENCH FOOD PAIR OPENING TOMORROW AT A DEPARTMENT STORE.
...IS A JOKE, RIGHT ?!
SO DON'T LOSE THIS CHANCE TO MEET NATSU AZUMI YOURSELF!
IF I WERE TO RUN INTO NATSU AS I AM NOW...
KOMOMO-SAMA...
GUSH
WHAT HAPPENED TO YOU WHILE I WAS AWAY? YOU PITIFUL THING...!
I SHOULD HAVE NEVER LEFT. PLEASE FORGIVE ME!
I ABSOLUTELY DON'T WANT TO MEET HIM!
NEXT DAY

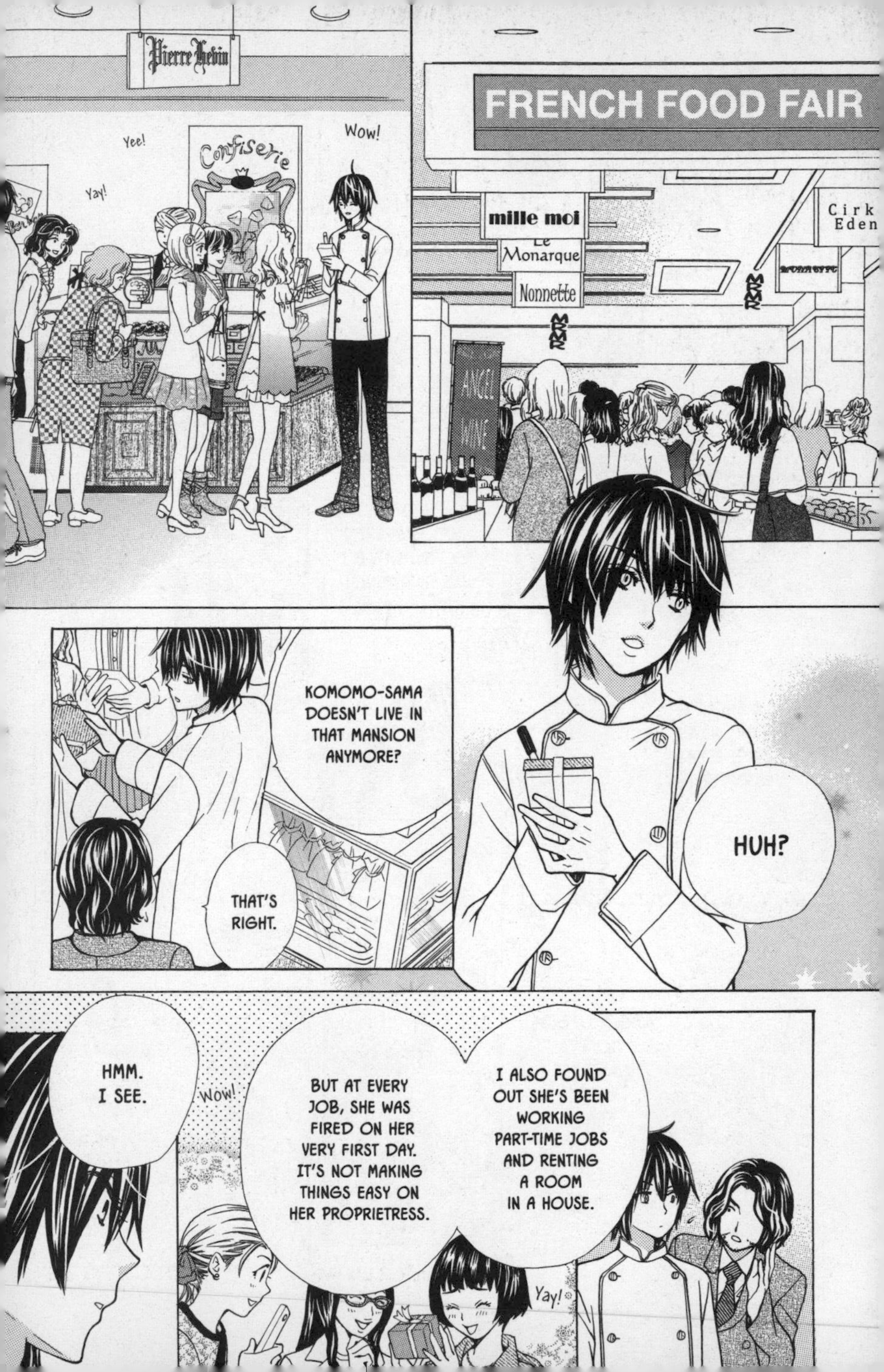
FRENCH FOOD FAIR
Cirk Eden
mille moi
Le Monarque
Nonnette
MRMR
MRMR
ANGEL WINE
Pierre Hebin
Wow!
Confiserie
Yee!
Yay!
HUH?
KOMOMO-SAMA DOESN'T LIVE IN THAT MANSION ANYMORE?
THAT'S RIGHT.
I ALSO FOUND OUT SHE'S BEEN WORKING PART-TIME JOBS AND RENTING A ROOM IN A HOUSE.
Yay!
BUT AT EVERY JOB, SHE WAS FIRED ON HER VERY FIRST DAY. IT'S NOT MAKING THINGS EASY ON HER PROPRIETRESS.
Wow!
HMM. I SEE.

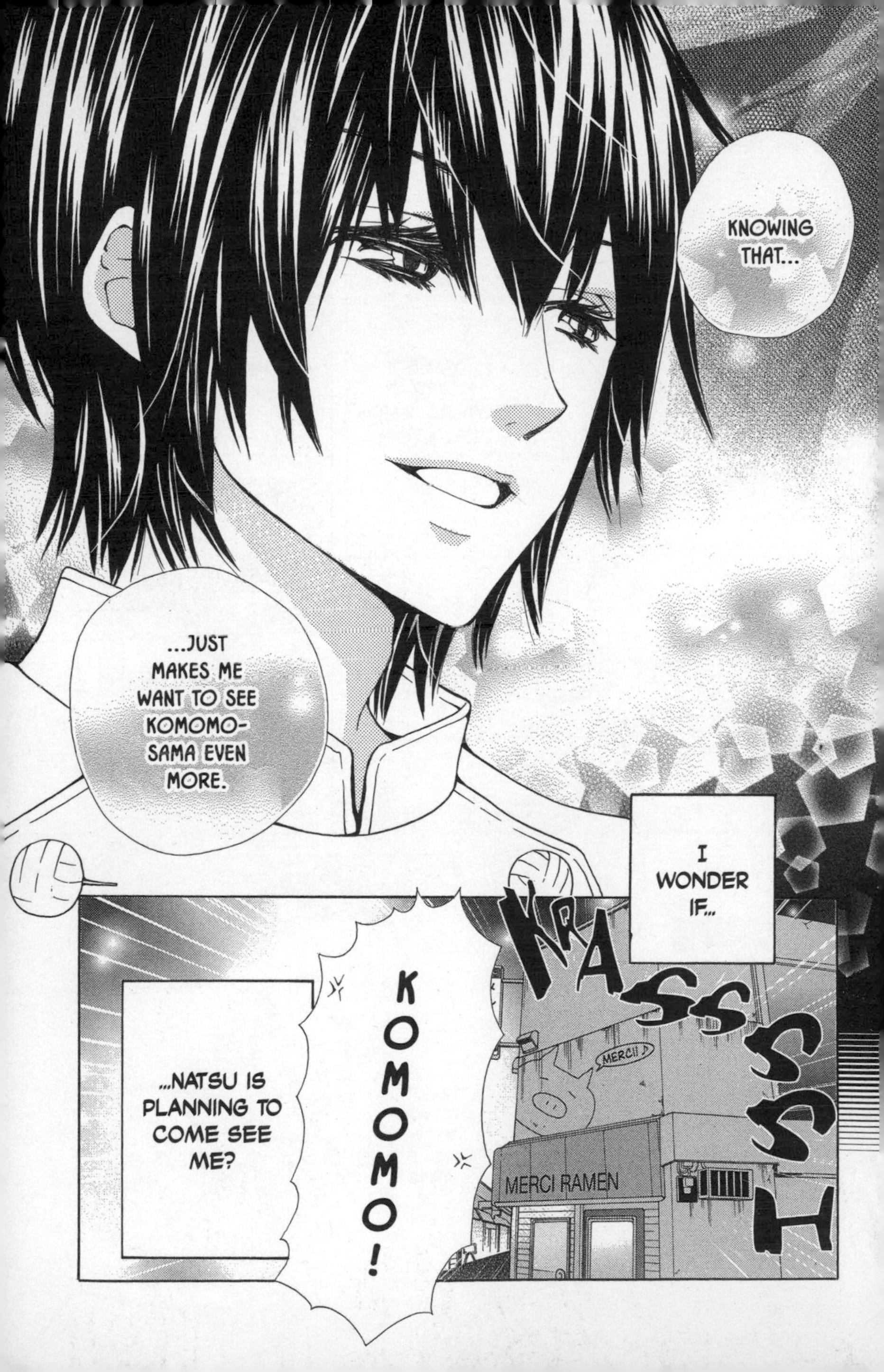
KNOWING THAT...
...JUST MAKES ME WANT TO SEE KOMOMO-SAMA EVEN MORE.
I WONDER IF...
KRASSSH
MERCI!♪
MERCI RAMEN
KOMOMO!
...NATSU IS PLANNING TO COME SEE ME?

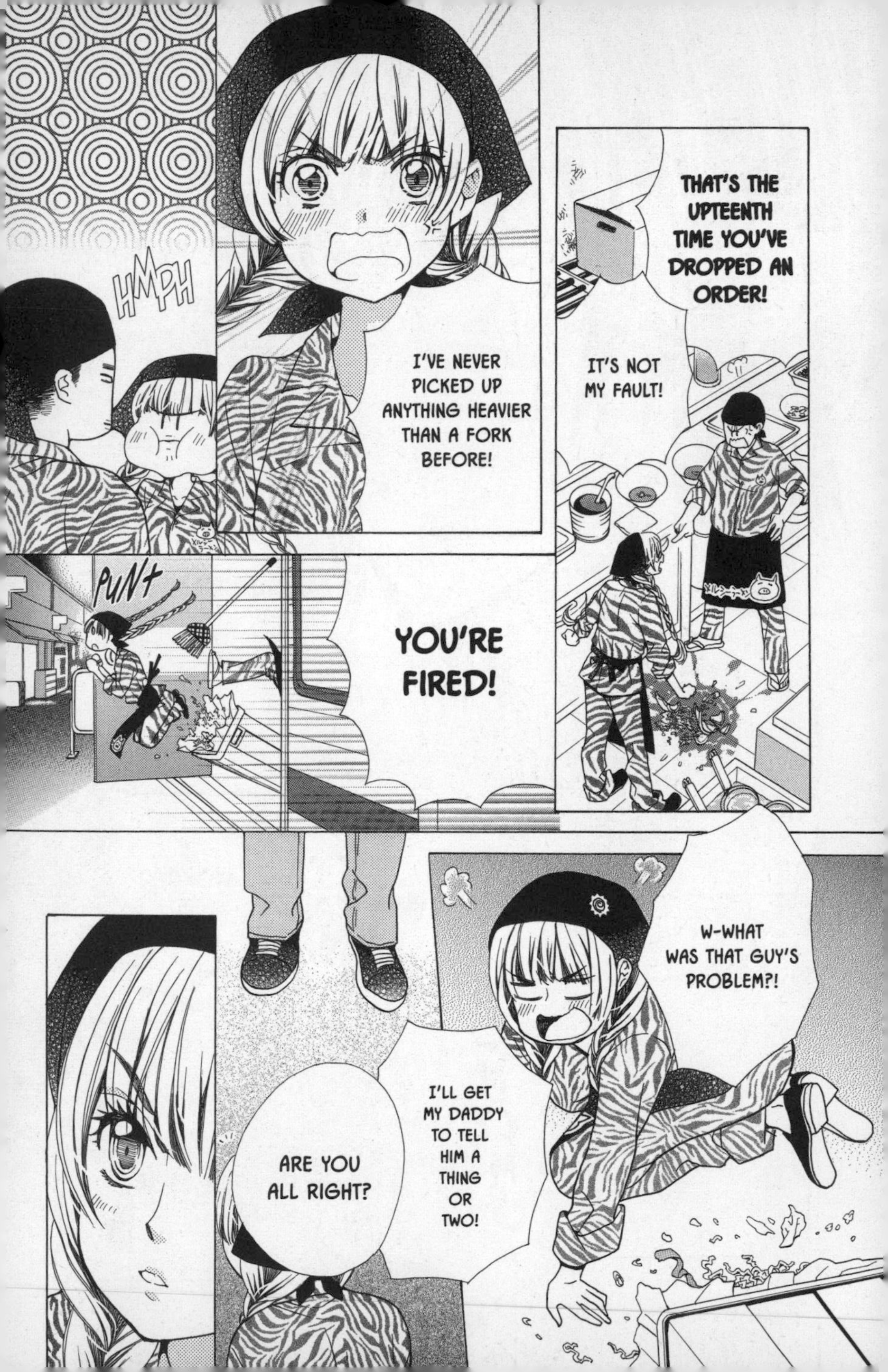
THAT'S THE UPTEENTH TIME YOU'VE DROPPED AN ORDER!
IT'S NOT MY FAULT!
I'VE NEVER PICKED UP ANYTHING HEAVIER THAN A FORK BEFORE!
HMPH
YOU'RE FIRED!
PUNT
W-WHAT WAS THAT GUY'S PROBLEM?!
I'LL GET MY DADDY TO TELL HIM A THING OR TWO!
ARE YOU ALL RIGHT?

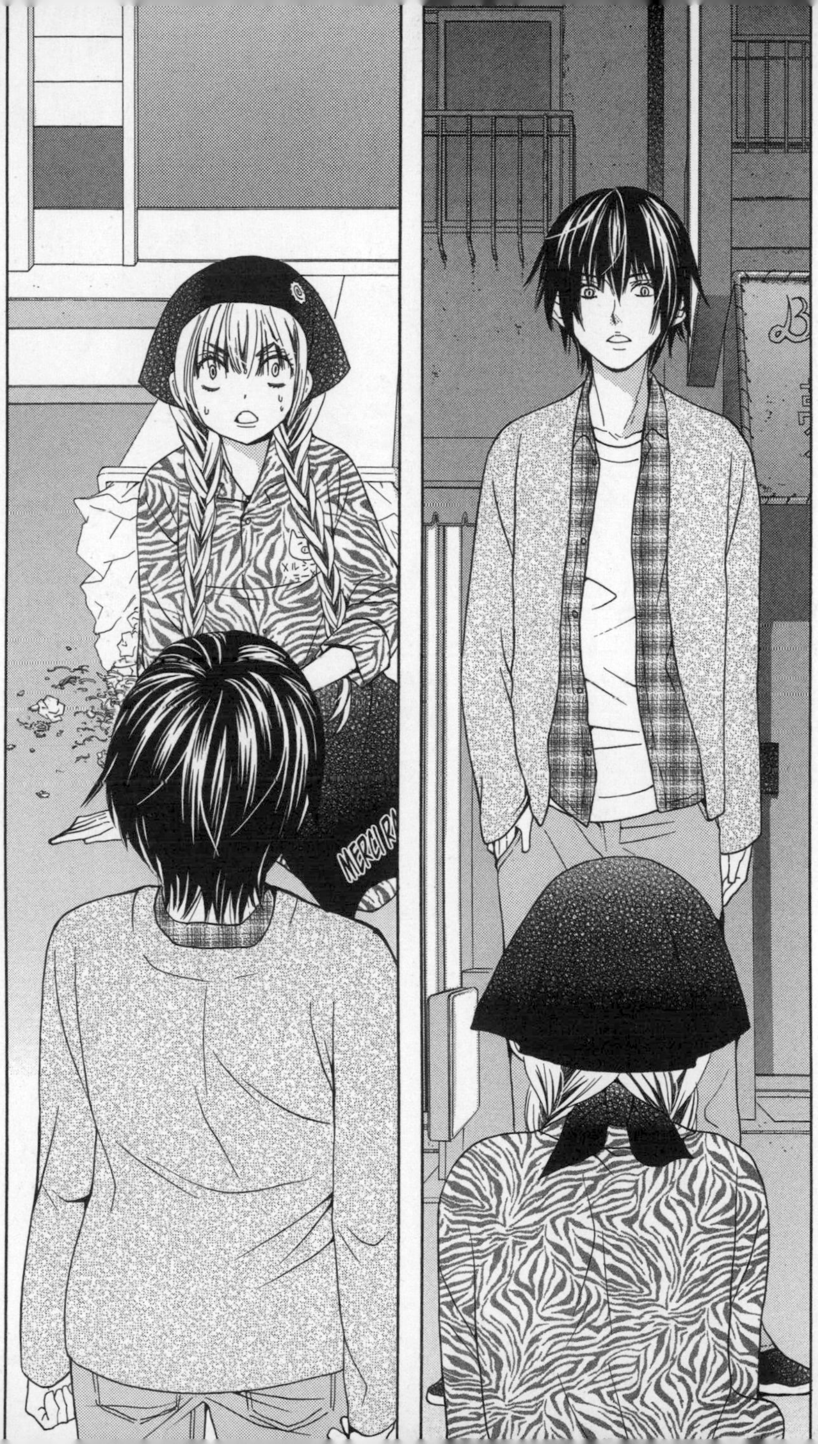

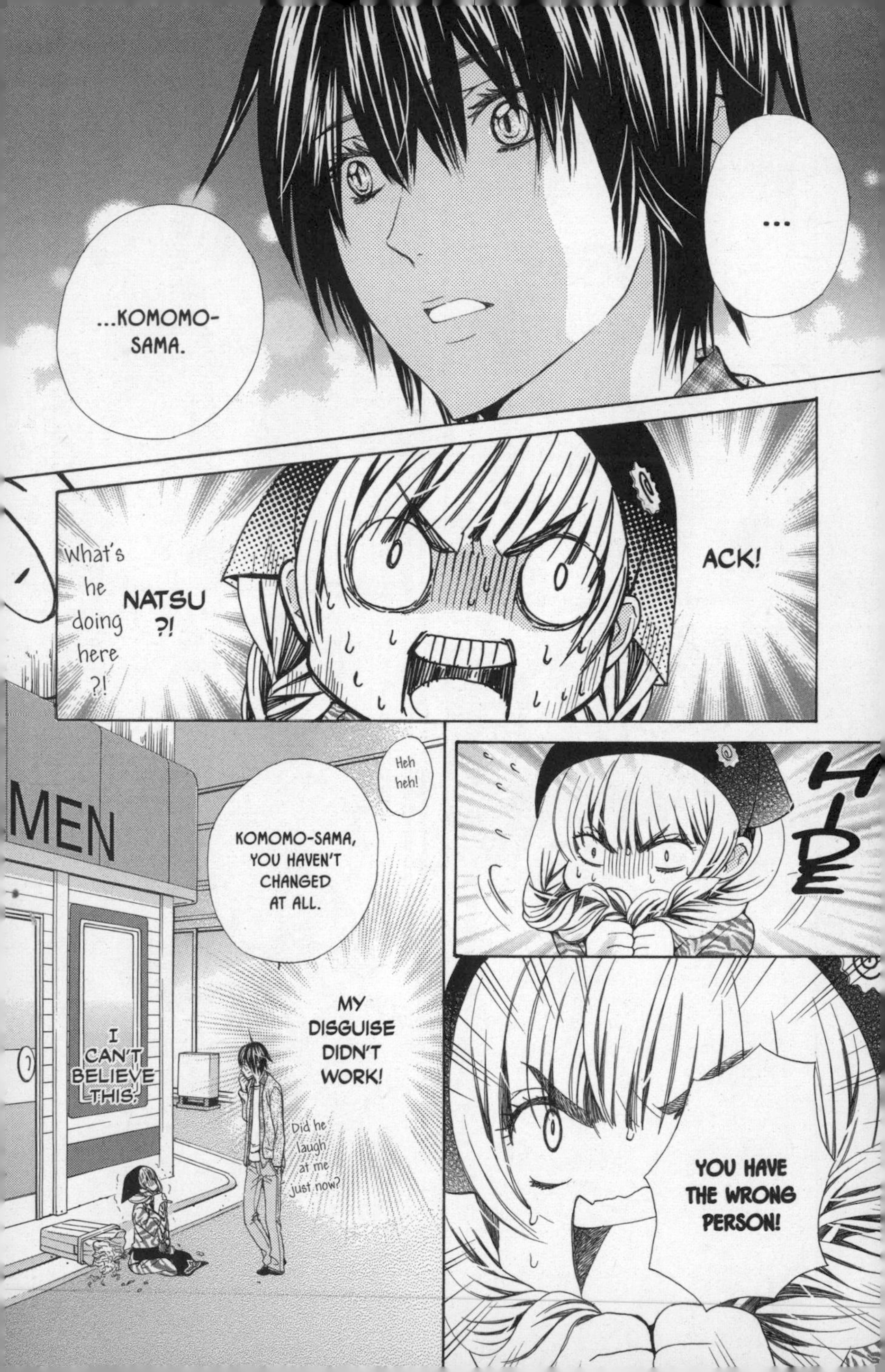
...
...KOMOMO-SAMA.
ACK!
NATSU?!
What's he doing here?!
HIDE
YOU HAVE THE WRONG PERSON!
Heh heh!
KOMOMO-SAMA, YOU HAVEN'T CHANGED AT ALL.
MY DISGUISE DIDN'T WORK!
Did he laugh at me just now?
I CAN'T BELIEVE THIS.
MEN

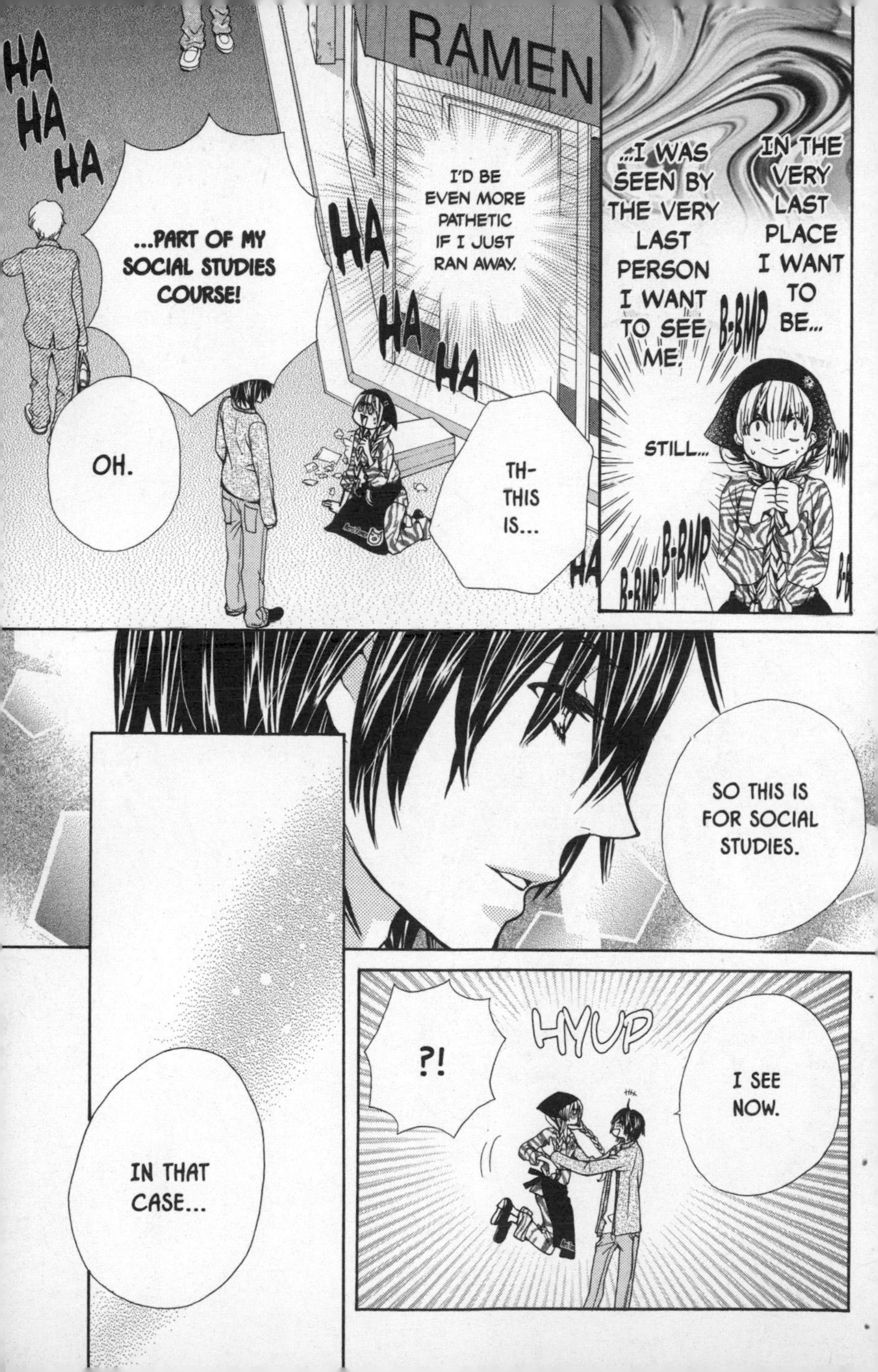
IN THE VERY LAST PLACE I WANT TO BE...
...I WAS SEEN BY THE VERY LAST PERSON I WANT TO SEE ME.
B-BMP
STILL...
B-BMP
B-BMP
B-BMP
RAMEN
I'D BE EVEN MORE PATHETIC IF I JUST RAN AWAY.
TH-THIS IS...
HA HA HA HA
...PART OF MY SOCIAL STUDIES COURSE!
HA HA HA
OH.
SO THIS IS FOR SOCIAL STUDIES.
I SEE NOW.
HYUP
?!
IN THAT CASE...

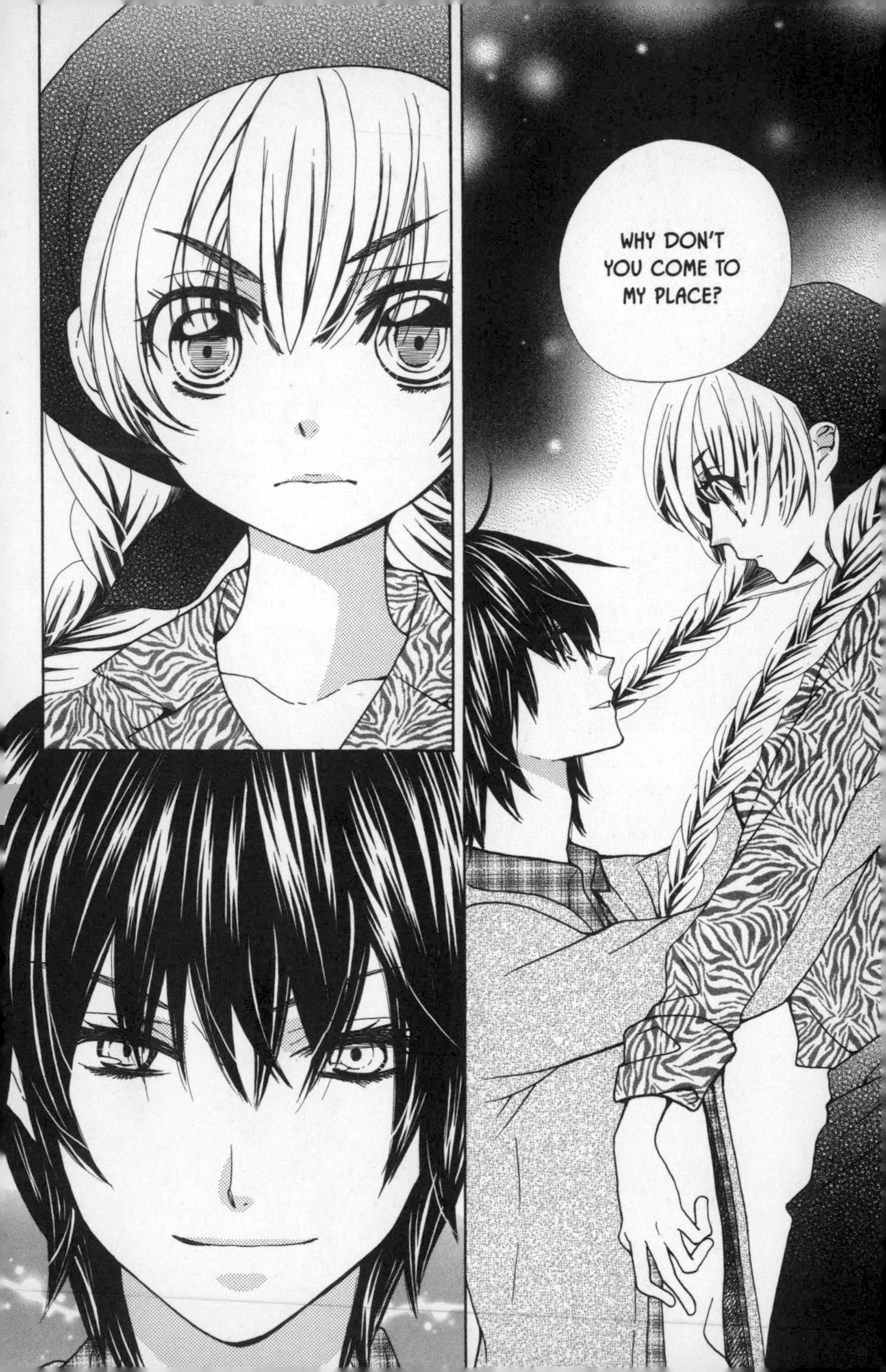
WHY DON'T YOU COME TO MY PLACE?

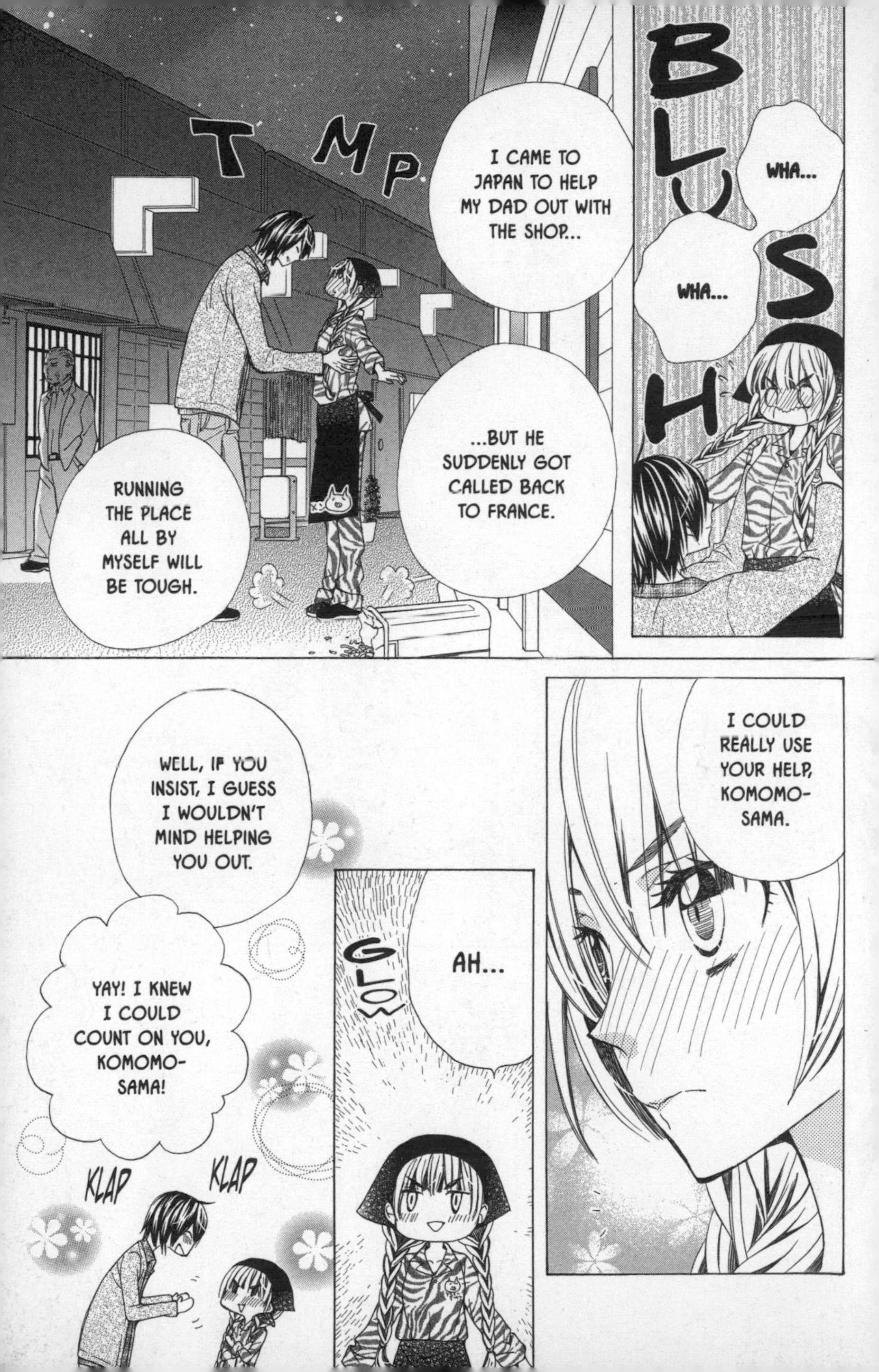
BLUSH
WHA...
WHA...
TMP
I CAME TO JAPAN TO HELP MY DAD OUT WITH THE SHOP...
...BUT HE SUDDENLY GOT CALLED BACK TO FRANCE.
RUNNING THE PLACE ALL BY MYSELF WILL BE TOUGH.
I COULD REALLY USE YOUR HELP, KOMOMO-SAMA.
WELL, IF YOU INSIST, I GUESS I WOULDN'T MIND HELPING YOU OUT.
GLOW
AH...
YAY! I KNEW I COULD COUNT ON YOU, KOMOMO-SAMA!
KLAP
KLAP

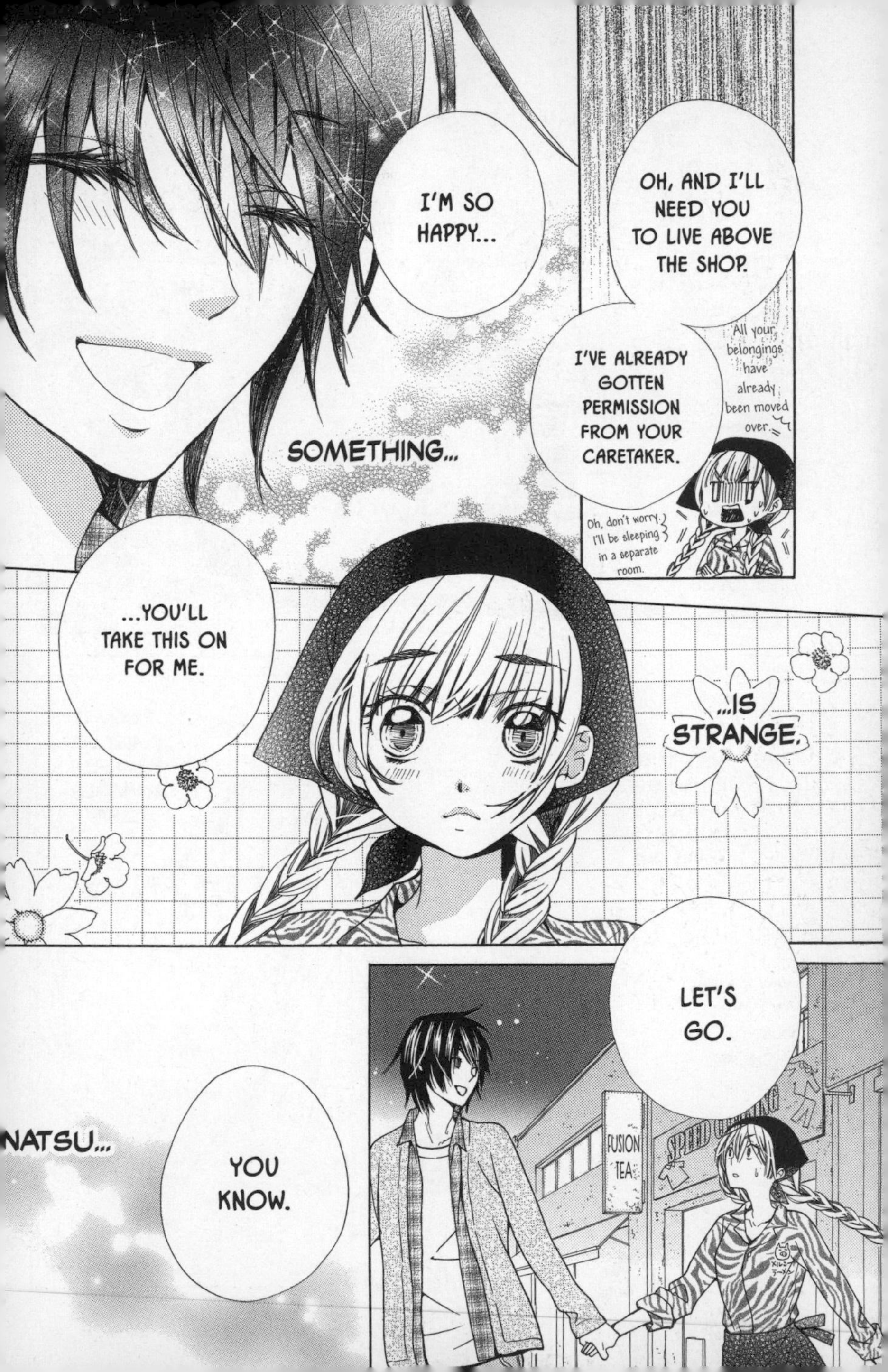
OH, AND I'LL NEED YOU TO LIVE ABOVE THE SHOP.
I'VE ALREADY GOTTEN PERMISSION FROM YOUR CARETAKER.
All your belongings have already been moved over.
Oh, don't worry. I'll be sleeping in a separate room.
I'M SO HAPPY...
SOMETHING...
...YOU'LL TAKE THIS ON FOR ME.
...IS STRANGE.
LET'S GO.
FUSION TEA
YOU KNOW.
NATSU...

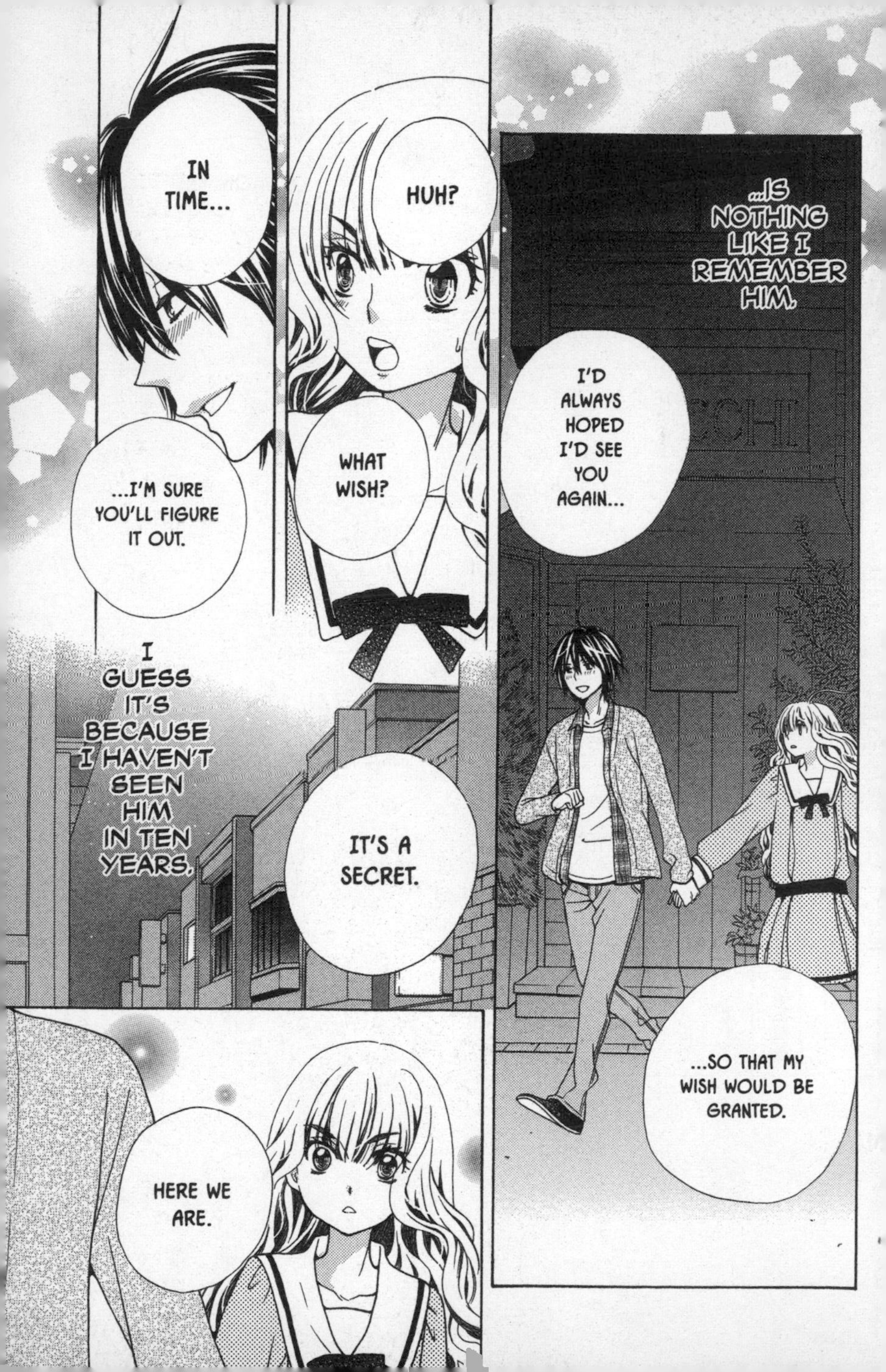
...IS NOTHING LIKE I REMEMBER HIM.
I'D ALWAYS HOPED I'D SEE YOU AGAIN...
...SO THAT MY WISH WOULD BE GRANTED.
HUH?
WHAT WISH?
IN TIME...
...I'M SURE YOU'LL FIGURE IT OUT.
I GUESS IT'S BECAUSE I HAVEN'T SEEN HIM IN TEN YEARS.
IT'S A SECRET.
HERE WE ARE.

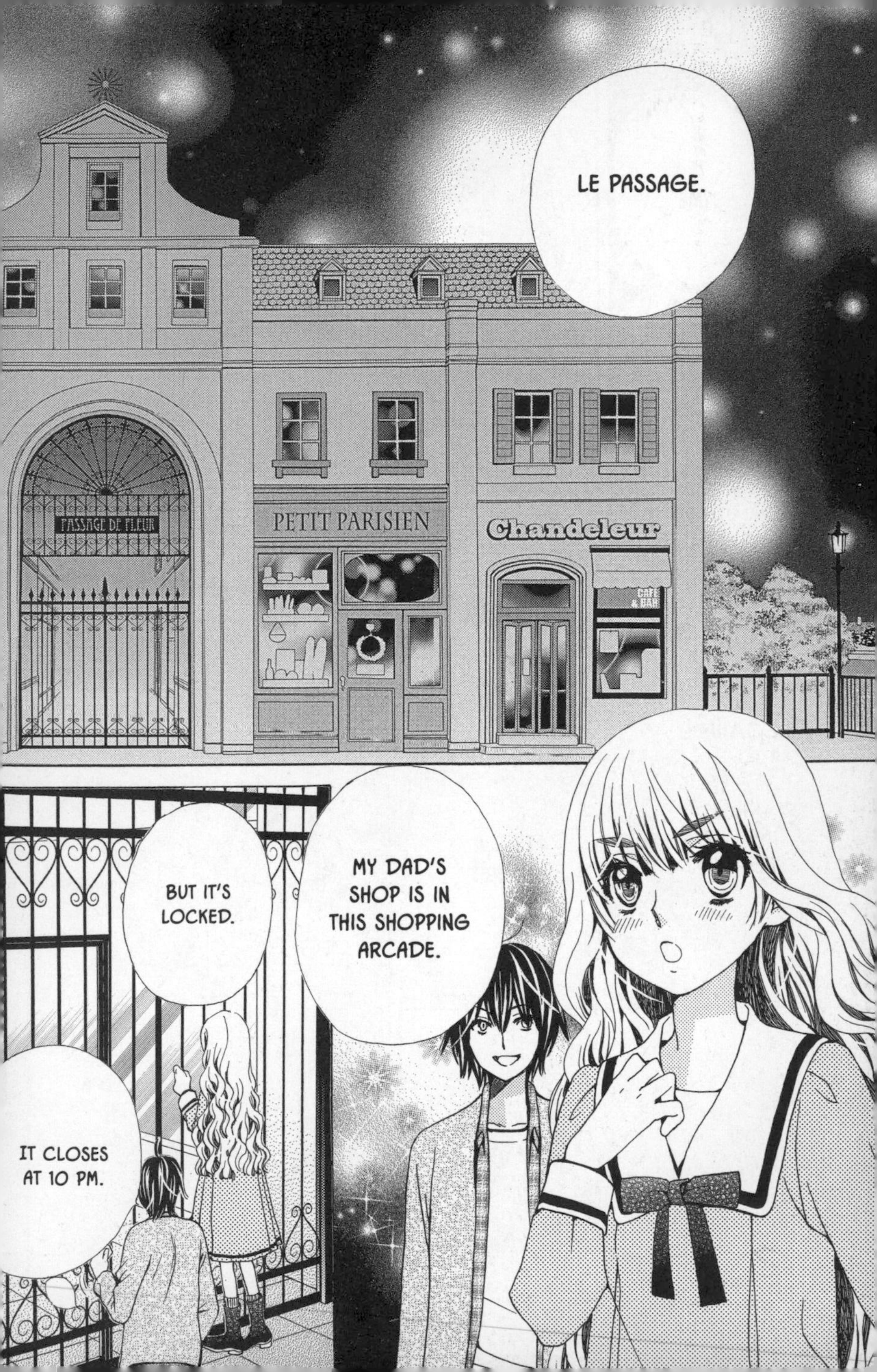
LE PASSAGE.
PASSAGE DE FLEUR
PETIT PARISIEN
Chandeleur
MY DAD'S SHOP IS IN THIS SHOPPING ARCADE.
BUT IT'S LOCKED.
IT CLOSES AT 10 PM.

FLEURISTE OLIVIER
CHAK
BUT WITH THE KEY, WE CAN GET IN.
KREAK
"LE PASSAGE."

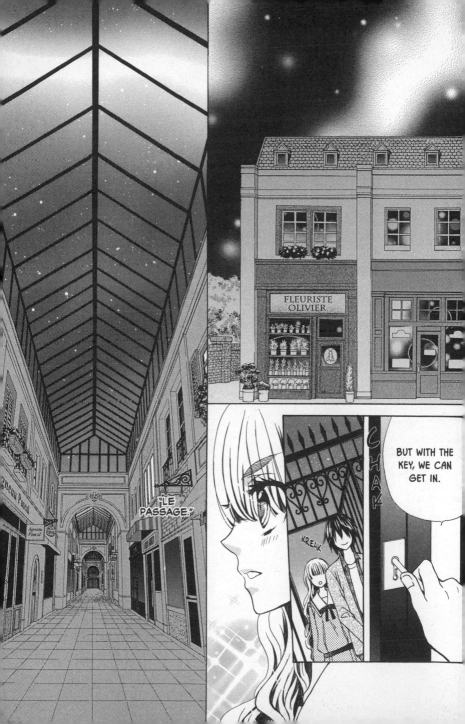

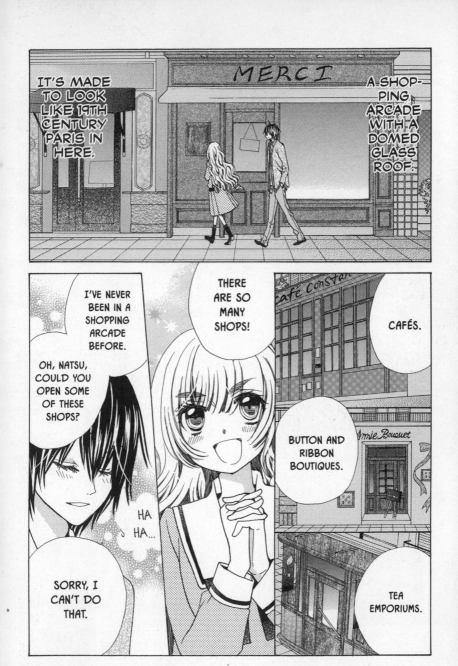

MERCI
A SHOPPING ARCADE WITH A DOMED GLASS ROOF.
IT'S MADE TO LOOK LIKE 19TH CENTURY PARIS IN HERE.
CAFÉS.
BUTTON AND RIBBON BOUTIQUES.
Amie Bouquet
TEA EMPORIUMS.
THERE ARE SO MANY SHOPS!
I'VE NEVER BEEN IN A SHOPPING ARCADE BEFORE.
OH, NATSU, COULD YOU OPEN SOME OF THESE SHOPS?
HA HA...
SORRY, I CAN'T DO THAT.

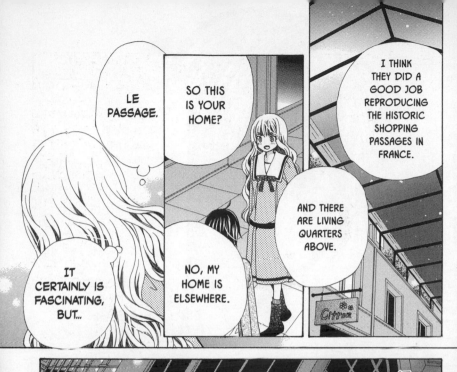

I THINK THEY DID A GOOD JOB REPRODUCING THE HISTORIC SHOPPING PASSAGES IN FRANCE.
AND THERE ARE LIVING QUARTERS ABOVE.
Citron
SO THIS IS YOUR HOME?
NO, MY HOME IS ELSEWHERE.
LE PASSAGE.
IT CERTAINLY IS FASCINATING, BUT...
...IT FEELS LIKE A LABY-RINTH I COULD GET LOST IN.
Editions de Paris
ALL RIGHT.
KOMOMO-SAMA.

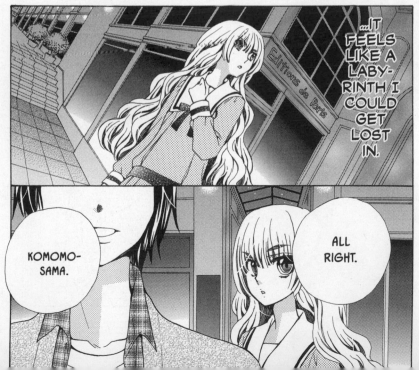

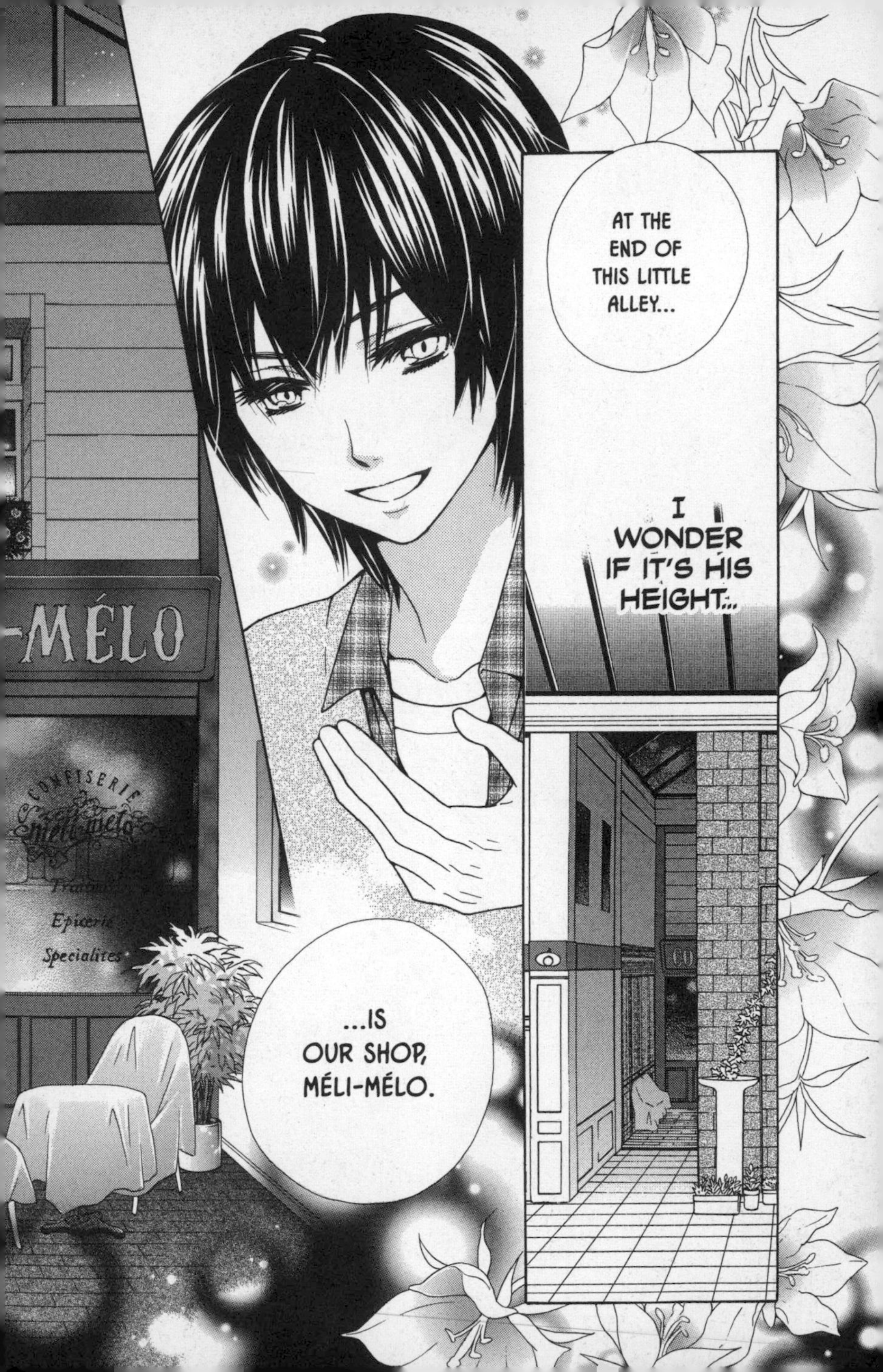

AT THE END OF THIS LITTLE ALLEY...
I WONDER IF IT'S HIS HEIGHT...
-MÉLO
CONFISERIE
méli-mélo
Epicerie
Specialites
...IS OUR SHOP, MÉLI-MÉLO.

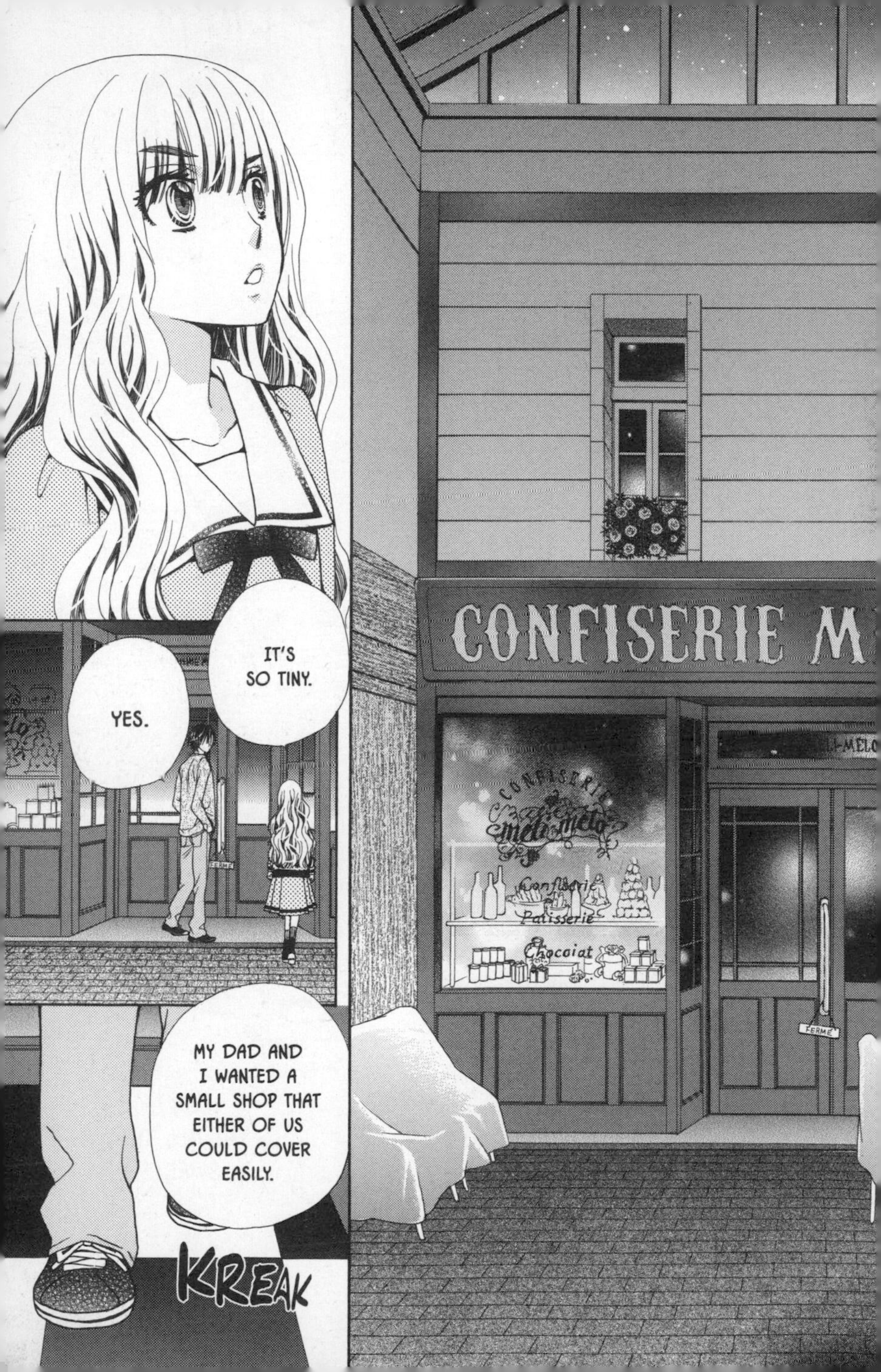

CONFISERIE M
CONFISERIE
meli-melo
Confiserie
Patisserie
Chocolat
FERMÉ
IT'S SO TINY.
YES.
MY DAD AND I WANTED A SMALL SHOP THAT EITHER OF US COULD COVER EASILY.
KREAK

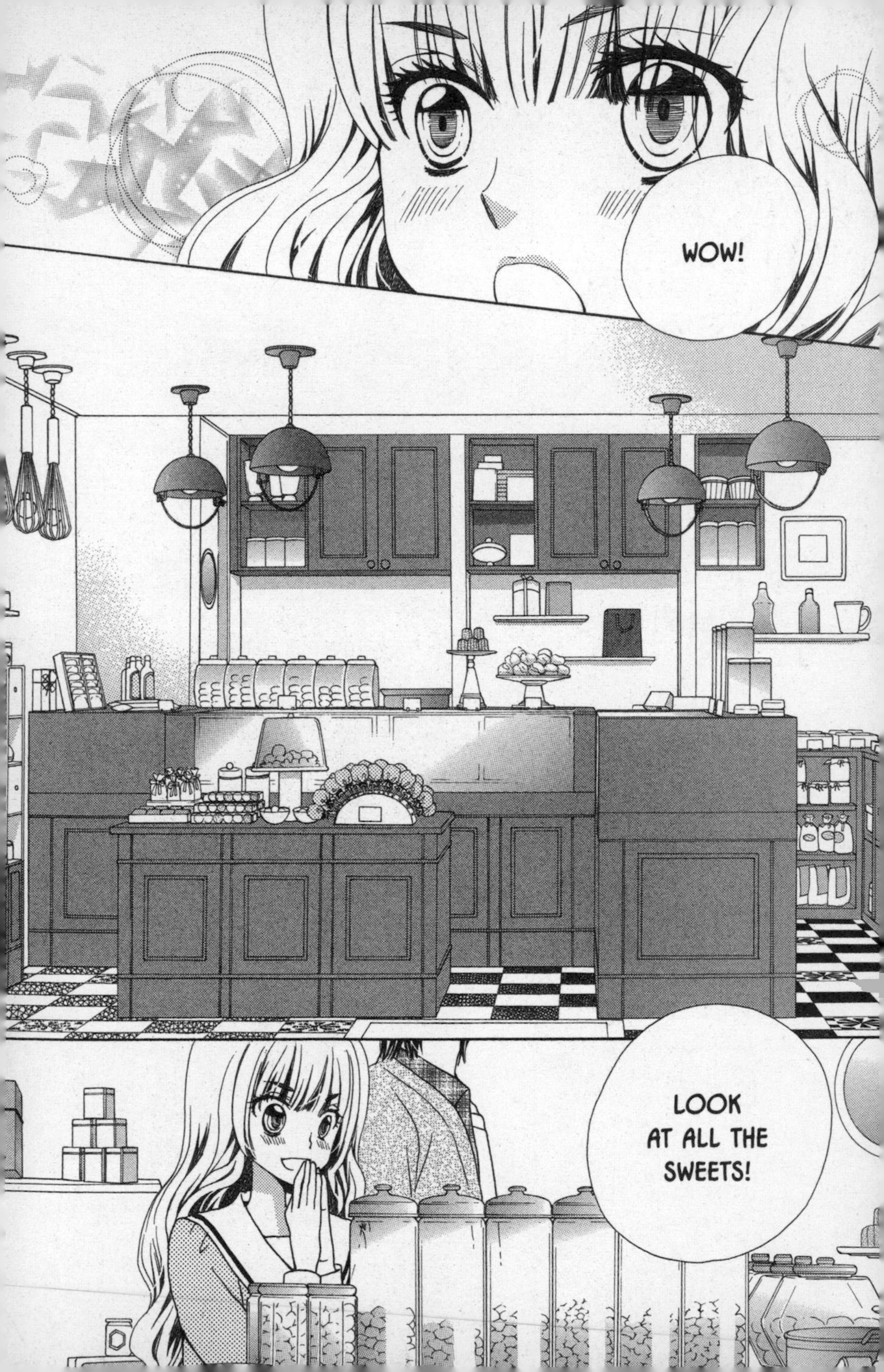
WOW!
LOOK AT ALL THE SWEETS!

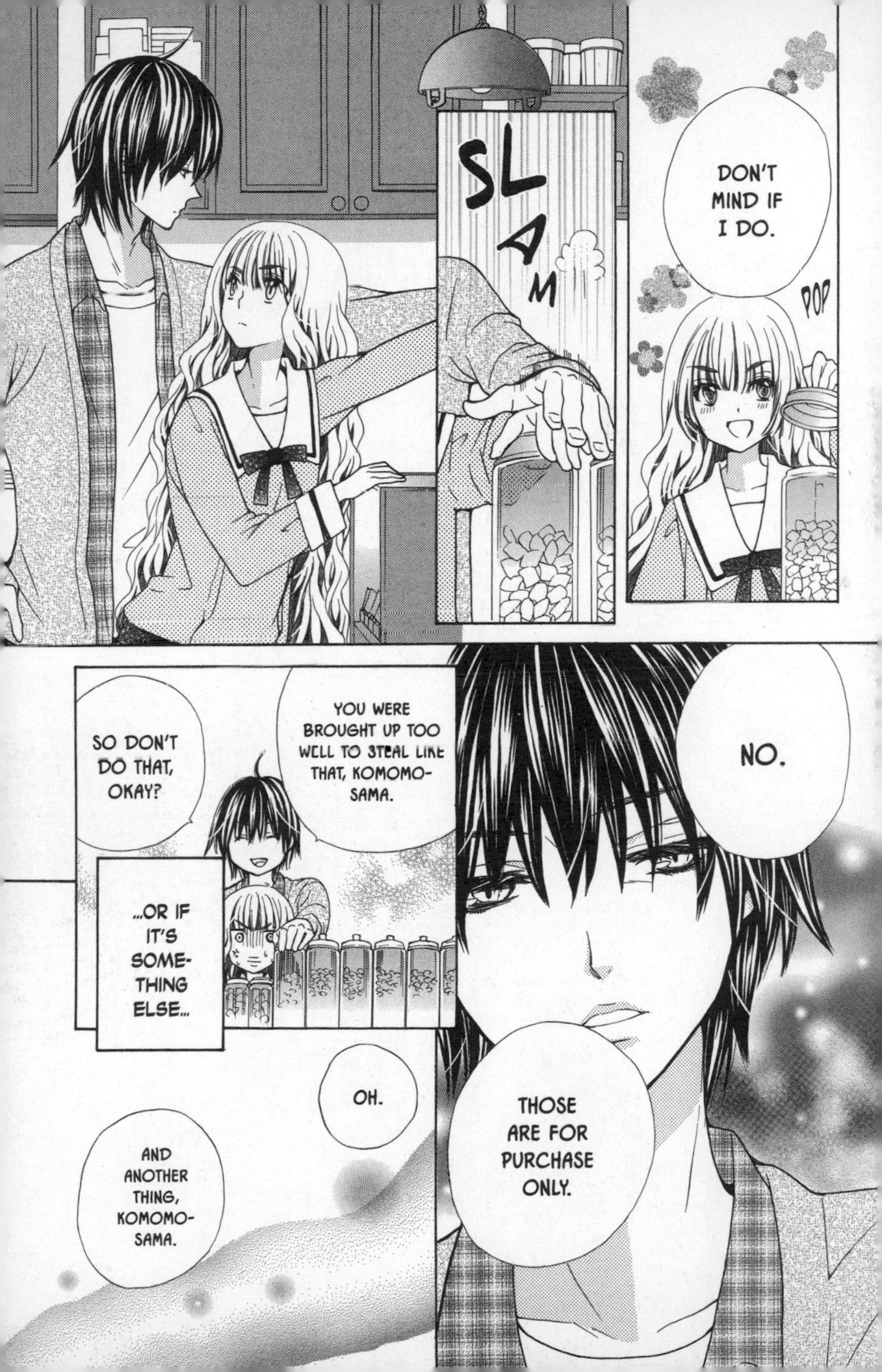
DON'T MIND IF I DO.
POP
SLAM
NO.
THOSE ARE FOR PURCHASE ONLY.
YOU WERE BROUGHT UP TOO WELL TO STEAL LIKE THAT, KOMOMO-SAMA.
SO DON'T DO THAT, OKAY?
...OR IF IT'S SOME-THING ELSE...
OH.
AND ANOTHER THING, KOMOMO-SAMA.

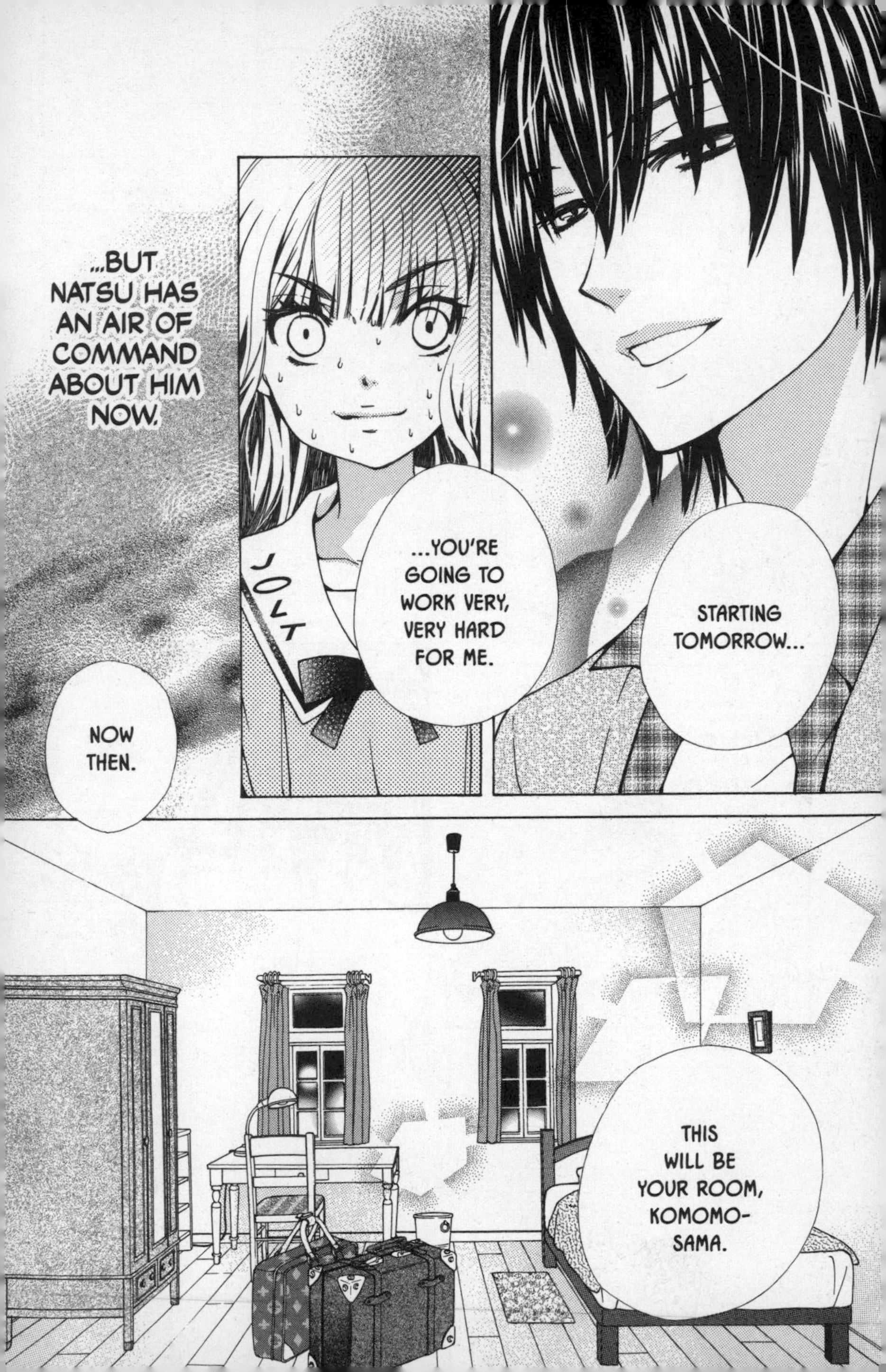
STARTING TOMORROW...
...YOU'RE GOING TO WORK VERY, VERY HARD FOR ME.
JOLT
...BUT NATSU HAS AN AIR OF COMMAND ABOUT HIM NOW.
NOW THEN.
THIS WILL BE YOUR ROOM, KOMOMO-SAMA.

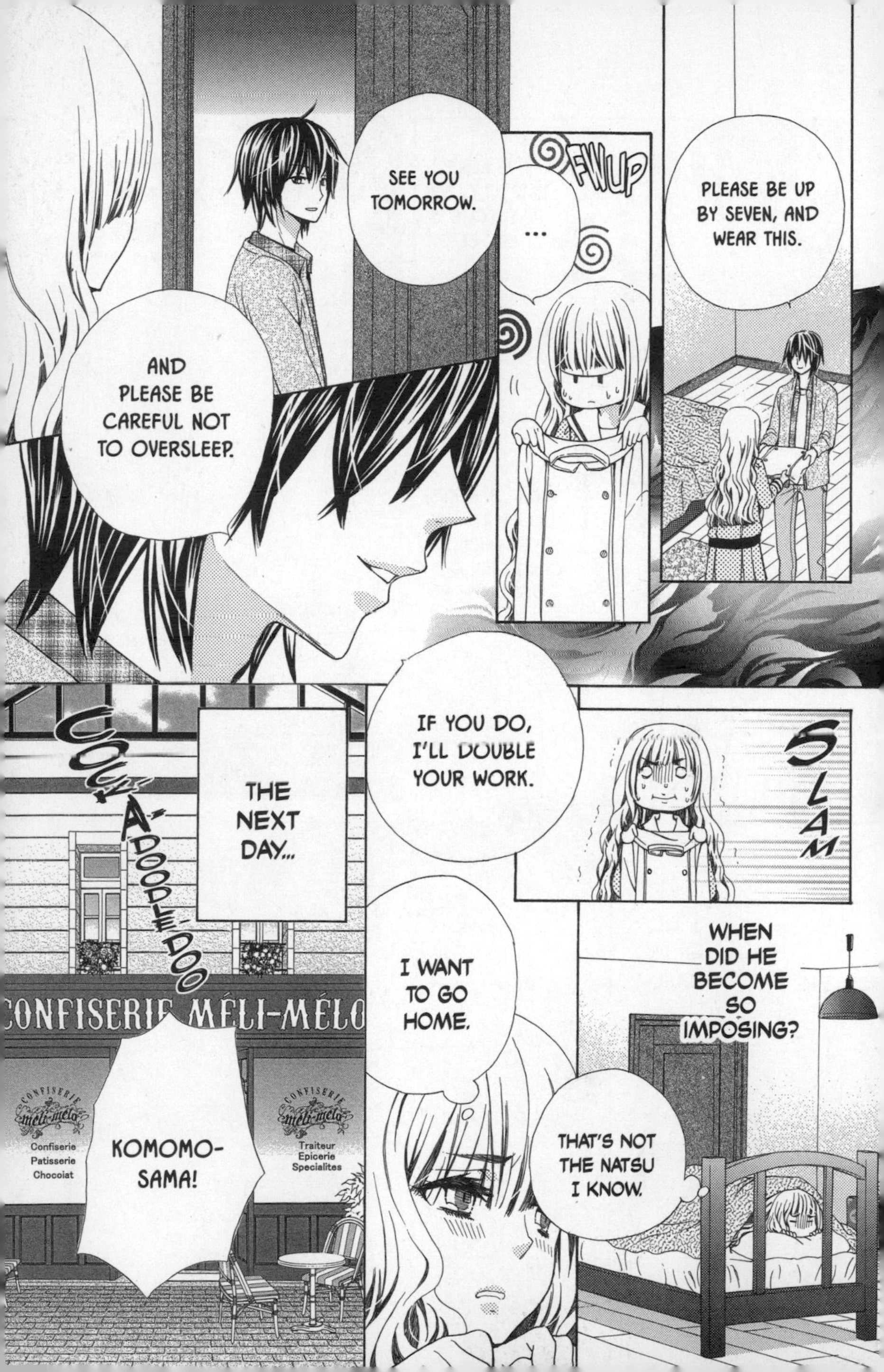

PLEASE BE UP BY SEVEN, AND WEAR THIS.
FWUP
...
SEE YOU TOMORROW.
AND PLEASE BE CAREFUL NOT TO OVERSLEEP.
IF YOU DO, I'LL DOUBLE YOUR WORK.
SLAM
WHEN DID HE BECOME SO IMPOSING?
I WANT TO GO HOME.
THAT'S NOT THE NATSU I KNOW.
COCK-A-DOODLE-DOO
THE NEXT DAY...
CONFISERIE MÉLI-MÉLO
CONFISERIE méli-mélo
Confiserie Patisserie Chocoiat
CONFISERIE méli-mélo
Traiteur Epicerie Specialites
KOMOMO-SAMA!

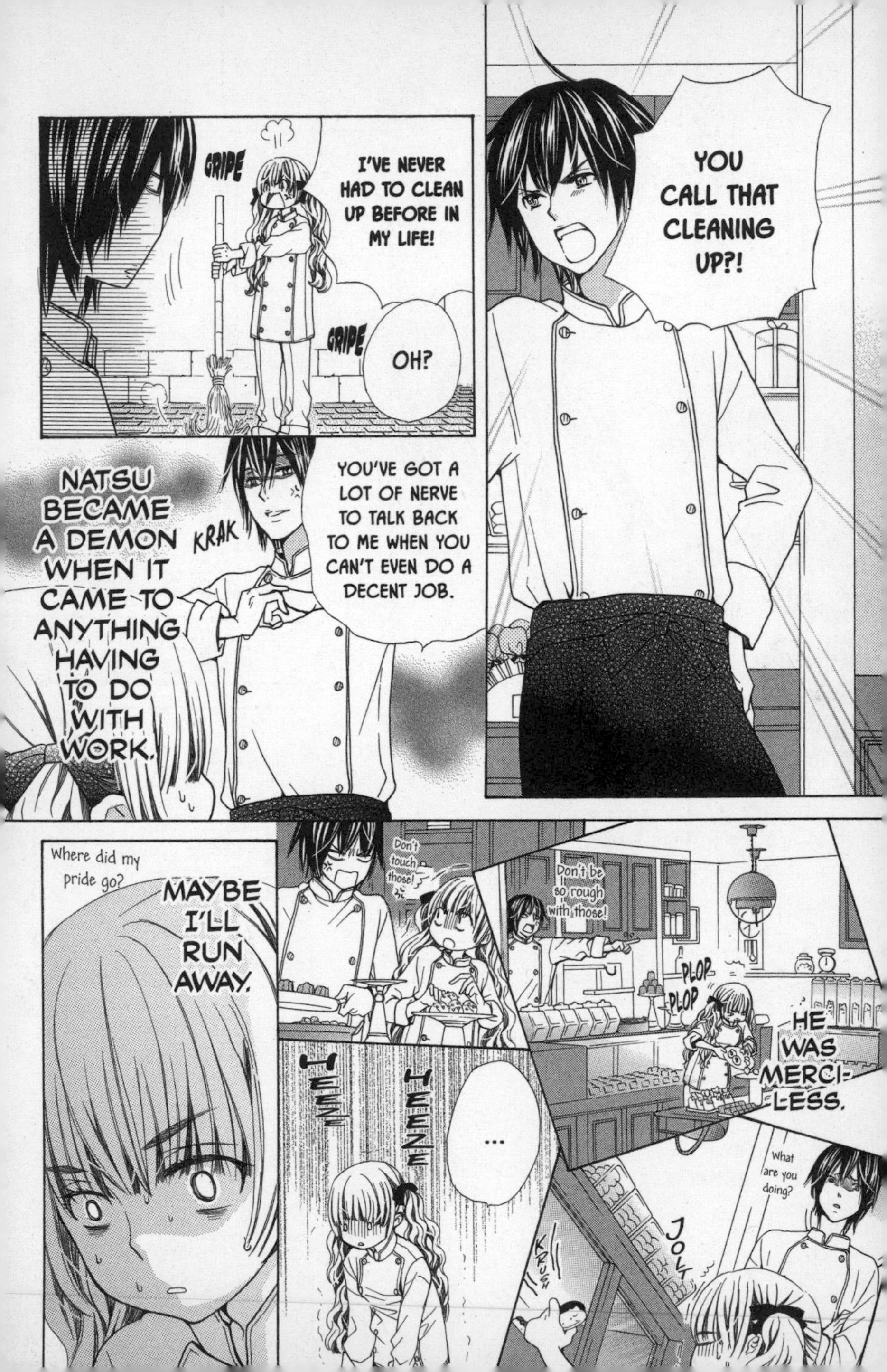
YOU CALL THAT CLEANING UP?!
GRIPE
I'VE NEVER HAD TO CLEAN UP BEFORE IN MY LIFE!
GRIPE
OH?
YOU'VE GOT A LOT OF NERVE TO TALK BACK TO ME WHEN YOU CAN'T EVEN DO A DECENT JOB.
KRAK
NATSU BECAME A DEMON WHEN IT CAME TO ANYTHING HAVING TO DO WITH WORK.
Don't be so rough with those!
PLOP
PLOP
HE WAS MERCILESS.
Don't touch those!
What are you doing?
JOLT
KRUSH
...
HEEZE
HEEZE
Where did my pride go?
MAYBE I'LL RUN AWAY.

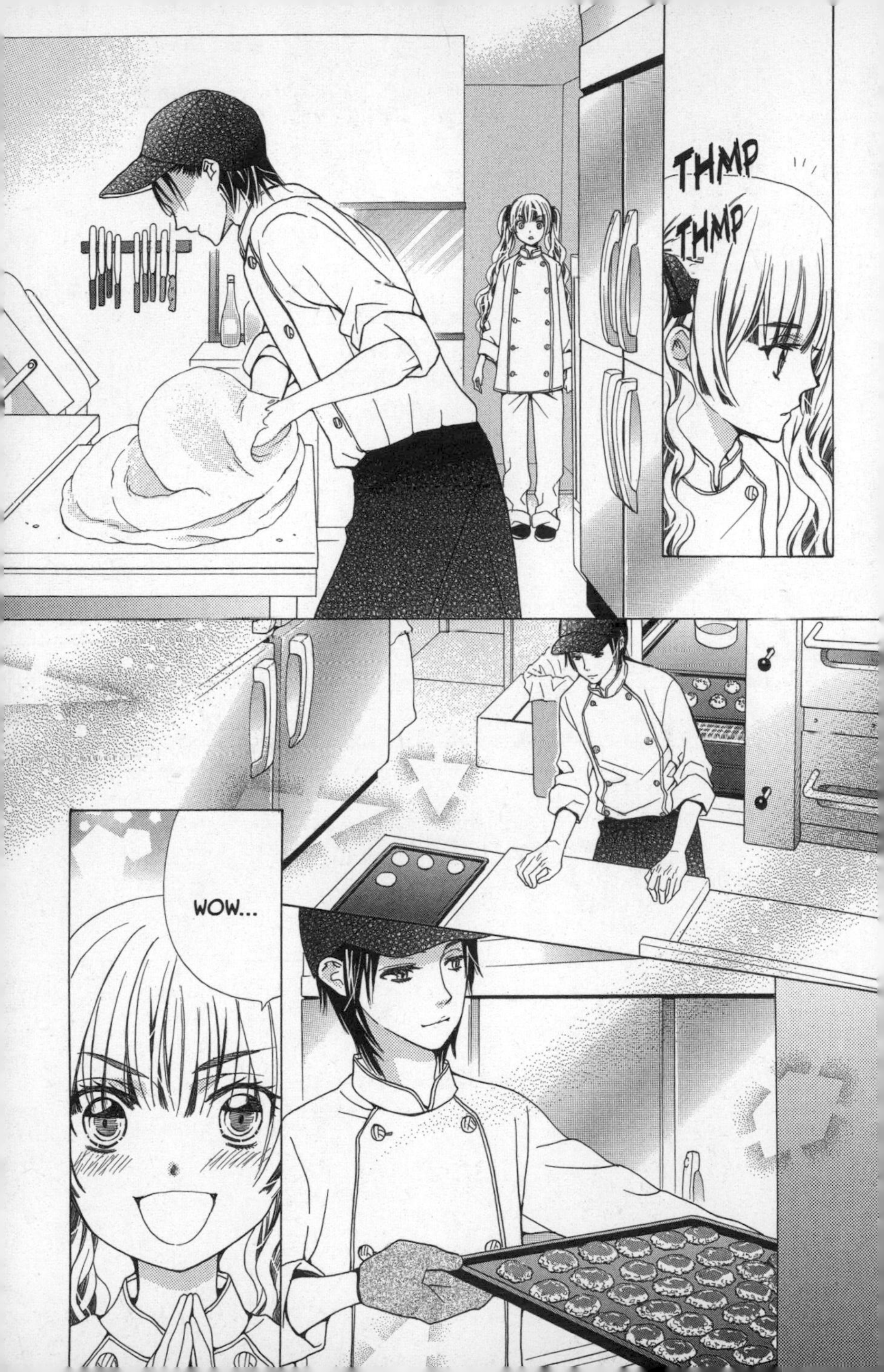
THMP THMP
WOW...

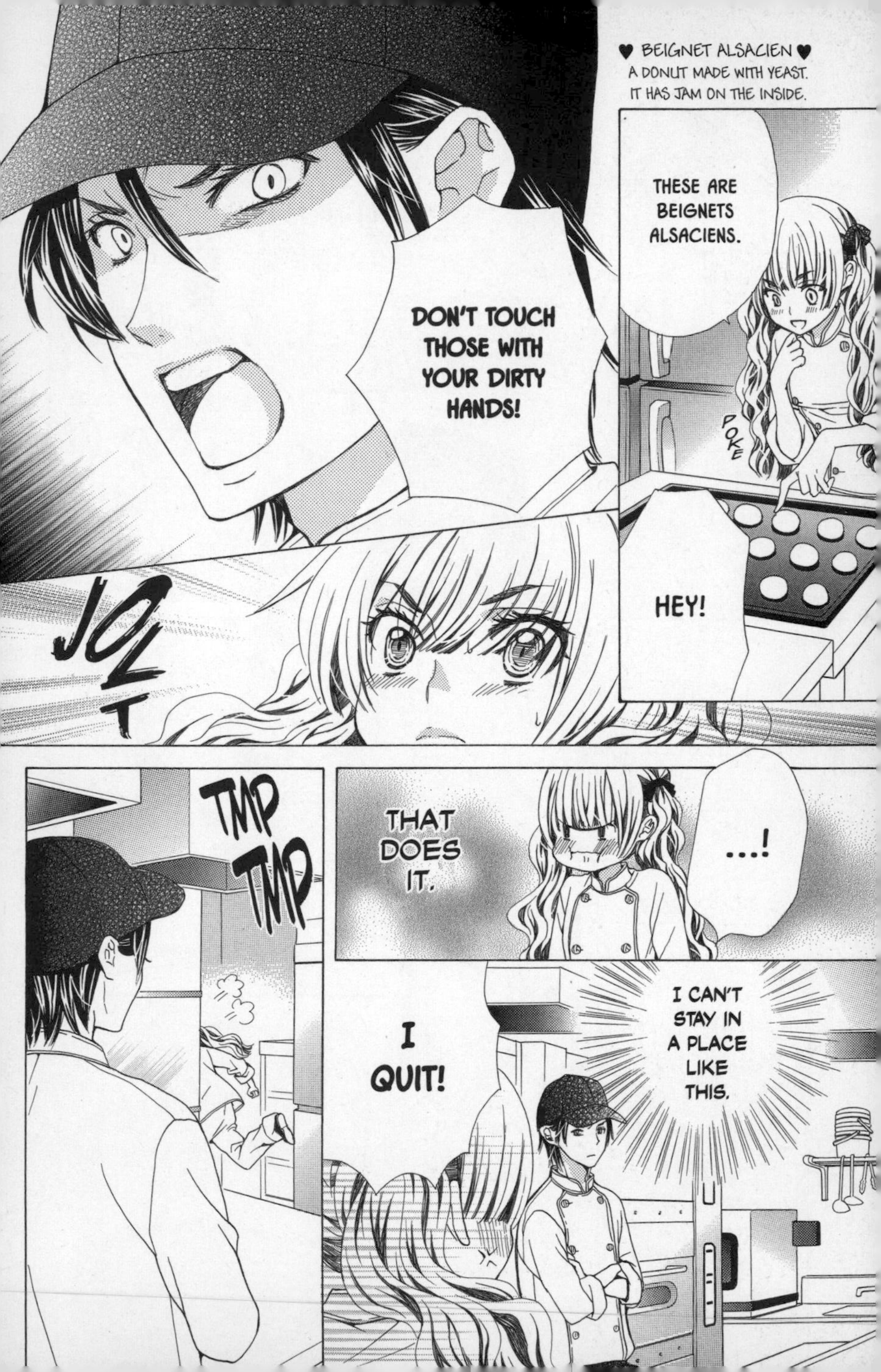
♥ BEIGNET ALSACIEN ♥
A DONUT MADE WITH YEAST.
IT HAS JAM ON THE INSIDE.
THESE ARE BEIGNETS ALSACIENS.
POKE
HEY!
DON'T TOUCH THOSE WITH YOUR DIRTY HANDS!
JOLT
...!
THAT DOES IT.
I CAN'T STAY IN A PLACE LIKE THIS.
I QUIT!
TMP TMP

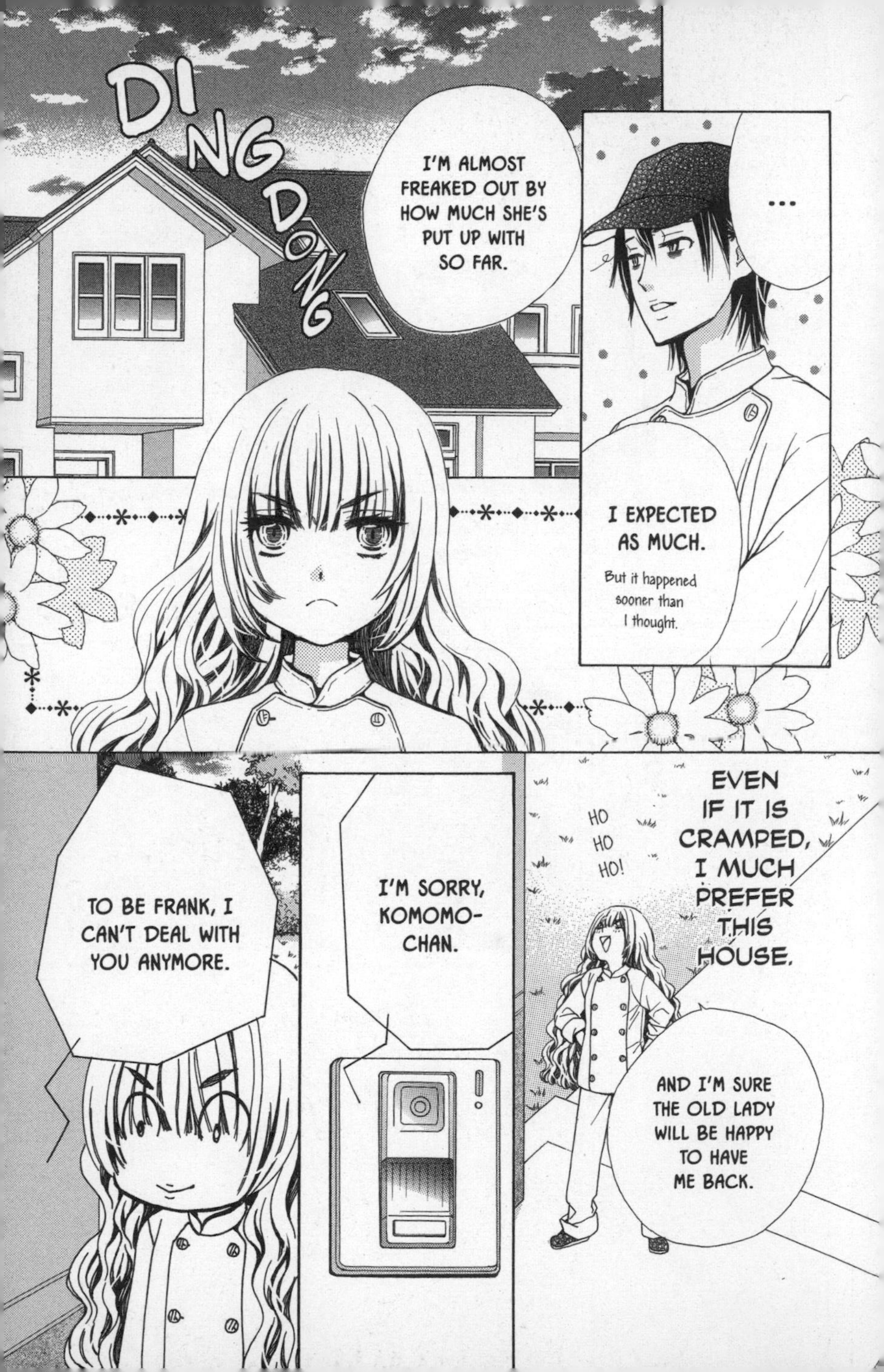

DING DONG
I'M ALMOST FREAKED OUT BY HOW MUCH SHE'S PUT UP WITH SO FAR.
...
I EXPECTED AS MUCH.
But it happened sooner than I thought.
EVEN IF IT IS CRAMPED, I MUCH PREFER THIS HOUSE.
HO HO HO!
AND I'M SURE THE OLD LADY WILL BE HAPPY TO HAVE ME BACK.
I'M SORRY, KOMOMO-CHAN.
TO BE FRANK, I CAN'T DEAL WITH YOU ANYMORE.

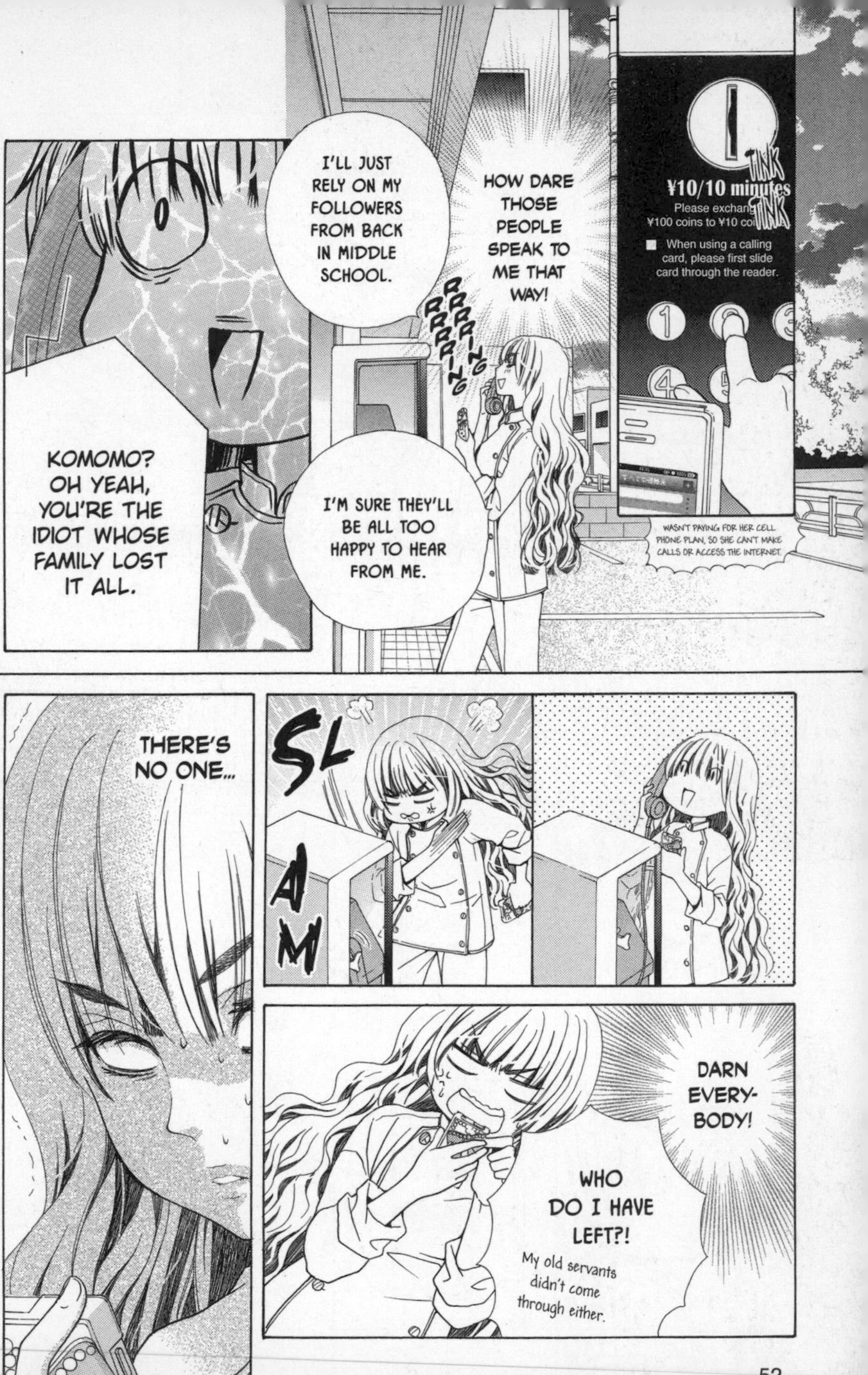
¥10/10 minutes
Please exchang
¥100 coins to ¥10 coi
When using a calling card, please first slide card through the reader.
TINK TINK
WASN'T PAYING FOR HER CELL PHONE PLAN, SO SHE CAN'T MAKE CALLS OR ACCESS THE INTERNET.
HOW DARE THOSE PEOPLE SPEAK TO ME THAT WAY!
I'LL JUST RELY ON MY FOLLOWERS FROM BACK IN MIDDLE SCHOOL.
RRRING RRRING
I'M SURE THEY'LL BE ALL TOO HAPPY TO HEAR FROM ME.
KOMOMO? OH YEAH, YOU'RE THE IDIOT WHOSE FAMILY LOST IT ALL.
SLAM
DARN EVERY-BODY!
WHO DO I HAVE LEFT?!
My old servants didn't come through either.
THERE'S NO ONE...

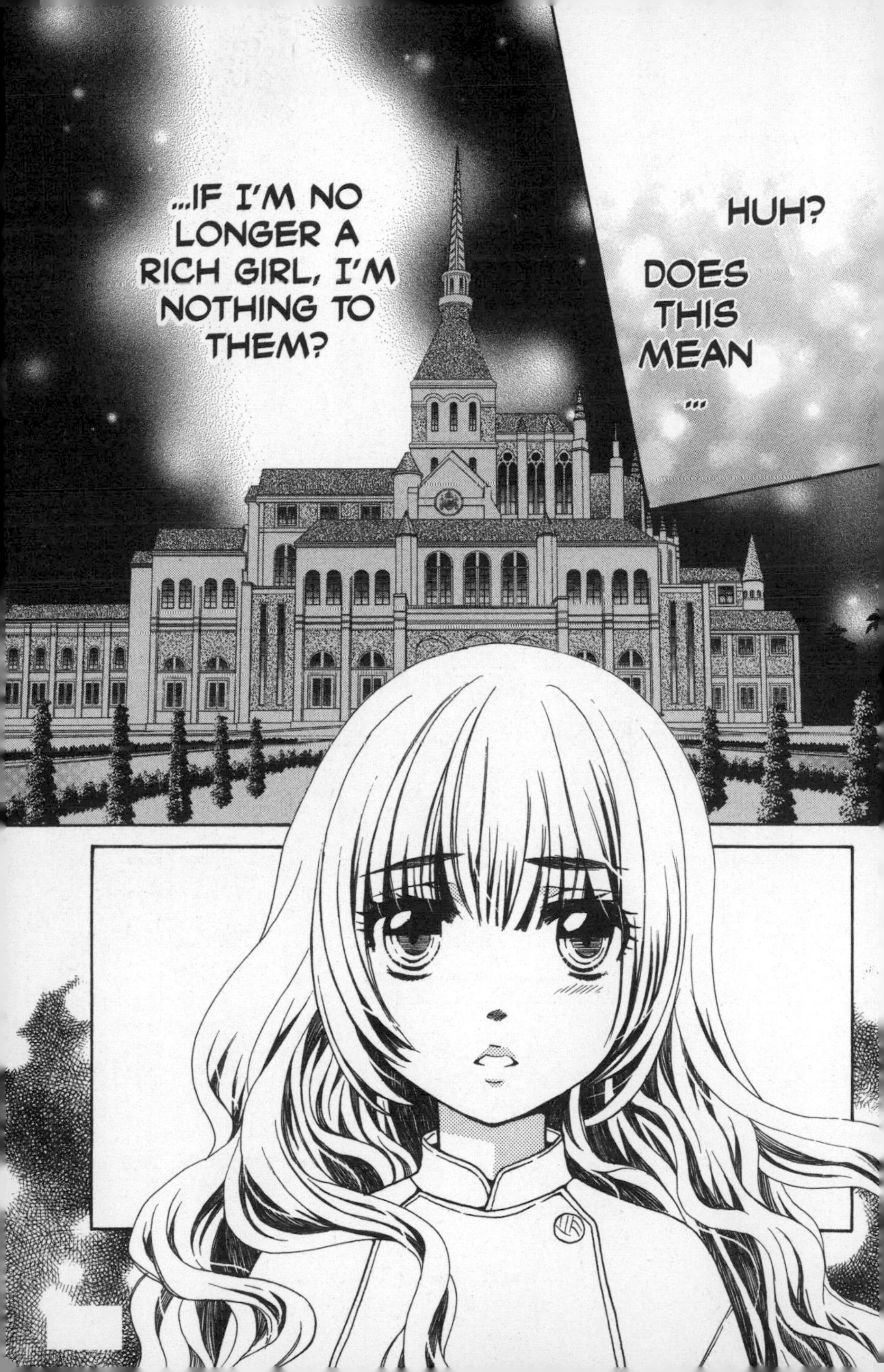
HUH?
DOES THIS MEAN ...
...IF I'M NO LONGER A RICH GIRL, I'M NOTHING TO THEM?

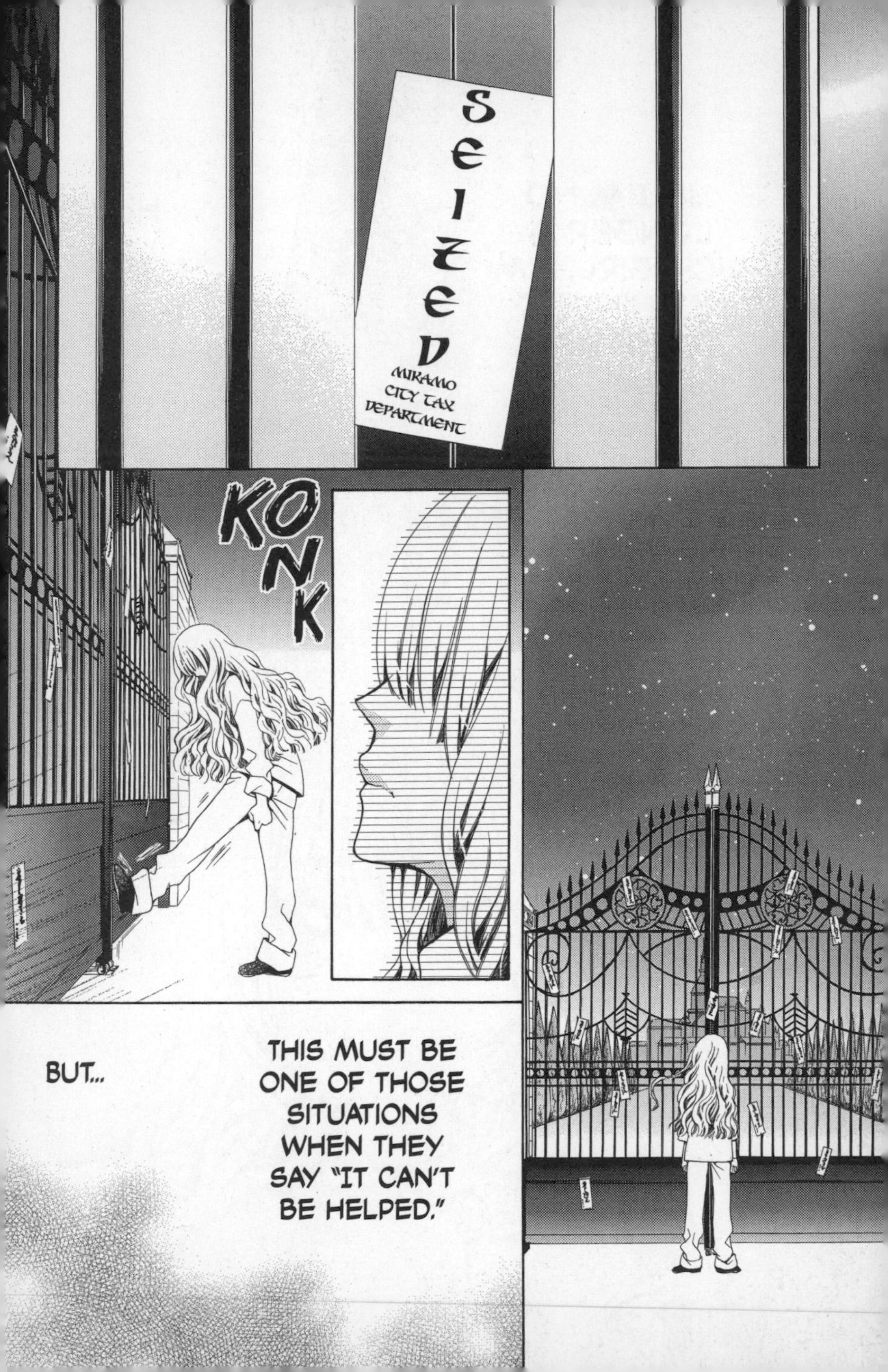
SEIZED
MIKAMO CITY TAX DEPARTMENT
KONK
THIS MUST BE ONE OF THOSE SITUATIONS WHEN THEY SAY "IT CAN'T BE HELPED."
BUT...

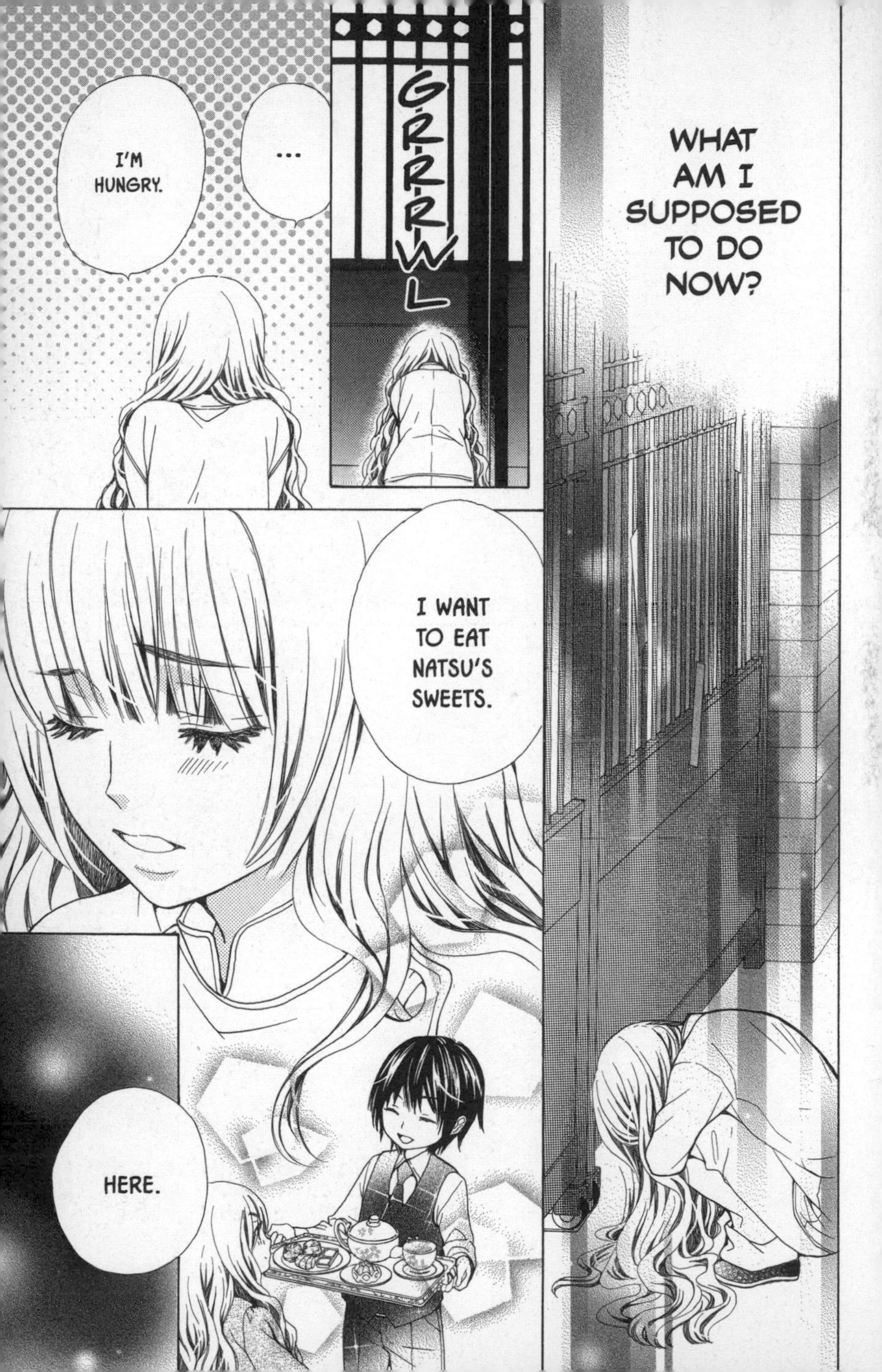
WHAT AM I SUPPOSED TO DO NOW?
GRRRWL
...
I'M HUNGRY.
I WANT TO EAT NATSU'S SWEETS.
HERE.

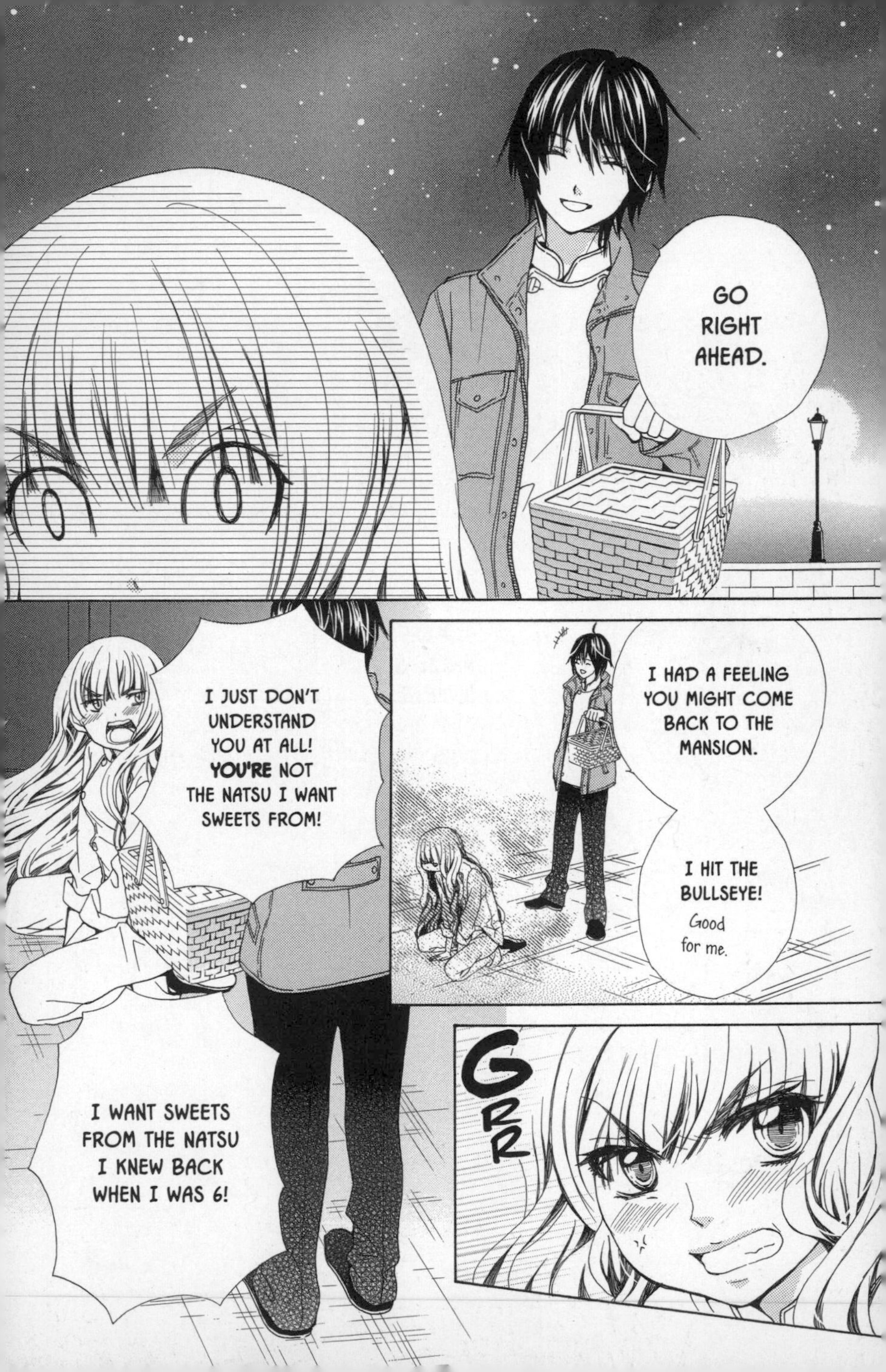
GO RIGHT AHEAD.
I HAD A FEELING YOU MIGHT COME BACK TO THE MANSION.
I HIT THE BULLSEYE!
Good for me.
GRR
I JUST DON'T UNDERSTAND YOU AT ALL! **YOU'RE** NOT THE NATSU I WANT SWEETS FROM!
I WANT SWEETS FROM THE NATSU I KNEW BACK WHEN I WAS 6!

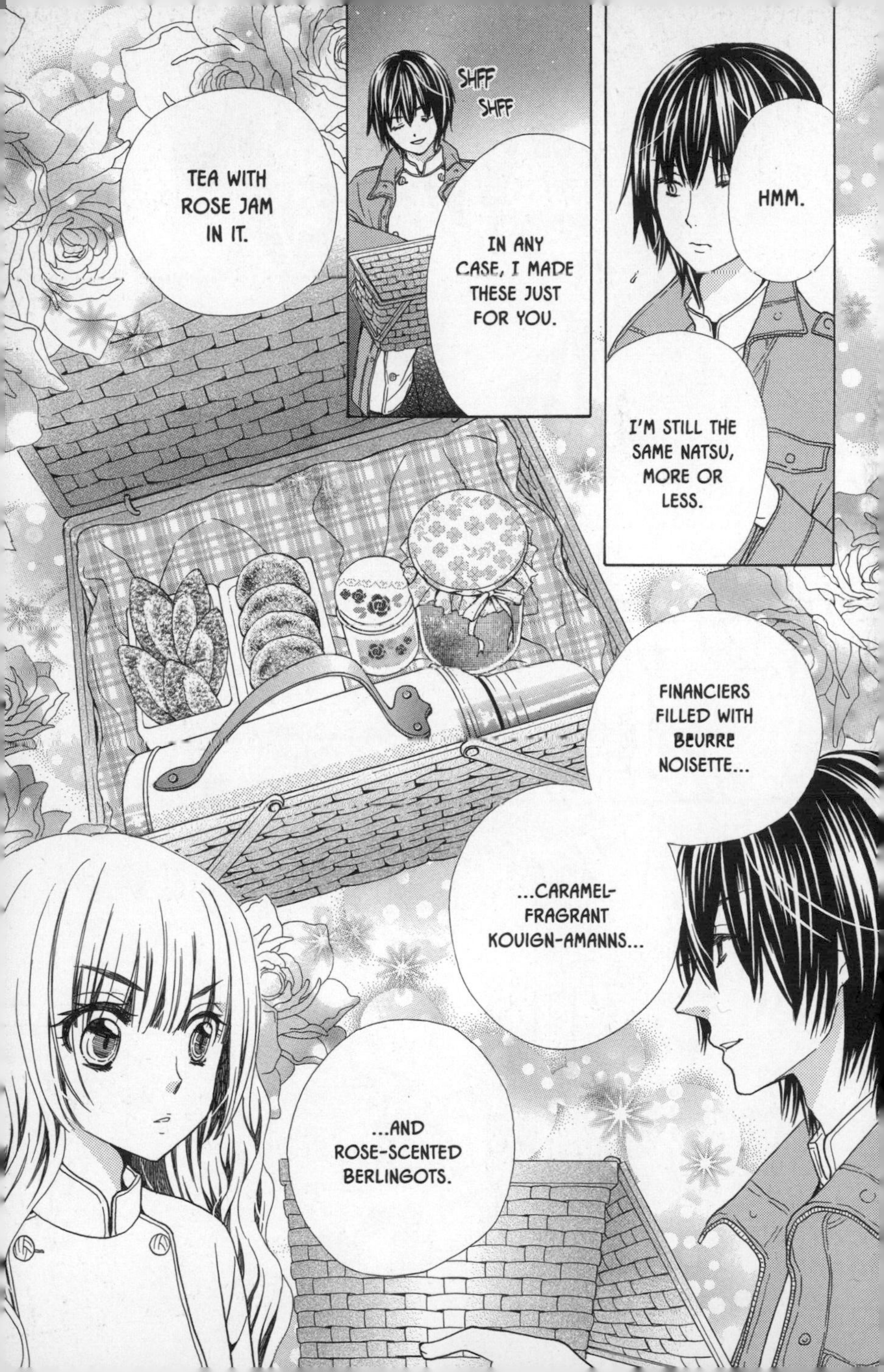
HMM.
I'M STILL THE SAME NATSU, MORE OR LESS.
SHFF SHFF
IN ANY CASE, I MADE THESE JUST FOR YOU.
TEA WITH ROSE JAM IN IT.
FINANCIERS FILLED WITH BEURRE NOISETTE...
...CARAMEL-FRAGRANT KOUIGN-AMANNS...
...AND ROSE-SCENTED BERLINGOTS.

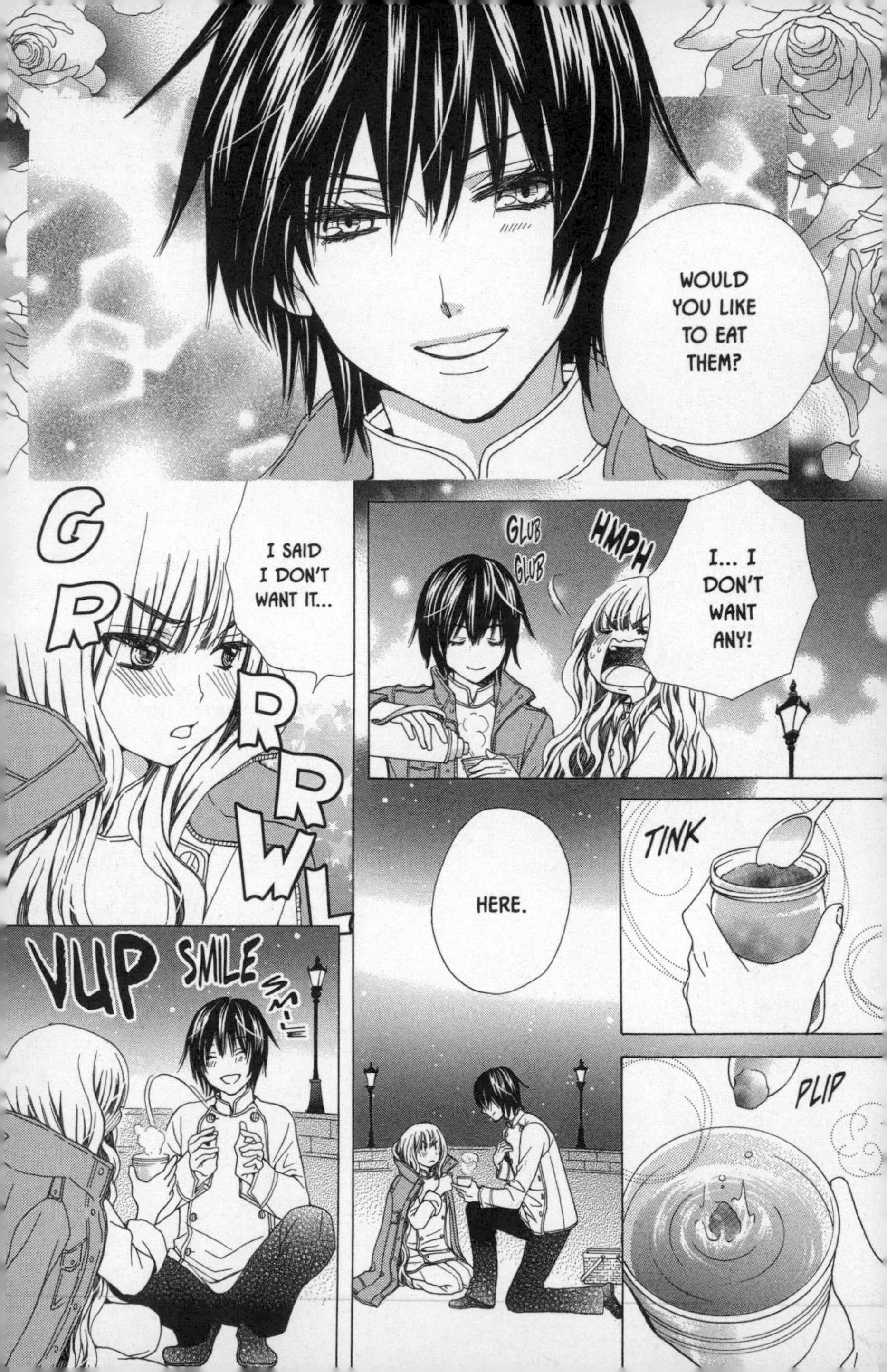
WOULD YOU LIKE TO EAT THEM?
I... I DON'T WANT ANY!
HMPH
GLUB GLUB
I SAID I DON'T WANT IT...
GRRRWL
TINK
PLIP
HERE.
SMILE SMILE
VUP

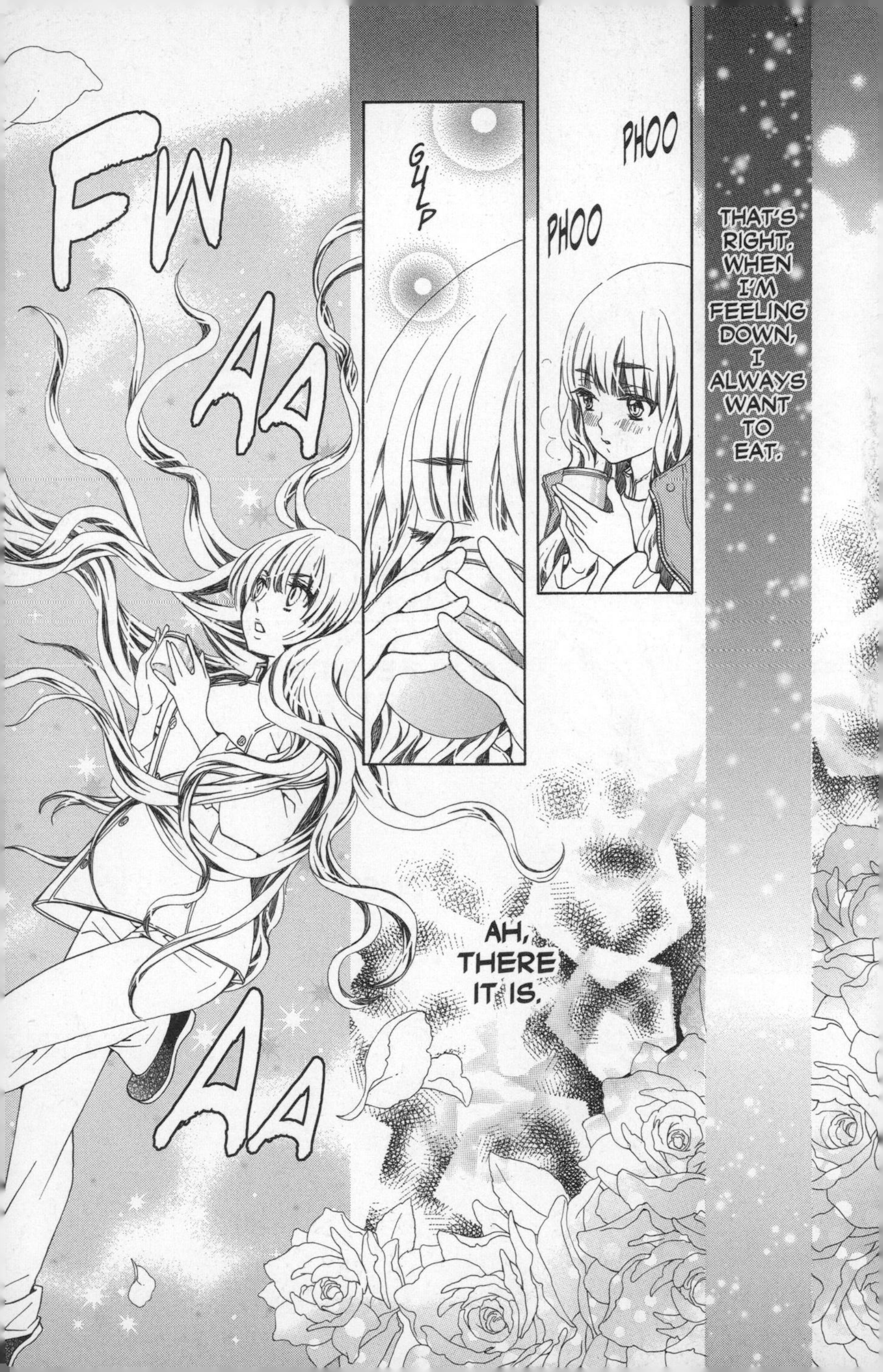
THAT'S RIGHT. WHEN I'M FEELING DOWN, I ALWAYS WANT TO EAT.
PHOO
PHOO
GULP
FWAAAA
AH, THERE IT IS.

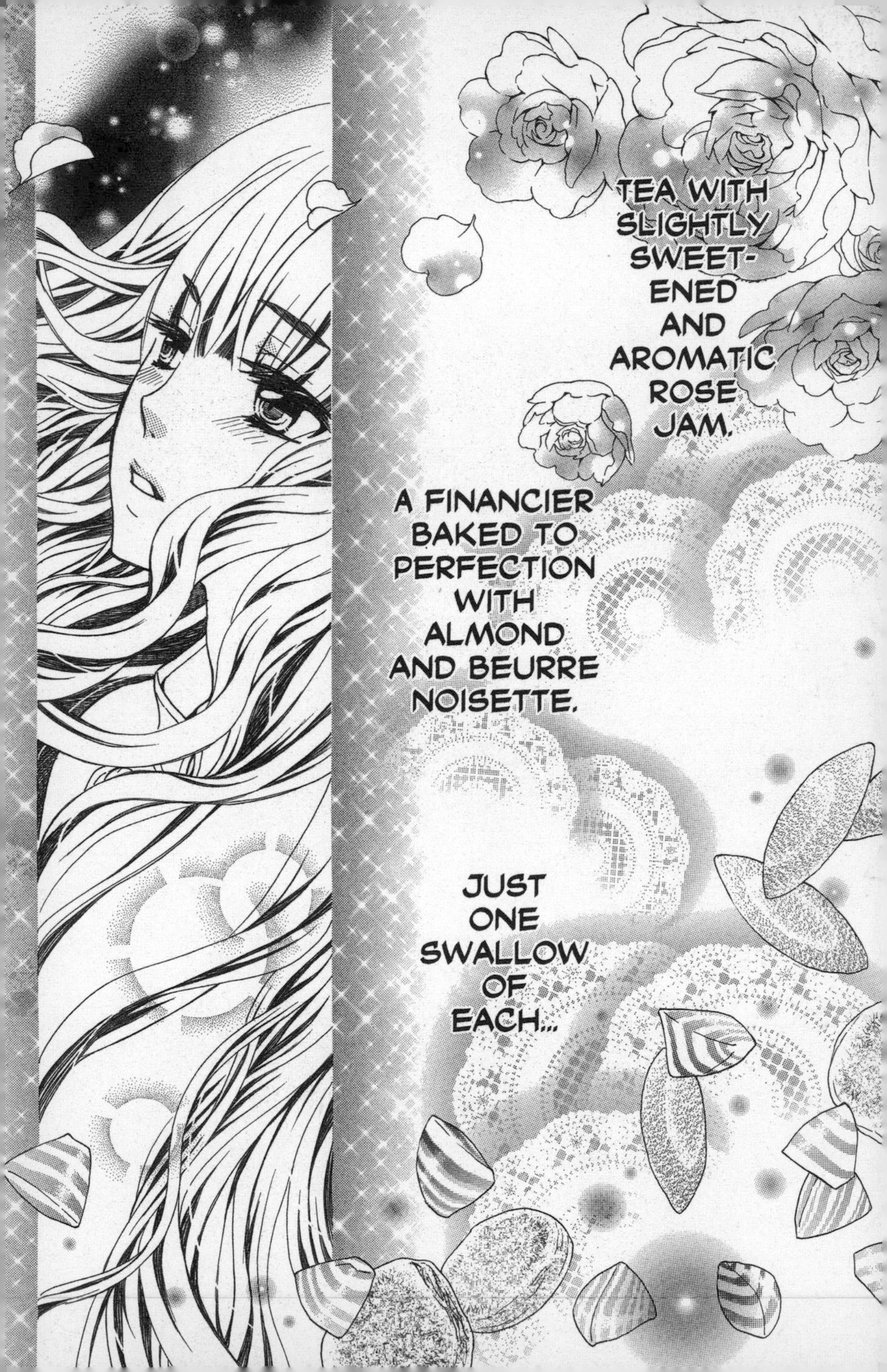
TEA WITH SLIGHTLY SWEET-ENED AND AROMATIC ROSE JAM.
A FINANCIER BAKED TO PERFECTION WITH ALMOND AND BEURRE NOISETTE.
JUST ONE SWALLOW OF EACH...

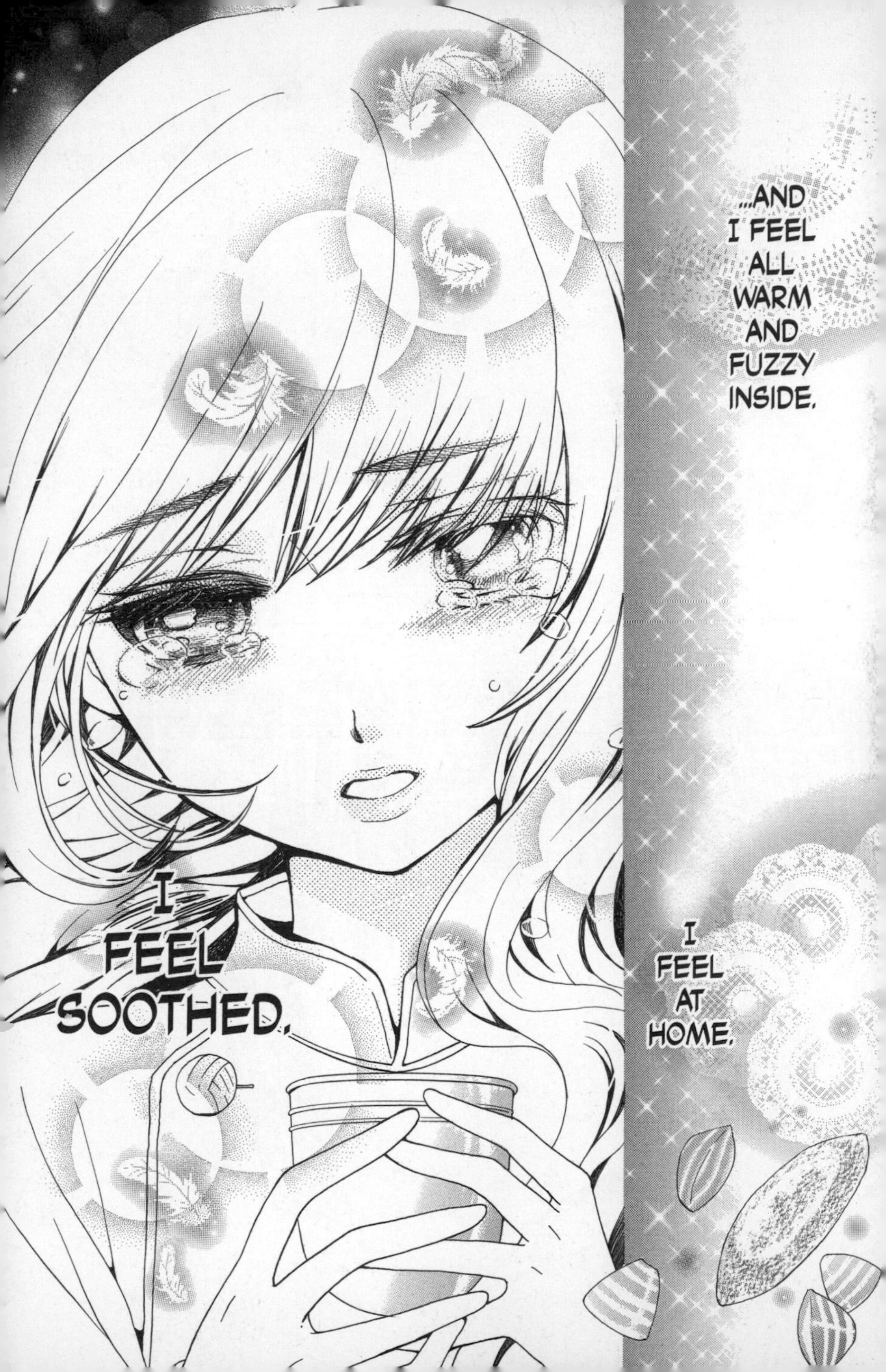
...AND I FEEL ALL WARM AND FUZZY INSIDE.
I FEEL AT HOME.
I FEEL SOOTHED.

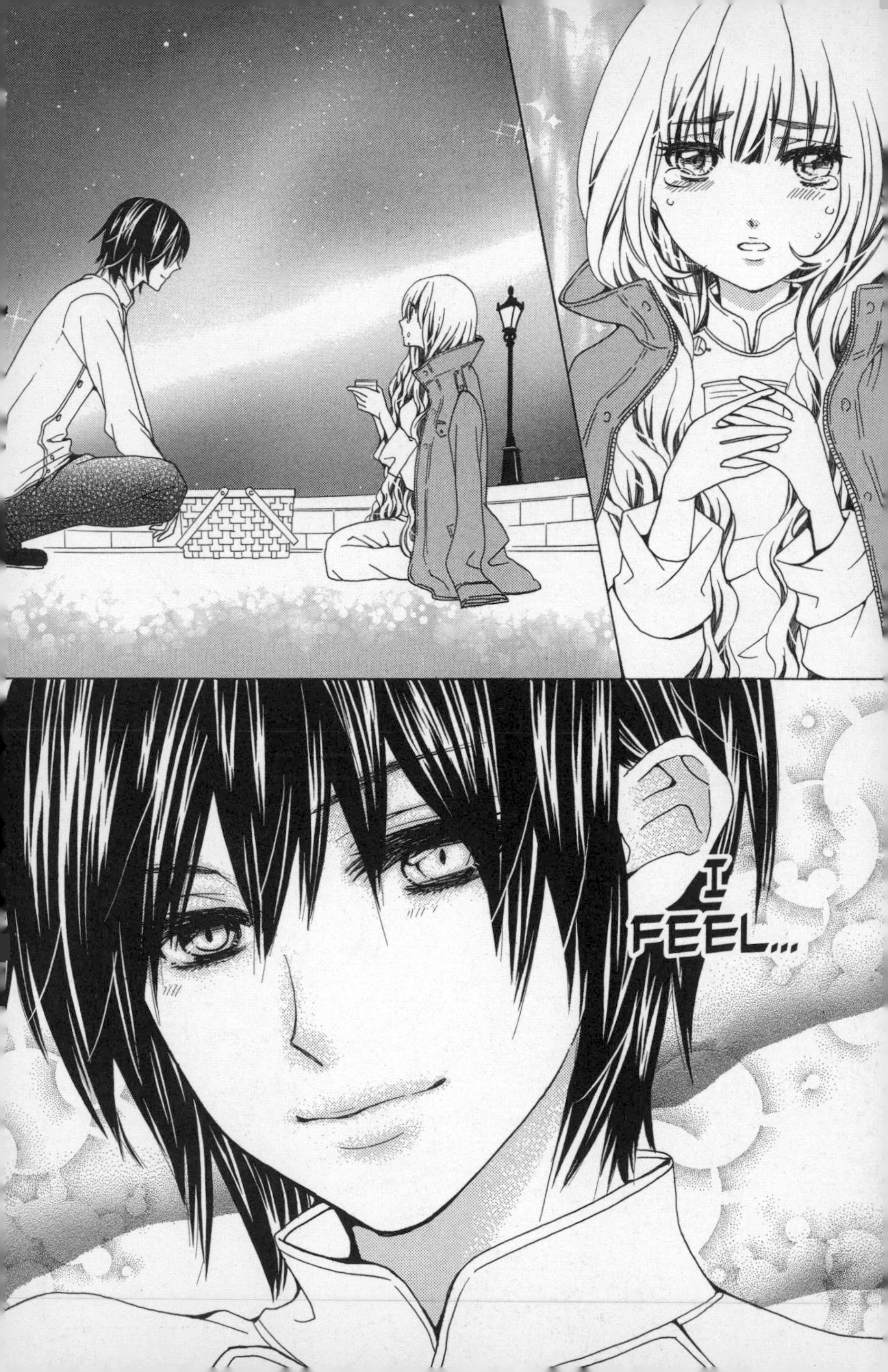
I FEEL...

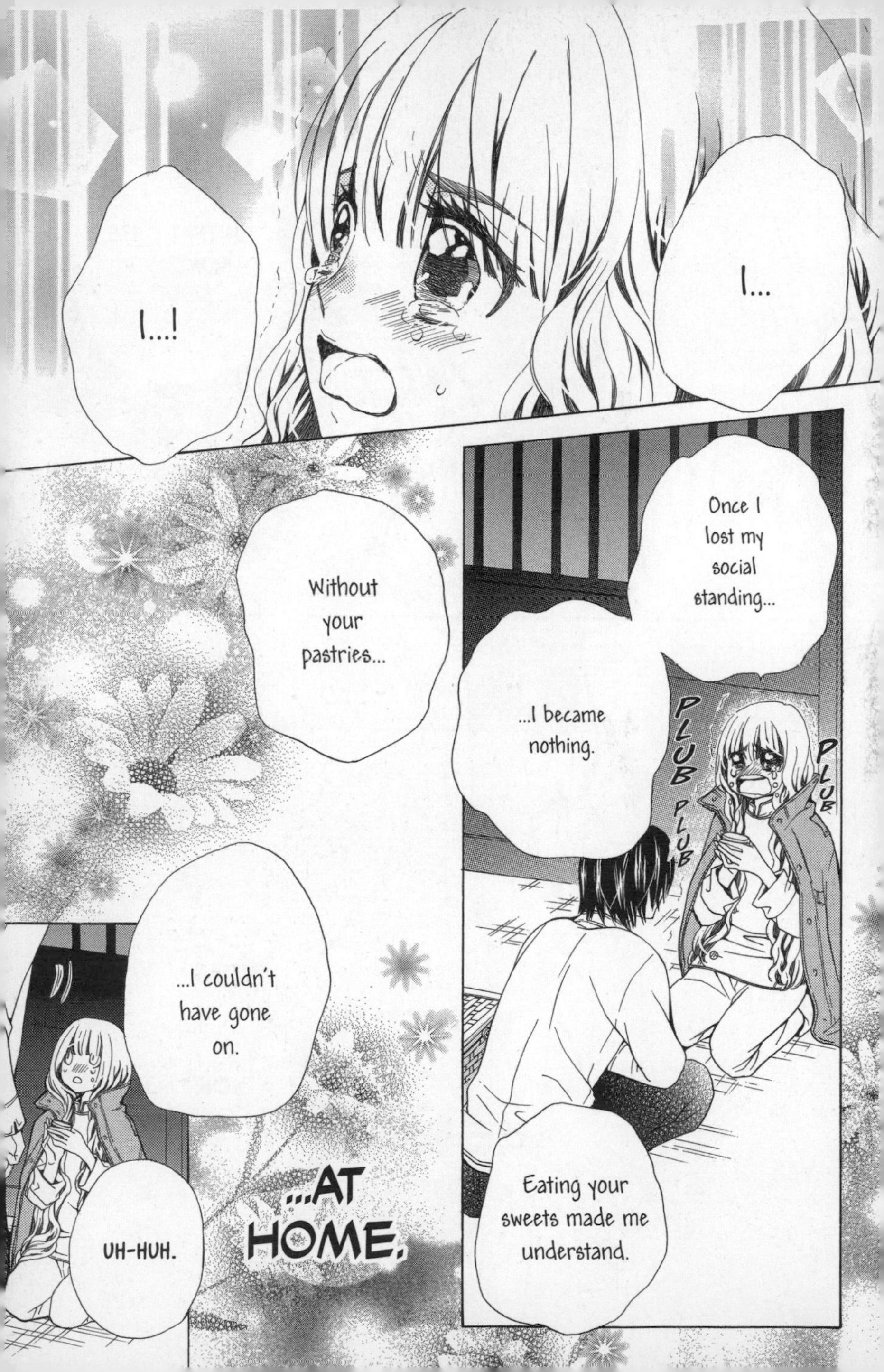
I...
I...!
Once I lost my social standing...
...I became nothing.
PLUB
PLUB
PLUB
Eating your sweets made me understand.
Without your pastries...
...I couldn't have gone on.
...AT HOME.
UH-HUH.

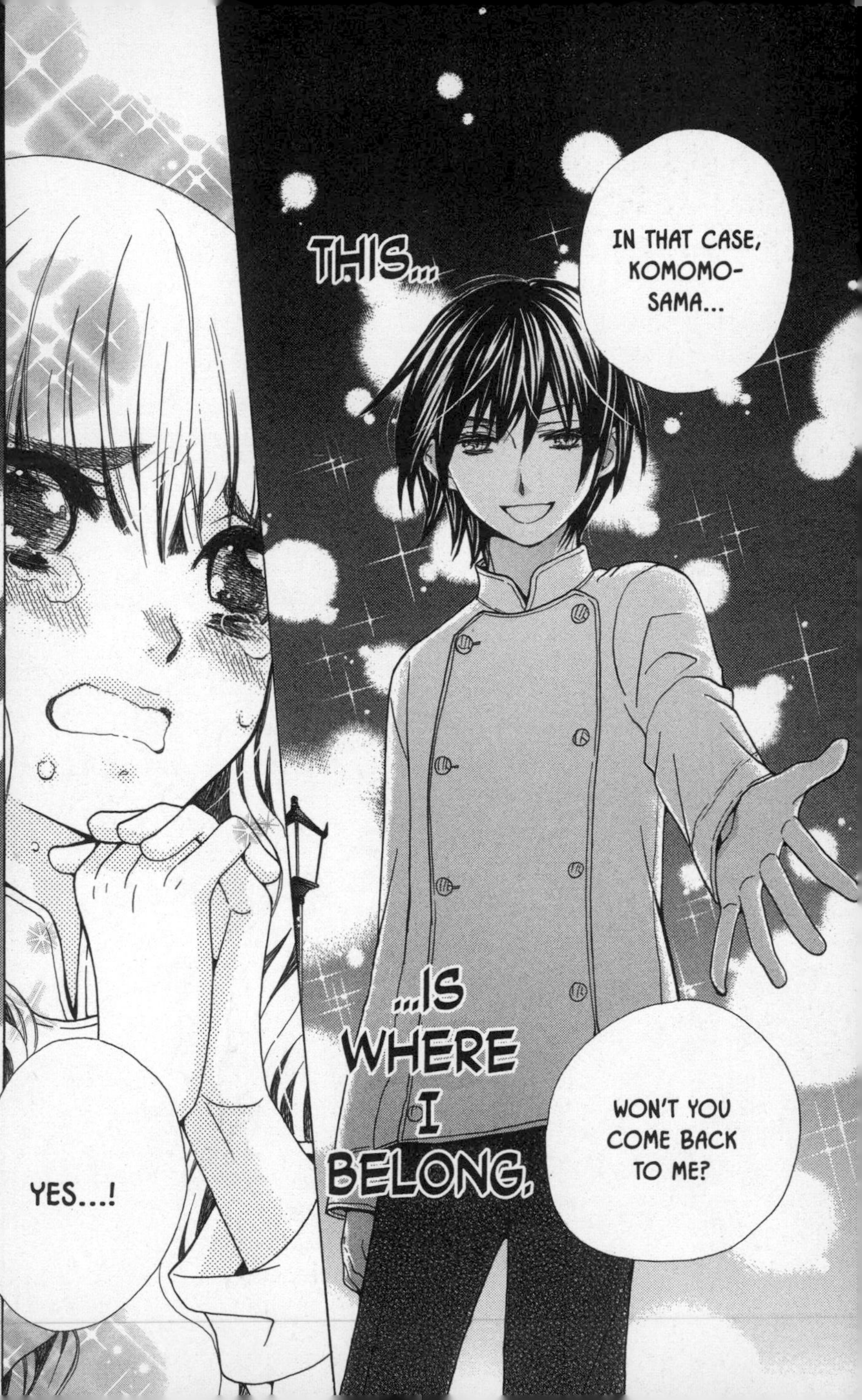
IN THAT CASE, KOMOMO-SAMA...
THIS...
...IS WHERE I BELONG.
WON'T YOU COME BACK TO ME?
YES...!

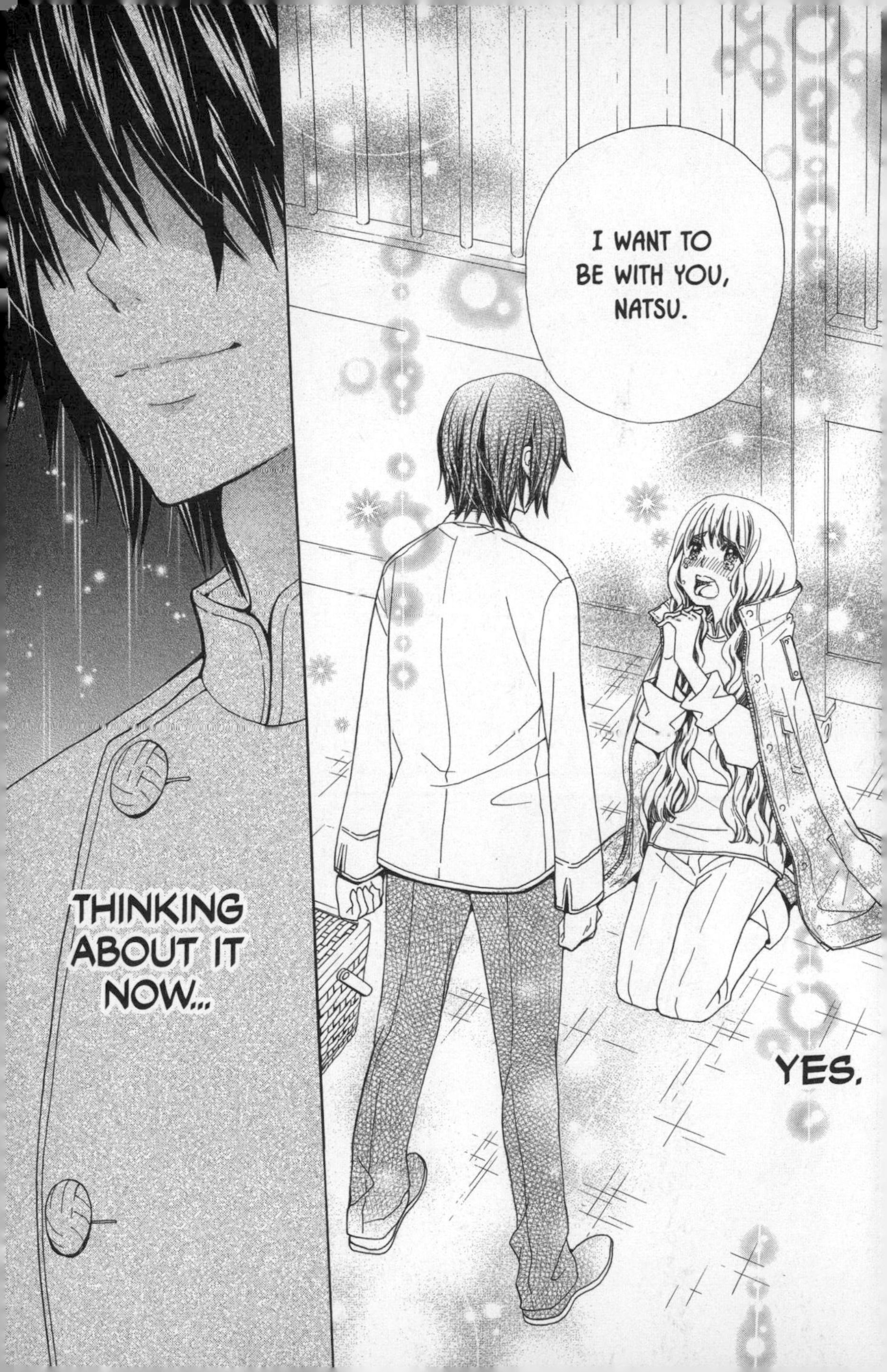
I WANT TO BE WITH YOU, NATSU.
YES.
THINKING ABOUT IT NOW...

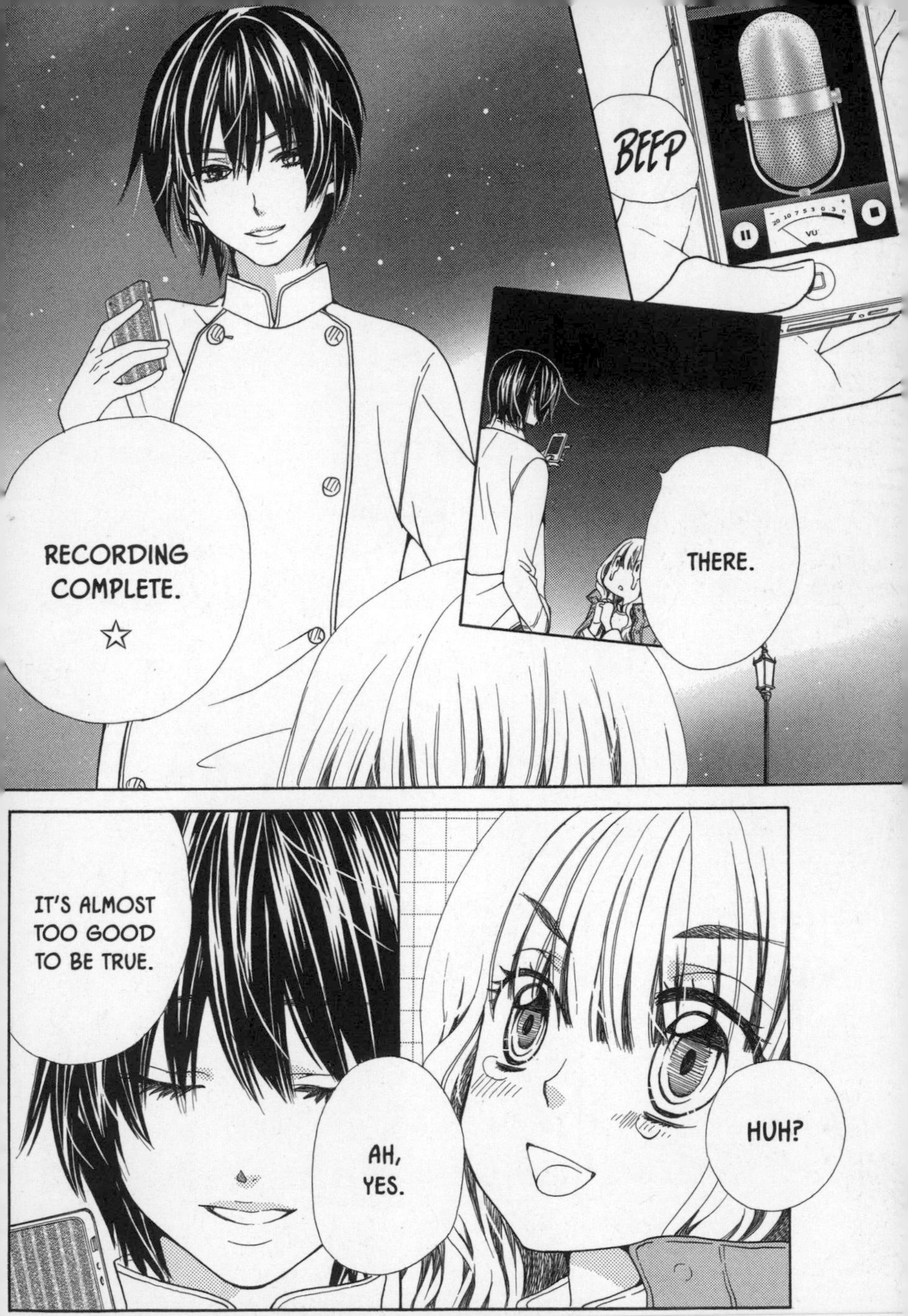
BEEP
THERE.
RECORDING COMPLETE. ☆
HUH?
IT'S ALMOST TOO GOOD TO BE TRUE.
AH, YES.

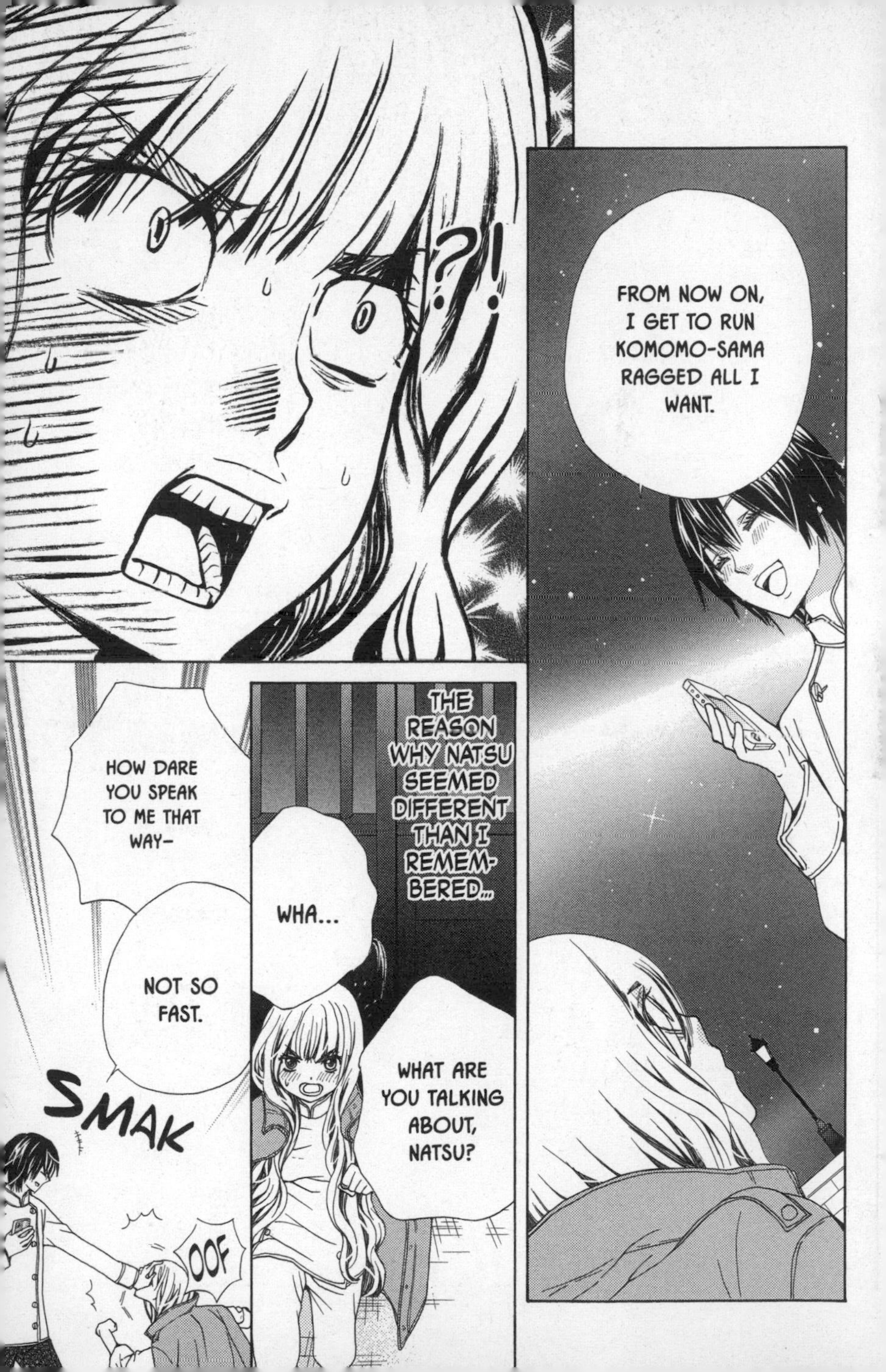
FROM NOW ON, I GET TO RUN KOMOMO-SAMA RAGGED ALL I WANT.
?!
THE REASON WHY NATSU SEEMED DIFFERENT THAN I REMEM-BERED...
WHA...
WHAT ARE YOU TALKING ABOUT, NATSU?
HOW DARE YOU SPEAK TO ME THAT WAY–
NOT SO FAST.
SMAK
OOF

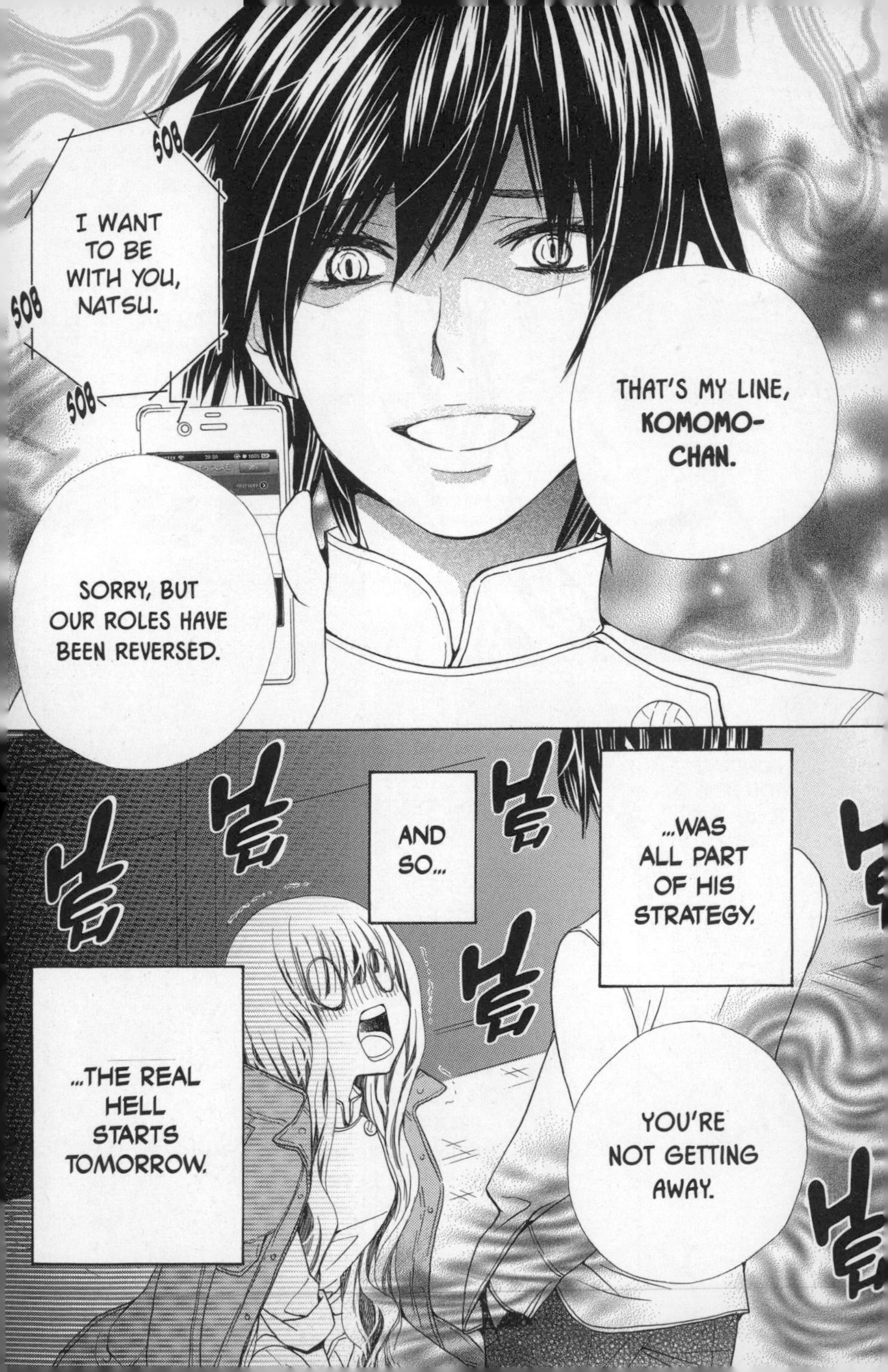
SOB
SOB
SOB
I WANT TO BE WITH YOU, NATSU.
THAT'S MY LINE, KOMOMO-CHAN.
SORRY, BUT OUR ROLES HAVE BEEN REVERSED.
...WAS ALL PART OF HIS STRATEGY.
YOU'RE NOT GETTING AWAY.
AND SO...
...THE REAL HELL STARTS TOMORROW.

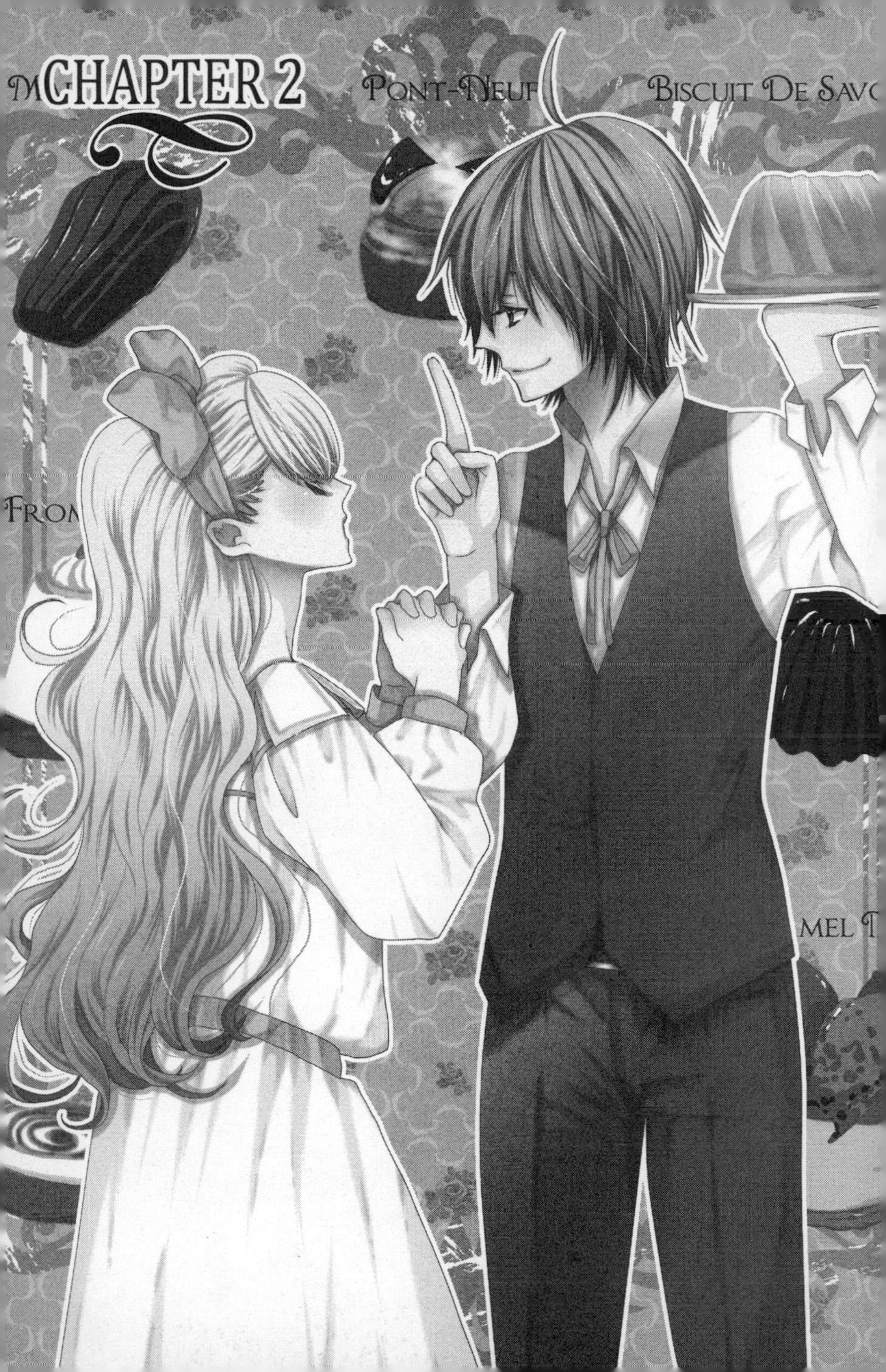
CHAPTER 2
Pont-Neuf
Biscuit De Savo

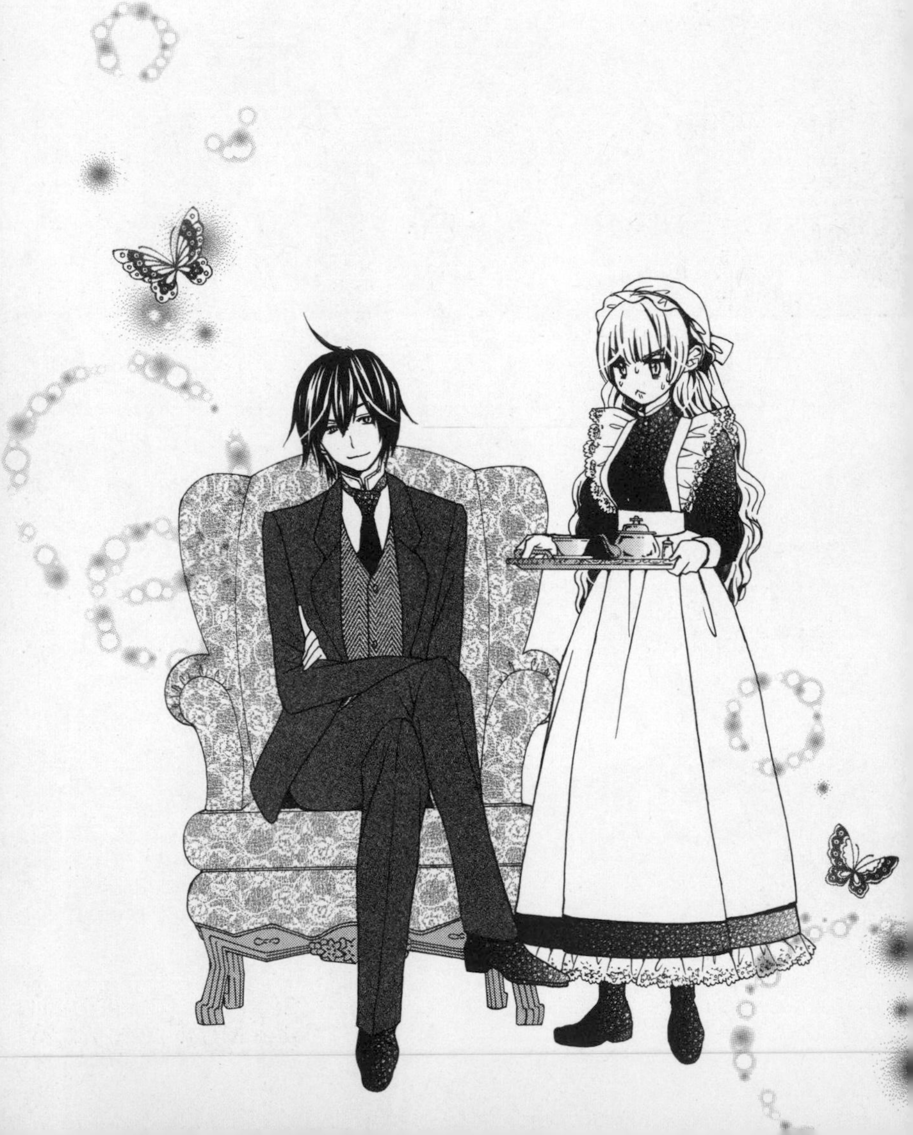

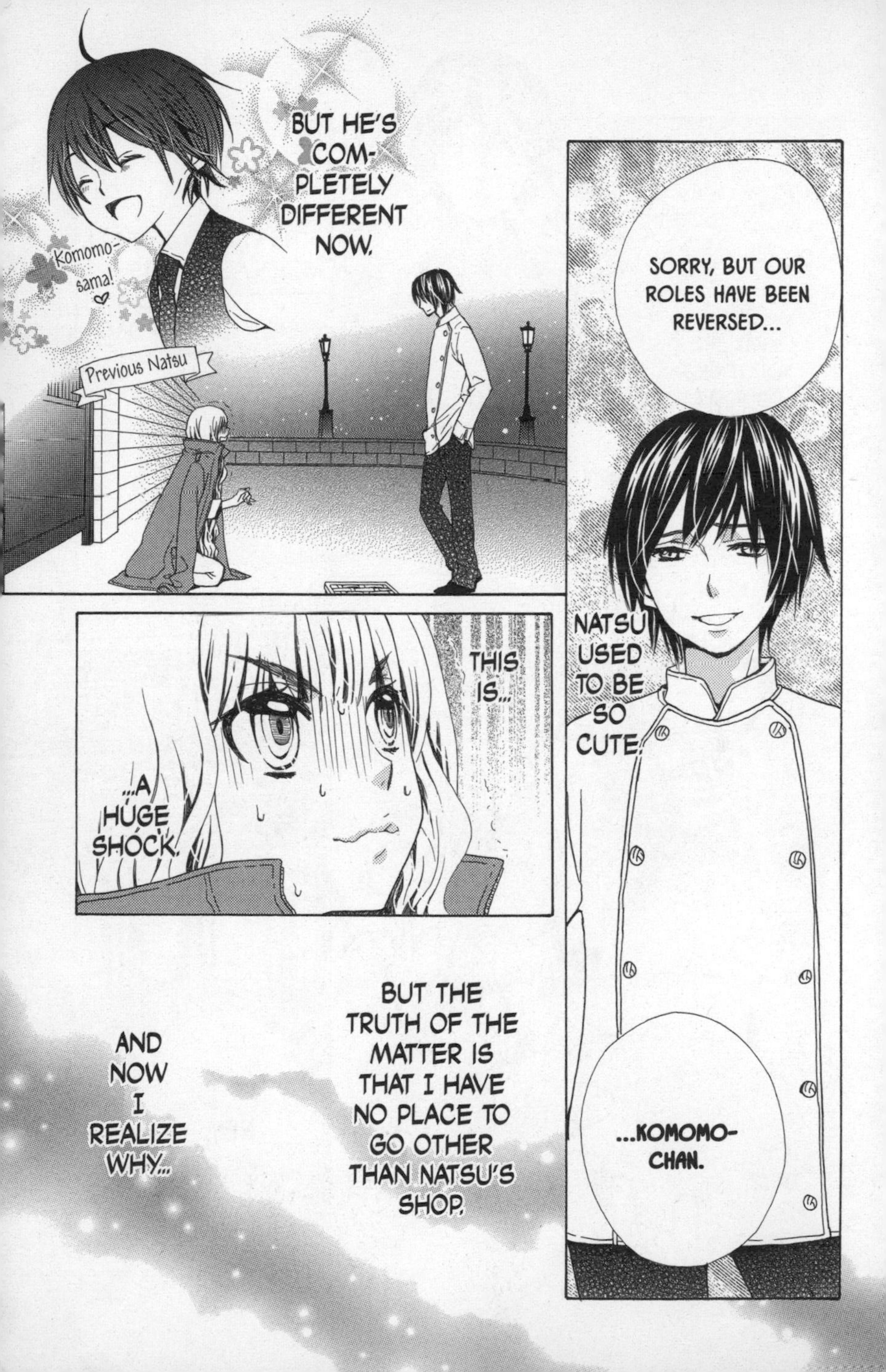
SORRY, BUT OUR ROLES HAVE BEEN REVERSED...
...KOMOMO-CHAN.
NATSU USED TO BE SO CUTE.
Komomo-sama!
Previous Natsu
BUT HE'S COMPLETELY DIFFERENT NOW.
THIS IS...
...A HUGE SHOCK.
BUT THE TRUTH OF THE MATTER IS THAT I HAVE NO PLACE TO GO OTHER THAN NATSU'S SHOP.
AND NOW I REALIZE WHY...

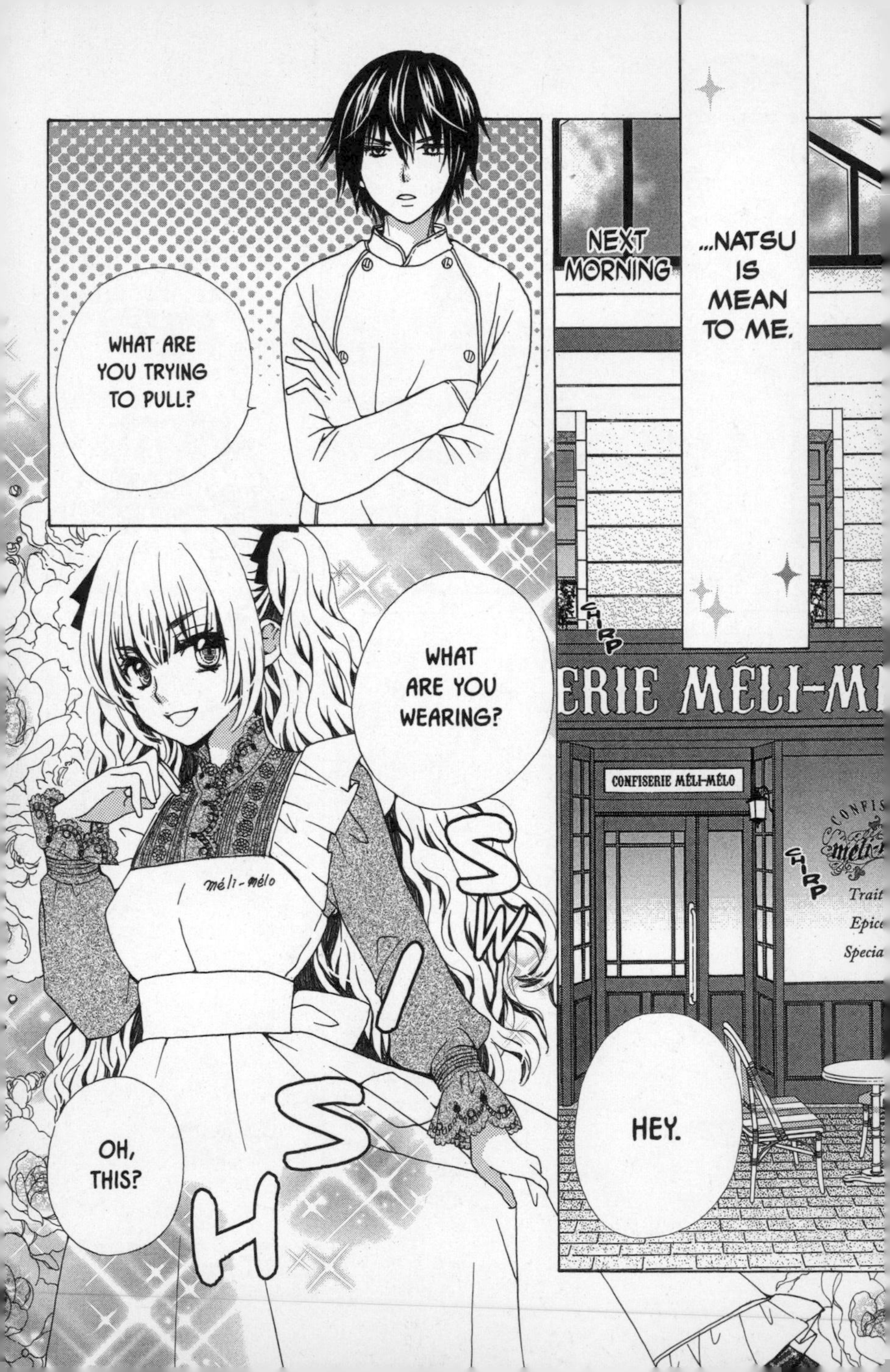

NEXT MORNING
...NATSU IS MEAN TO ME.
CHIRP
CONFISERIE MÉLI-MÉLO
CHIRP
HEY.
WHAT ARE YOU TRYING TO PULL?
WHAT ARE YOU WEARING?
méli-mélo
SWISH
OH, THIS?

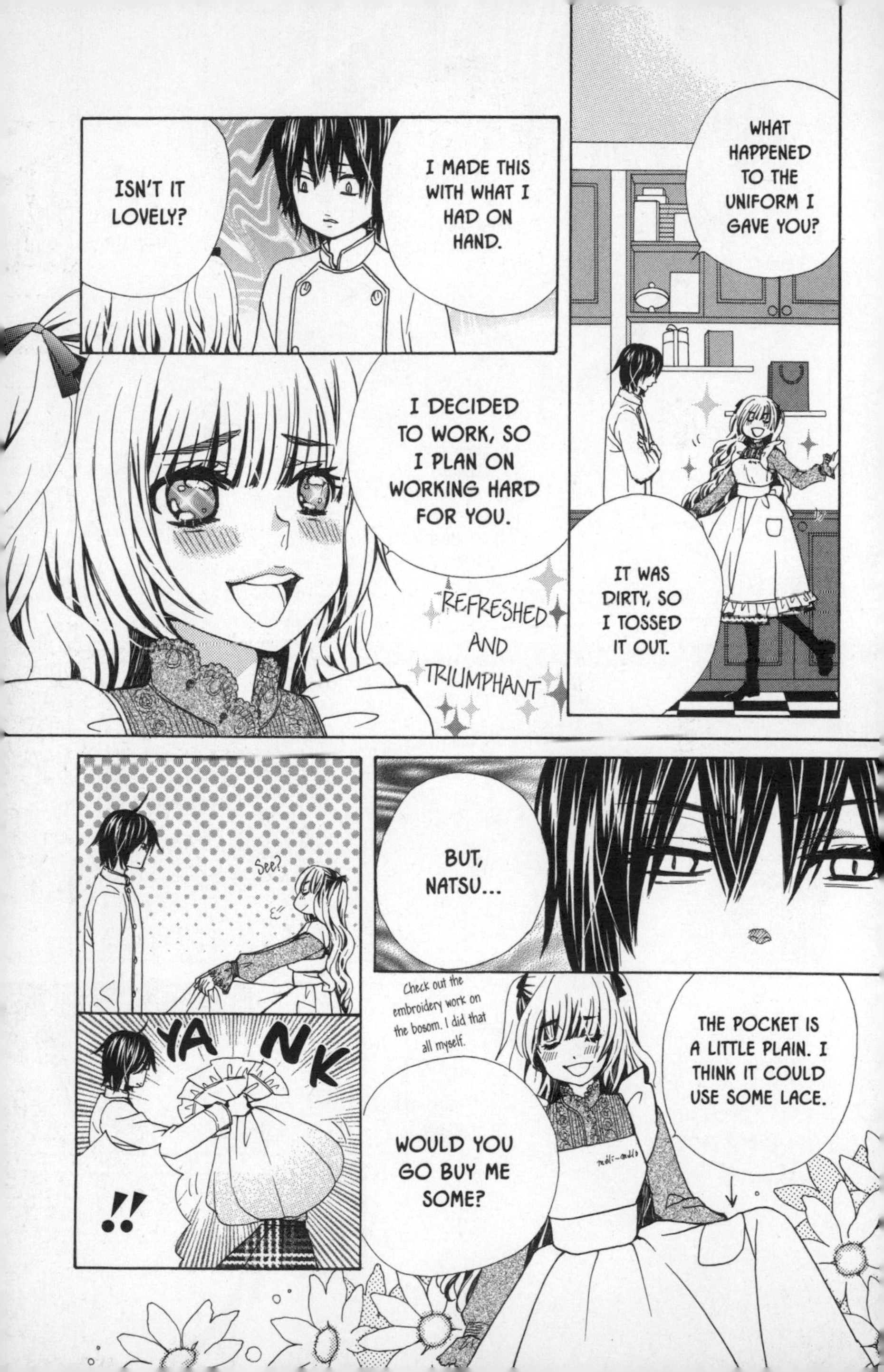
WHAT HAPPENED TO THE UNIFORM I GAVE YOU?
IT WAS DIRTY, SO I TOSSED IT OUT.
I MADE THIS WITH WHAT I HAD ON HAND.
ISN'T IT LOVELY?
I DECIDED TO WORK, SO I PLAN ON WORKING HARD FOR YOU.
REFRESHED AND TRIUMPHANT
BUT, NATSU...
See?
THE POCKET IS A LITTLE PLAIN. I THINK IT COULD USE SOME LACE.
WOULD YOU GO BUY ME SOME?
Check out the embroidery work on the bosom. I did that all myself.
YANK
!!

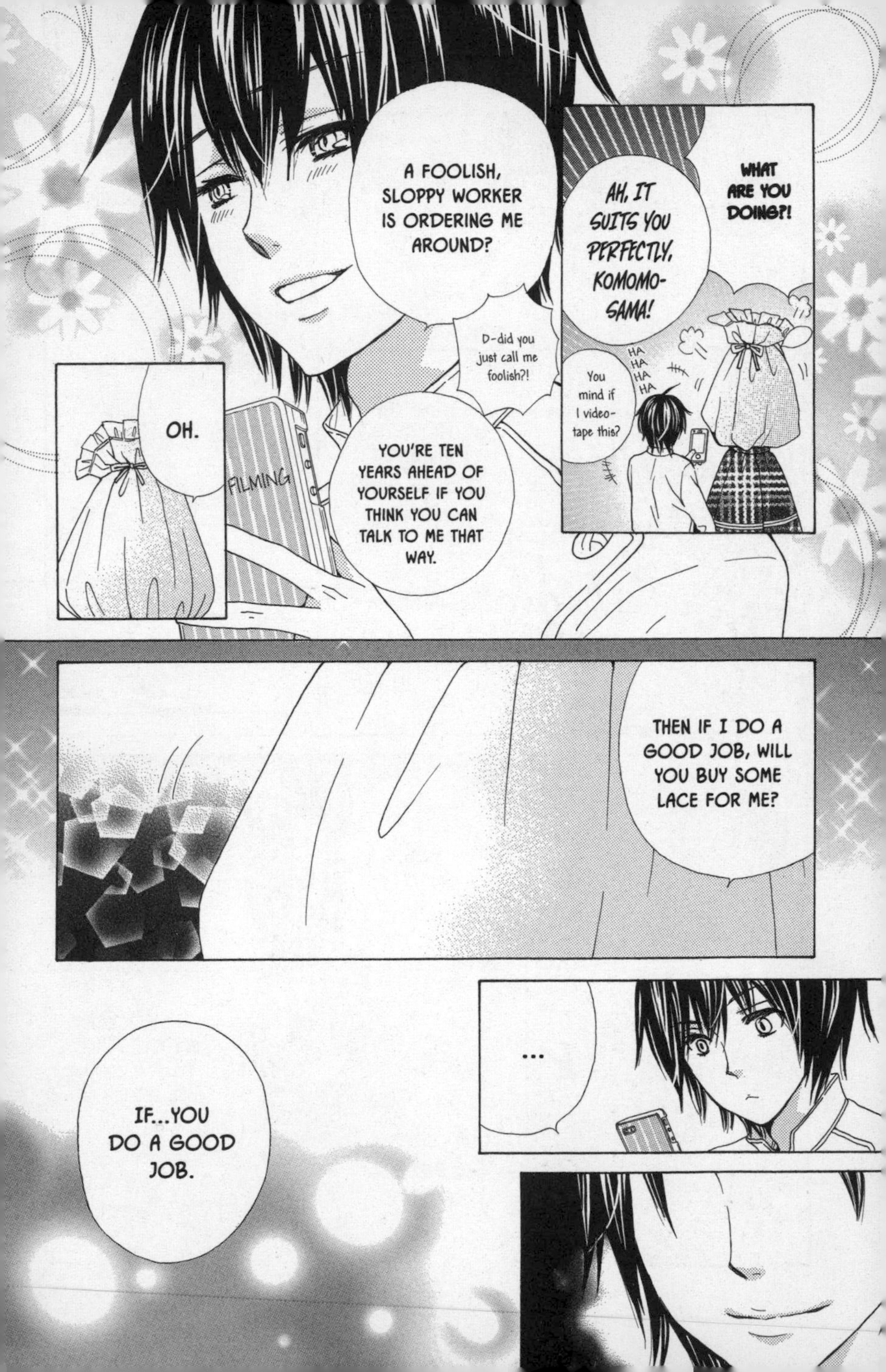
WHAT ARE YOU DOING?!
AH, IT SUITS YOU PERFECTLY, KOMOMO-SAMA!
HA HA HA HA
You mind if I videotape this?
A FOOLISH, SLOPPY WORKER IS ORDERING ME AROUND?
D-did you just call me foolish?!
YOU'RE TEN YEARS AHEAD OF YOURSELF IF YOU THINK YOU CAN TALK TO ME THAT WAY.
FILMING
OH.
THEN IF I DO A GOOD JOB, WILL YOU BUY SOME LACE FOR ME?
...
IF...YOU DO A GOOD JOB.

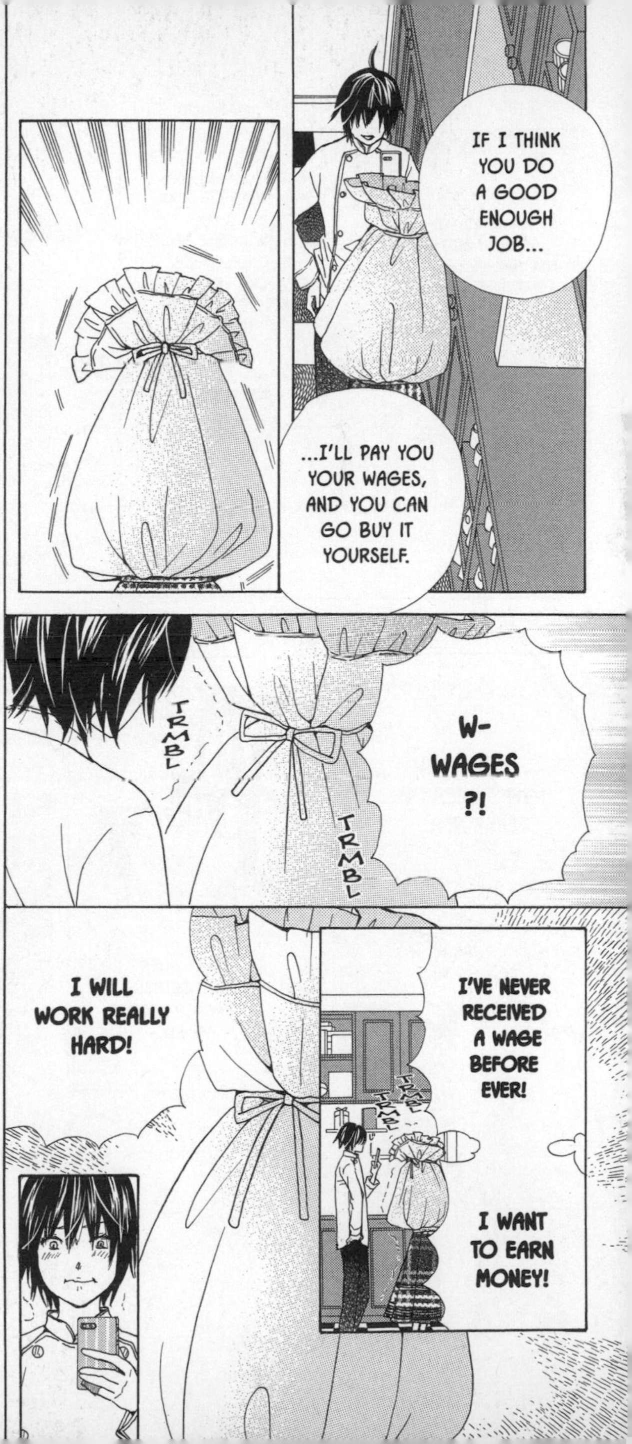
IF I THINK YOU DO A GOOD ENOUGH JOB...
...I'LL PAY YOU YOUR WAGES, AND YOU CAN GO BUY IT YOURSELF.
TRMBL
W-WAGES?!
TRMBL
I'VE NEVER RECEIVED A WAGE BEFORE EVER!
TRMBL
TRMBL
I WANT TO EARN MONEY!
I WILL WORK REALLY HARD!

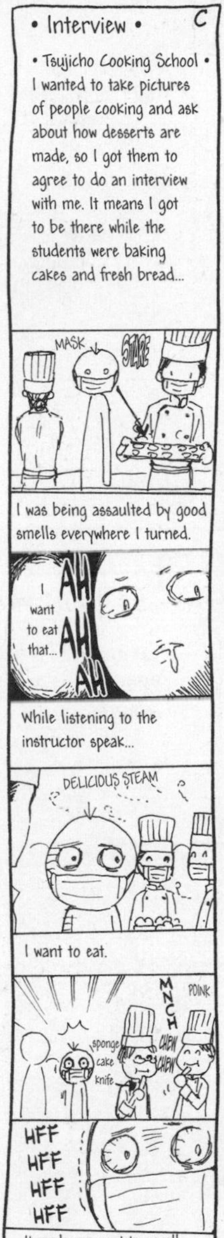
• Interview •
C
• Tsujicho Cooking School •
I wanted to take pictures of people cooking and ask about how desserts are made, so I got them to agree to do an interview with me. It means I got to be there while the students were baking cakes and fresh bread...
MASK
STARE
I was being assaulted by good smells everywhere I turned.
I want to eat that...
AH AH AH
While listening to the instructor speak...
DELICIOUS STEAM
I want to eat.
MNCH
POINK
sponge cake knife
CHEW CHEW
HFF HFF HFF HFF
It made me want to enroll. And thanks for everything!

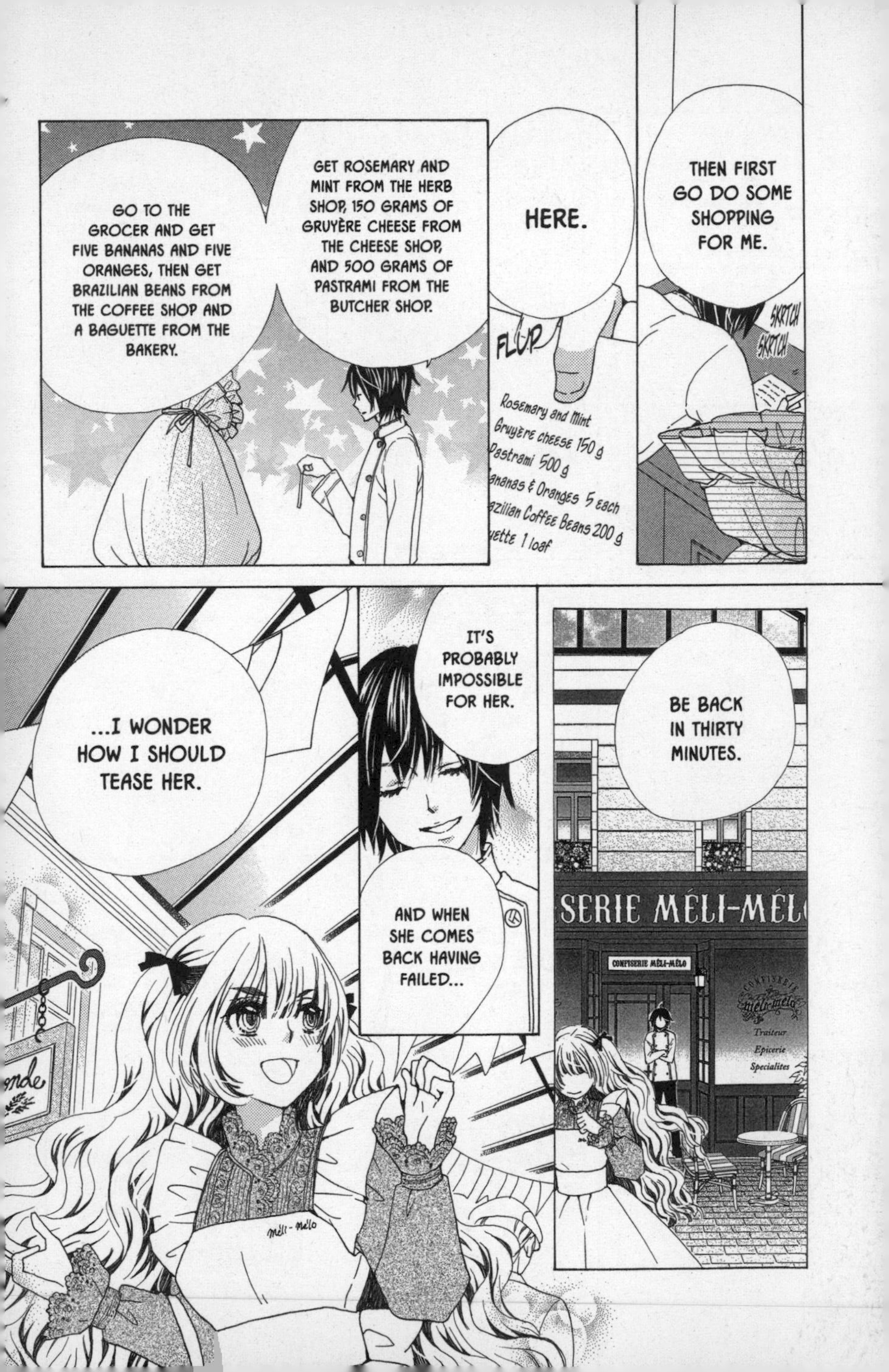
THEN FIRST GO DO SOME SHOPPING FOR ME.
SKRTCH SKRTCH
HERE.
FLUP
Rosemary and Mint
Gruyère cheese 150 g
Pastrami 500 g
ananas & Oranges 5 each
azilian Coffee Beans 200 g
uette 1 loaf
GET ROSEMARY AND MINT FROM THE HERB SHOP, 150 GRAMS OF GRUYÈRE CHEESE FROM THE CHEESE SHOP, AND 500 GRAMS OF PASTRAMI FROM THE BUTCHER SHOP.
GO TO THE GROCER AND GET FIVE BANANAS AND FIVE ORANGES, THEN GET BRAZILIAN BEANS FROM THE COFFEE SHOP AND A BAGUETTE FROM THE BAKERY.
BE BACK IN THIRTY MINUTES.
SERIE MÉLI-MÉLO
Traiteur
Epicerie
Specialites
IT'S PROBABLY IMPOSSIBLE FOR HER.
AND WHEN SHE COMES BACK HAVING FAILED...
...I WONDER HOW I SHOULD TEASE HER.
méli-mélo

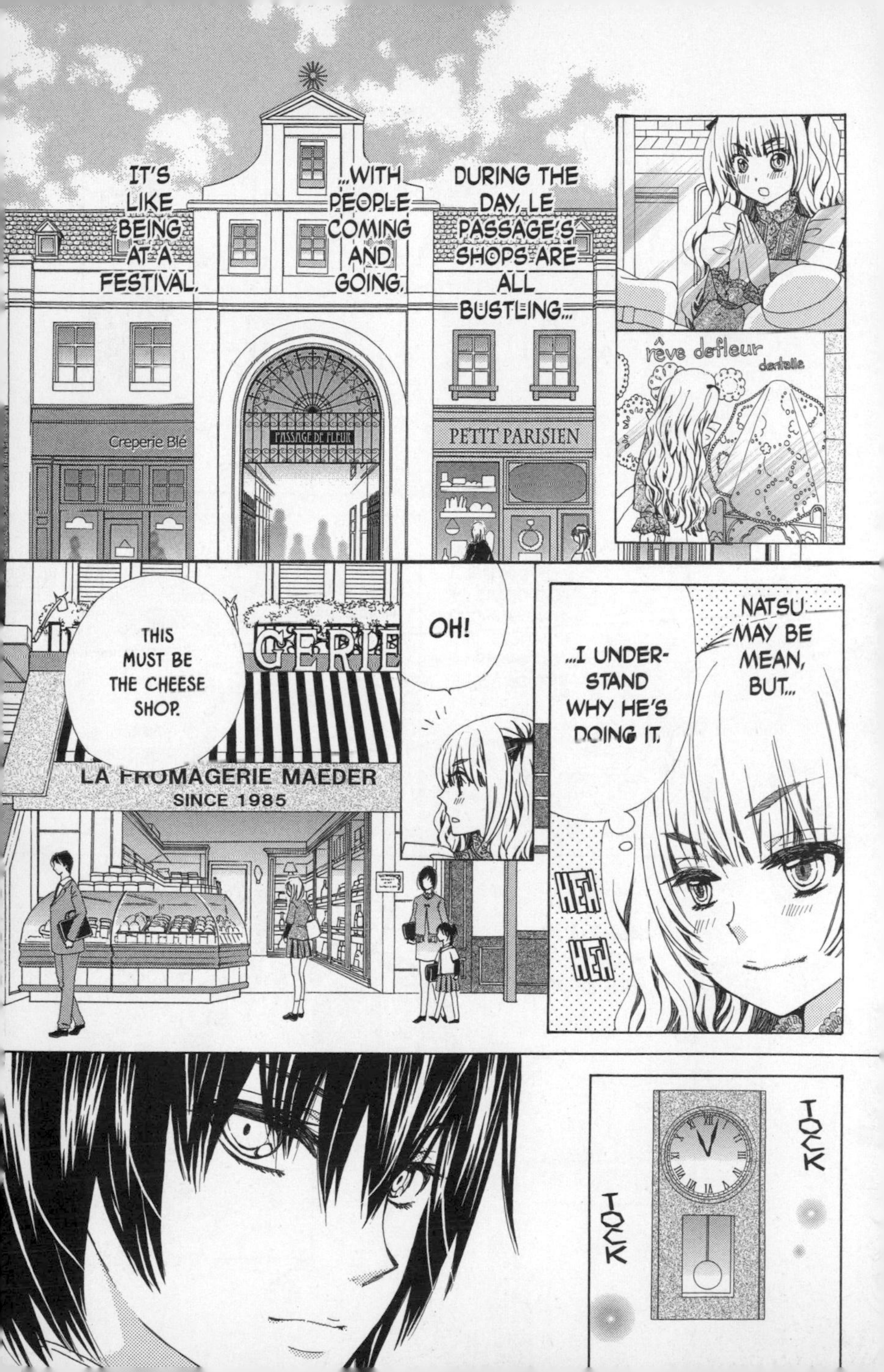
rêve defleur
dentelle
DURING THE DAY, LE PASSAGE'S SHOPS ARE ALL BUSTLING...
...WITH PEOPLE COMING AND GOING.
IT'S LIKE BEING AT A FESTIVAL.
PETIT PARISIEN
PASSAGE DE FLEUR
Creperie Blé
NATSU MAY BE MEAN, BUT...
...I UNDERSTAND WHY HE'S DOING IT.
HEH
HEH
OH!
THIS MUST BE THE CHEESE SHOP.
GERIE
LA FROMAGERIE MAEDER
SINCE 1985
TOCK
TOCK

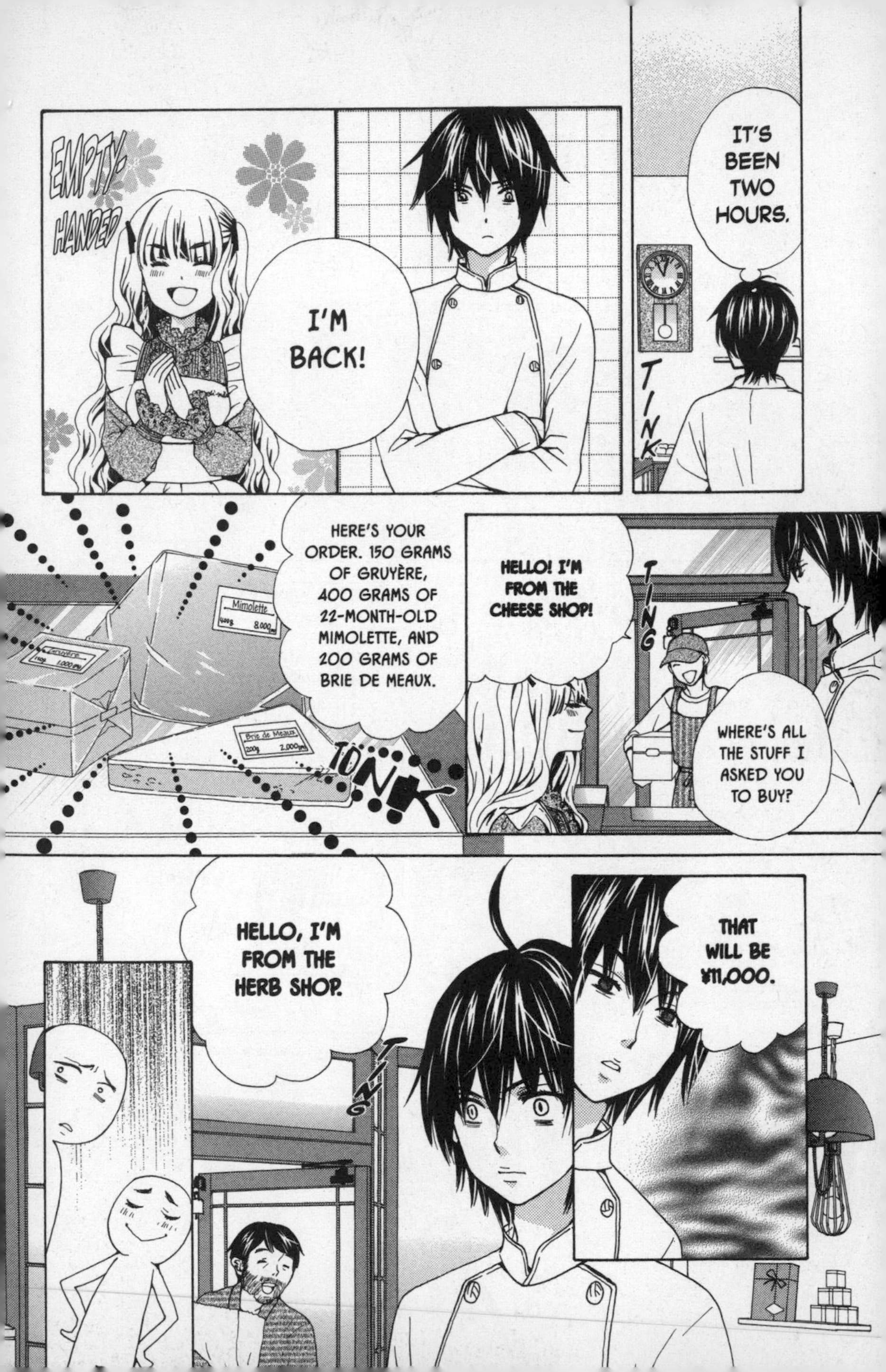
IT'S BEEN TWO HOURS.
TINK
I'M BACK!
EMPTY-HANDED
TING
HELLO! I'M FROM THE CHEESE SHOP!
WHERE'S ALL THE STUFF I ASKED YOU TO BUY?
HERE'S YOUR ORDER. 150 GRAMS OF GRUYÈRE, 400 GRAMS OF 22-MONTH-OLD MIMOLETTE, AND 200 GRAMS OF BRIE DE MEAUX.
Mimolette
Brie de Meaux
TONK
THAT WILL BE ¥11,000.
HELLO, I'M FROM THE HERB SHOP.
TING

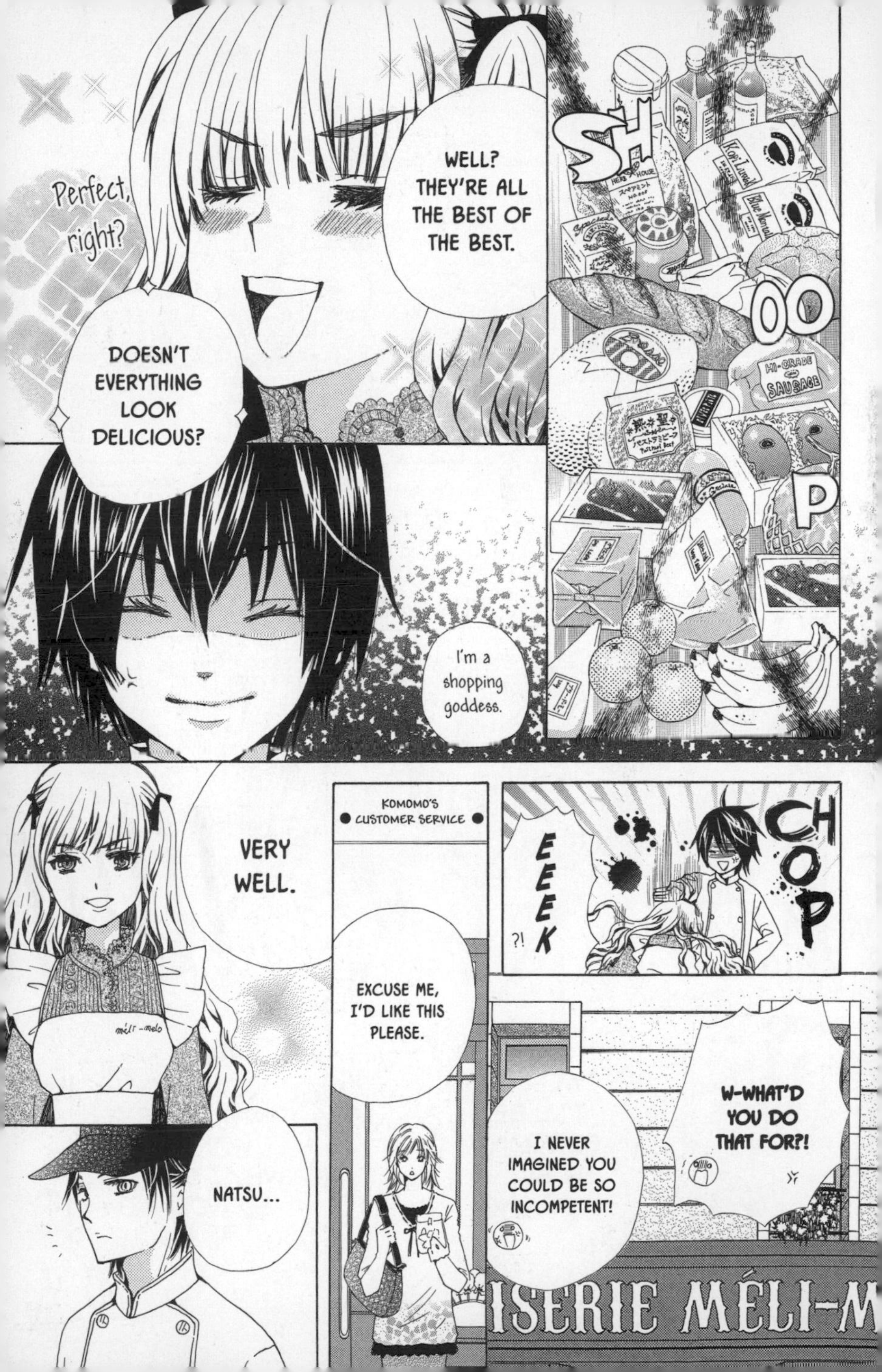
SHOOP
WELL? THEY'RE ALL THE BEST OF THE BEST.
Perfect, right?
DOESN'T EVERYTHING LOOK DELICIOUS?
I'm a shopping goddess.
CHOP
EEEK
?!
W-WHAT'D YOU DO THAT FOR?!
I NEVER IMAGINED YOU COULD BE SO INCOMPETENT!
ISERIE MÉLI-M
KOMOMO'S CUSTOMER SERVICE
EXCUSE ME, I'D LIKE THIS PLEASE.
VERY WELL.
NATSU...

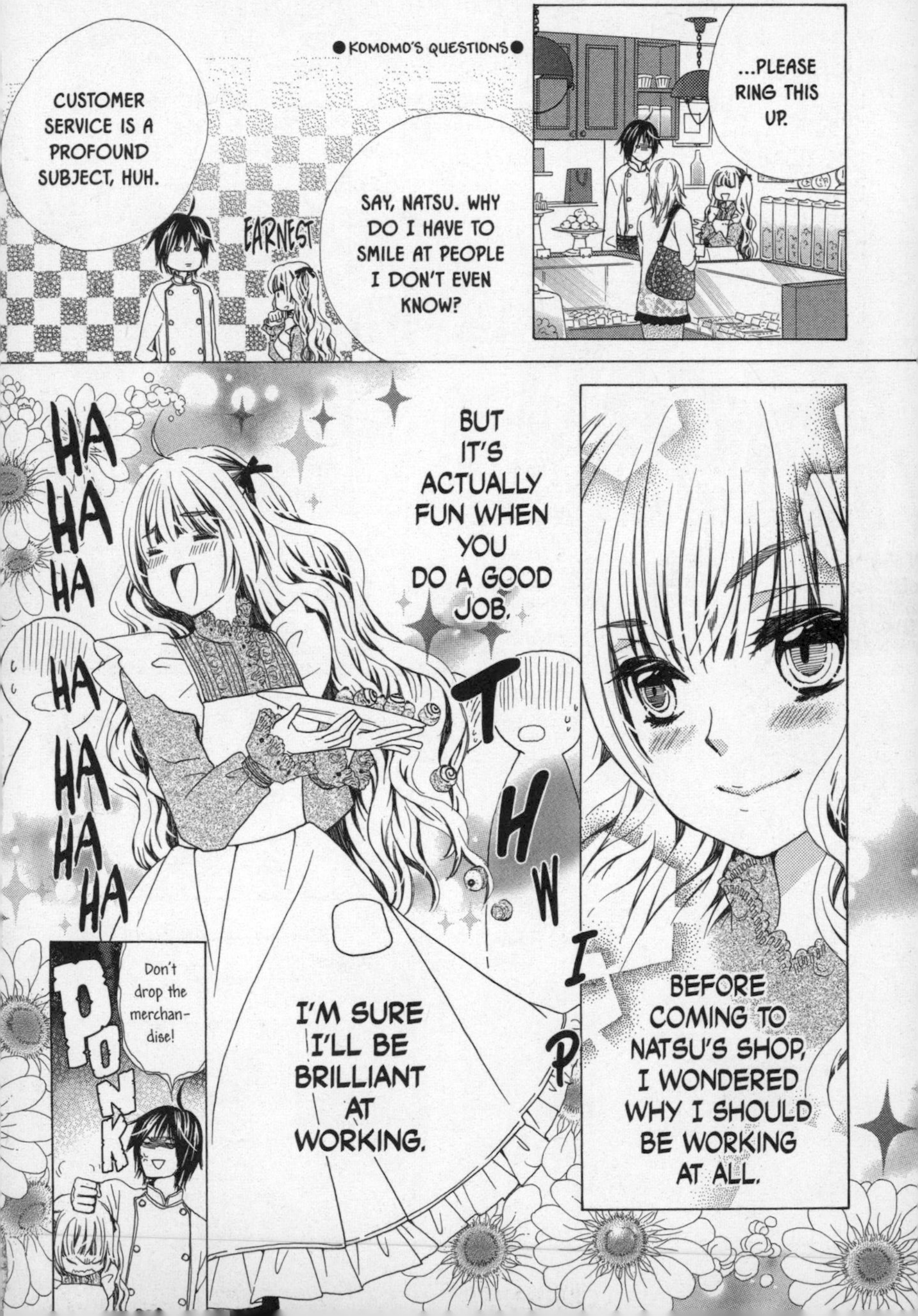
●KOMOMO'S QUESTIONS●
...PLEASE RING THIS UP.
SAY, NATSU. WHY DO I HAVE TO SMILE AT PEOPLE I DON'T EVEN KNOW?
EARNEST
CUSTOMER SERVICE IS A PROFOUND SUBJECT, HUH.
BEFORE COMING TO NATSU'S SHOP, I WONDERED WHY I SHOULD BE WORKING AT ALL.
BUT IT'S ACTUALLY FUN WHEN YOU DO A GOOD JOB.
I'M SURE I'LL BE BRILLIANT AT WORKING.
THWIP
HA HA HA HA HA HA HA HA HA
PONK
Don't drop the merchandise!

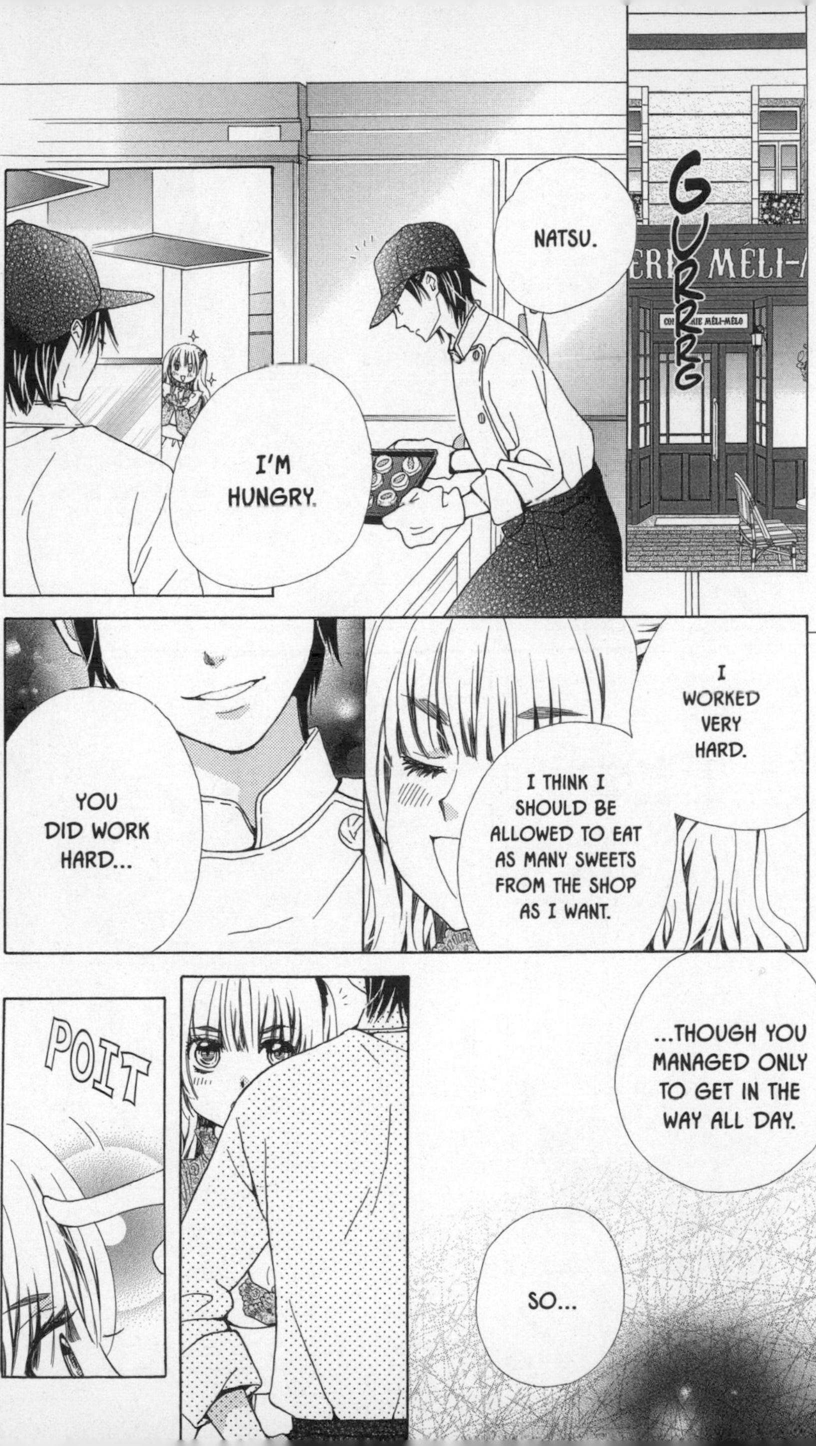
GURRRG
NATSU.
I'M HUNGRY.
I WORKED VERY HARD.
I THINK I SHOULD BE ALLOWED TO EAT AS MANY SWEETS FROM THE SHOP AS I WANT.
YOU DID WORK HARD...
...THOUGH YOU MANAGED ONLY TO GET IN THE WAY ALL DAY.
SO...
POIT

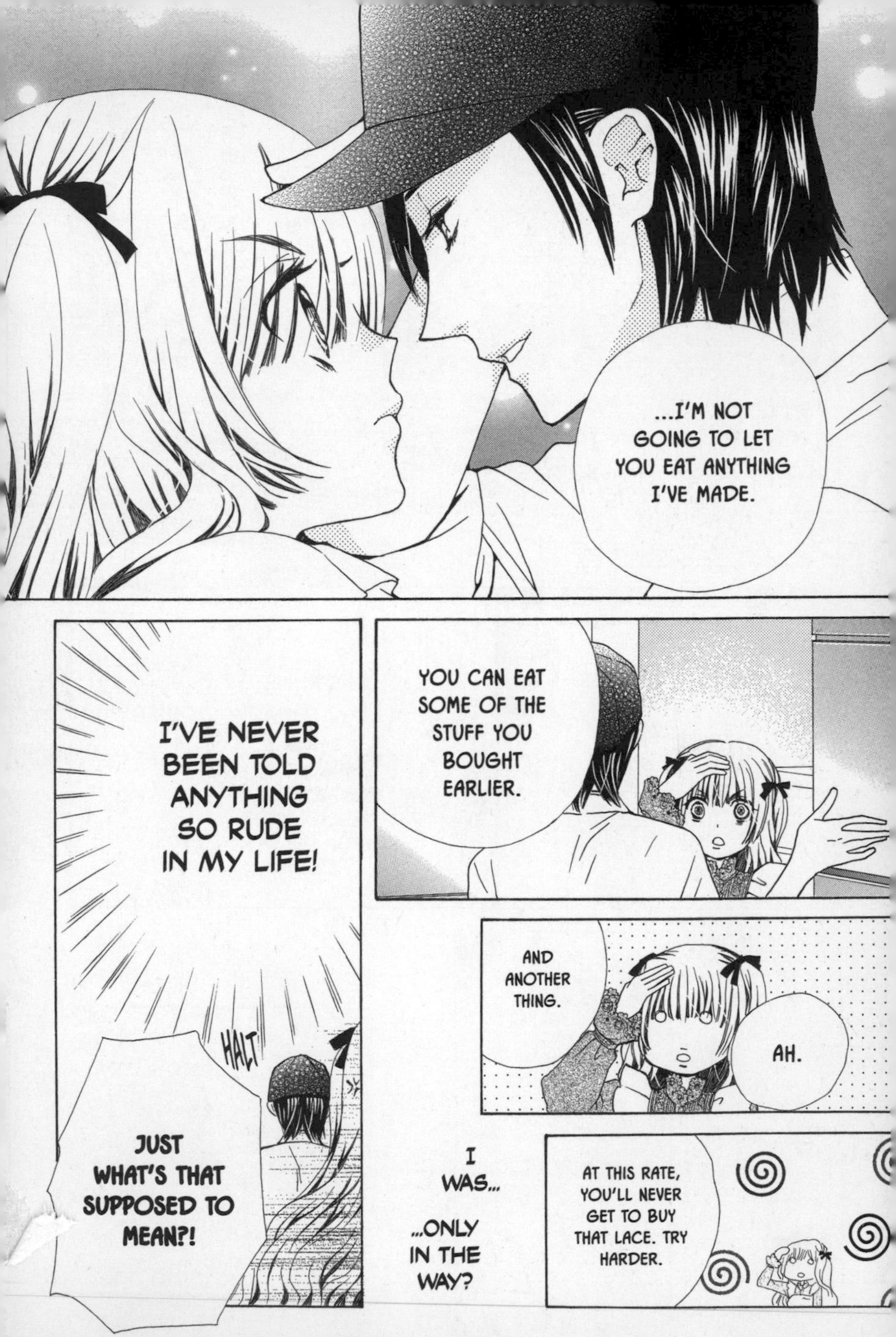

...I'M NOT GOING TO LET YOU EAT ANYTHING I'VE MADE.
YOU CAN EAT SOME OF THE STUFF YOU BOUGHT EARLIER.
AH.
AND ANOTHER THING.
AT THIS RATE, YOU'LL NEVER GET TO BUY THAT LACE. TRY HARDER.
I WAS...
...ONLY IN THE WAY?
I'VE NEVER BEEN TOLD ANYTHING SO RUDE IN MY LIFE!
HALT
JUST WHAT'S THAT SUPPOSED TO MEAN?!

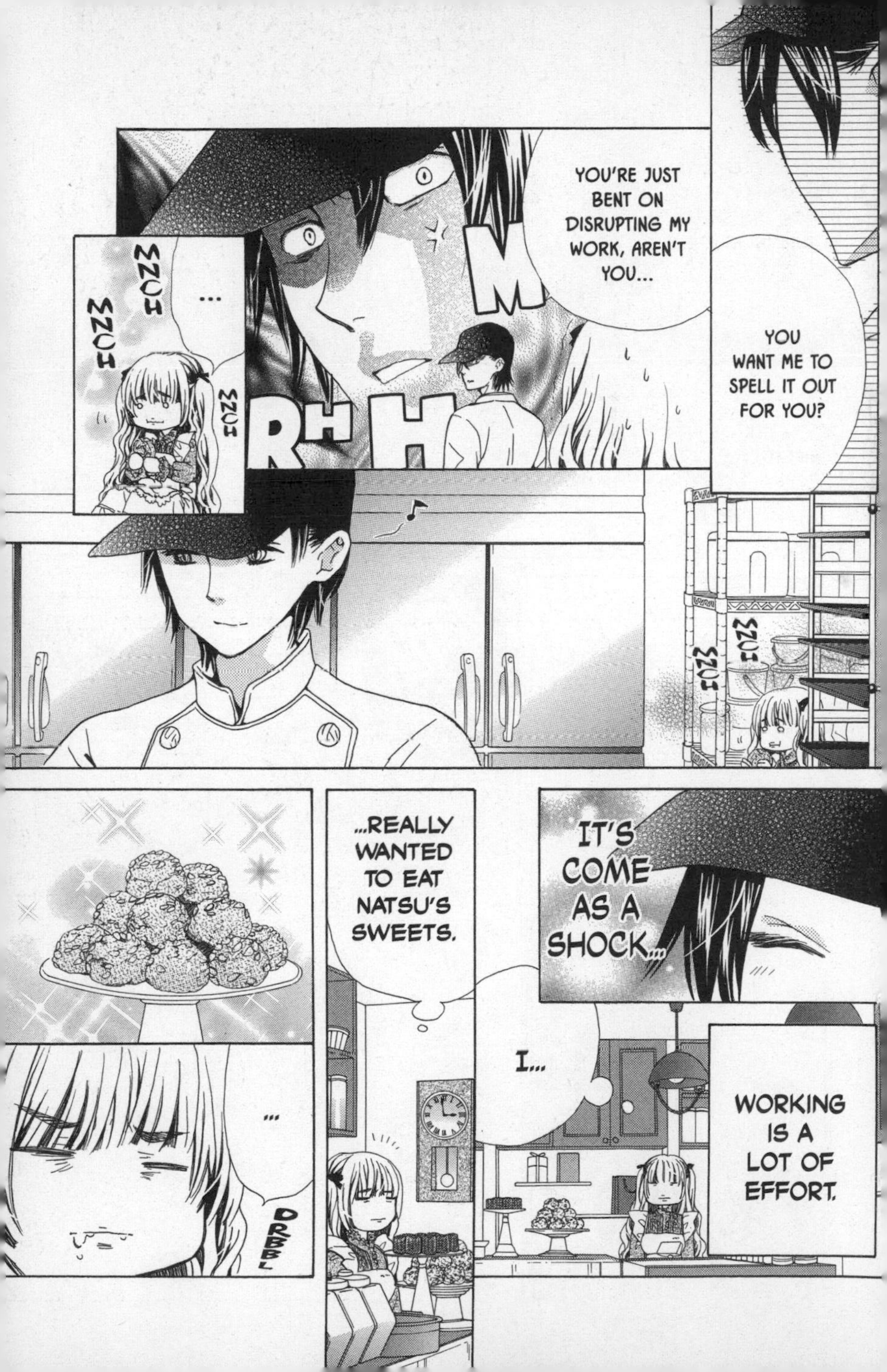
YOU WANT ME TO SPELL IT OUT FOR YOU?
YOU'RE JUST BENT ON DISRUPTING MY WORK, AREN'T YOU...
MNCH
MNCH
...
MNCH
MNCH
MNCH
IT'S COME AS A SHOCK...
WORKING IS A LOT OF EFFORT.
I...
...REALLY WANTED TO EAT NATSU'S SWEETS.
...
DRBBL

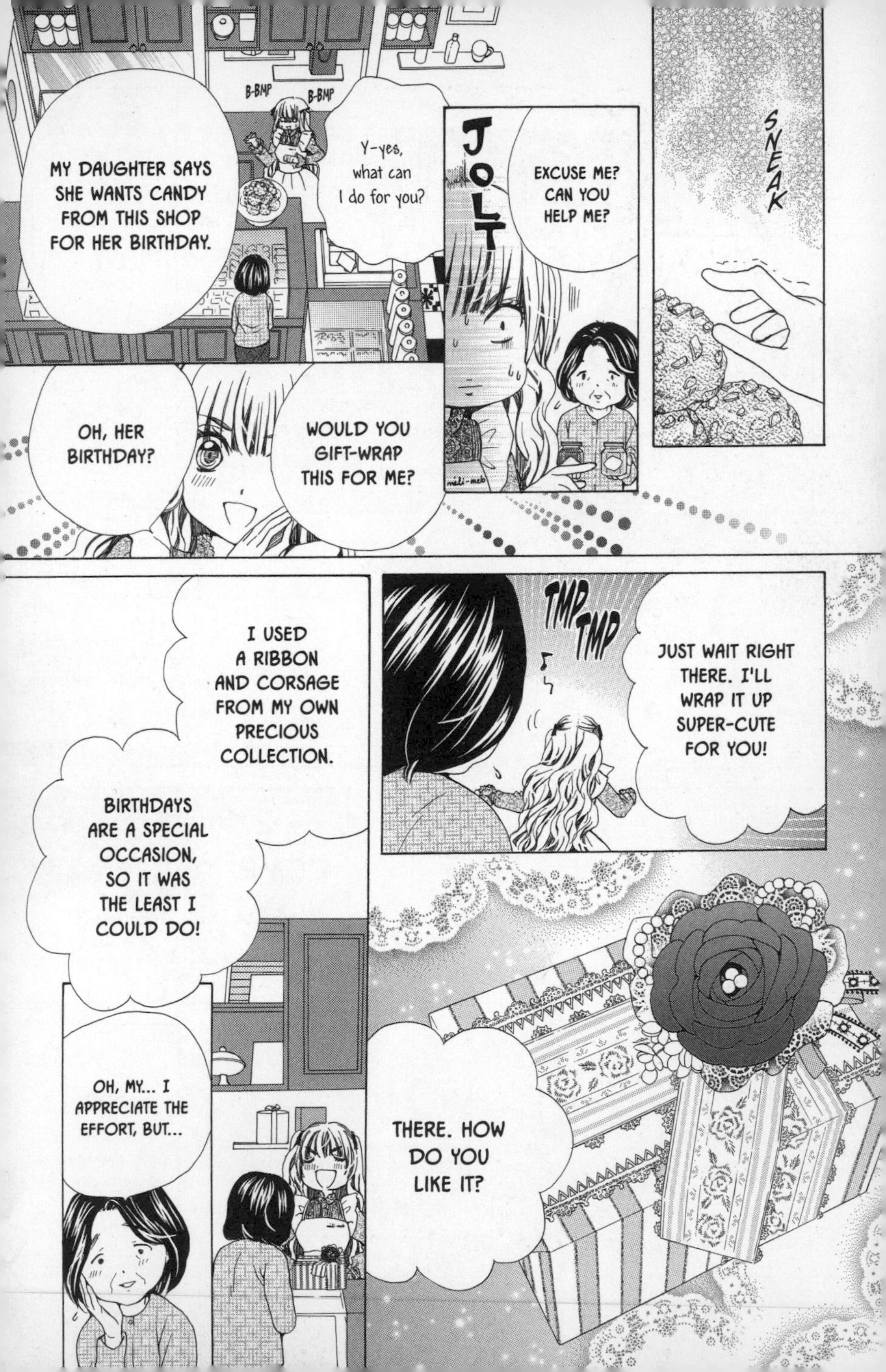
SNEAK
JOLT
EXCUSE ME? CAN YOU HELP ME?
B-BMP B-BMP
Y-yes, what can I do for you?
MY DAUGHTER SAYS SHE WANTS CANDY FROM THIS SHOP FOR HER BIRTHDAY.
WOULD YOU GIFT-WRAP THIS FOR ME?
OH, HER BIRTHDAY?
TMP TMP
JUST WAIT RIGHT THERE. I'LL WRAP IT UP SUPER-CUTE FOR YOU!
THERE. HOW DO YOU LIKE IT?
I USED A RIBBON AND CORSAGE FROM MY OWN PRECIOUS COLLECTION.
BIRTHDAYS ARE A SPECIAL OCCASION, SO IT WAS THE LEAST I COULD DO!
OH, MY... I APPRECIATE THE EFFORT, BUT...

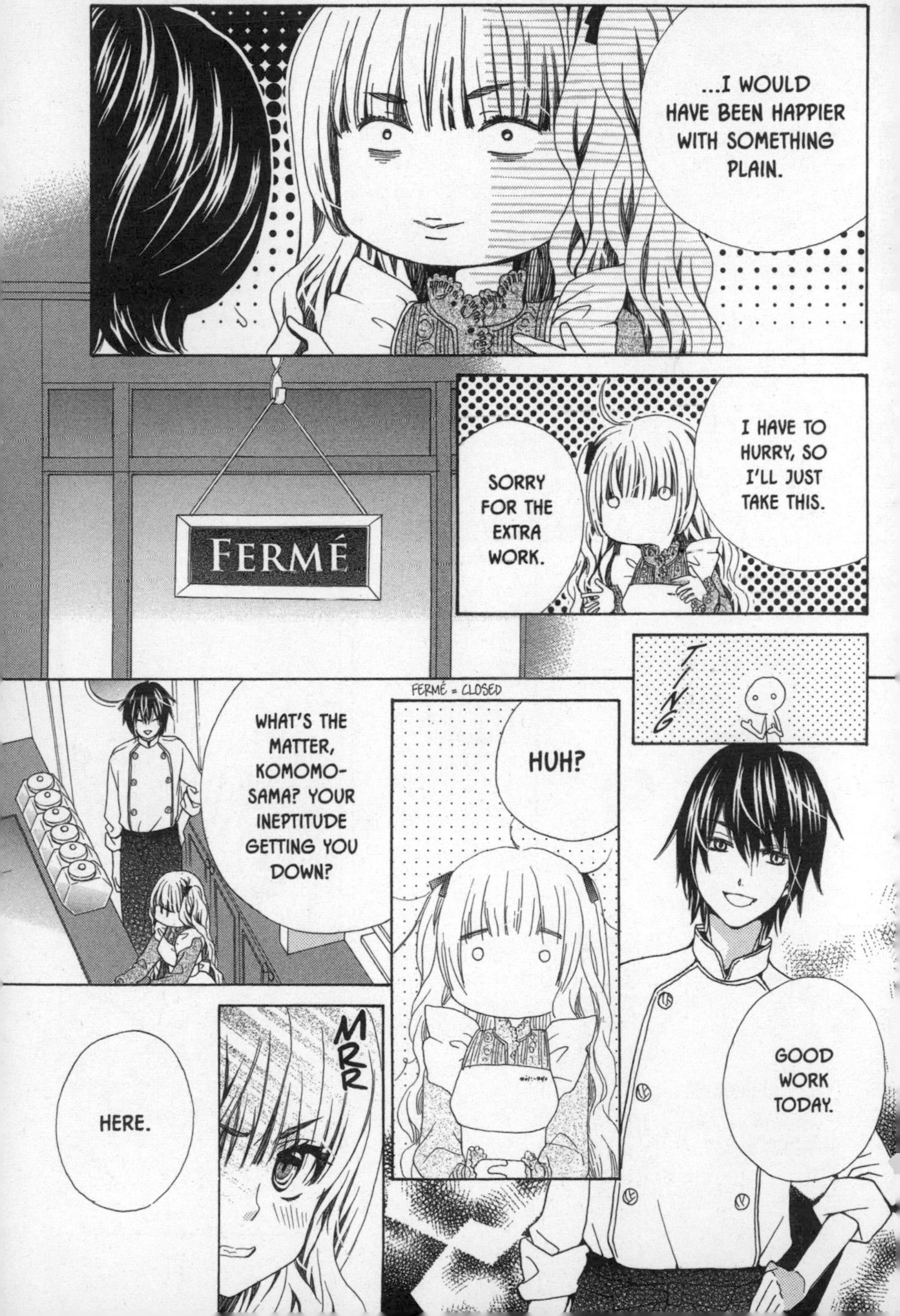
...I WOULD HAVE BEEN HAPPIER WITH SOMETHING PLAIN.
I HAVE TO HURRY, SO I'LL JUST TAKE THIS.
SORRY FOR THE EXTRA WORK.
FERMÉ
FERMÉ = CLOSED
TING
GOOD WORK TODAY.
HUH?
WHAT'S THE MATTER, KOMOMO-SAMA? YOUR INEPTITUDE GETTING YOU DOWN?
MRR
HERE.

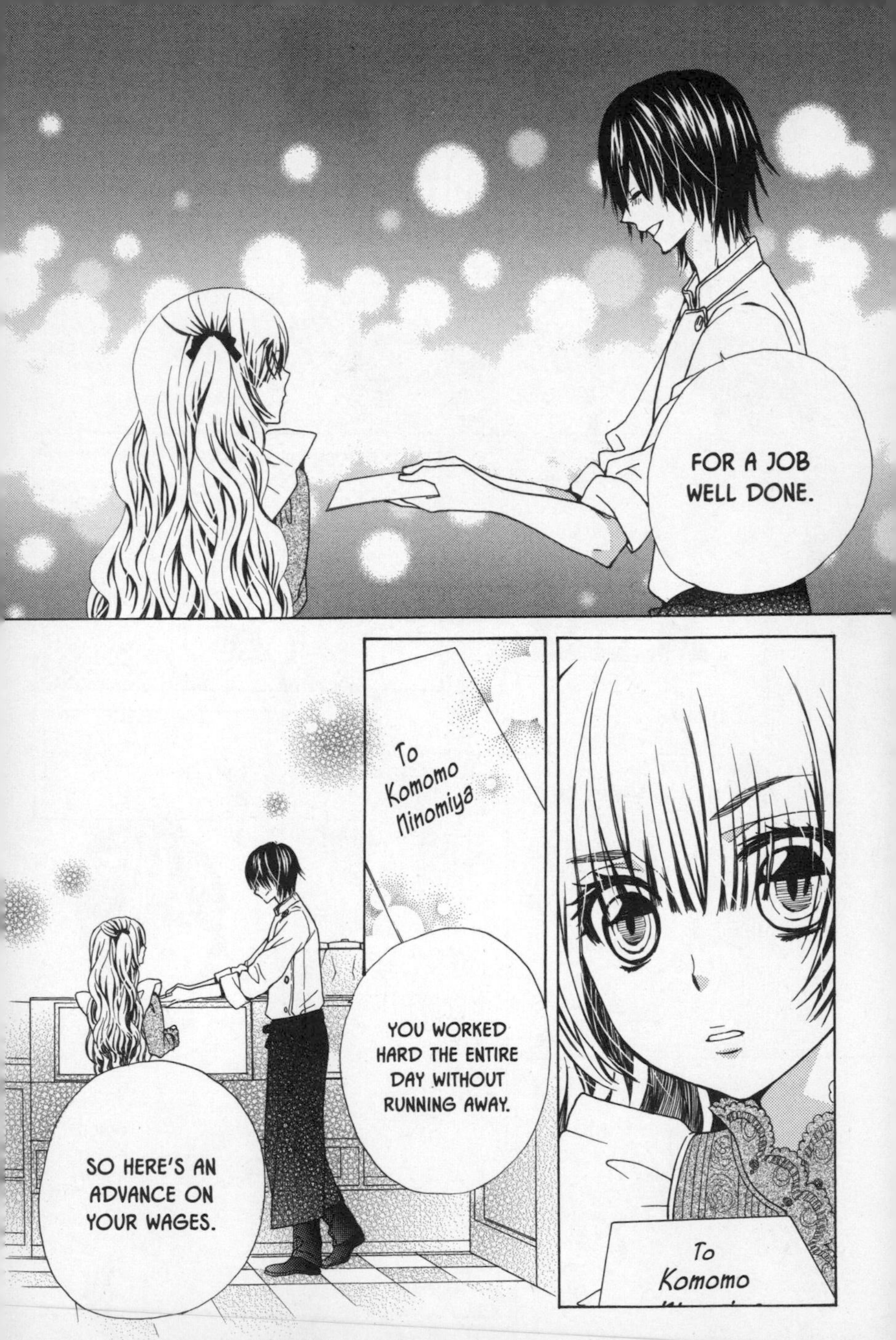
FOR A JOB WELL DONE.
To Komomo
To Komomo Ninomiya
YOU WORKED HARD THE ENTIRE DAY WITHOUT RUNNING AWAY.
SO HERE'S AN ADVANCE ON YOUR WAGES.

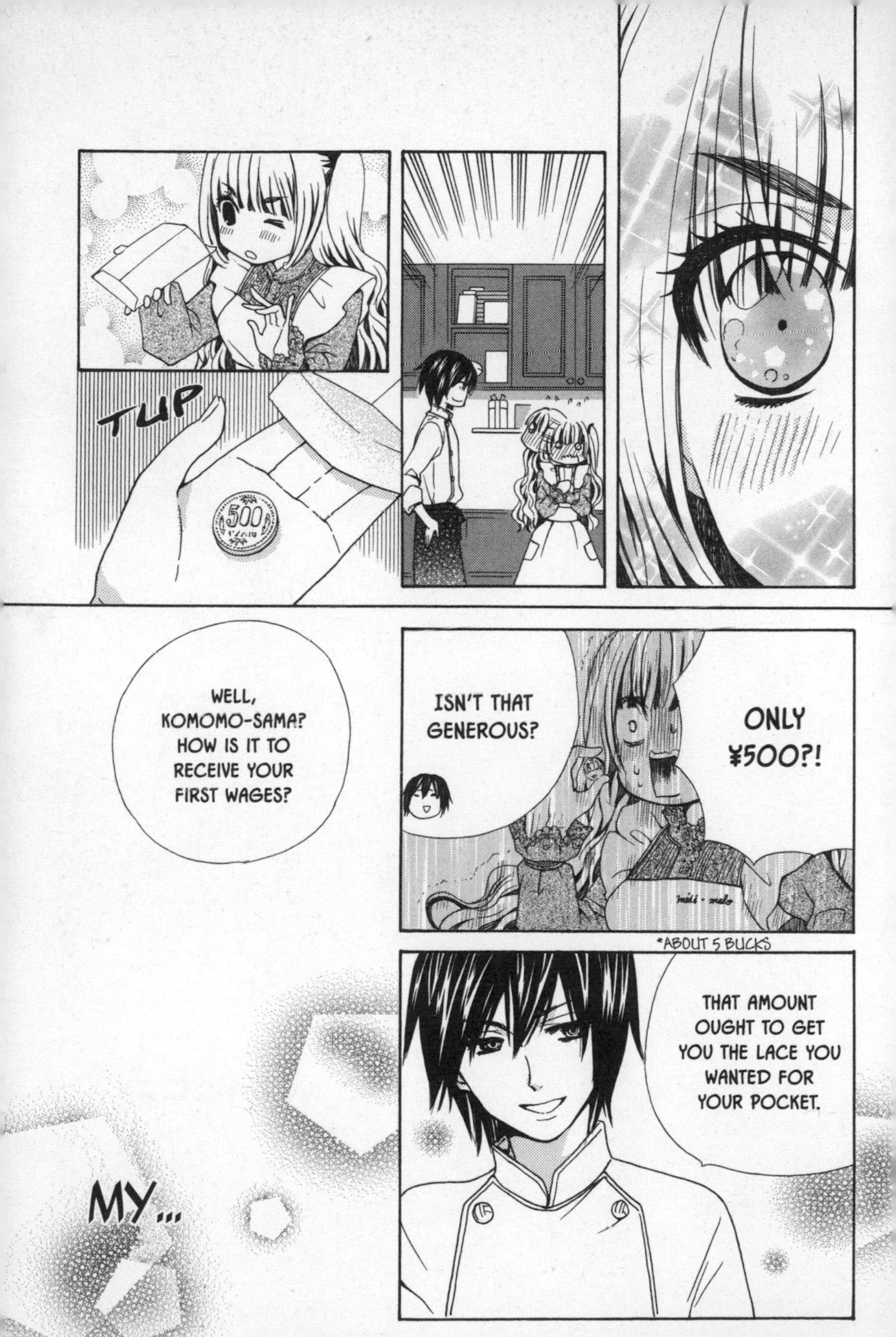
TUP
ONLY ¥500?!
ISN'T THAT GENEROUS?
WELL, KOMOMO-SAMA? HOW IS IT TO RECEIVE YOUR FIRST WAGES?
*ABOUT 5 BUCKS
THAT AMOUNT OUGHT TO GET YOU THE LACE YOU WANTED FOR YOUR POCKET.
MY...

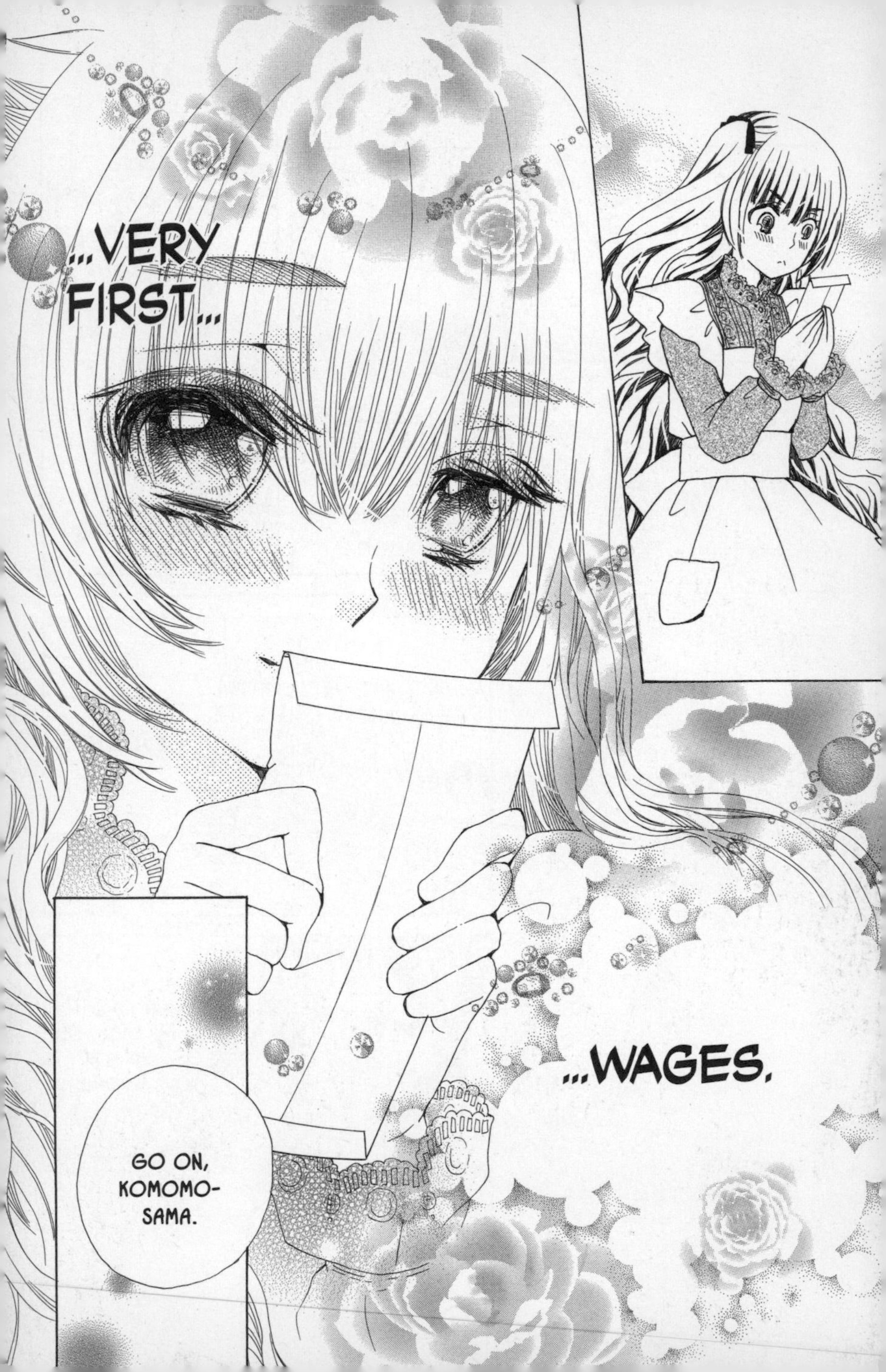
...VERY FIRST...
...WAGES.
GO ON, KOMOMO-SAMA.

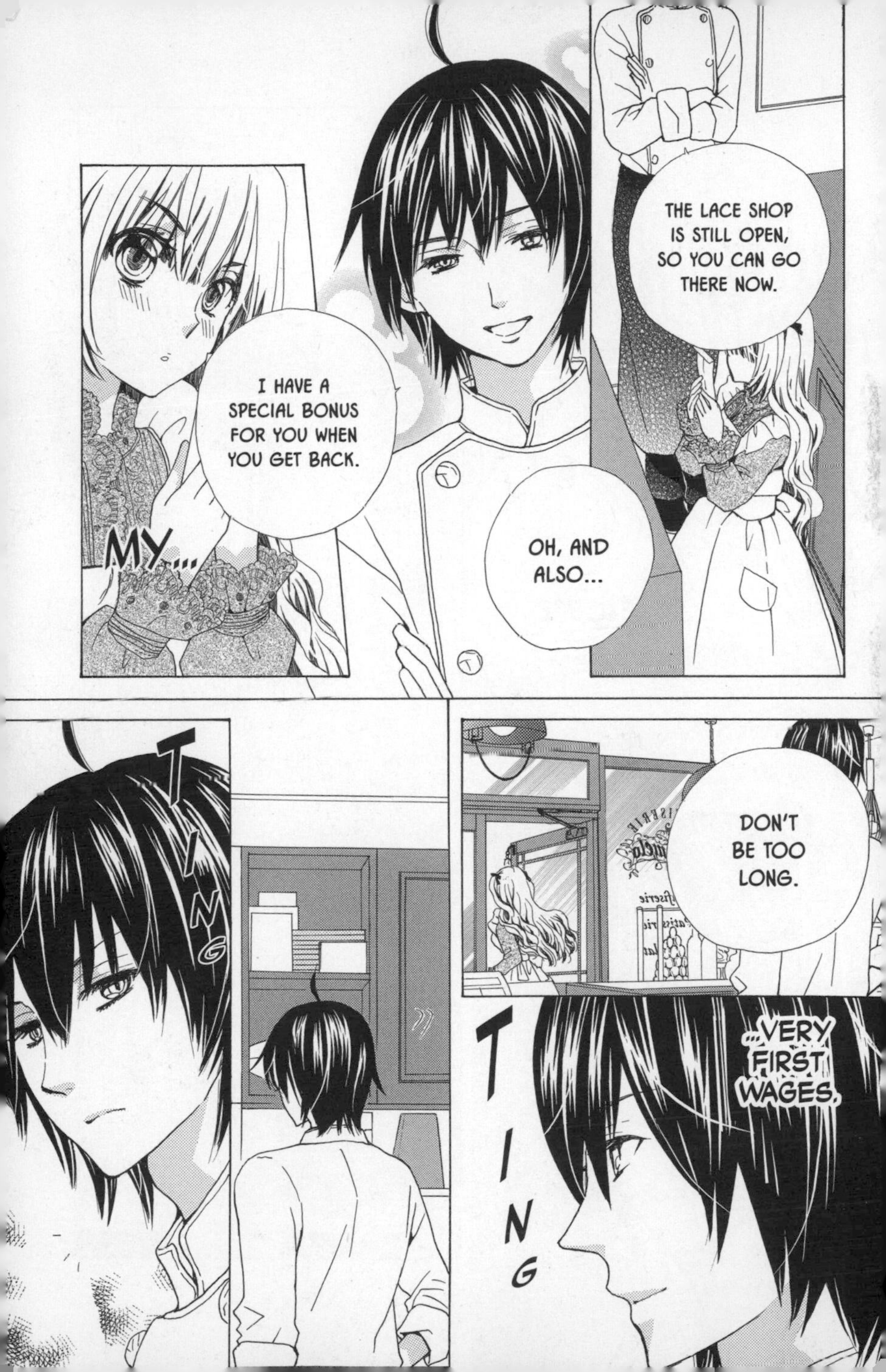
THE LACE SHOP IS STILL OPEN, SO YOU CAN GO THERE NOW.
OH, AND ALSO...
I HAVE A SPECIAL BONUS FOR YOU WHEN YOU GET BACK.
MY...
DON'T BE TOO LONG.
TING
...VERY FIRST WAGES.
TING

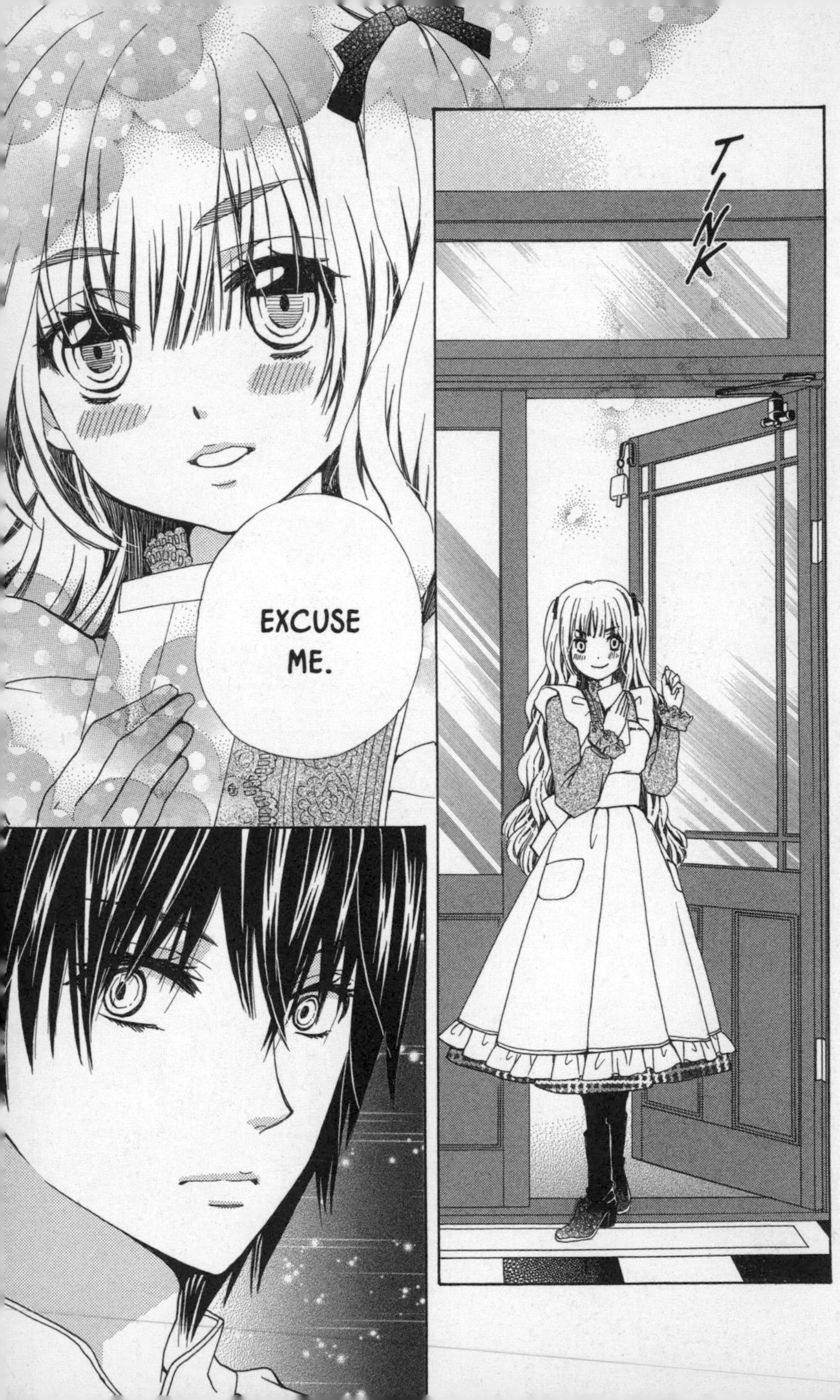
TINK
EXCUSE ME.

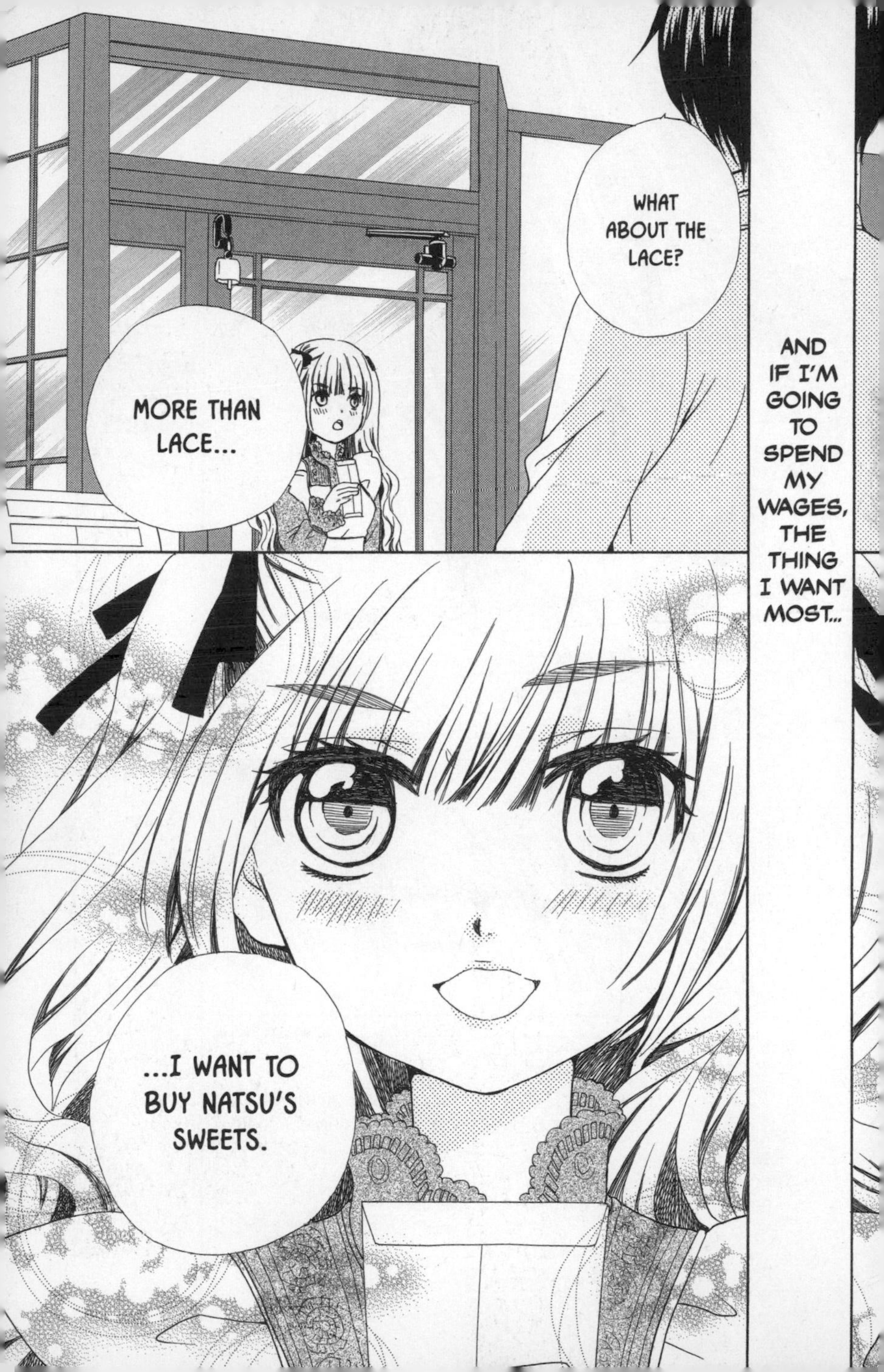
WHAT ABOUT THE LACE?
MORE THAN LACE...
AND IF I'M GOING TO SPEND MY WAGES, THE THING I WANT MOST...
...I WANT TO BUY NATSU'S SWEETS.

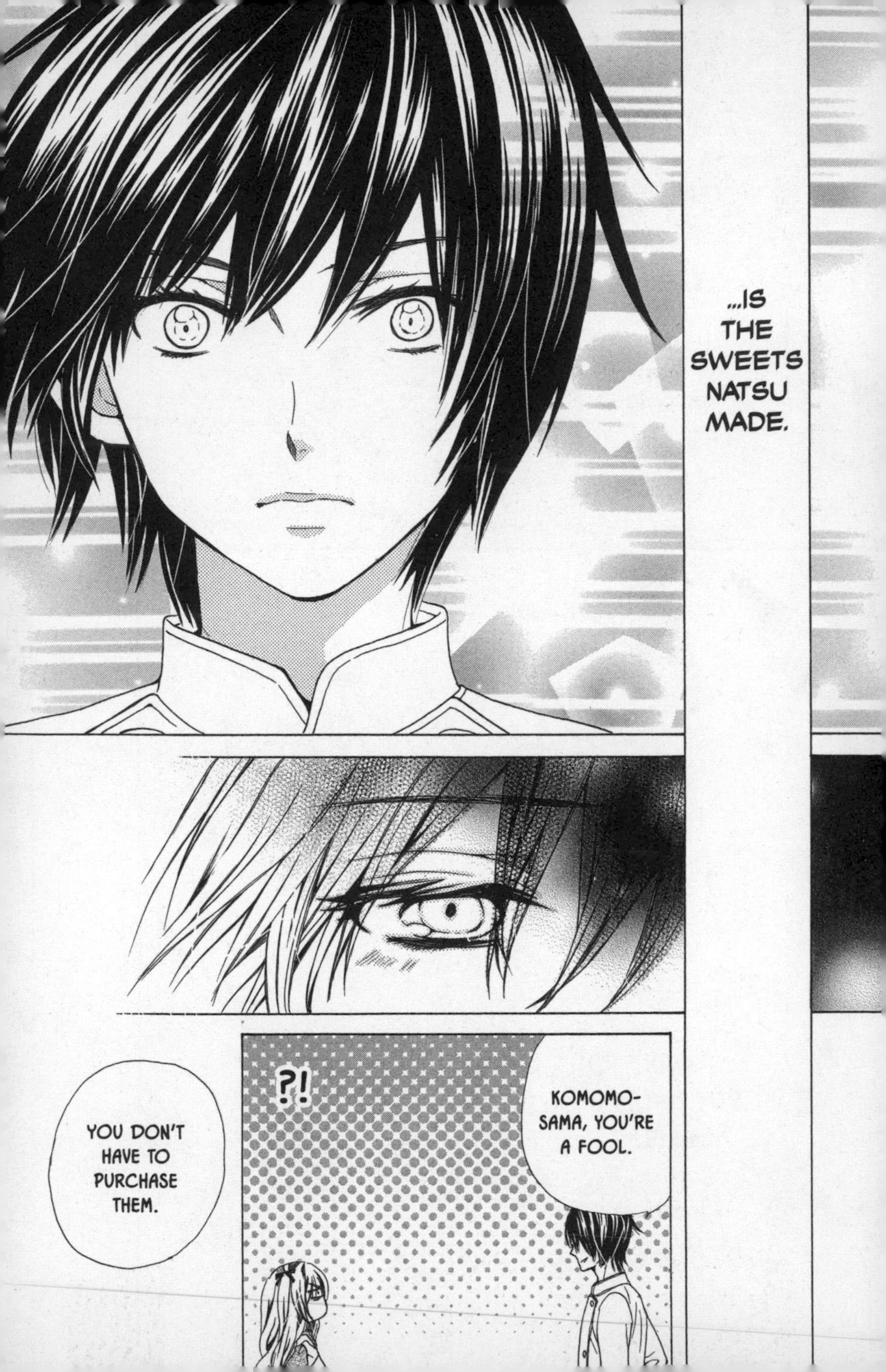
...IS THE SWEETS NATSU MADE.
KOMOMO-SAMA, YOU'RE A FOOL.
?!
YOU DON'T HAVE TO PURCHASE THEM.

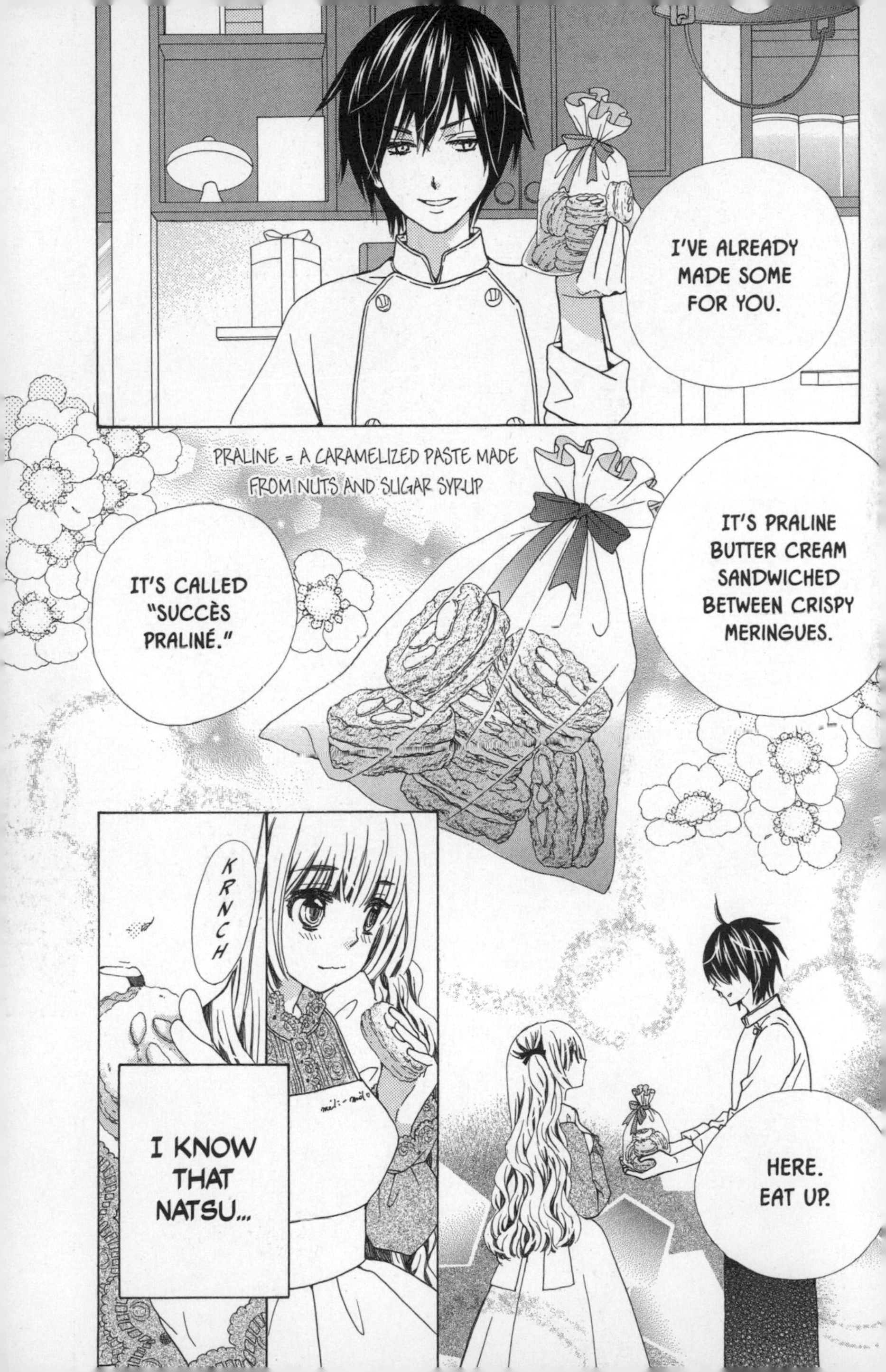
I'VE ALREADY MADE SOME FOR YOU.
IT'S PRALINE BUTTER CREAM SANDWICHED BETWEEN CRISPY MERINGUES.
PRALINE = A CARAMELIZED PASTE MADE FROM NUTS AND SUGAR SYRUP
IT'S CALLED "SUCCÈS PRALINÉ."
HERE. EAT UP.
KRNCH
I KNOW THAT NATSU...

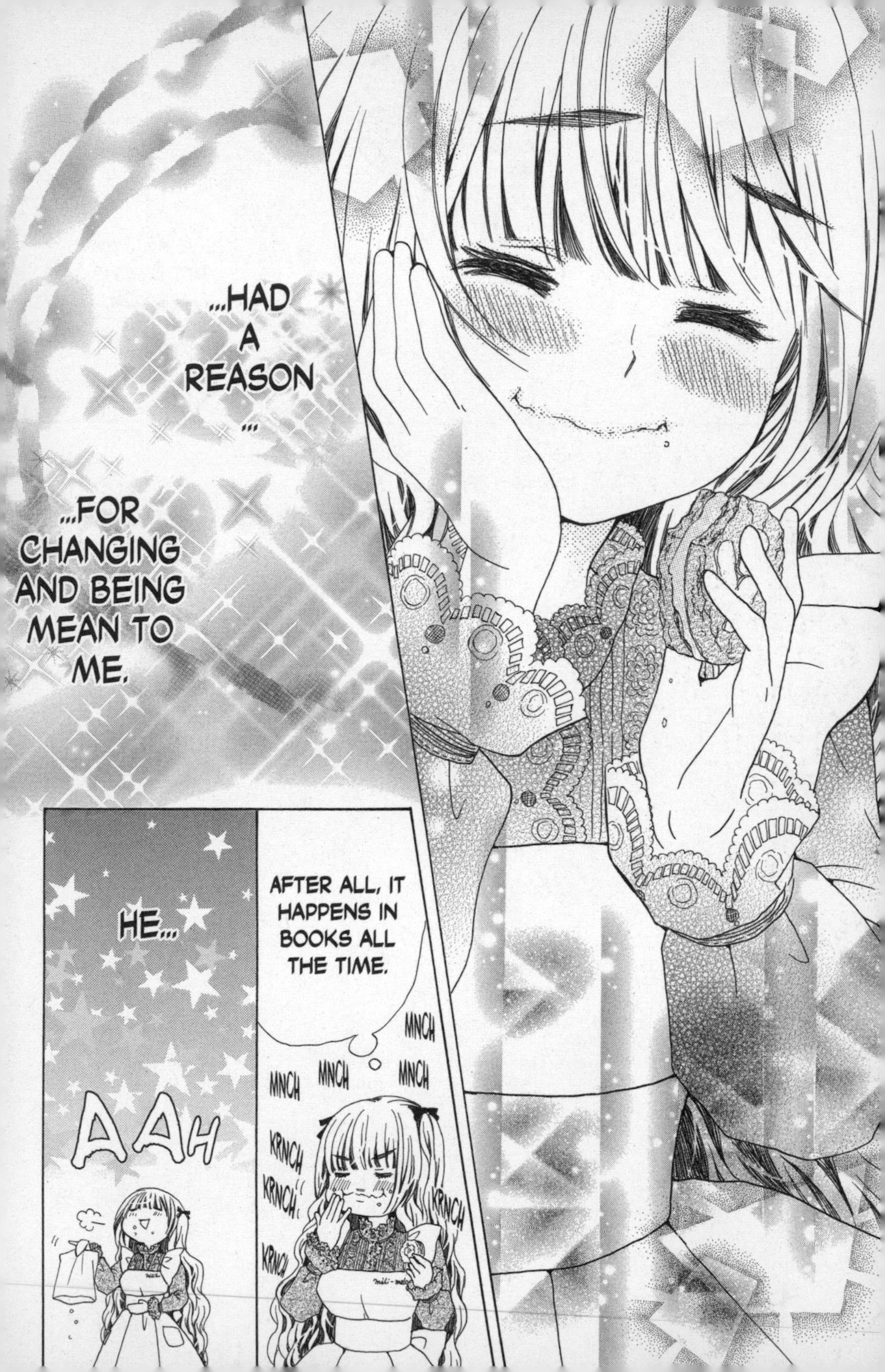
...HAD A REASON ...
...FOR CHANGING AND BEING MEAN TO ME.
AFTER ALL, IT HAPPENS IN BOOKS ALL THE TIME.
MNCH
MNCH
MNCH
MNCH
KRNCH
KRNCH
KRNCH
KRNCH
HE...
AAH

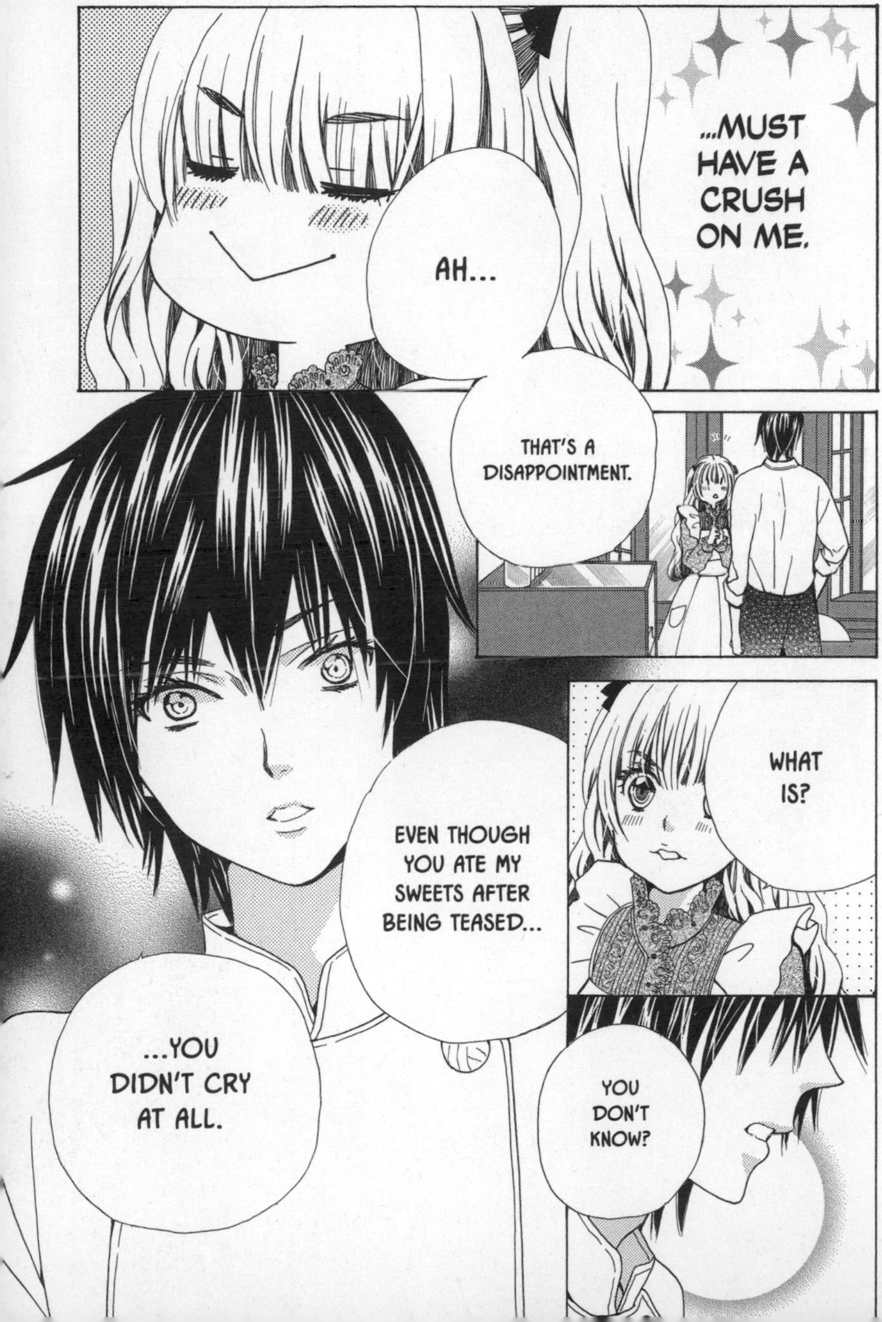
...MUST HAVE A CRUSH ON ME.
AH...
THAT'S A DISAPPOINTMENT.
WHAT IS?
YOU DON'T KNOW?
EVEN THOUGH YOU ATE MY SWEETS AFTER BEING TEASED...
...YOU DIDN'T CRY AT ALL.

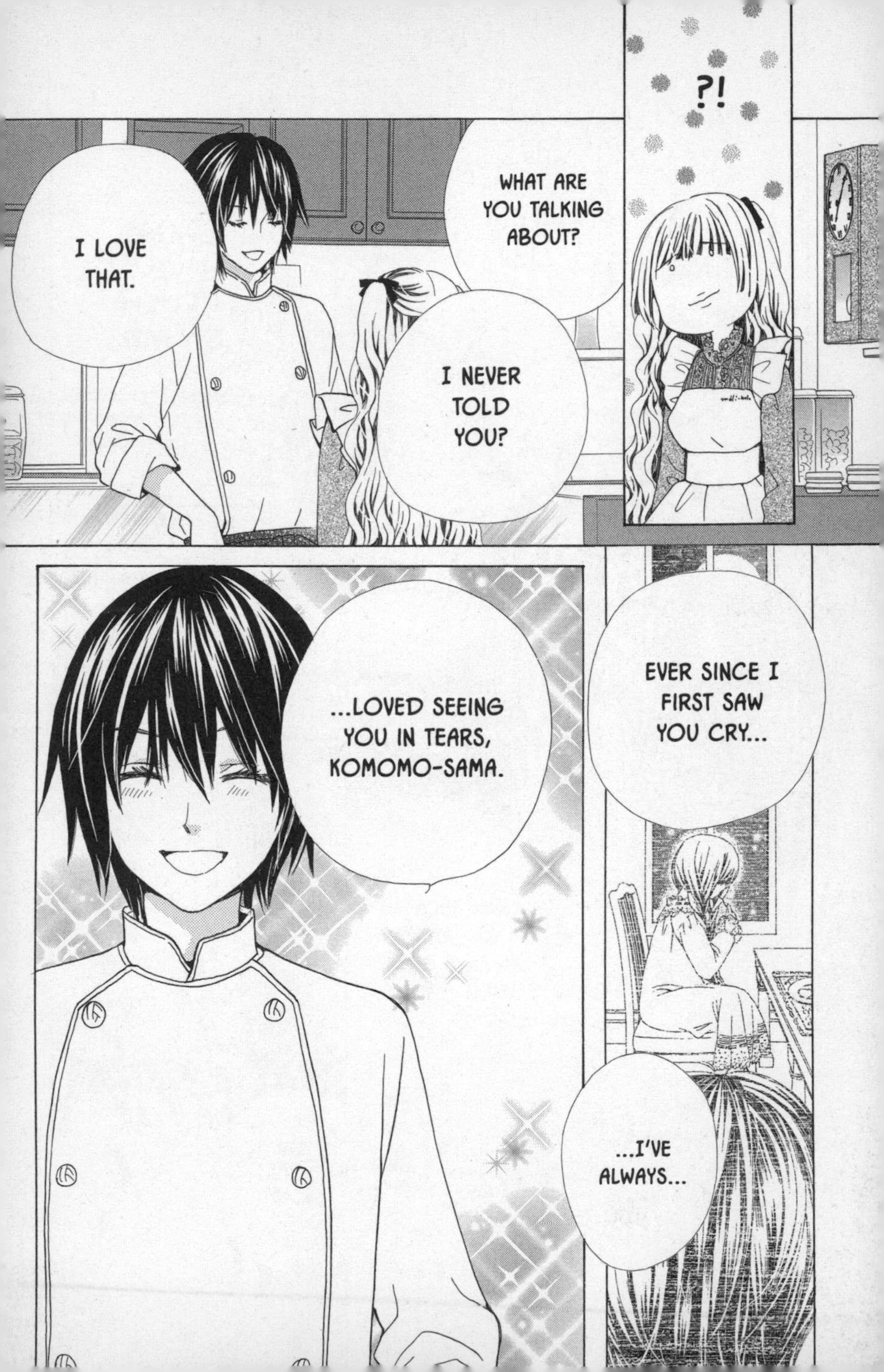
?!
WHAT ARE YOU TALKING ABOUT?
I NEVER TOLD YOU?
I LOVE THAT.
EVER SINCE I FIRST SAW YOU CRY...
...I'VE ALWAYS...
...LOVED SEEING YOU IN TEARS, KOMOMO-SAMA.

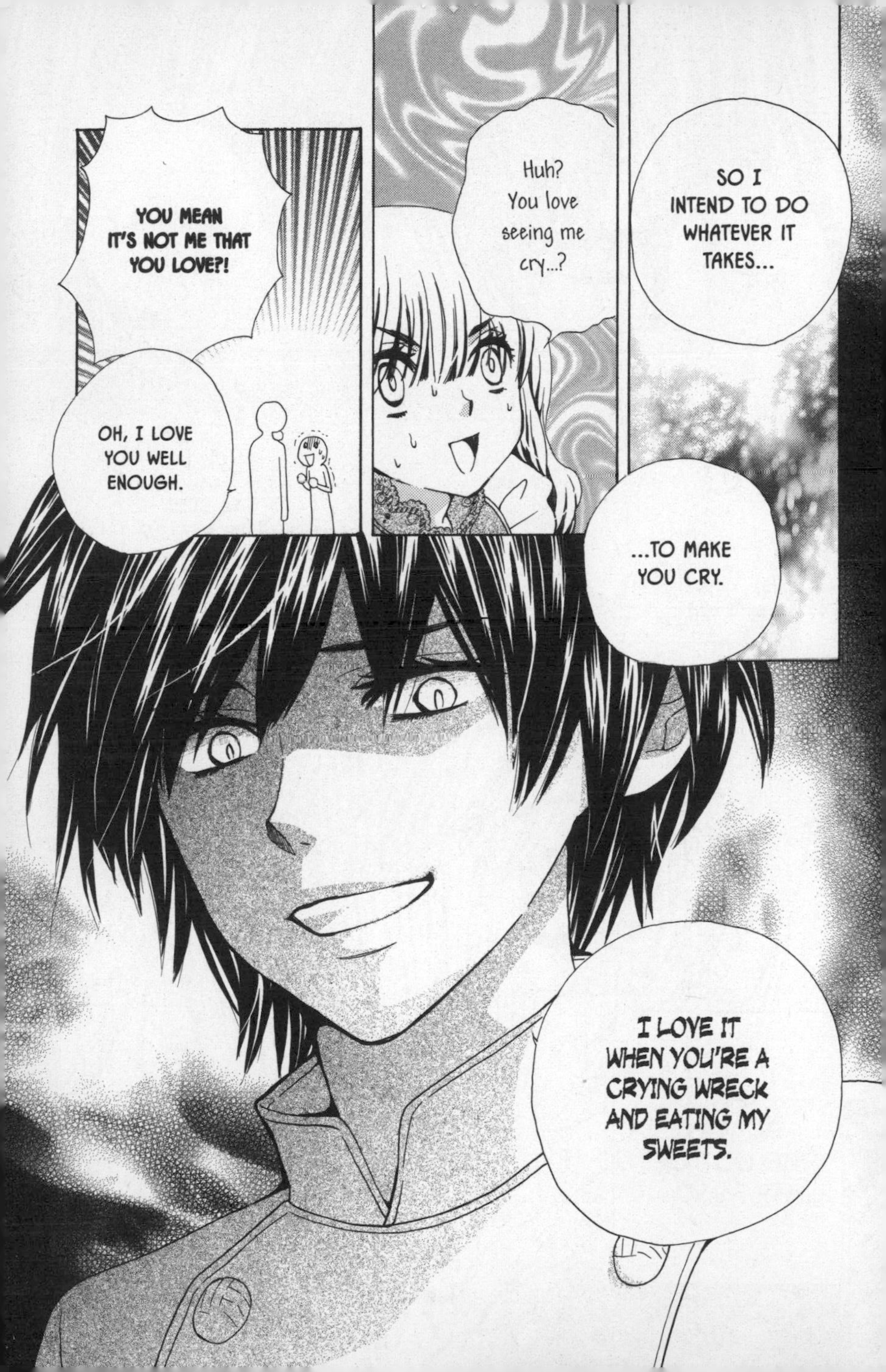
SO I INTEND TO DO WHATEVER IT TAKES...
Huh? You love seeing me cry...?
YOU MEAN IT'S NOT ME THAT YOU LOVE?!
OH, I LOVE YOU WELL ENOUGH.
...TO MAKE YOU CRY.
I LOVE IT WHEN YOU'RE A CRYING WRECK AND EATING MY SWEETS.

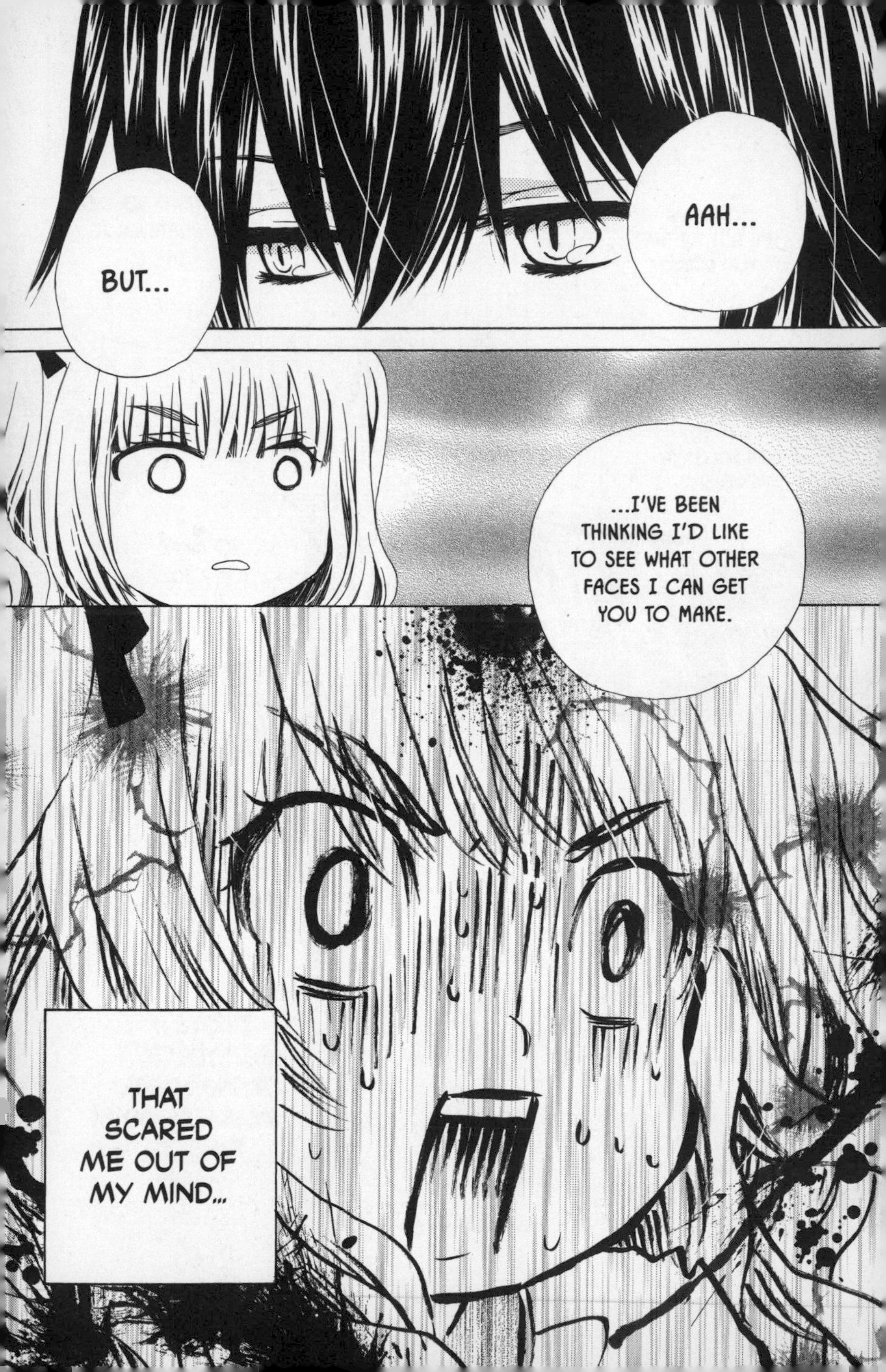
AAH...
BUT...
...I'VE BEEN THINKING I'D LIKE TO SEE WHAT OTHER FACES I CAN GET YOU TO MAKE.
THAT SCARED ME OUT OF MY MIND...

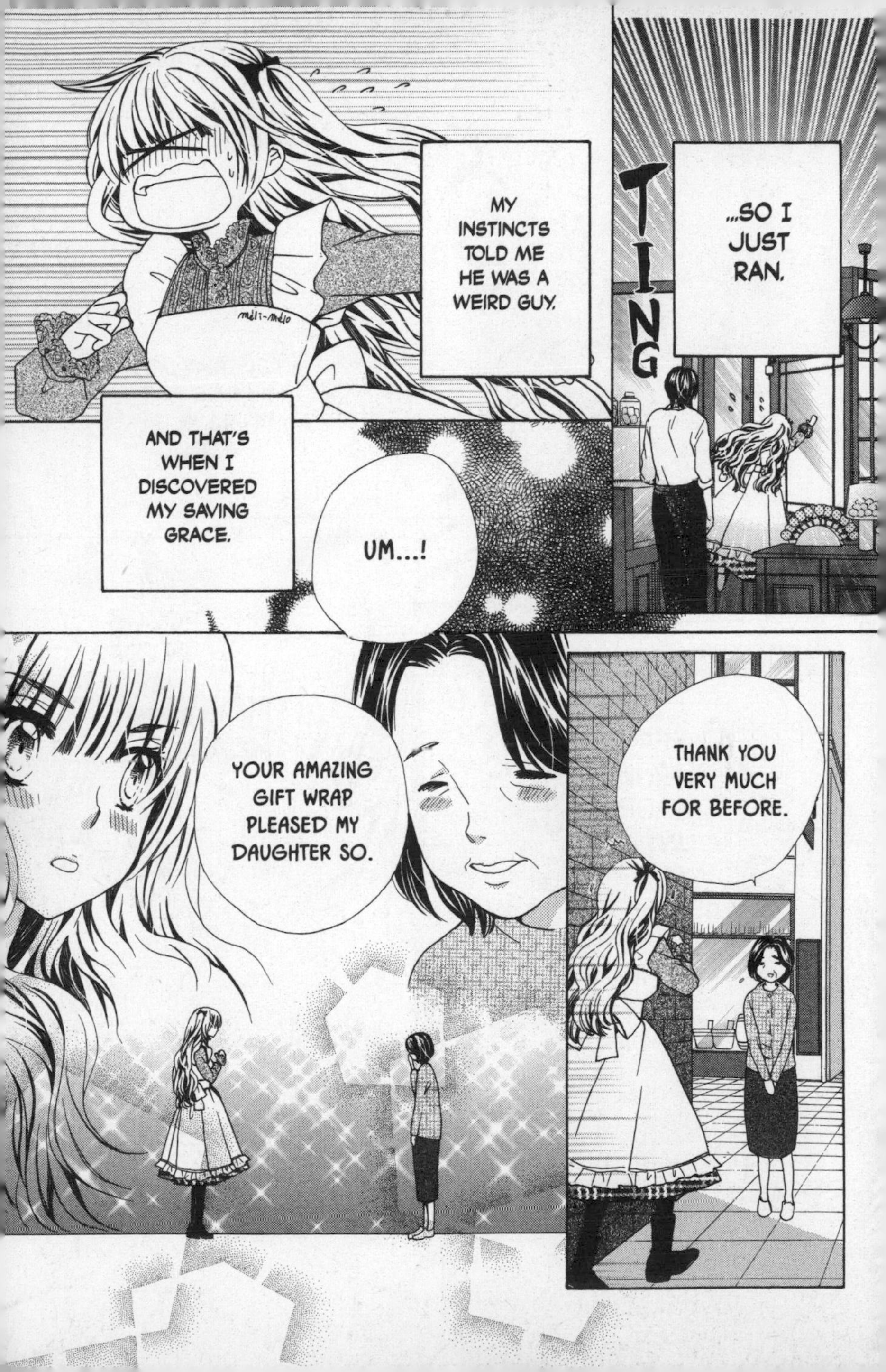
TING
...SO I JUST RAN.
MY INSTINCTS TOLD ME HE WAS A WEIRD GUY.
AND THAT'S WHEN I DISCOVERED MY SAVING GRACE.
UM...!
THANK YOU VERY MUCH FOR BEFORE.
YOUR AMAZING GIFT WRAP PLEASED MY DAUGHTER SO.

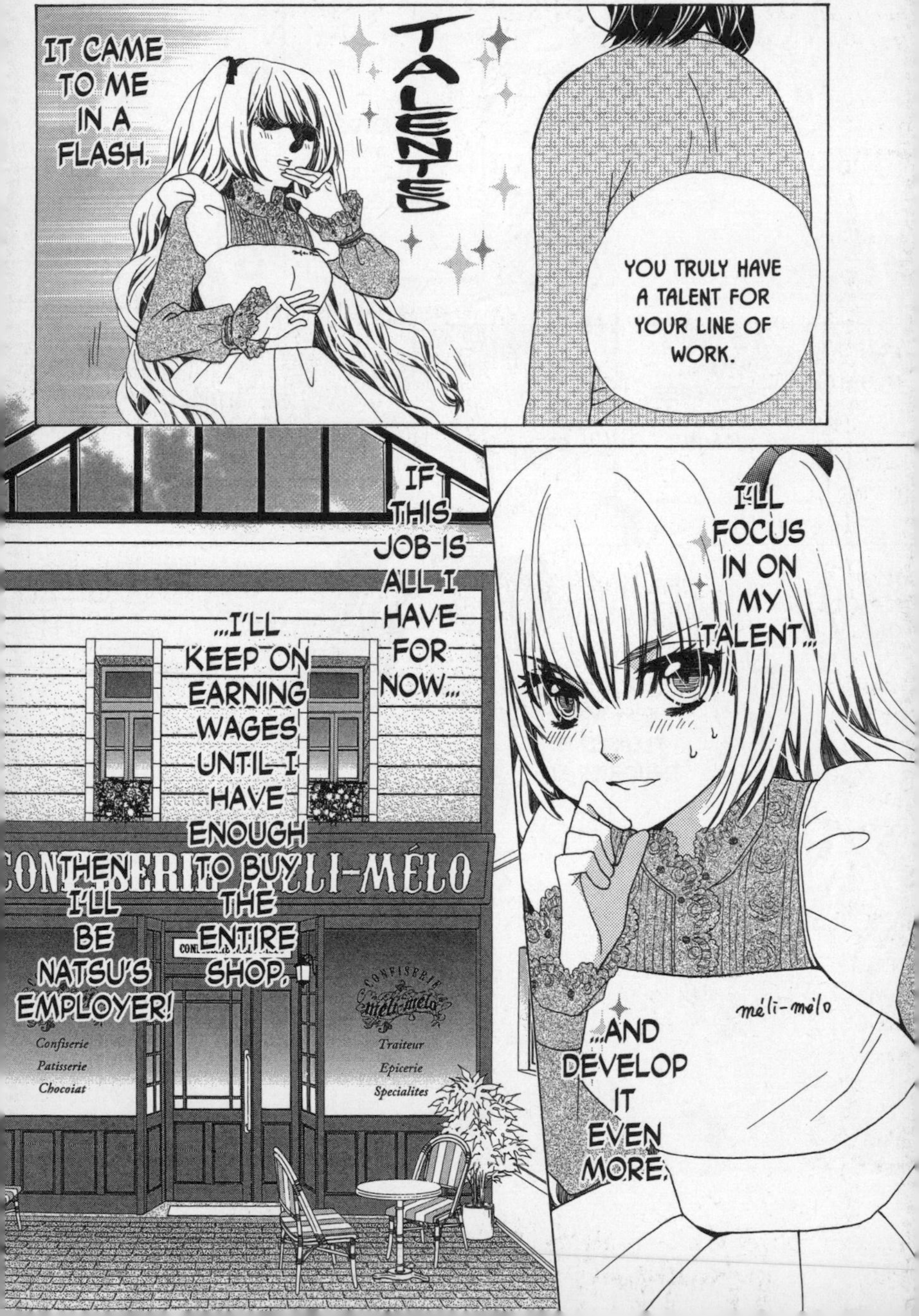
YOU TRULY HAVE A TALENT FOR YOUR LINE OF WORK.
TALENTS
IT CAME TO ME IN A FLASH.
I'LL FOCUS IN ON MY TALENT...
...AND DEVELOP IT EVEN MORE.
méli-mélo
IF THIS JOB IS ALL I HAVE FOR NOW...
...I'LL KEEP ON EARNING WAGES UNTIL I HAVE ENOUGH TO BUY THE ENTIRE SHOP.
THEN I'LL BE NATSU'S EMPLOYER!
CONFISERIE
méli-mélo
Confiserie
Patisserie
Chocoiat
Traiteur
Epicerie
Specialites

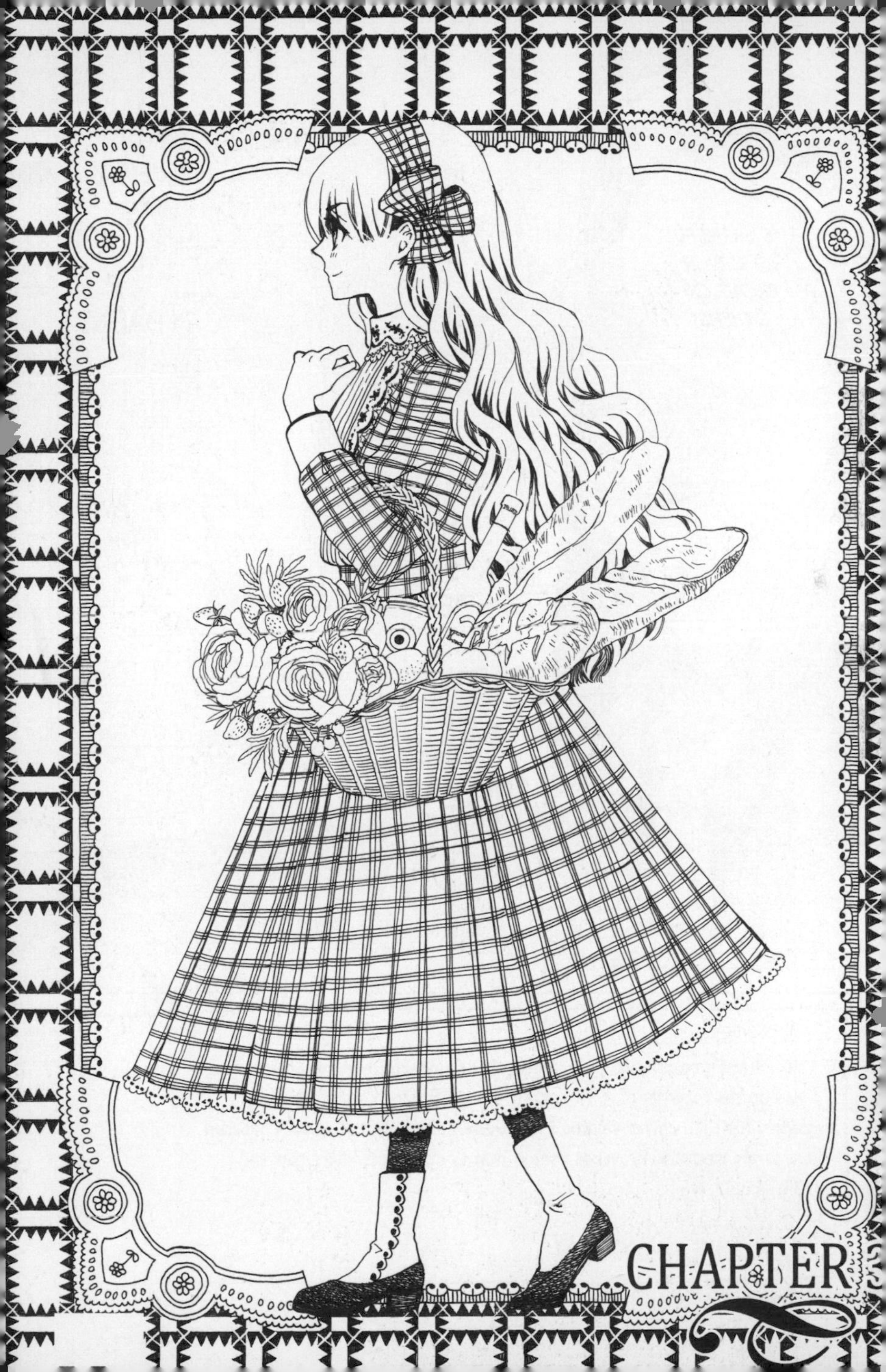
CHAPTER

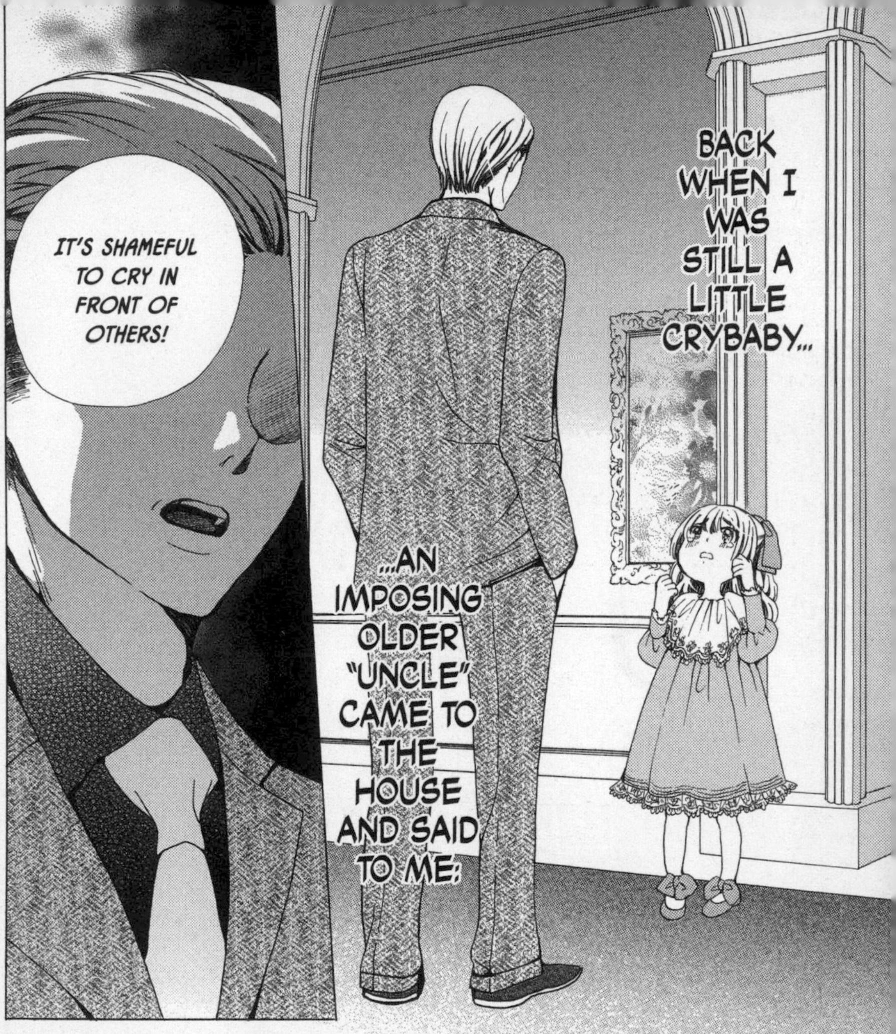
BACK WHEN I WAS STILL A LITTLE CRYBABY...
...AN IMPOSING OLDER "UNCLE" CAME TO THE HOUSE AND SAID TO ME:
IT'S SHAMEFUL TO CRY IN FRONT OF OTHERS!

• The Cover •

This volume's cover uses the publisher's new design! Now the illustration takes up the majority of it. I think I'll try a different color theme and dessert for each cover. Volume 1 is a white color with *calisson.* A *calisson* is a candy from the Provence region that is made with marzipan and fruit syrup.

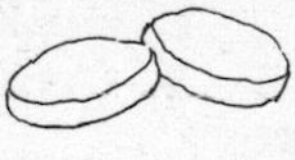

1

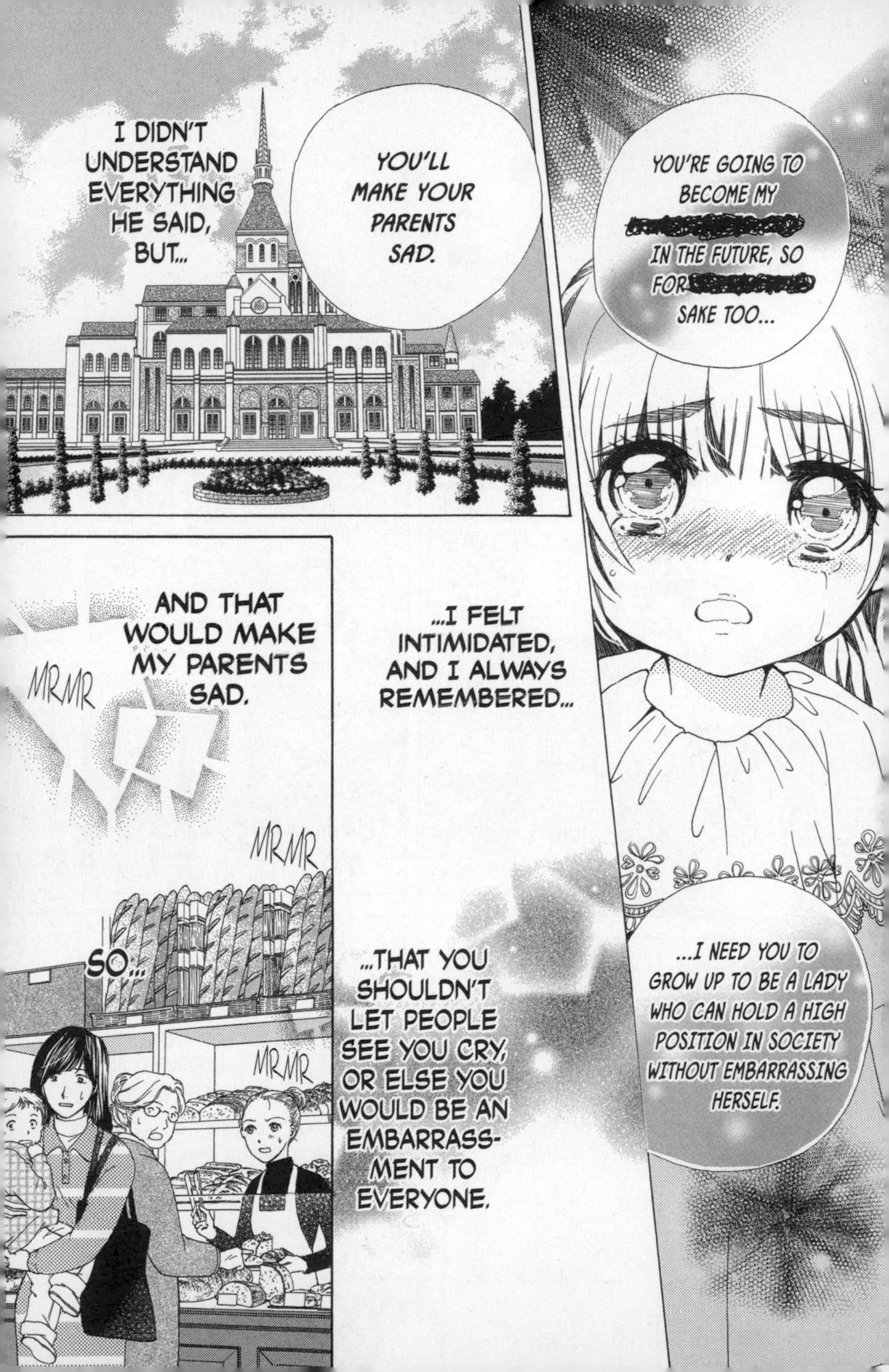
YOU'RE GOING TO BECOME MY [redacted] IN THE FUTURE, SO FOR [redacted] SAKE TOO...
...I NEED YOU TO GROW UP TO BE A LADY WHO CAN HOLD A HIGH POSITION IN SOCIETY WITHOUT EMBARRASSING HERSELF.
YOU'LL MAKE YOUR PARENTS SAD.
I DIDN'T UNDERSTAND EVERYTHING HE SAID, BUT...
...I FELT INTIMIDATED, AND I ALWAYS REMEMBERED...
...THAT YOU SHOULDN'T LET PEOPLE SEE YOU CRY, OR ELSE YOU WOULD BE AN EMBARRASS-MENT TO EVERYONE.
AND THAT WOULD MAKE MY PARENTS SAD.
MRMR
MRMR
SO...
MRMR

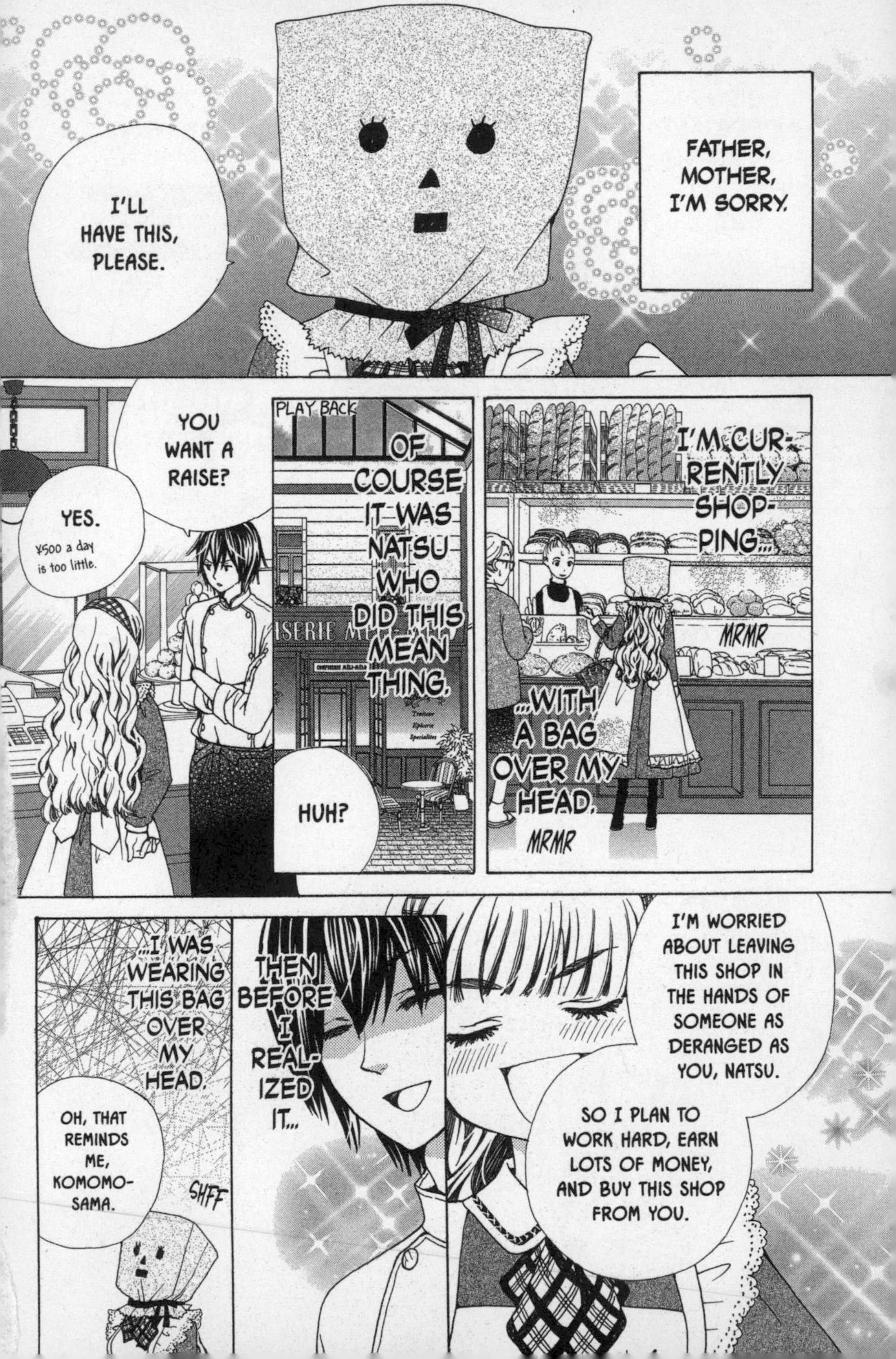
FATHER, MOTHER, I'M SORRY.
I'LL HAVE THIS, PLEASE.
I'M CUR-RENTLY SHOP-PING...
...WITH A BAG OVER MY HEAD.
MRMR
MRMR
PLAY BACK
OF COURSE IT WAS NATSU WHO DID THIS MEAN THING.
HUH?
YOU WANT A RAISE?
YES.
¥500 a day is too little.
I'M WORRIED ABOUT LEAVING THIS SHOP IN THE HANDS OF SOMEONE AS DERANGED AS YOU, NATSU.
SO I PLAN TO WORK HARD, EARN LOTS OF MONEY, AND BUY THIS SHOP FROM YOU.
THEN BEFORE I REAL-IZED IT...
...I WAS WEARING THIS BAG OVER MY HEAD.
OH, THAT REMINDS ME, KOMOMO-SAMA.
SHFF

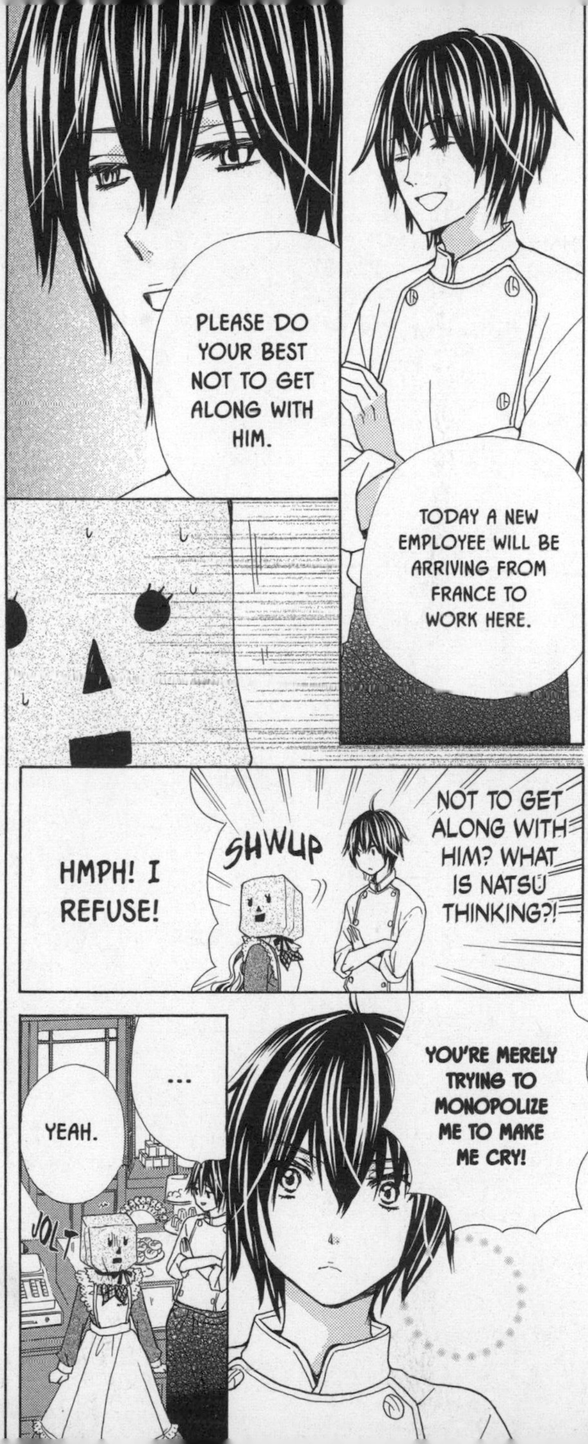
TODAY A NEW EMPLOYEE WILL BE ARRIVING FROM FRANCE TO WORK HERE.
PLEASE DO YOUR BEST NOT TO GET ALONG WITH HIM.
NOT TO GET ALONG WITH HIM? WHAT IS NATSU THINKING?!
SHWUP
HMPH! I REFUSE!
YOU'RE MERELY TRYING TO MONOPOLIZE ME TO MAKE ME CRY!
...
YEAH.
JOLT

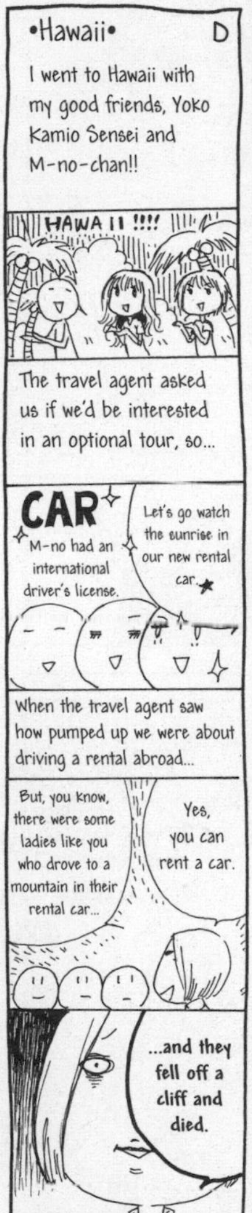
•Hawaii•
D
I went to Hawaii with my good friends, Yoko Kamio Sensei and M-no-chan!!
HAWAII !!!!
The travel agent asked us if we'd be interested in an optional tour, so...
CAR
M-no had an international driver's license.
Let's go watch the sunrise in our new rental car.
When the travel agent saw how pumped up we were about driving a rental abroad...
Yes, you can rent a car.
But, you know, there were some ladies like you who drove to a mountain in their rental car...
...and they fell off a cliff and died.
?!
Are you trying to jinx us...?

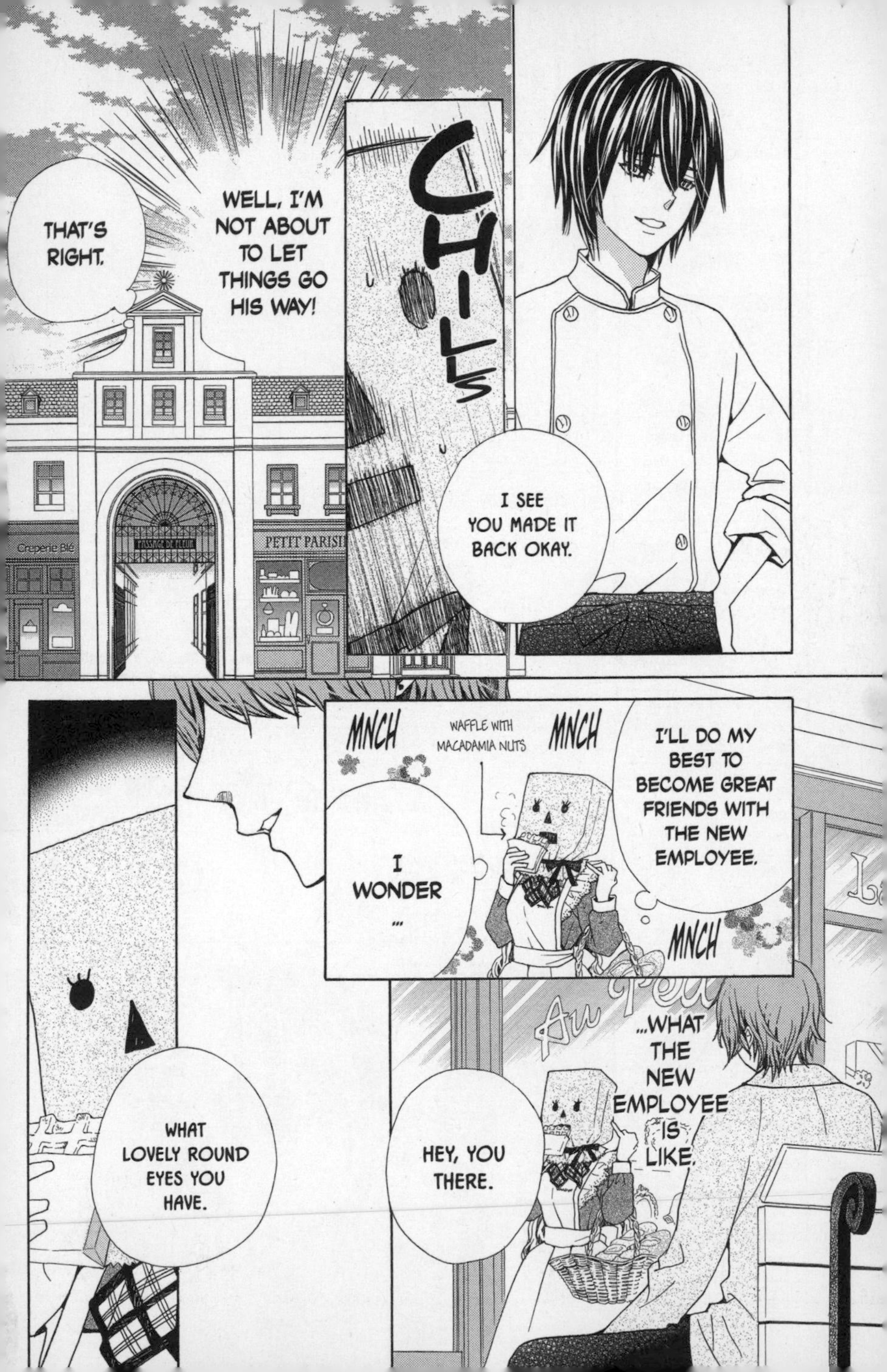
I SEE YOU MADE IT BACK OKAY.
CHILLS
WELL, I'M NOT ABOUT TO LET THINGS GO HIS WAY!
THAT'S RIGHT.
Creperie Blé
PASSAGE DE FLEUR
PETIT PARISI
MNCH
MNCH
WAFFLE WITH MACADAMIA NUTS
I'LL DO MY BEST TO BECOME GREAT FRIENDS WITH THE NEW EMPLOYEE.
MNCH
I WONDER ...
...WHAT THE NEW EMPLOYEE IS LIKE.
HEY, YOU THERE.
WHAT LOVELY ROUND EYES YOU HAVE.

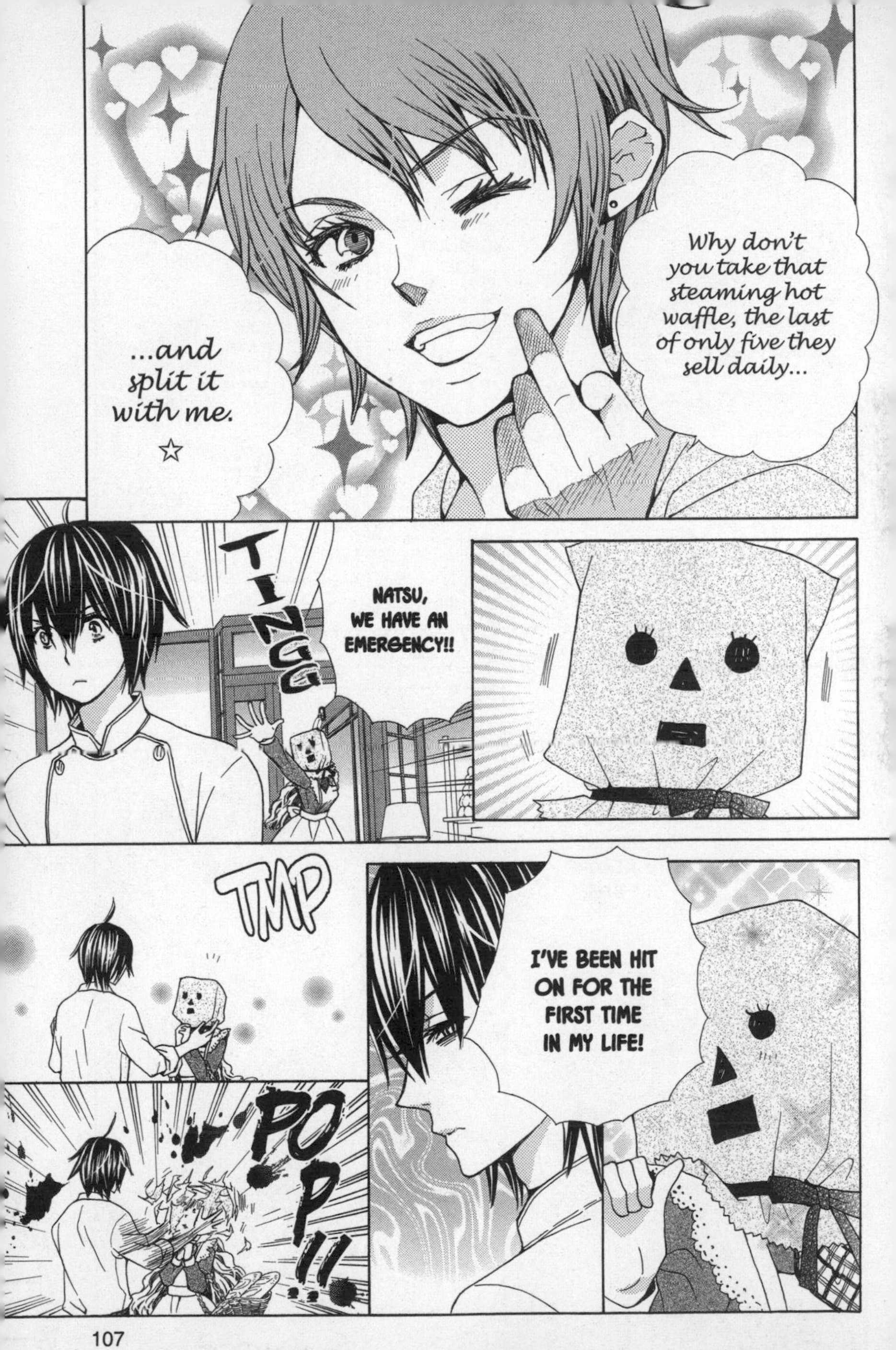

Why don't you take that steaming hot waffle, the last of only five they sell daily...
...and split it with me. ☆
TINGG
NATSU, WE HAVE AN EMERGENCY!!
I'VE BEEN HIT ON FOR THE FIRST TIME IN MY LIFE!
TMP
POP!!

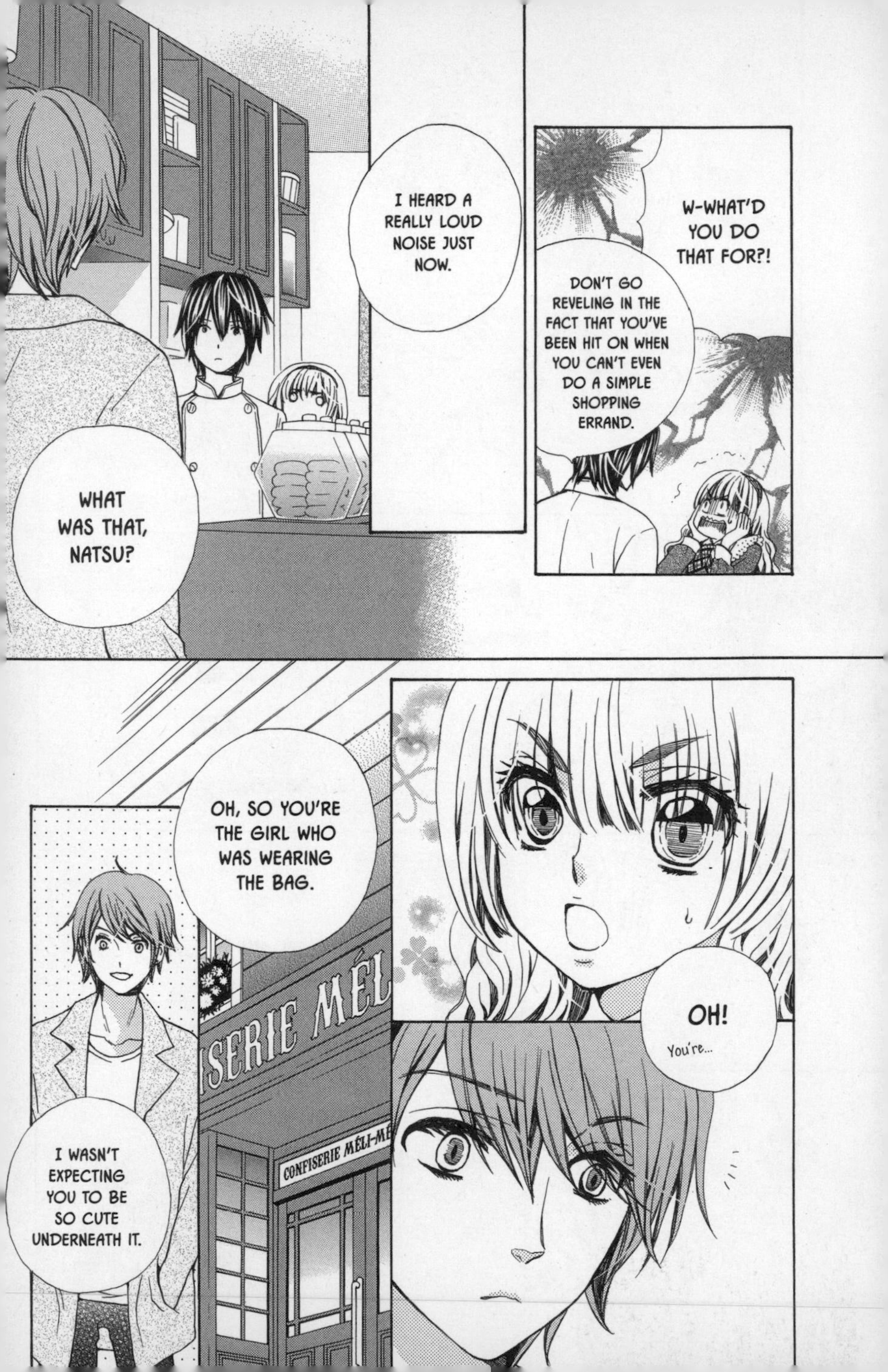
W-WHAT'D YOU DO THAT FOR?!
DON'T GO REVELING IN THE FACT THAT YOU'VE BEEN HIT ON WHEN YOU CAN'T EVEN DO A SIMPLE SHOPPING ERRAND.
I HEARD A REALLY LOUD NOISE JUST NOW.
WHAT WAS THAT, NATSU?
OH! You're...
OH, SO YOU'RE THE GIRL WHO WAS WEARING THE BAG.
I WASN'T EXPECTING YOU TO BE SO CUTE UNDERNEATH IT.
CONFISERIE MÉLI-MÉ
ISERIE MÉL

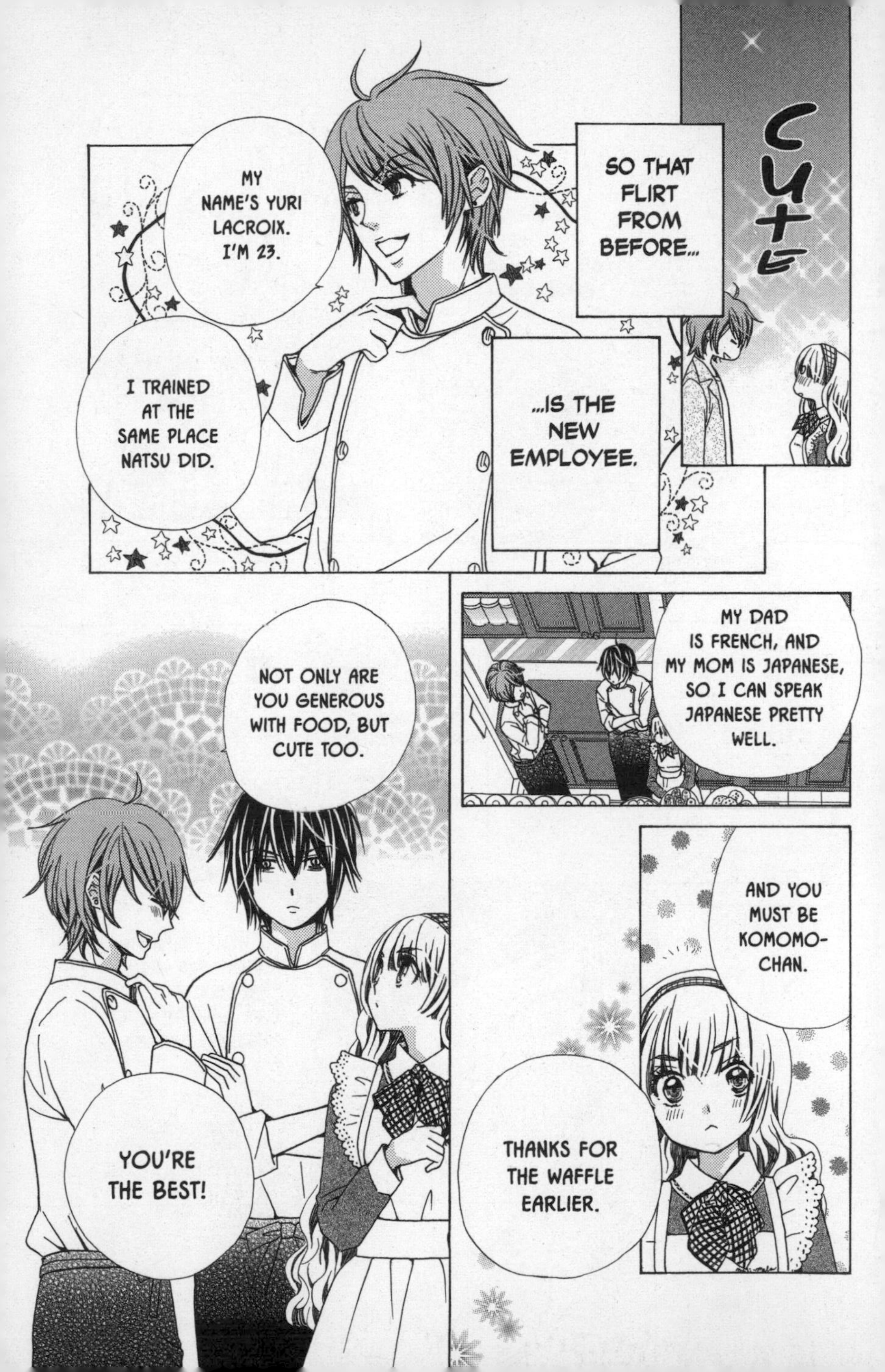
CUTE
SO THAT FLIRT FROM BEFORE...
...IS THE NEW EMPLOYEE.
MY NAME'S YURI LACROIX. I'M 23.
I TRAINED AT THE SAME PLACE NATSU DID.
MY DAD IS FRENCH, AND MY MOM IS JAPANESE, SO I CAN SPEAK JAPANESE PRETTY WELL.
AND YOU MUST BE KOMOMO-CHAN.
THANKS FOR THE WAFFLE EARLIER.
NOT ONLY ARE YOU GENEROUS WITH FOOD, BUT CUTE TOO.
YOU'RE THE BEST!

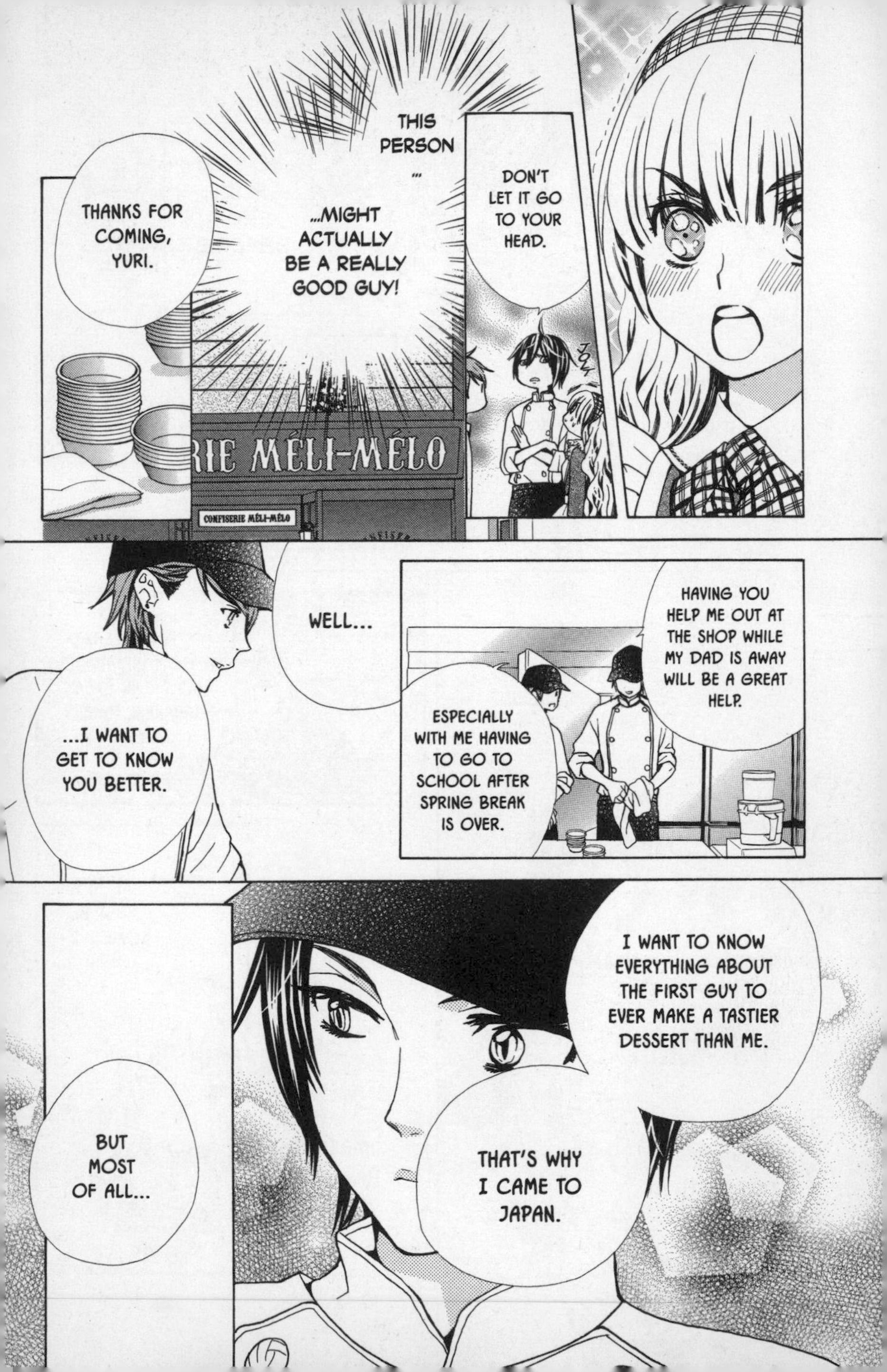
DON'T LET IT GO TO YOUR HEAD.
THIS PERSON ...
...MIGHT ACTUALLY BE A REALLY GOOD GUY!
RIE MÉLI-MÉLO
CONFISERIE MÉLI-MÉLO
THANKS FOR COMING, YURI.
HAVING YOU HELP ME OUT AT THE SHOP WHILE MY DAD IS AWAY WILL BE A GREAT HELP.
ESPECIALLY WITH ME HAVING TO GO TO SCHOOL AFTER SPRING BREAK IS OVER.
WELL...
...I WANT TO GET TO KNOW YOU BETTER.
I WANT TO KNOW EVERYTHING ABOUT THE FIRST GUY TO EVER MAKE A TASTIER DESSERT THAN ME.
THAT'S WHY I CAME TO JAPAN.
BUT MOST OF ALL...

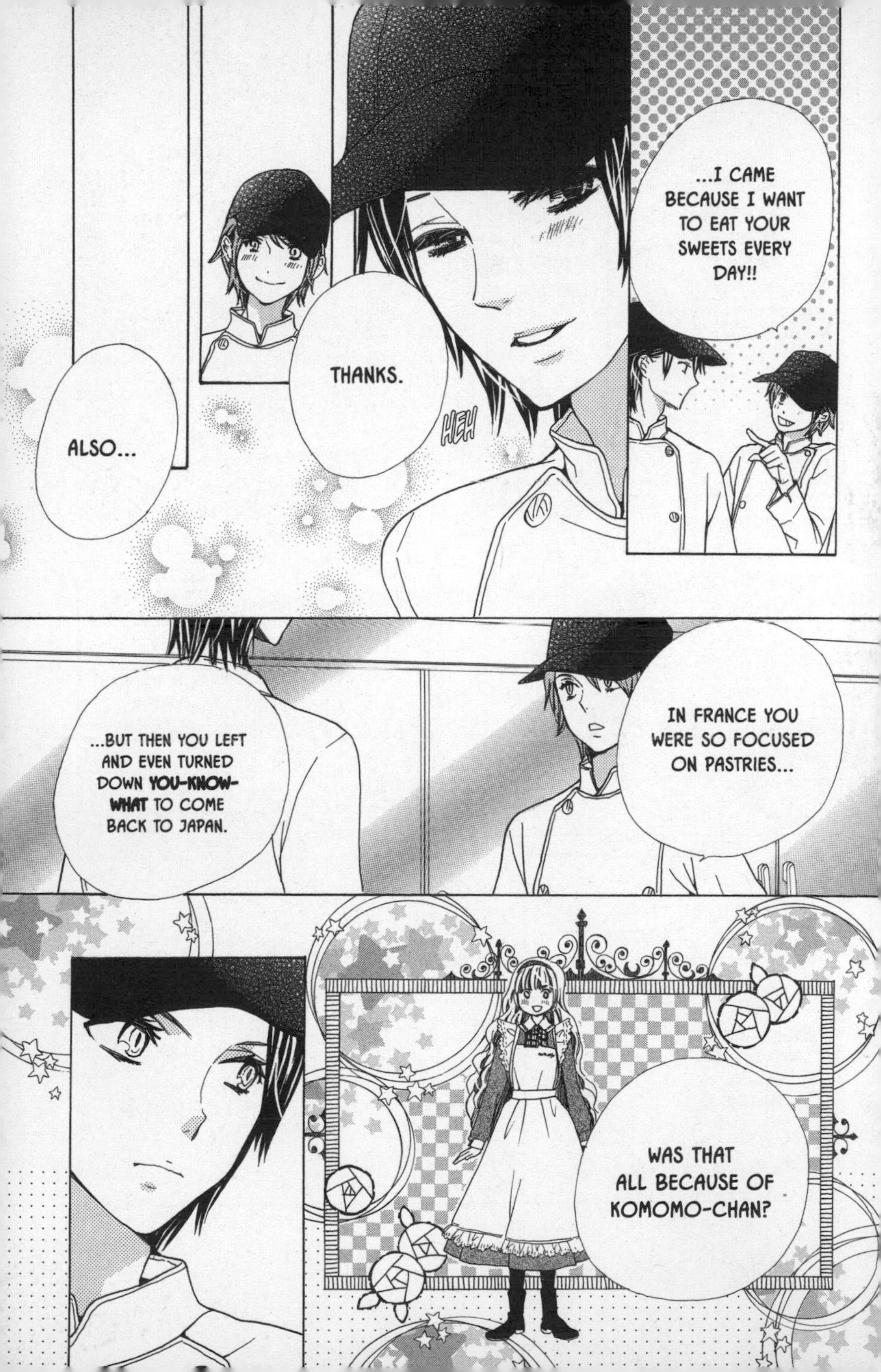
...I CAME BECAUSE I WANT TO EAT YOUR SWEETS EVERY DAY!!
THANKS.
HEH
ALSO...
IN FRANCE YOU WERE SO FOCUSED ON PASTRIES...
...BUT THEN YOU LEFT AND EVEN TURNED DOWN **YOU-KNOW-WHAT** TO COME BACK TO JAPAN.
WAS THAT ALL BECAUSE OF KOMOMO-CHAN?

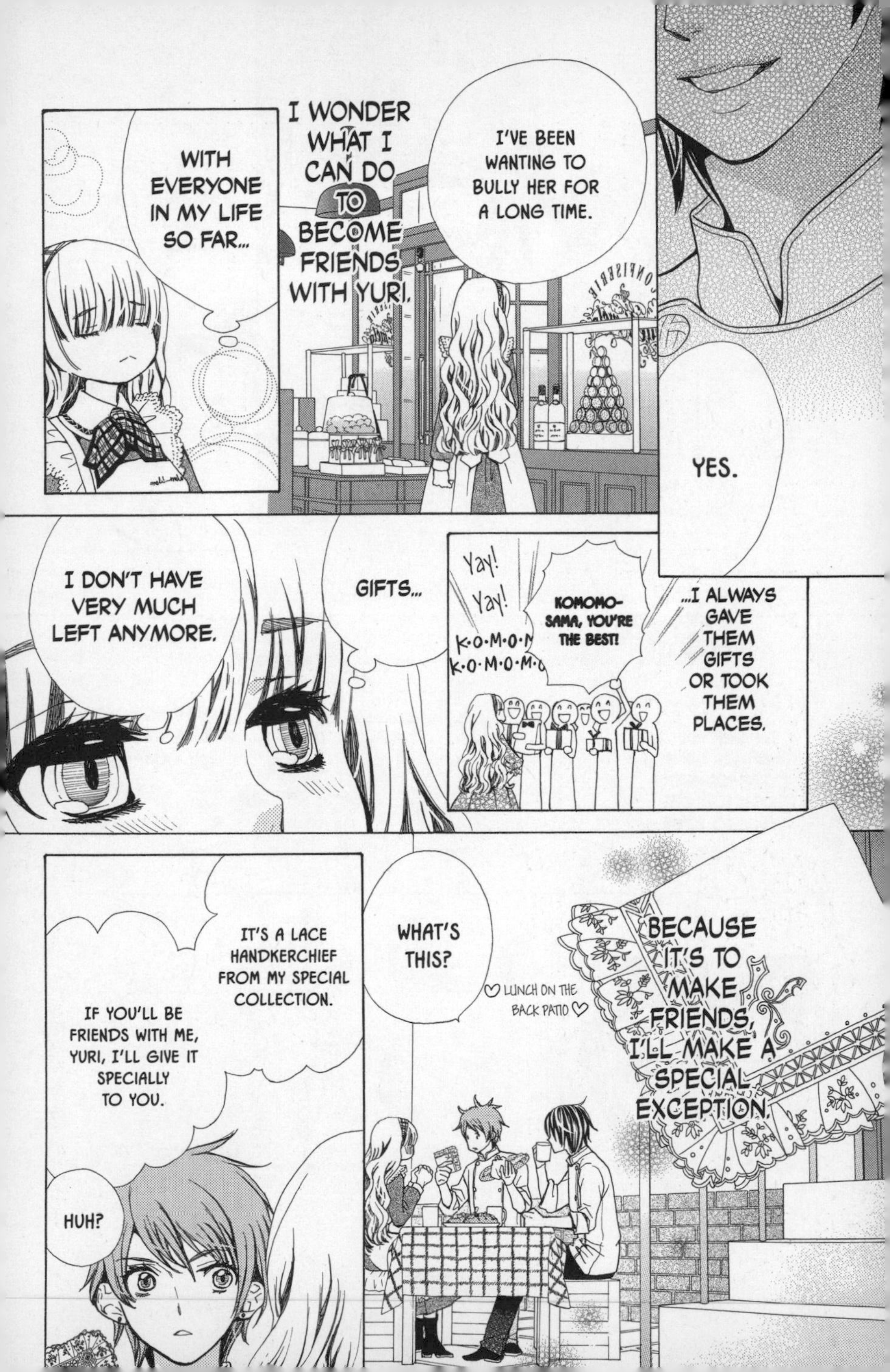
YES.
I'VE BEEN WANTING TO BULLY HER FOR A LONG TIME.
I WONDER WHAT I CAN DO TO BECOME FRIENDS WITH YURI.
WITH EVERYONE IN MY LIFE SO FAR...
...I ALWAYS GAVE THEM GIFTS OR TOOK THEM PLACES.
KOMOMO-SAMA, YOU'RE THE BEST!
Yay!
Yay!
K·O·M·O·M
K·O·M·O·M·O
GIFTS...
I DON'T HAVE VERY MUCH LEFT ANYMORE.
BECAUSE IT'S TO MAKE FRIENDS, I'LL MAKE A SPECIAL EXCEPTION.
LUNCH ON THE BACK PATIO
WHAT'S THIS?
IT'S A LACE HANDKERCHIEF FROM MY SPECIAL COLLECTION.
IF YOU'LL BE FRIENDS WITH ME, YURI, I'LL GIVE IT SPECIALLY TO YOU.
HUH?

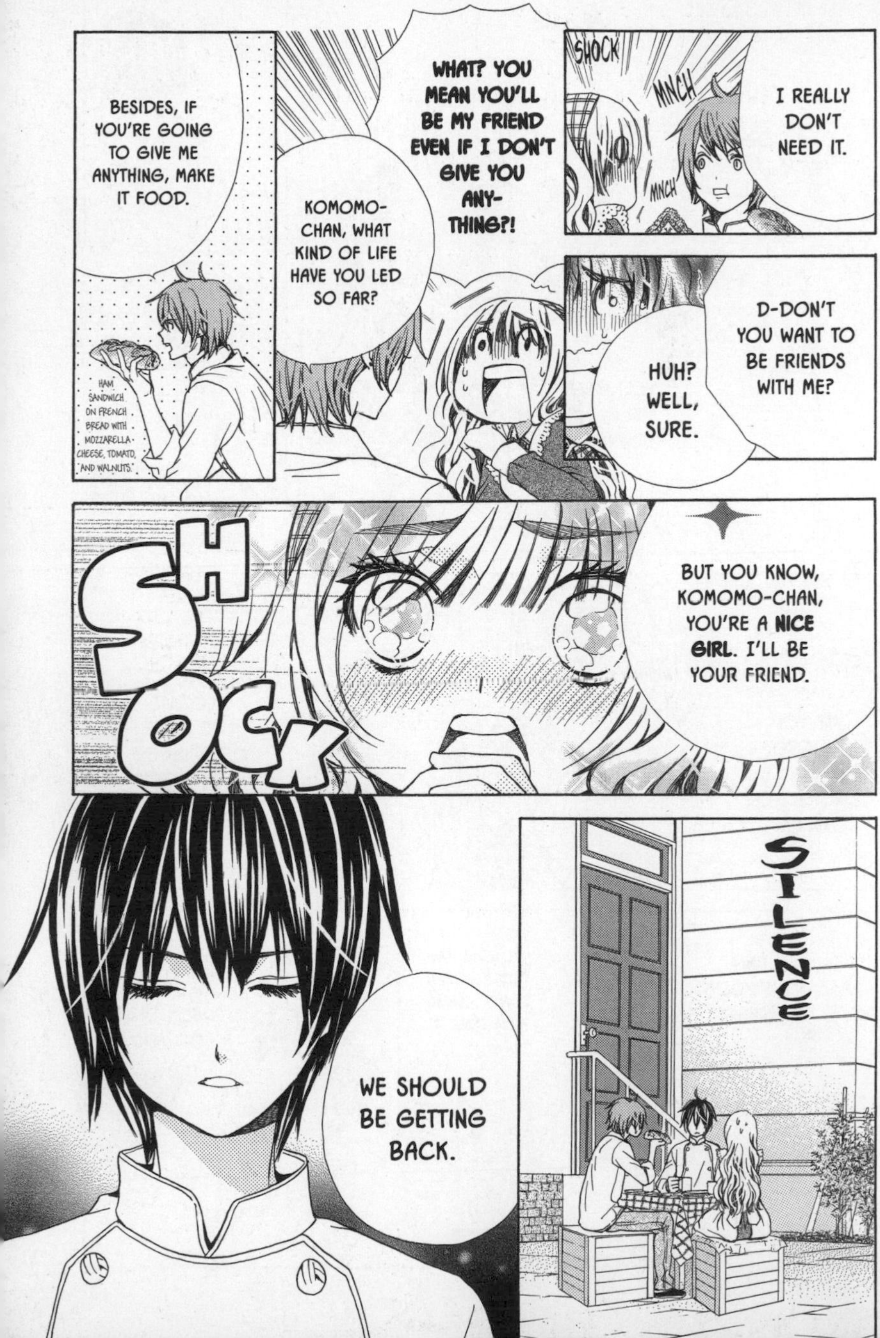
SHOCK
MNCH
MNCH
I REALLY DON'T NEED IT.
D-DON'T YOU WANT TO BE FRIENDS WITH ME?
HUH? WELL, SURE.
WHAT? YOU MEAN YOU'LL BE MY FRIEND EVEN IF I DON'T GIVE YOU ANY-THING?!
KOMOMO-CHAN, WHAT KIND OF LIFE HAVE YOU LED SO FAR?
BESIDES, IF YOU'RE GOING TO GIVE ME ANYTHING, MAKE IT FOOD.
HAM SANDWICH ON FRENCH BREAD WITH MOZZARELLA CHEESE, TOMATO, AND WALNUTS.
BUT YOU KNOW, KOMOMO-CHAN, YOU'RE A NICE GIRL. I'LL BE YOUR FRIEND.
SHOCK
SILENCE
WE SHOULD BE GETTING BACK.

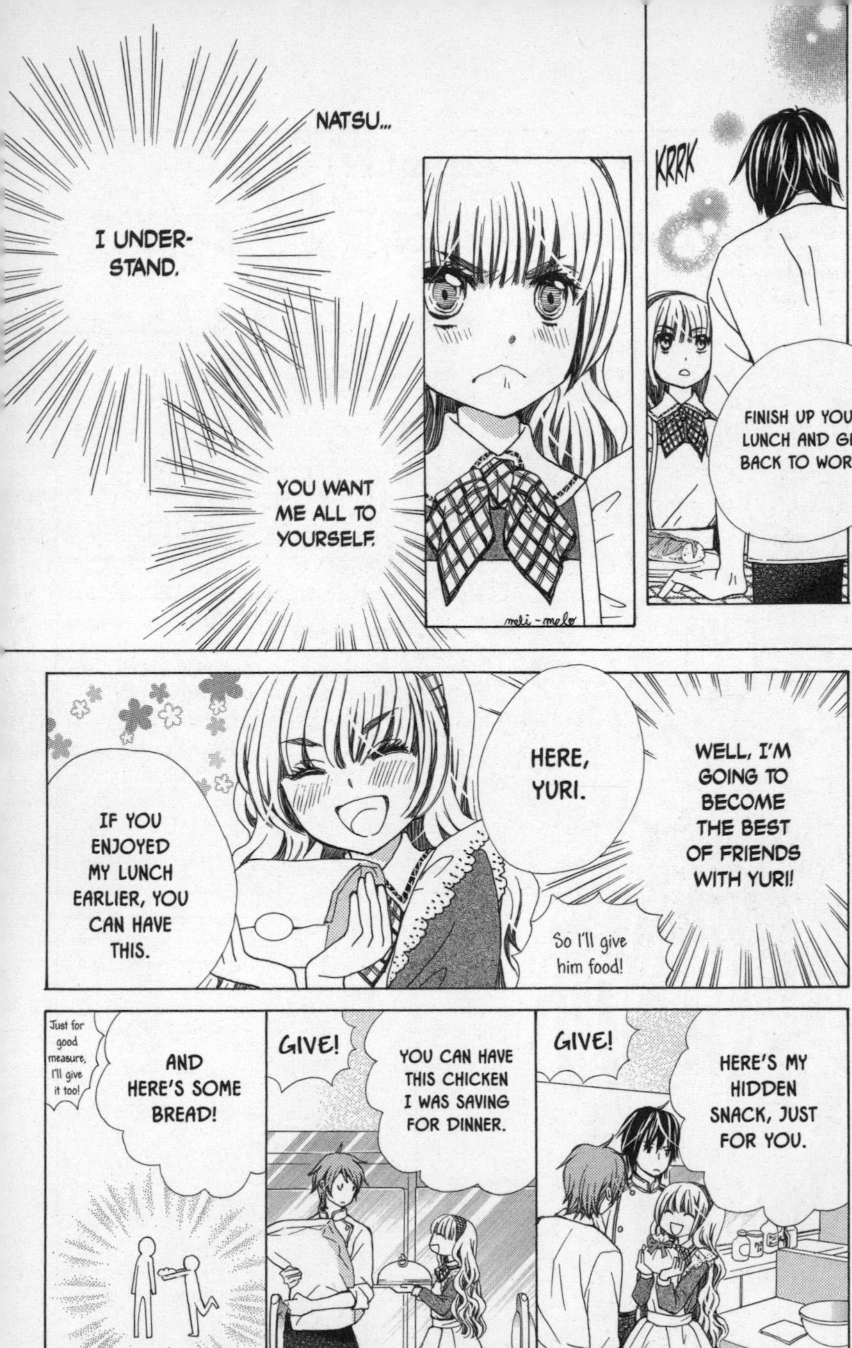
KRRK
FINISH UP YOUR LUNCH AND GET BACK TO WORK.
meli-melo
NATSU...
I UNDER-STAND.
YOU WANT ME ALL TO YOURSELF.
WELL, I'M GOING TO BECOME THE BEST OF FRIENDS WITH YURI!
HERE, YURI.
So I'll give him food!
IF YOU ENJOYED MY LUNCH EARLIER, YOU CAN HAVE THIS.
GIVE!
HERE'S MY HIDDEN SNACK, JUST FOR YOU.
GIVE!
YOU CAN HAVE THIS CHICKEN I WAS SAVING FOR DINNER.
AND HERE'S SOME BREAD!
Just for good measure, I'll give it too!

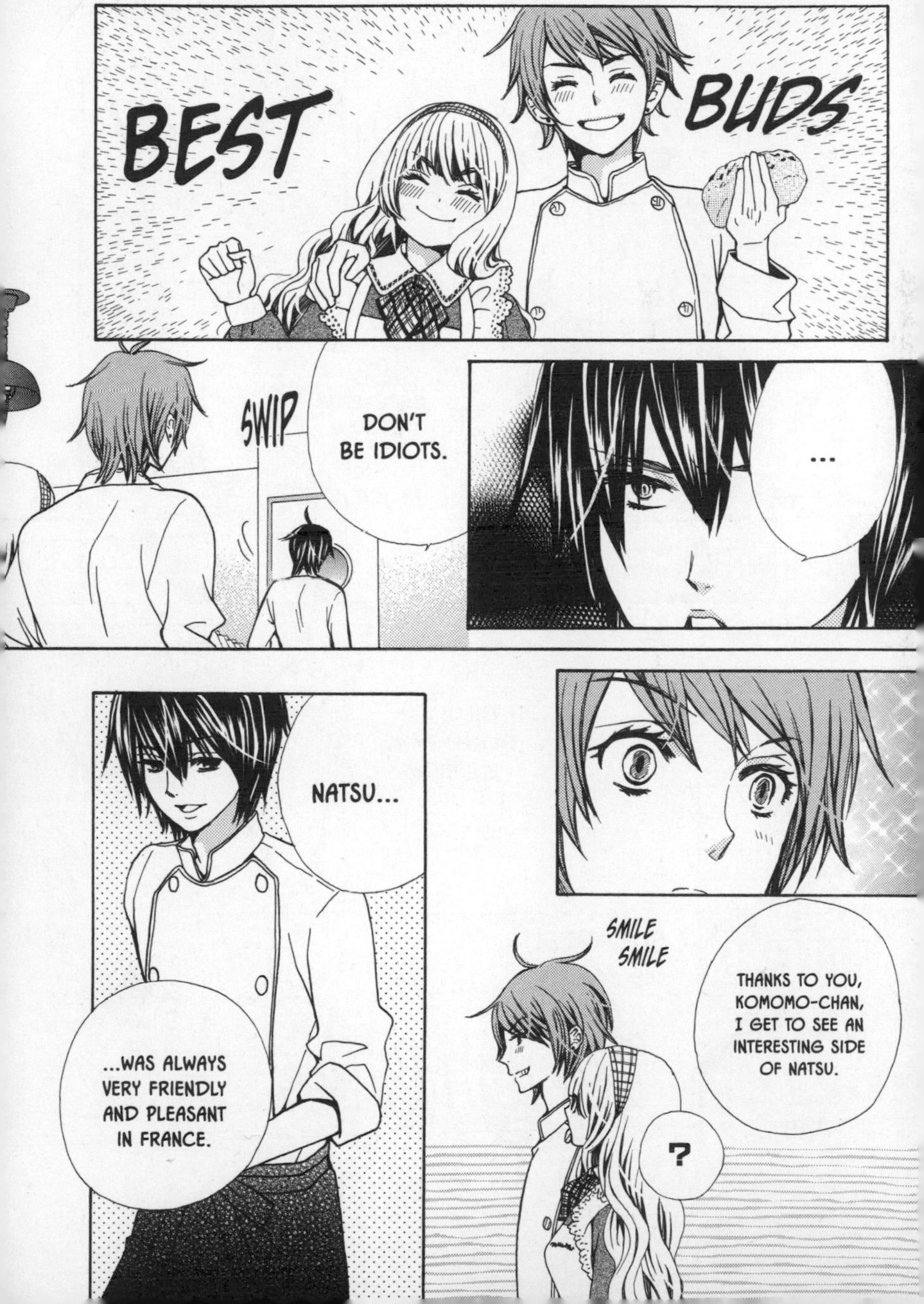

BEST BUDS
...
DON'T BE IDIOTS.
SWIP
THANKS TO YOU, KOMOMO-CHAN, I GET TO SEE AN INTERESTING SIDE OF NATSU.
SMILE SMILE
?
NATSU...
...WAS ALWAYS VERY FRIENDLY AND PLEASANT IN FRANCE.

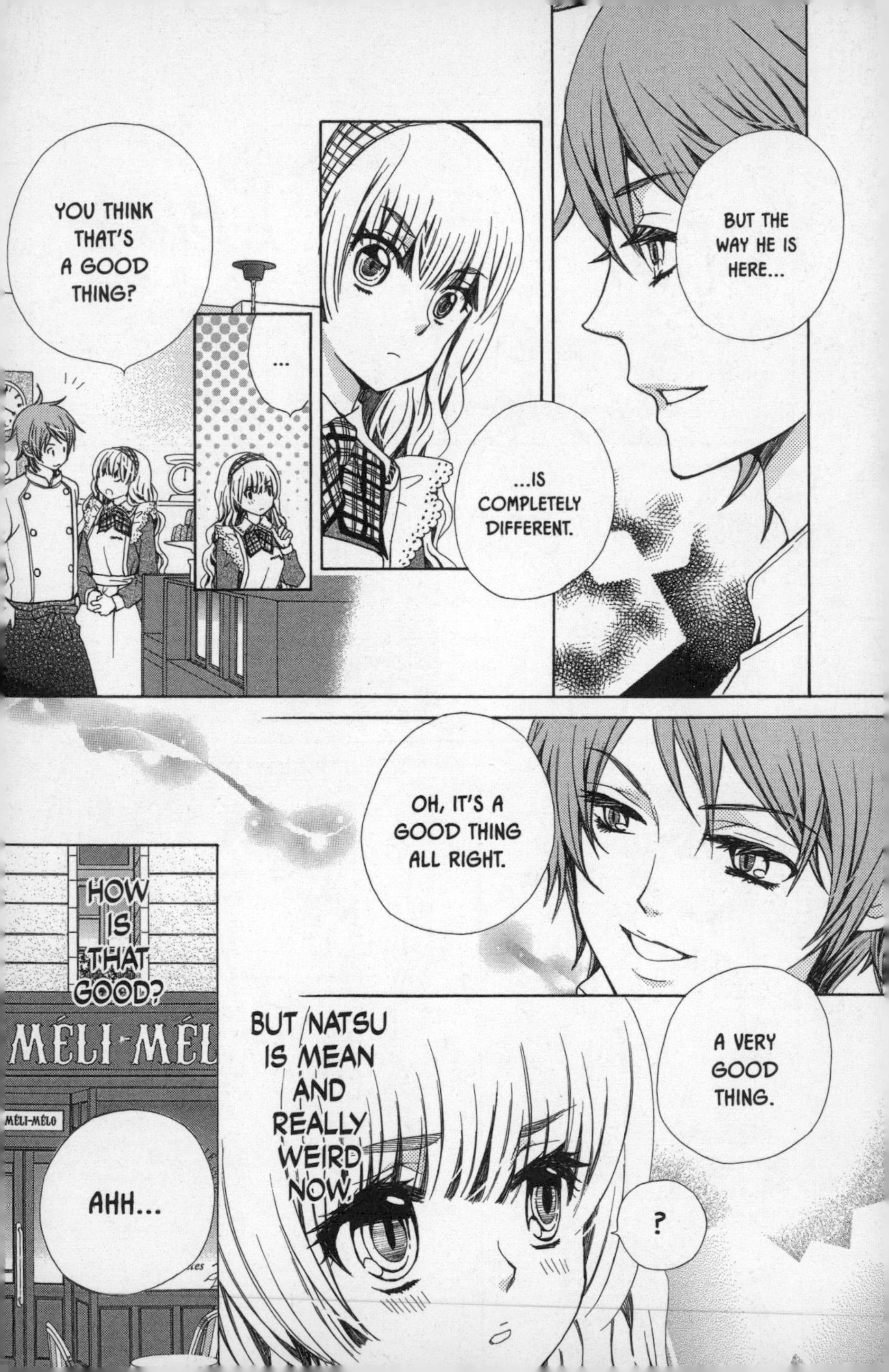
BUT THE WAY HE IS HERE...
...IS COMPLETELY DIFFERENT.
...
YOU THINK THAT'S A GOOD THING?
OH, IT'S A GOOD THING ALL RIGHT.
A VERY GOOD THING.
?
BUT NATSU IS MEAN AND REALLY WEIRD NOW.
HOW IS THAT GOOD?
MÉLI-MÉL
MÉLI-MÉLO
AHH...

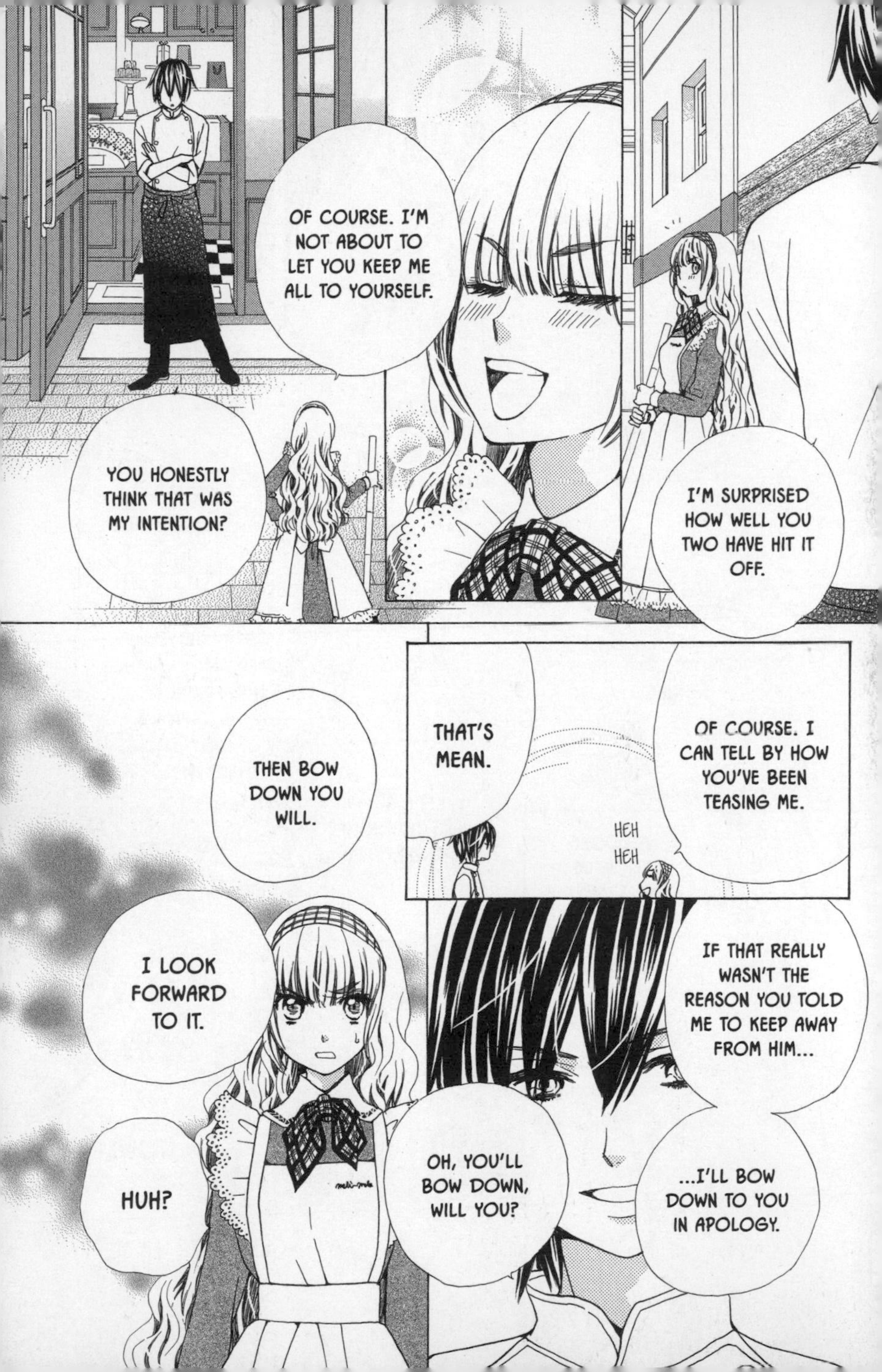
I'M SURPRISED HOW WELL YOU TWO HAVE HIT IT OFF.
OF COURSE. I'M NOT ABOUT TO LET YOU KEEP ME ALL TO YOURSELF.
YOU HONESTLY THINK THAT WAS MY INTENTION?
OF COURSE. I CAN TELL BY HOW YOU'VE BEEN TEASING ME.
HEH HEH
THAT'S MEAN.
IF THAT REALLY WASN'T THE REASON YOU TOLD ME TO KEEP AWAY FROM HIM...
...I'LL BOW DOWN TO YOU IN APOLOGY.
HUH?
OH, YOU'LL BOW DOWN, WILL YOU?
THEN BOW DOWN YOU WILL.
I LOOK FORWARD TO IT.

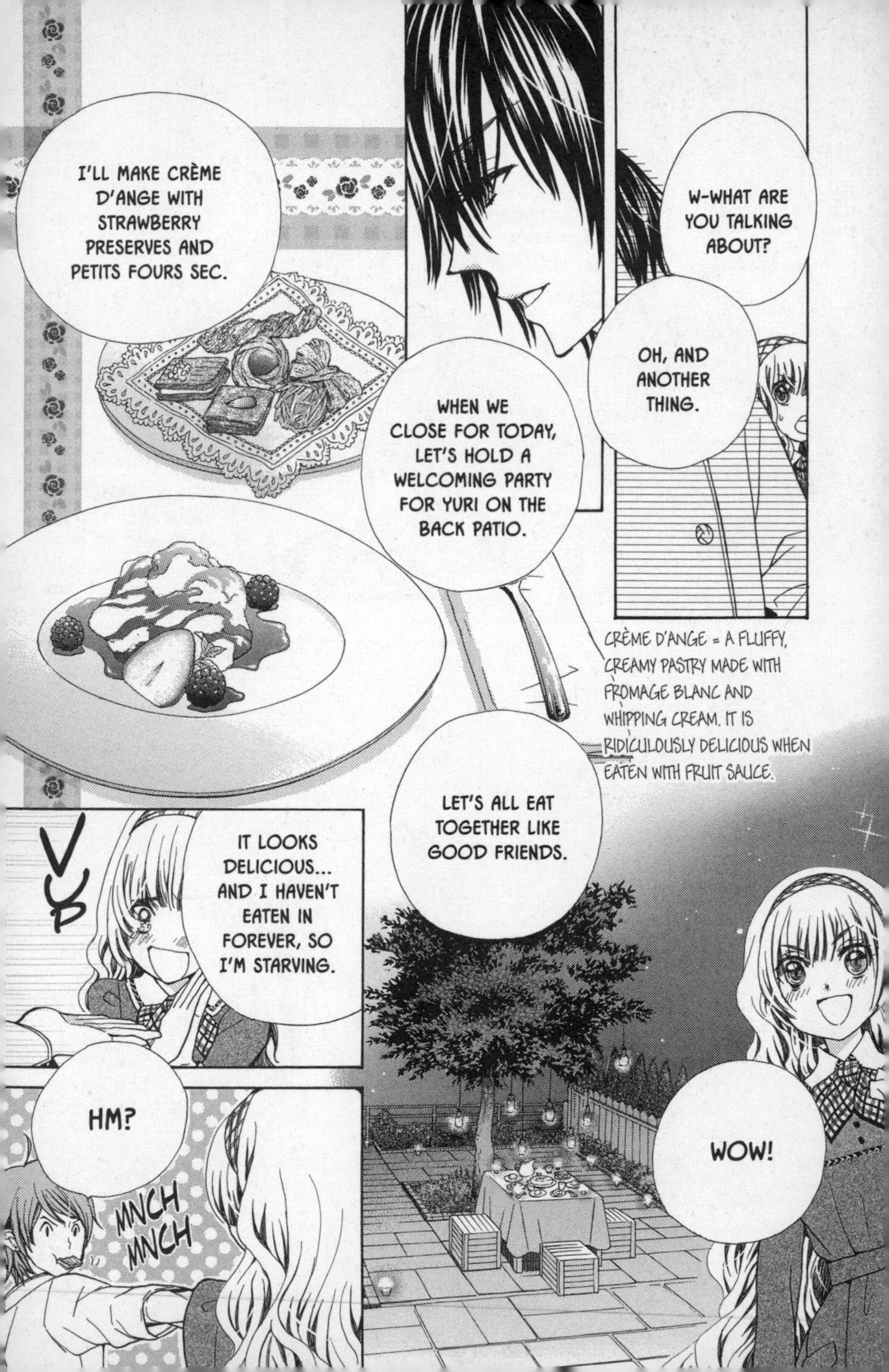
W-WHAT ARE YOU TALKING ABOUT?
OH, AND ANOTHER THING.
WHEN WE CLOSE FOR TODAY, LET'S HOLD A WELCOMING PARTY FOR YURI ON THE BACK PATIO.
I'LL MAKE CRÈME D'ANGE WITH STRAWBERRY PRESERVES AND PETITS FOURS SEC.
CRÈME D'ANGE = A FLUFFY, CREAMY PASTRY MADE WITH FROMAGE BLANC AND WHIPPING CREAM. IT IS RIDICULOUSLY DELICIOUS WHEN EATEN WITH FRUIT SAUCE.
LET'S ALL EAT TOGETHER LIKE GOOD FRIENDS.
WOW!
IT LOOKS DELICIOUS... AND I HAVEN'T EATEN IN FOREVER, SO I'M STARVING.
HM?
MNCH MNCH

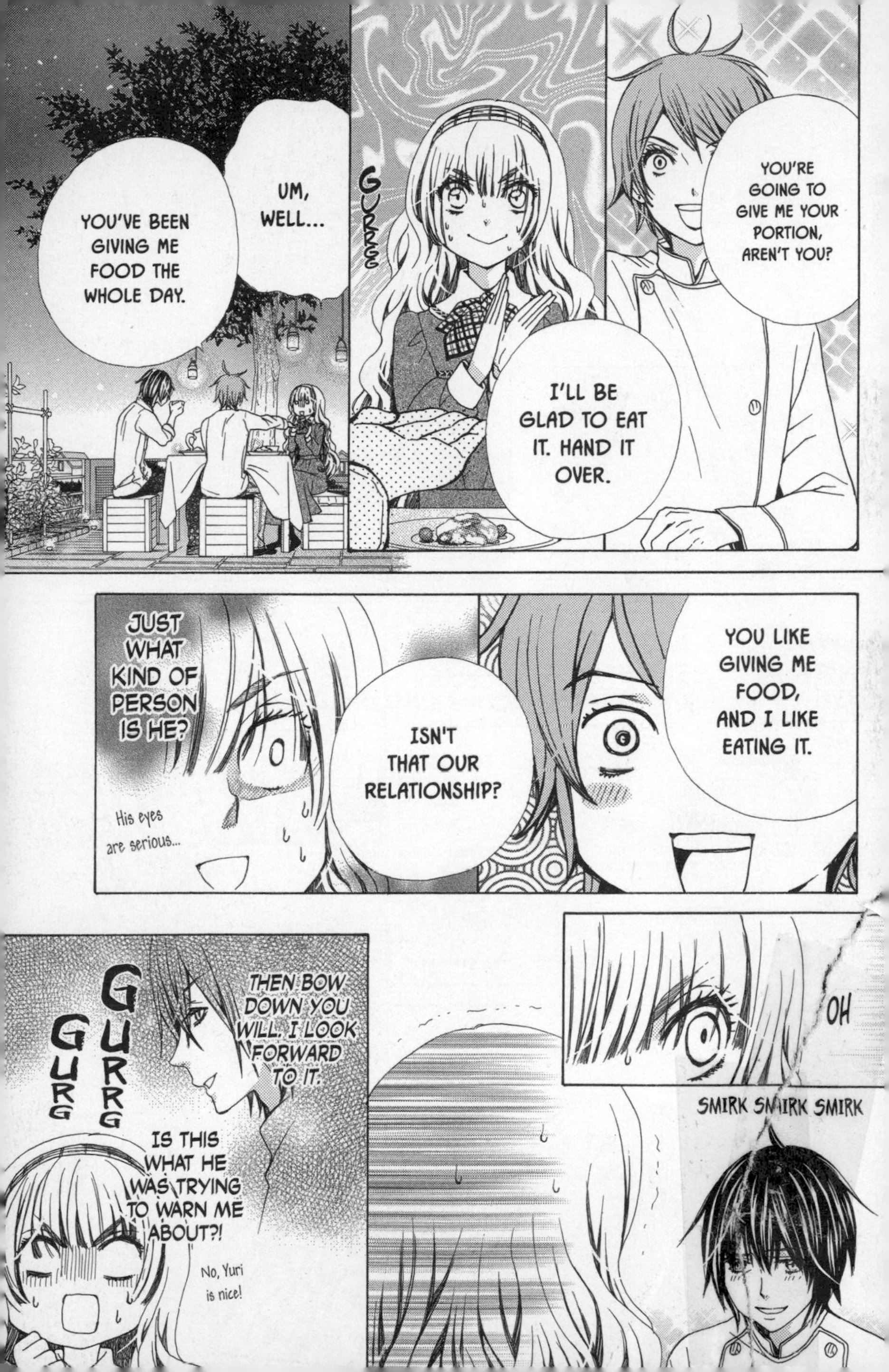
YOU'RE GOING TO GIVE ME YOUR PORTION, AREN'T YOU?
GURRGG
I'LL BE GLAD TO EAT IT. HAND IT OVER.
UM, WELL...
YOU'VE BEEN GIVING ME FOOD THE WHOLE DAY.
YOU LIKE GIVING ME FOOD, AND I LIKE EATING IT.
ISN'T THAT OUR RELATIONSHIP?
JUST WHAT KIND OF PERSON IS HE?
His eyes are serious...
OH
SMIRK SMIRK SMIRK
THEN BOW DOWN YOU WILL. I LOOK FORWARD TO IT.
GURRG
GURG
IS THIS WHAT HE WAS TRYING TO WARN ME ABOUT?!
No, Yuri is nice!

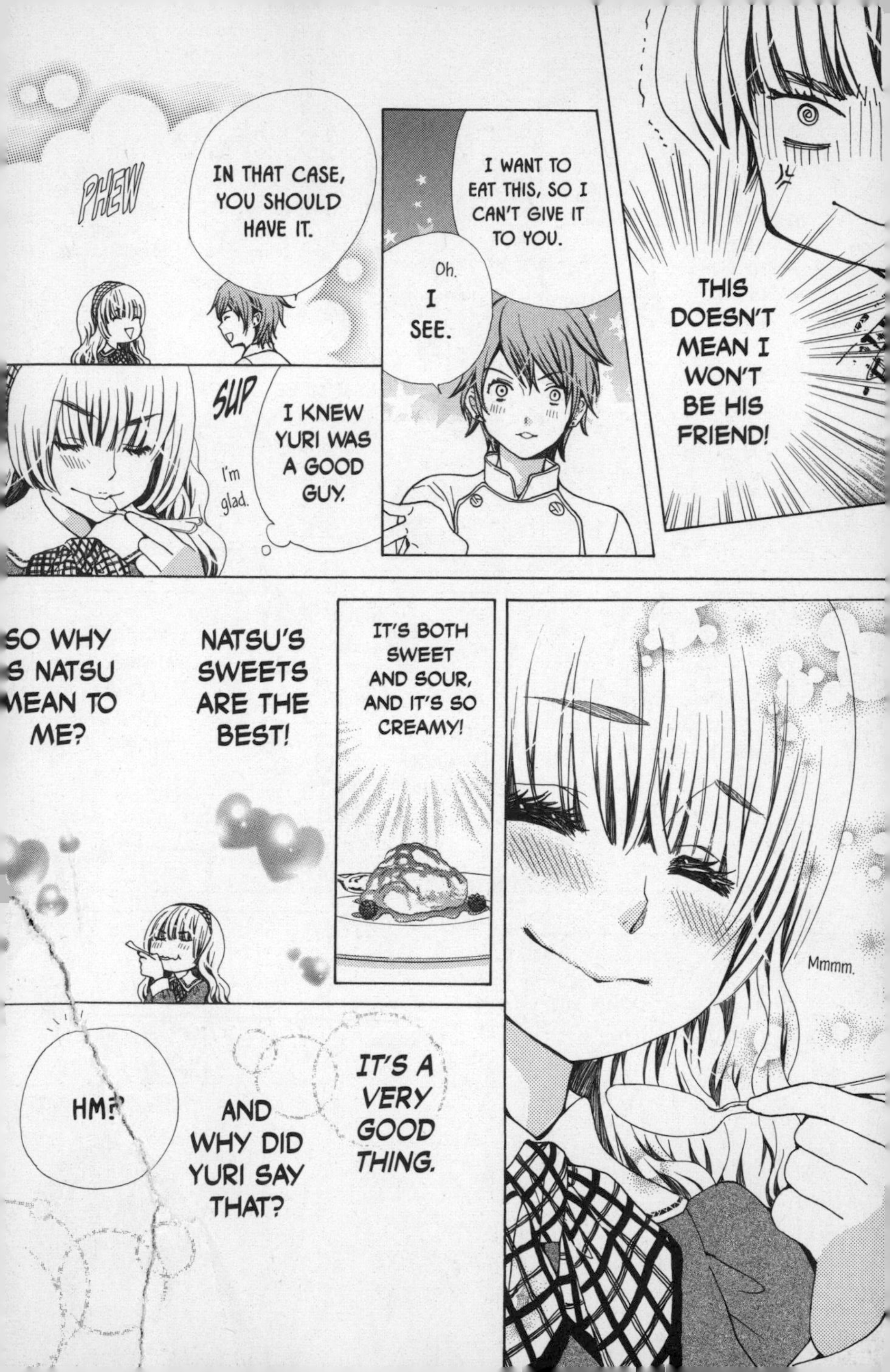
THIS DOESN'T MEAN I WON'T BE HIS FRIEND!
I WANT TO EAT THIS, SO I CAN'T GIVE IT TO YOU.
Oh. I SEE.
PHEW
IN THAT CASE, YOU SHOULD HAVE IT.
SUP
I KNEW YURI WAS A GOOD GUY.
I'm glad.
Mmmm.
IT'S BOTH SWEET AND SOUR, AND IT'S SO CREAMY!
NATSU'S SWEETS ARE THE BEST!
SO WHY S NATSU MEAN TO ME?
IT'S A VERY GOOD THING.
AND WHY DID YURI SAY THAT?
HM?

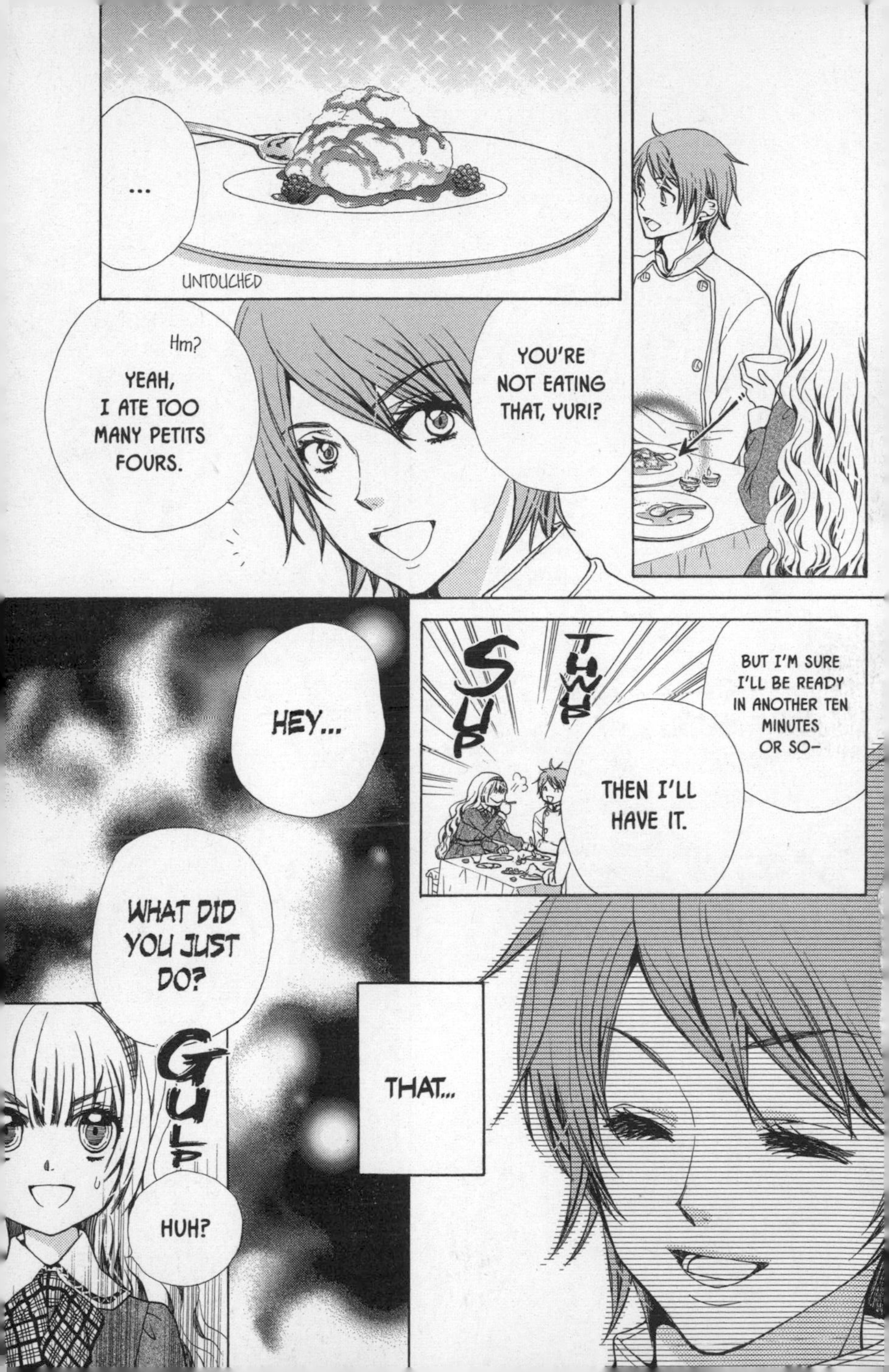
YOU'RE NOT EATING THAT, YURI?
Hm?
YEAH, I ATE TOO MANY PETITS FOURS.
...
UNTOUCHED
BUT I'M SURE I'LL BE READY IN ANOTHER TEN MINUTES OR SO–
THEN I'LL HAVE IT.
THWUP
SLUP
THAT...
HEY...
WHAT DID YOU JUST DO?
GULP
HUH?

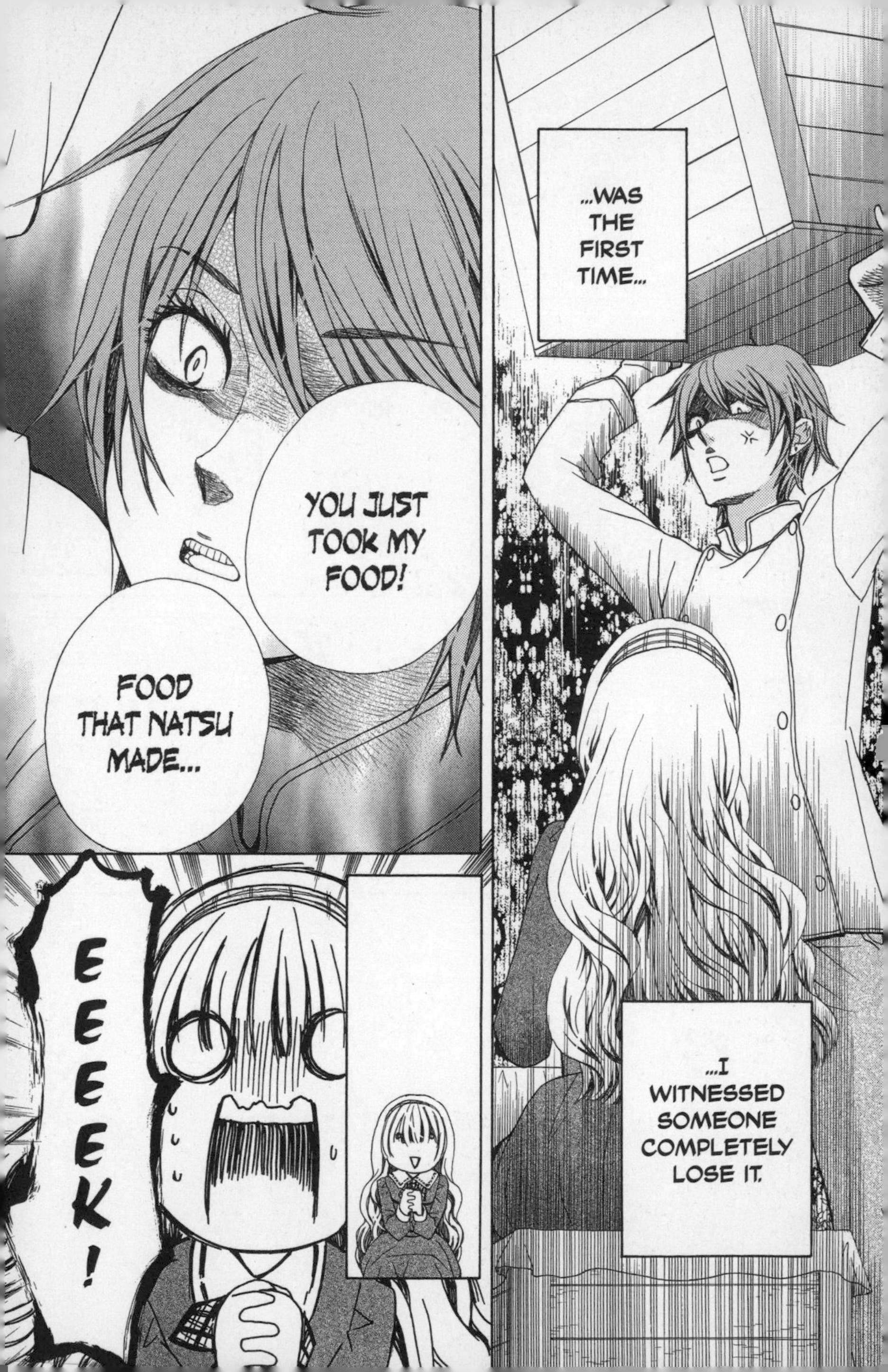
...WAS THE FIRST TIME...
...I WITNESSED SOMEONE COMPLETELY LOSE IT.
YOU JUST TOOK MY FOOD!
FOOD THAT NATSU MADE...
EEEEEK!

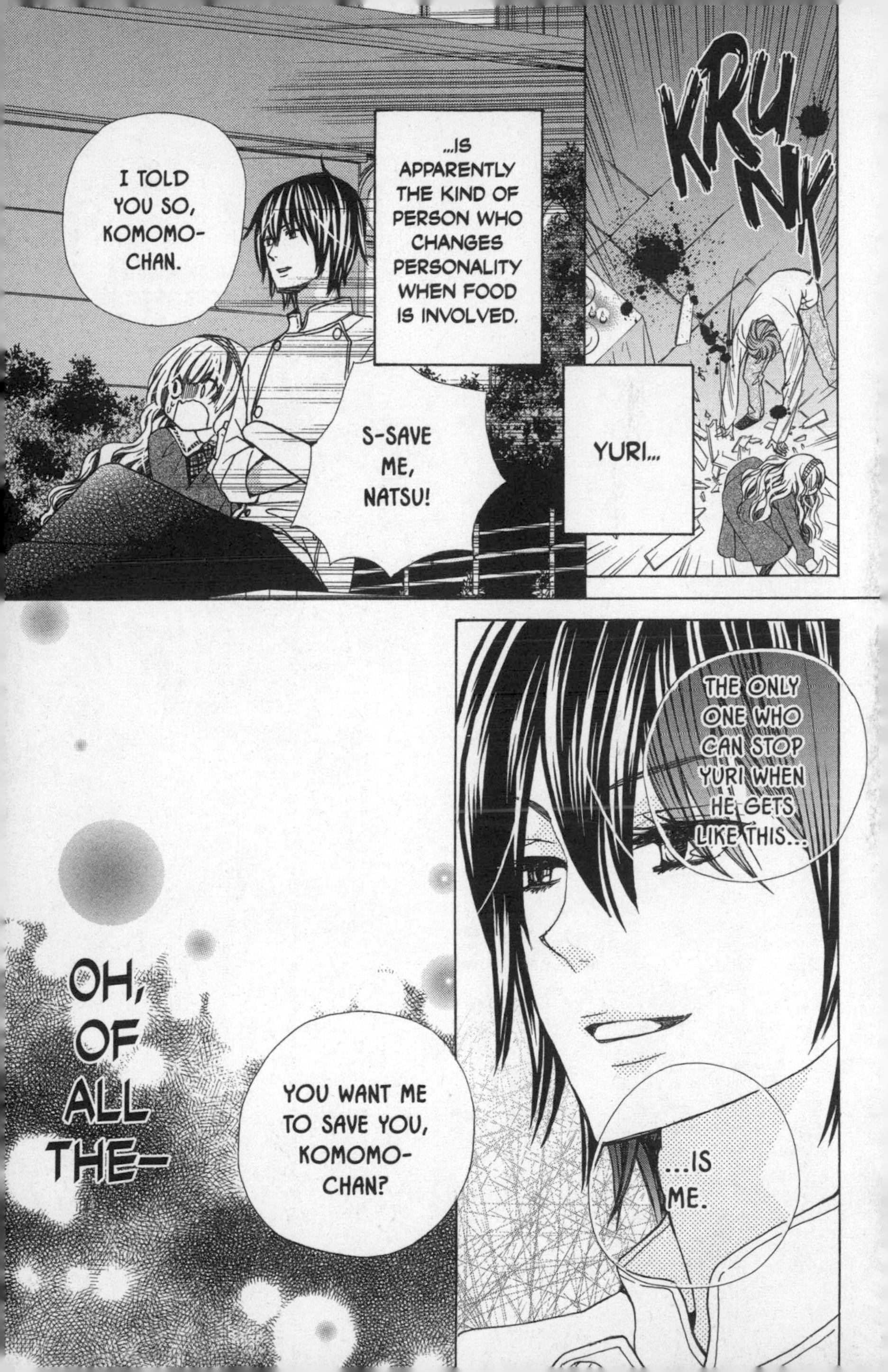
KRUNK
YURI...
...IS APPARENTLY THE KIND OF PERSON WHO CHANGES PERSONALITY WHEN FOOD IS INVOLVED.
S-SAVE ME, NATSU!
I TOLD YOU SO, KOMOMO-CHAN.
THE ONLY ONE WHO CAN STOP YURI WHEN HE GETS LIKE THIS...
...IS ME.
YOU WANT ME TO SAVE YOU, KOMOMO-CHAN?
OH, OF ALL THE-

WHAT WAS THAT ABOUT ME TRYING TO KEEP YOU ALL TO MYSELF SO I COULD TEASE YOU?
I REALLY DID TRY TO WARN YOU OUT OF CONSIDERATION.
ACK!
ISN'T THERE SOMETHING YOU'RE SUPPOSED TO DO FOR ME NOW?
I'M GOING TO UPSET...
...THAT UNCLE AGAIN.

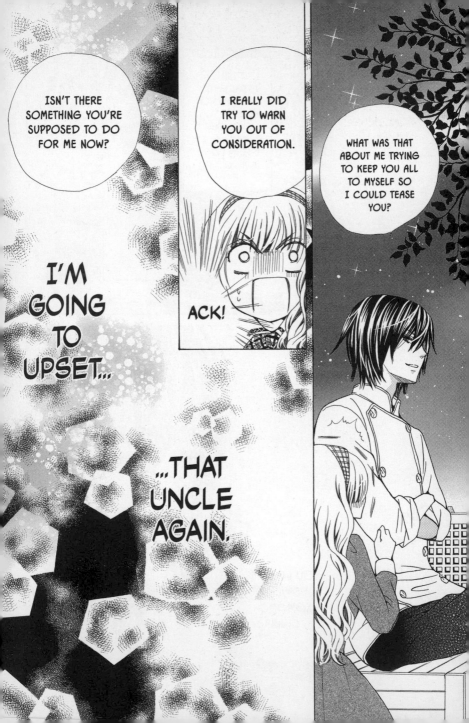

...I'M KNEELING BEFORE SOMEONE.

I'M SORRY I DOUBTED YOU.

FOR THE FIRST TIME IN MY LIFE...

BUT THIS IS MY SHOP.

IN THE PAST, I'VE ALWAYS STOPPED YOU AS GENTLY AS I COULD.

HUFF HUFF

NEW WEAPON ↓

SORRY, YURI.

VOOSH
SLAM
I'LL HAVE TO BE A LITTLE ROUGH WITH YOU.

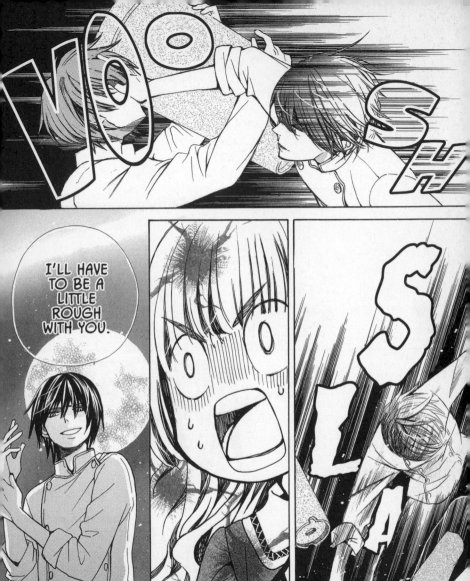

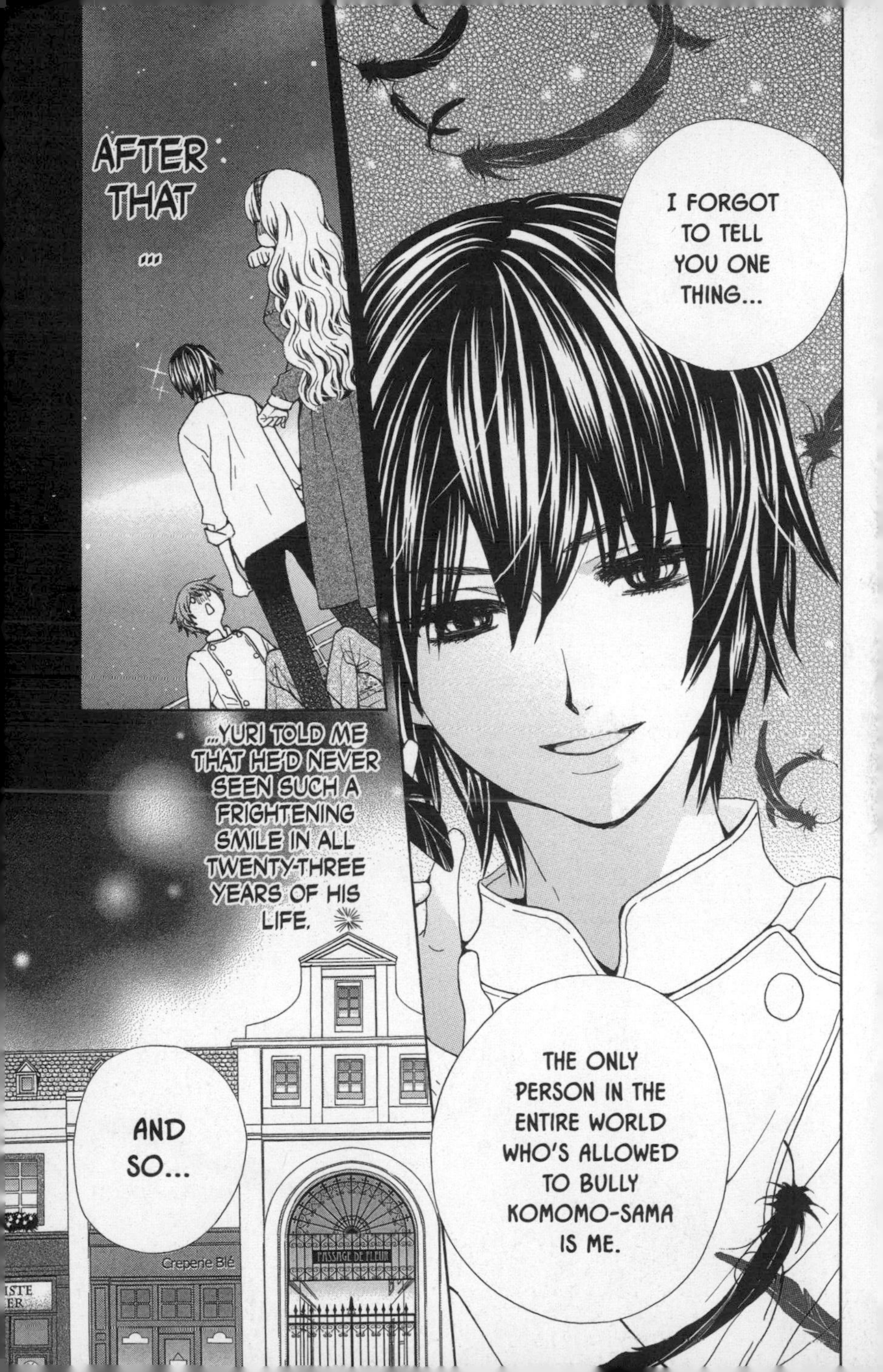
I FORGOT TO TELL YOU ONE THING...
THE ONLY PERSON IN THE ENTIRE WORLD WHO'S ALLOWED TO BULLY KOMOMO-SAMA IS ME.
AFTER THAT ...
...YURI TOLD ME THAT HE'D NEVER SEEN SUCH A FRIGHTENING SMILE IN ALL TWENTY-THREE YEARS OF HIS LIFE.
AND SO...
Creperie Blé
PASSAGE DE FLEUR

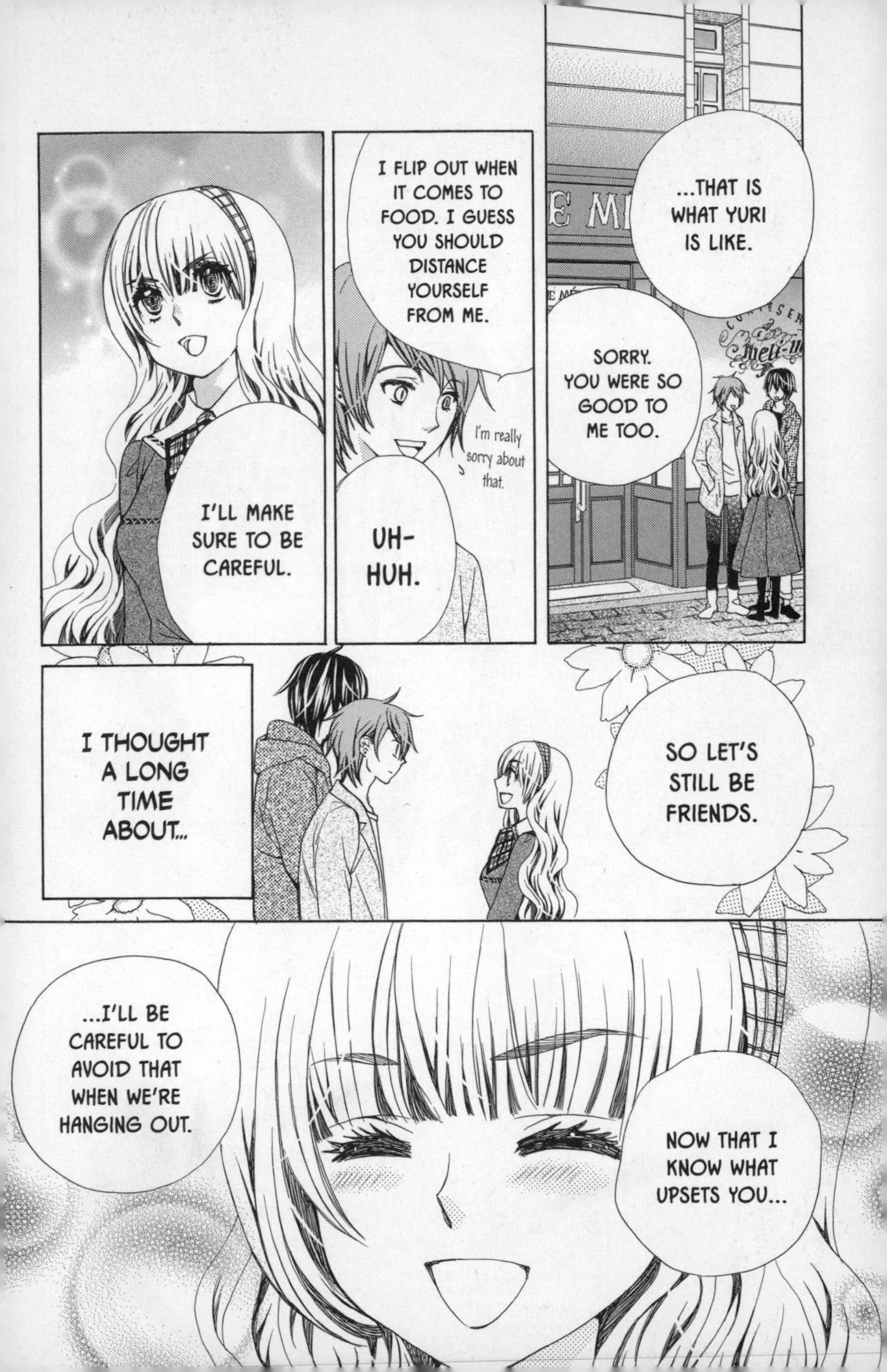
...THAT IS WHAT YURI IS LIKE.
SORRY. YOU WERE SO GOOD TO ME TOO.
I FLIP OUT WHEN IT COMES TO FOOD. I GUESS YOU SHOULD DISTANCE YOURSELF FROM ME.
I'm really sorry about that.
UH-HUH.
I'LL MAKE SURE TO BE CAREFUL.
SO LET'S STILL BE FRIENDS.
I THOUGHT A LONG TIME ABOUT...
NOW THAT I KNOW WHAT UPSETS YOU...
...I'LL BE CAREFUL TO AVOID THAT WHEN WE'RE HANGING OUT.

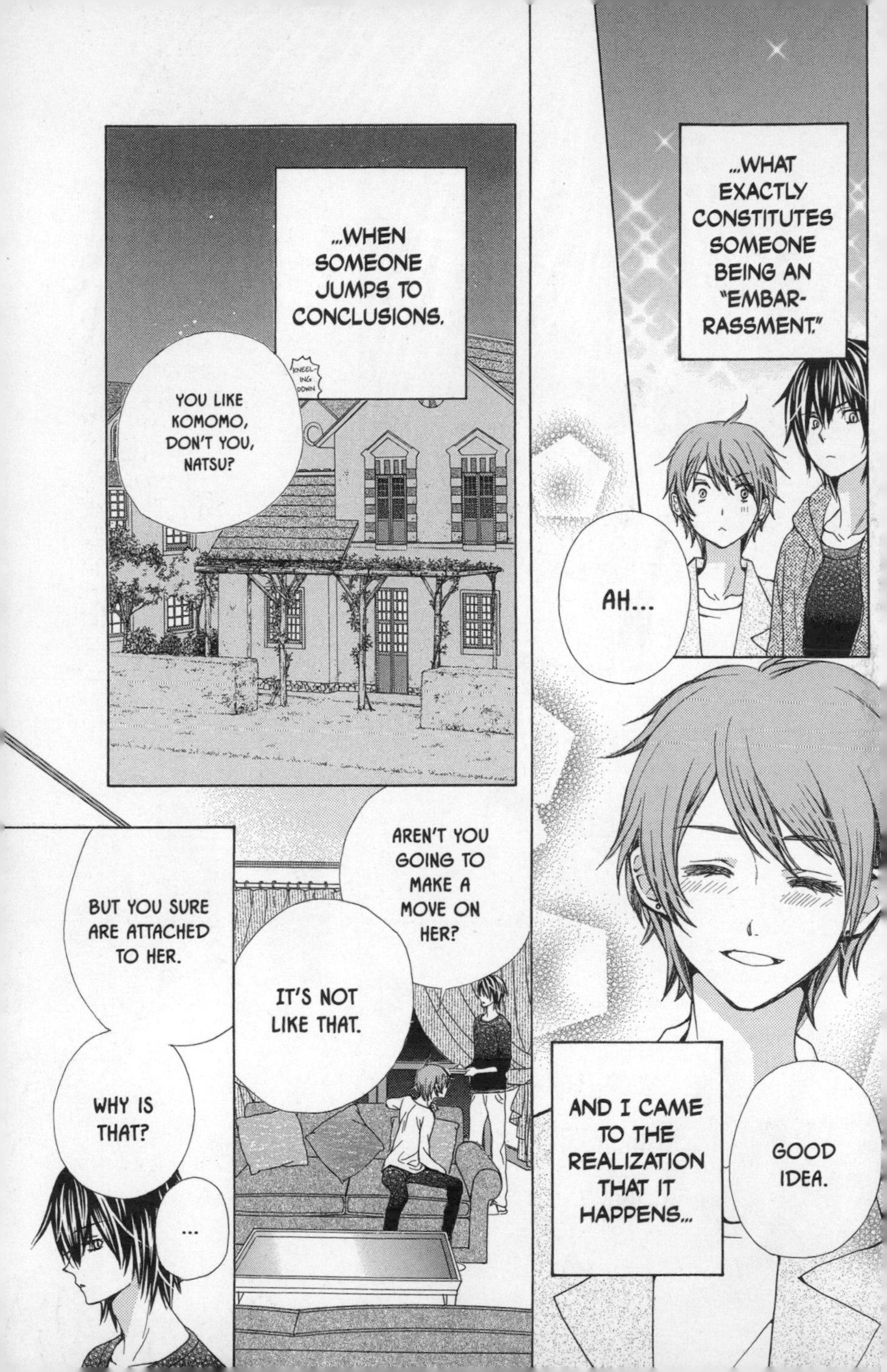
...WHAT EXACTLY CONSTITUTES SOMEONE BEING AN "EMBARRASSMENT."
AH...
GOOD IDEA.
AND I CAME TO THE REALIZATION THAT IT HAPPENS...
...WHEN SOMEONE JUMPS TO CONCLUSIONS.
KNEELING DOWN
YOU LIKE KOMOMO, DON'T YOU, NATSU?
AREN'T YOU GOING TO MAKE A MOVE ON HER?
IT'S NOT LIKE THAT.
BUT YOU SURE ARE ATTACHED TO HER.
WHY IS THAT?
...

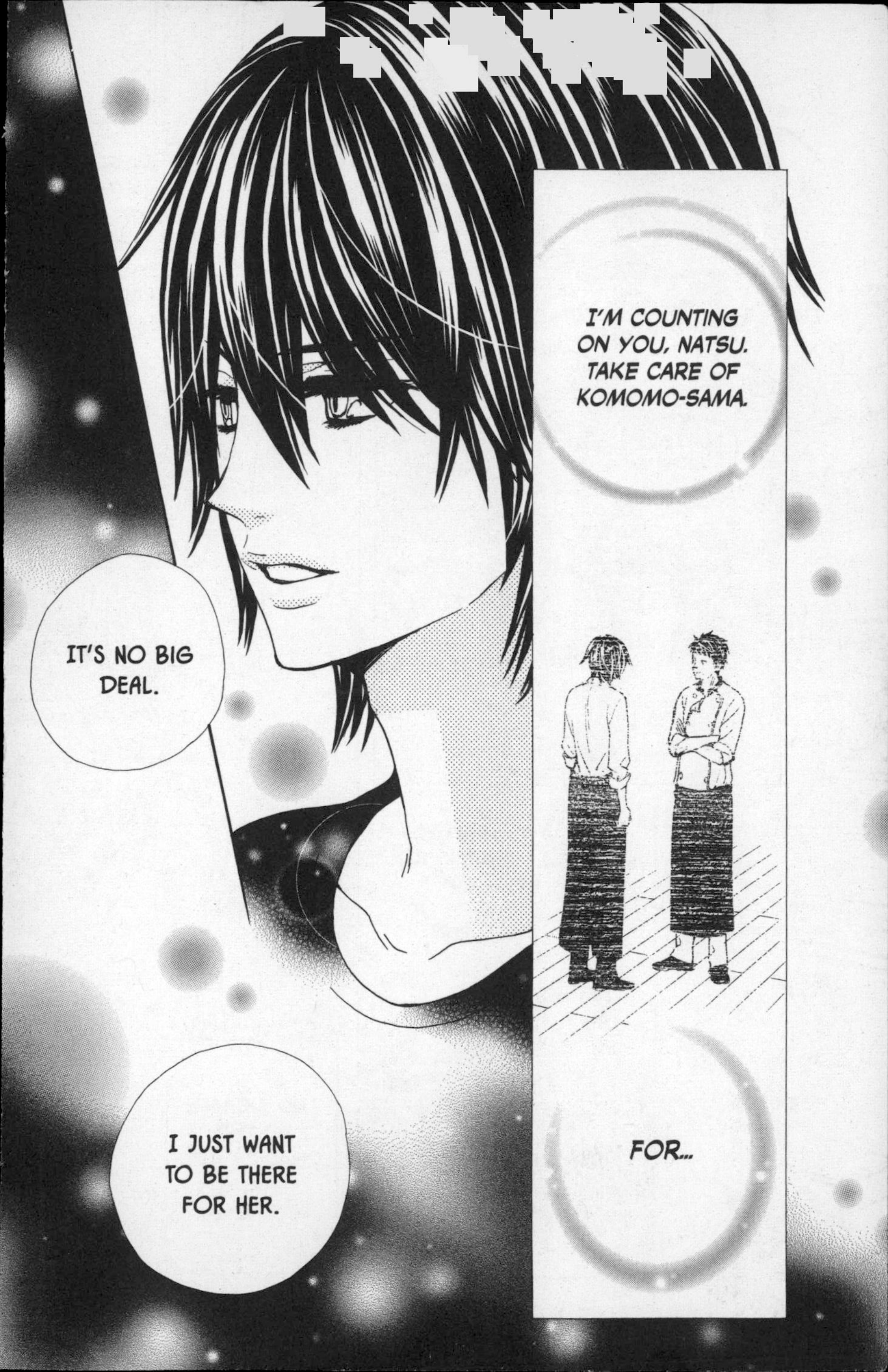
I'M COUNTING ON YOU, NATSU. TAKE CARE OF KOMOMO-SAMA.
FOR...
IT'S NO BIG DEAL.
I JUST WANT TO BE THERE FOR HER.

CHAPTER 4

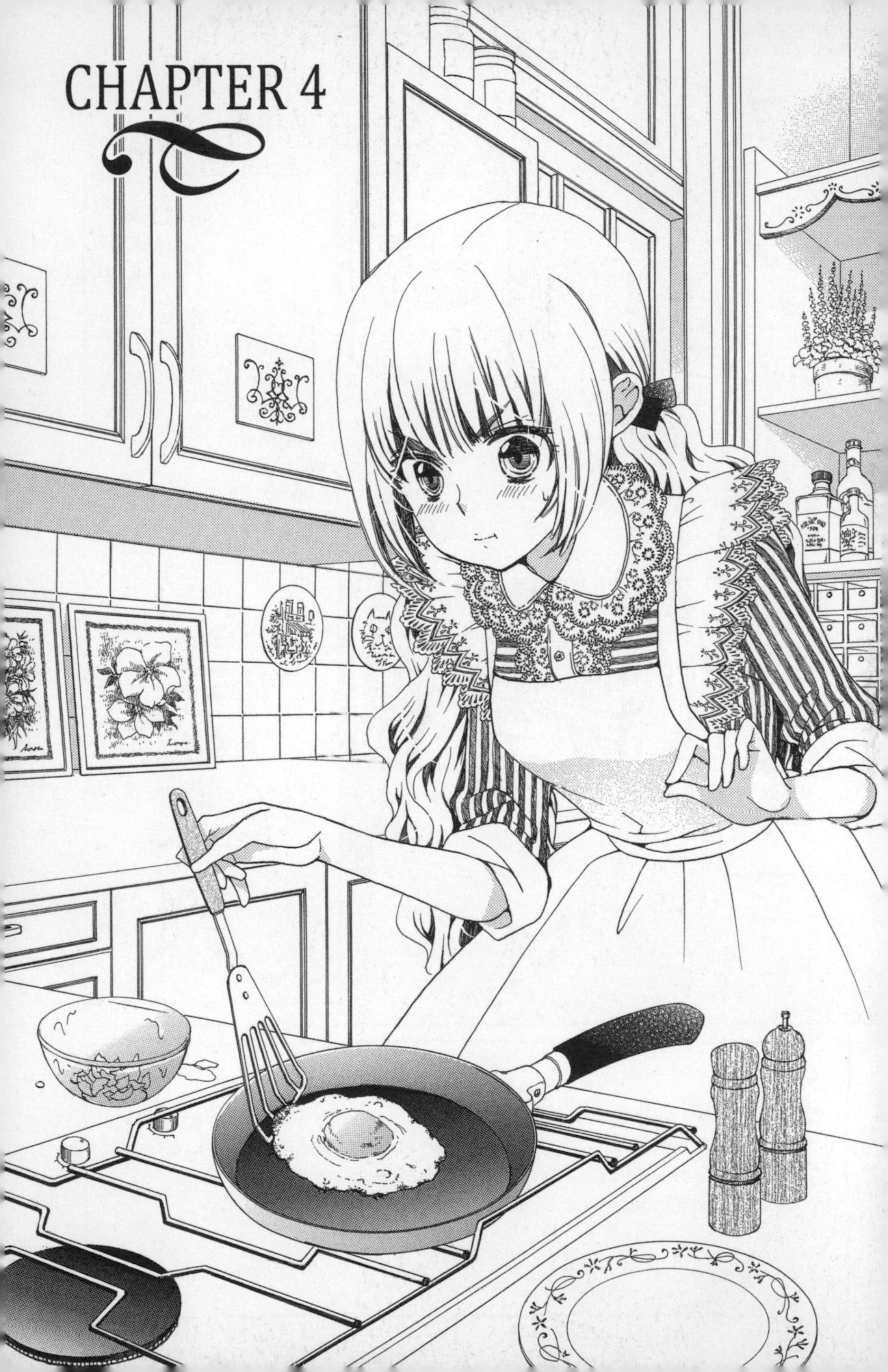

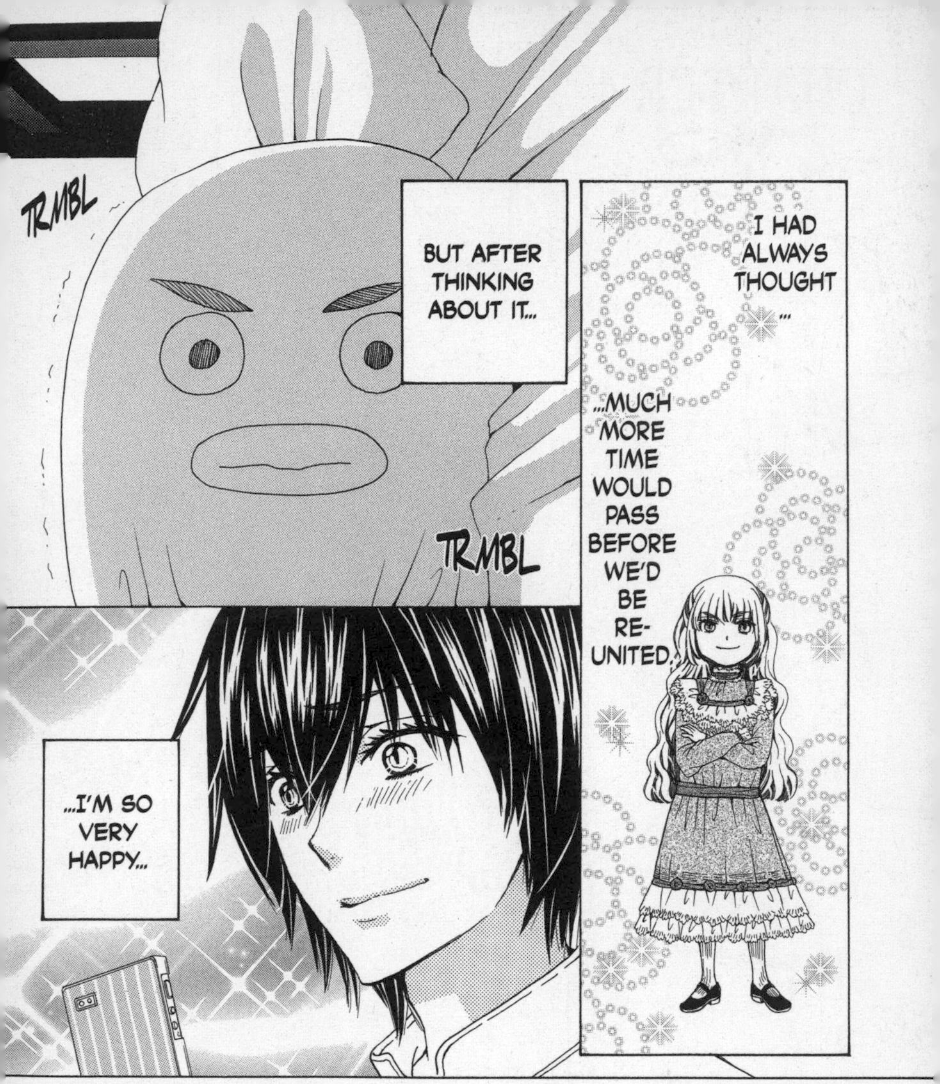
I HAD ALWAYS THOUGHT...
...MUCH MORE TIME WOULD PASS BEFORE WE'D BE RE-UNITED.
BUT AFTER THINKING ABOUT IT...
TRMBL
TRMBL
...I'M SO VERY HAPPY...

•France•

This story is set in Japan, but I made the atmosphere of the town like France, and the clothes Komomo wears are more European in style. I have her wearing aprons over her dresses and lacy blouses to conjure up a feeling of the early 1900s. But I think I'll have her wear more modern clothes every once in a while too.

2

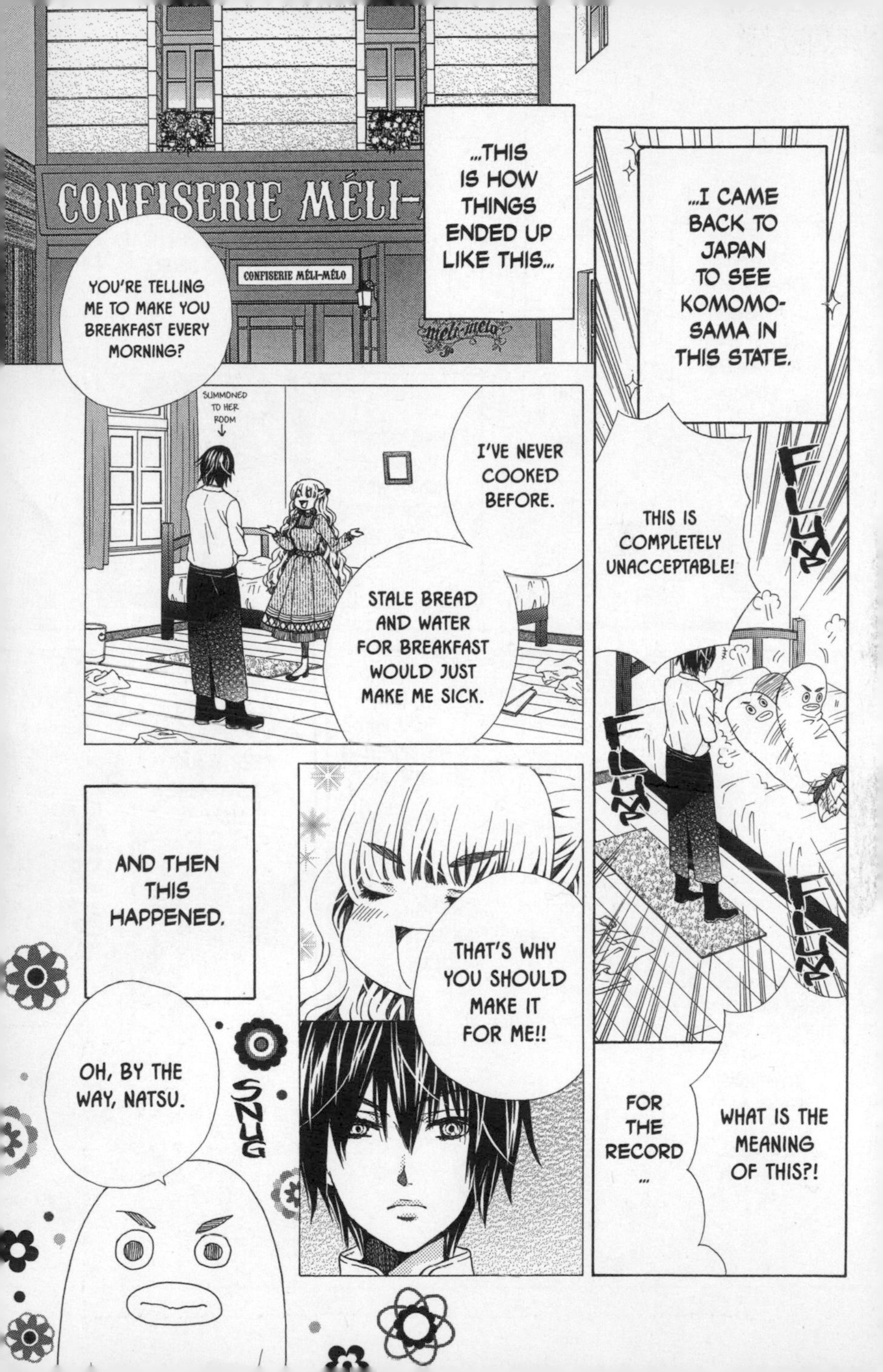
...I CAME BACK TO JAPAN TO SEE KOMOMO-SAMA IN THIS STATE.
THIS IS COMPLETELY UNACCEPTABLE!
FLUMP
FLUMP
FLUMP
WHAT IS THE MEANING OF THIS?!
FOR THE RECORD...
...THIS IS HOW THINGS ENDED UP LIKE THIS...
CONFISERIE MÉLI-
CONFISERIE MÉLI-MÉLO
méli-mélo
YOU'RE TELLING ME TO MAKE YOU BREAKFAST EVERY MORNING?
I'VE NEVER COOKED BEFORE.
STALE BREAD AND WATER FOR BREAKFAST WOULD JUST MAKE ME SICK.
SUMMONED TO HER ROOM
THAT'S WHY YOU SHOULD MAKE IT FOR ME!!
SNUG
AND THEN THIS HAPPENED.
OH, BY THE WAY, NATSU.

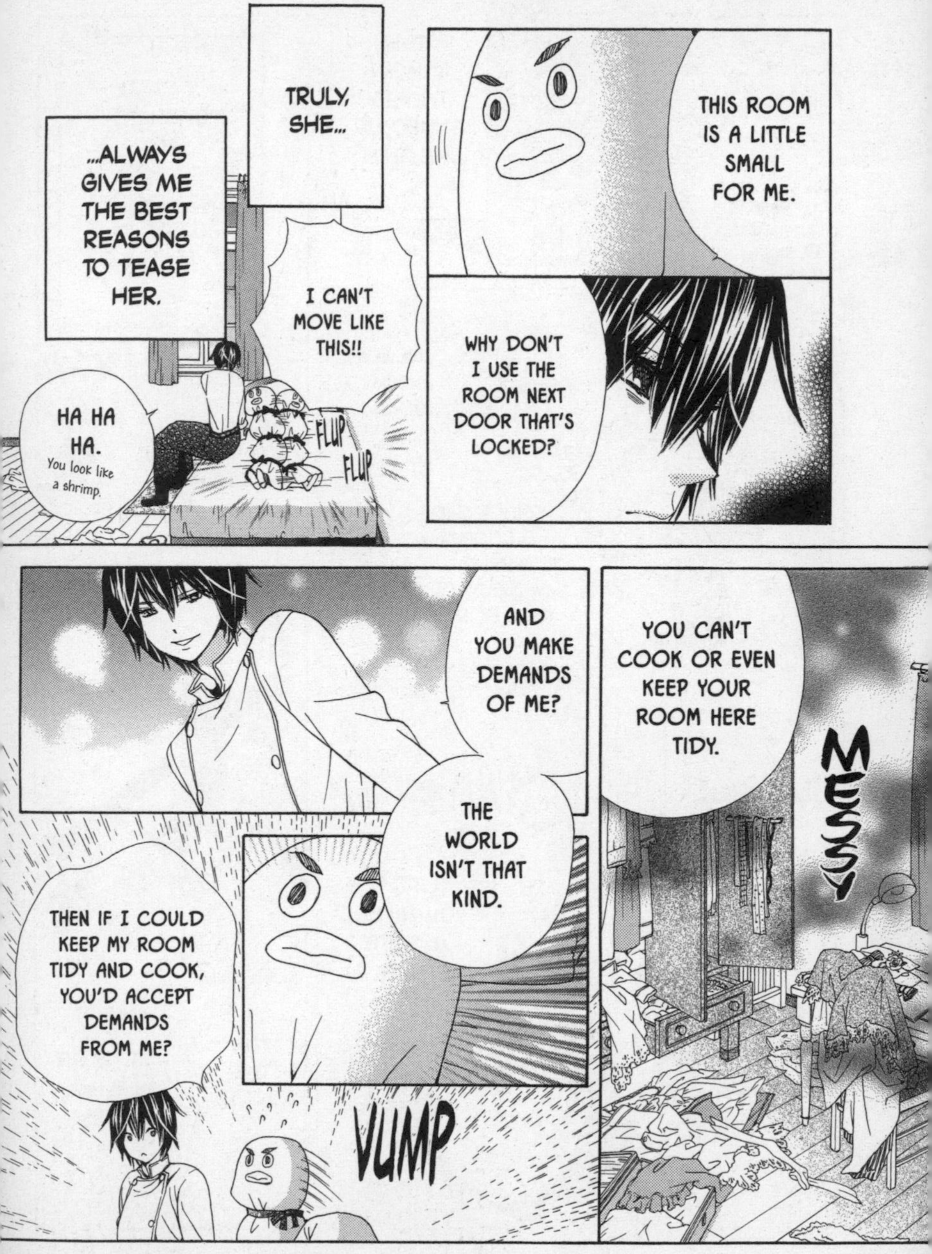
THIS ROOM IS A LITTLE SMALL FOR ME.
WHY DON'T I USE THE ROOM NEXT DOOR THAT'S LOCKED?
TRULY, SHE...
I CAN'T MOVE LIKE THIS!!
FLUP FLUP
...ALWAYS GIVES ME THE BEST REASONS TO TEASE HER.
HA HA HA.
You look like a shrimp.
YOU CAN'T COOK OR EVEN KEEP YOUR ROOM HERE TIDY.
MESSY
AND YOU MAKE DEMANDS OF ME?
THE WORLD ISN'T THAT KIND.
THEN IF I COULD KEEP MY ROOM TIDY AND COOK, YOU'D ACCEPT DEMANDS FROM ME?
VUMP

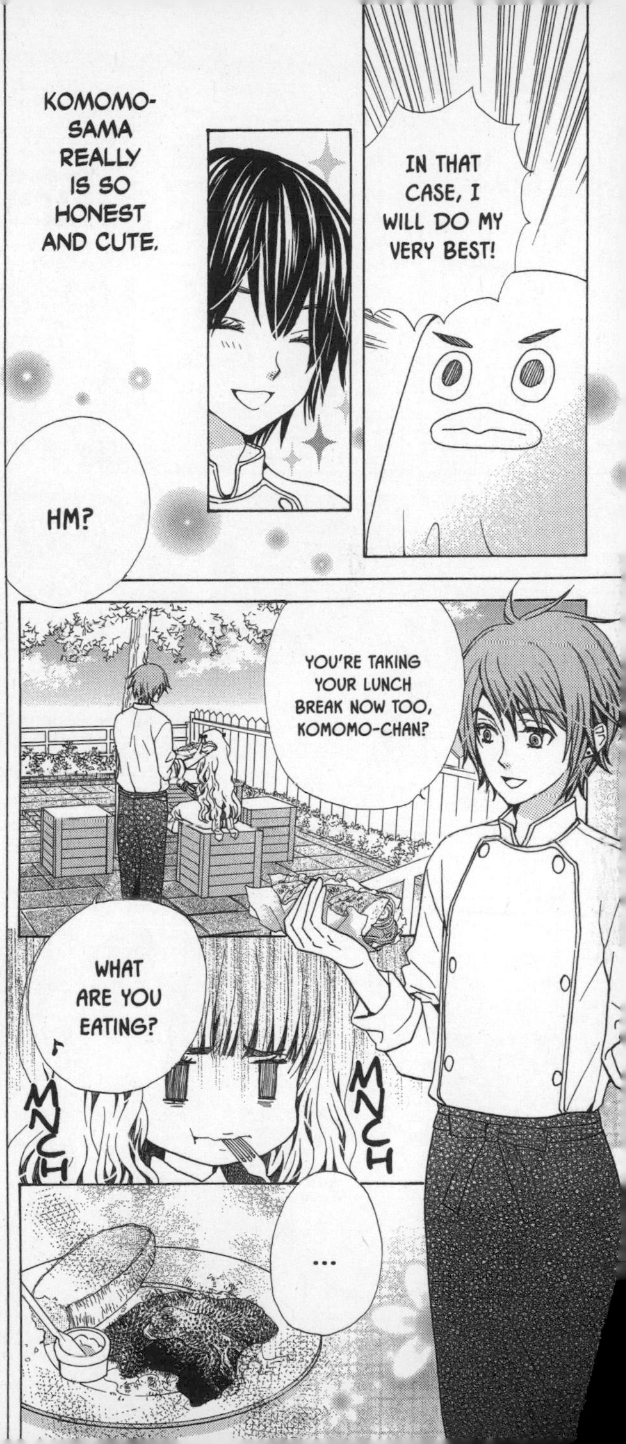
IN THAT CASE, I WILL DO MY VERY BEST!
KOMOMO-SAMA REALLY IS SO HONEST AND CUTE.
HM?
YOU'RE TAKING YOUR LUNCH BREAK NOW TOO, KOMOMO-CHAN?
WHAT ARE YOU EATING?
MNCH
MNCH
...

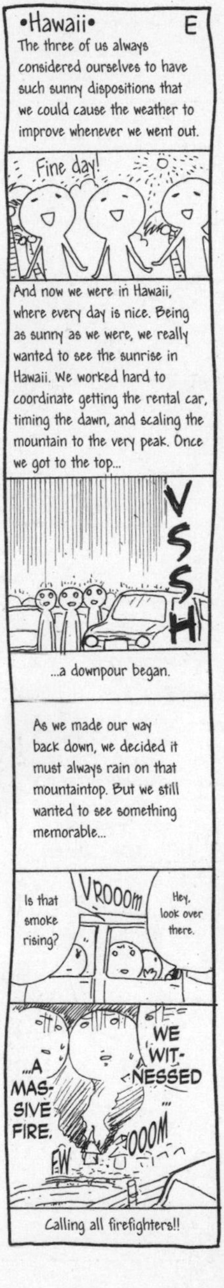
•Hawaii•
E
The three of us always considered ourselves to have such sunny dispositions that we could cause the weather to improve whenever we went out.
Fine day!
And now we were in Hawaii, where every day is nice. Being as sunny as we were, we really wanted to see the sunrise in Hawaii. We worked hard to coordinate getting the rental car, timing the dawn, and scaling the mountain to the very peak. Once we got to the top...
VSSH
...a downpour began.
As we made our way back down, we decided it must always rain on that mountaintop. But we still wanted to see something memorable...
Hey, look over there.
VROOOM
Is that smoke rising?
WE WIT-NESSED...
...A MAS-SIVE FIRE.
FWOOOM
Calling all firefighters!!

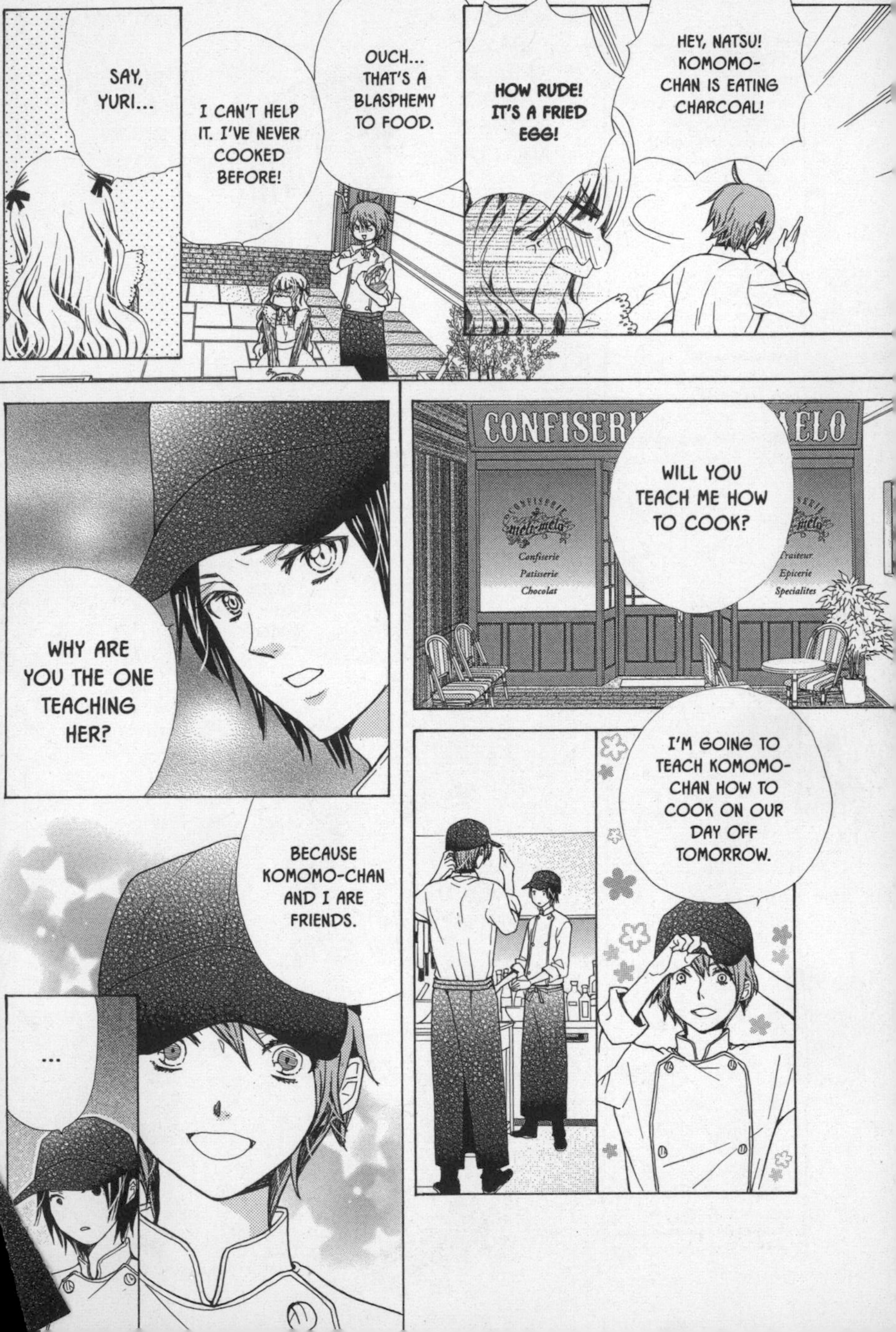
HEY, NATSU! KOMOMO-CHAN IS EATING CHARCOAL!
HOW RUDE! IT'S A FRIED EGG!
OUCH... THAT'S A BLASPHEMY TO FOOD.
I CAN'T HELP IT. I'VE NEVER COOKED BEFORE!
SAY, YURI...
CONFISERI
MÉLO
Confiserie
Patisserie
Chocolat
Traiteur
Epicerie
Specialites
WILL YOU TEACH ME HOW TO COOK?
WHY ARE YOU THE ONE TEACHING HER?
I'M GOING TO TEACH KOMOMO-CHAN HOW TO COOK ON OUR DAY OFF TOMORROW.
BECAUSE KOMOMO-CHAN AND I ARE FRIENDS.
...

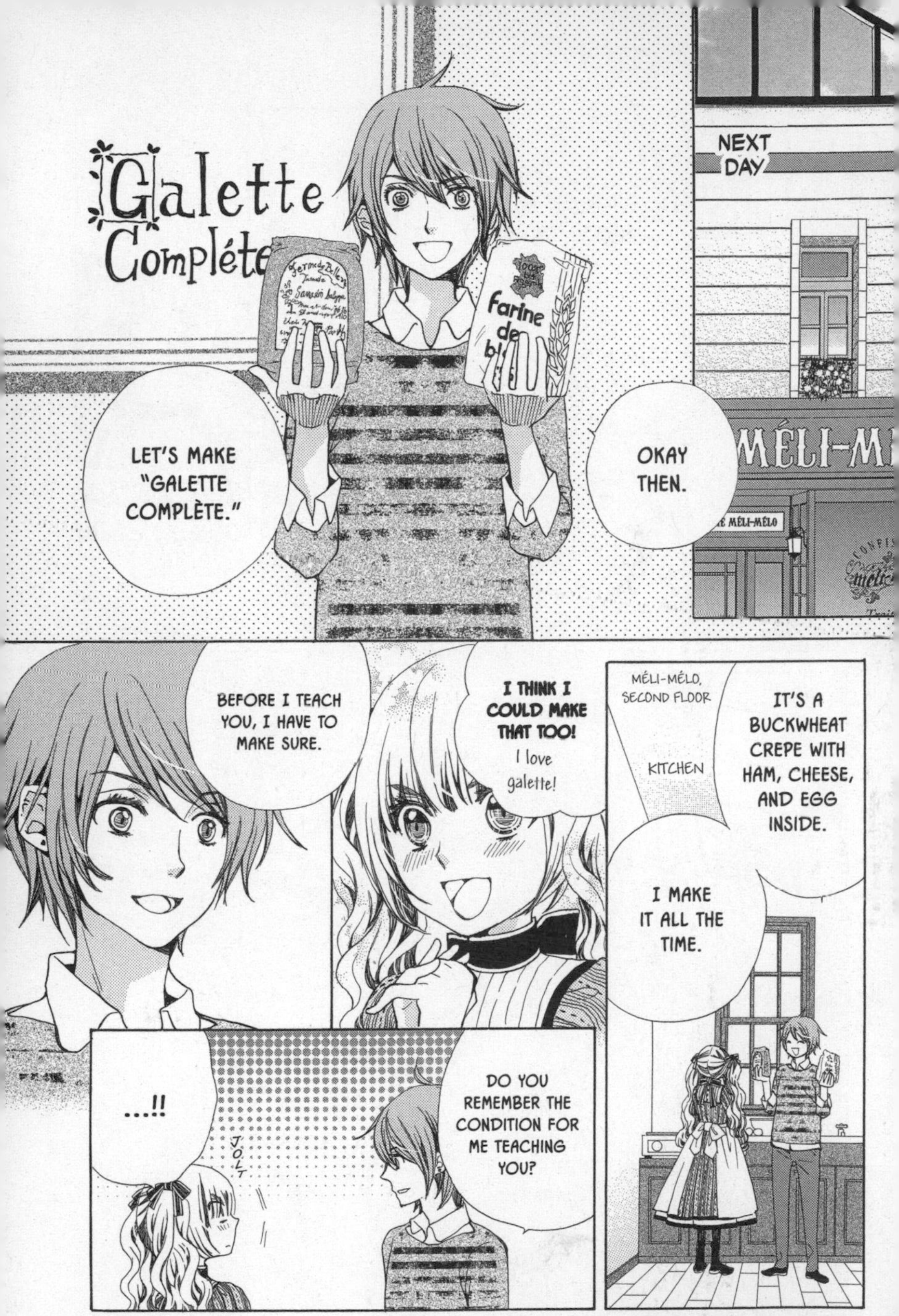
NEXT DAY
MÉLI-M
MÉLI-MÉLO
Galette Compléte
farine de
OKAY THEN.
LET'S MAKE "GALETTE COMPLÈTE."
MÉLI-MÉLO, SECOND FLOOR
KITCHEN
IT'S A BUCKWHEAT CREPE WITH HAM, CHEESE, AND EGG INSIDE.
I MAKE IT ALL THE TIME.
I THINK I COULD MAKE THAT TOO!
I love galette!
BEFORE I TEACH YOU, I HAVE TO MAKE SURE.
DO YOU REMEMBER THE CONDITION FOR ME TEACHING YOU?
JOLT
...!!

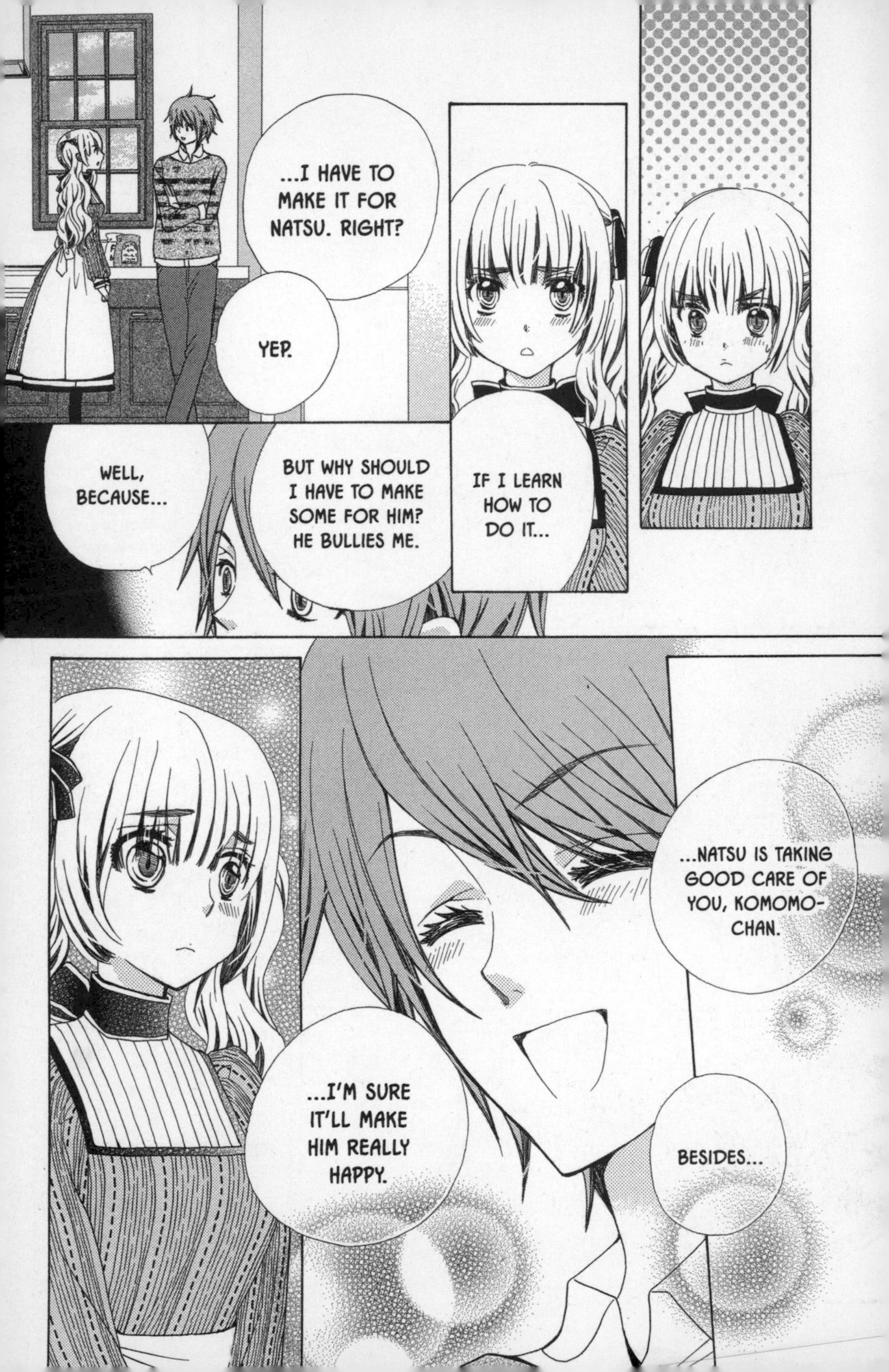
IF I LEARN HOW TO DO IT...
...I HAVE TO MAKE IT FOR NATSU. RIGHT?
YEP.
BUT WHY SHOULD I HAVE TO MAKE SOME FOR HIM? HE BULLIES ME.
WELL, BECAUSE...
...NATSU IS TAKING GOOD CARE OF YOU, KOMOMO-CHAN.
BESIDES...
...I'M SURE IT'LL MAKE HIM REALLY HAPPY.

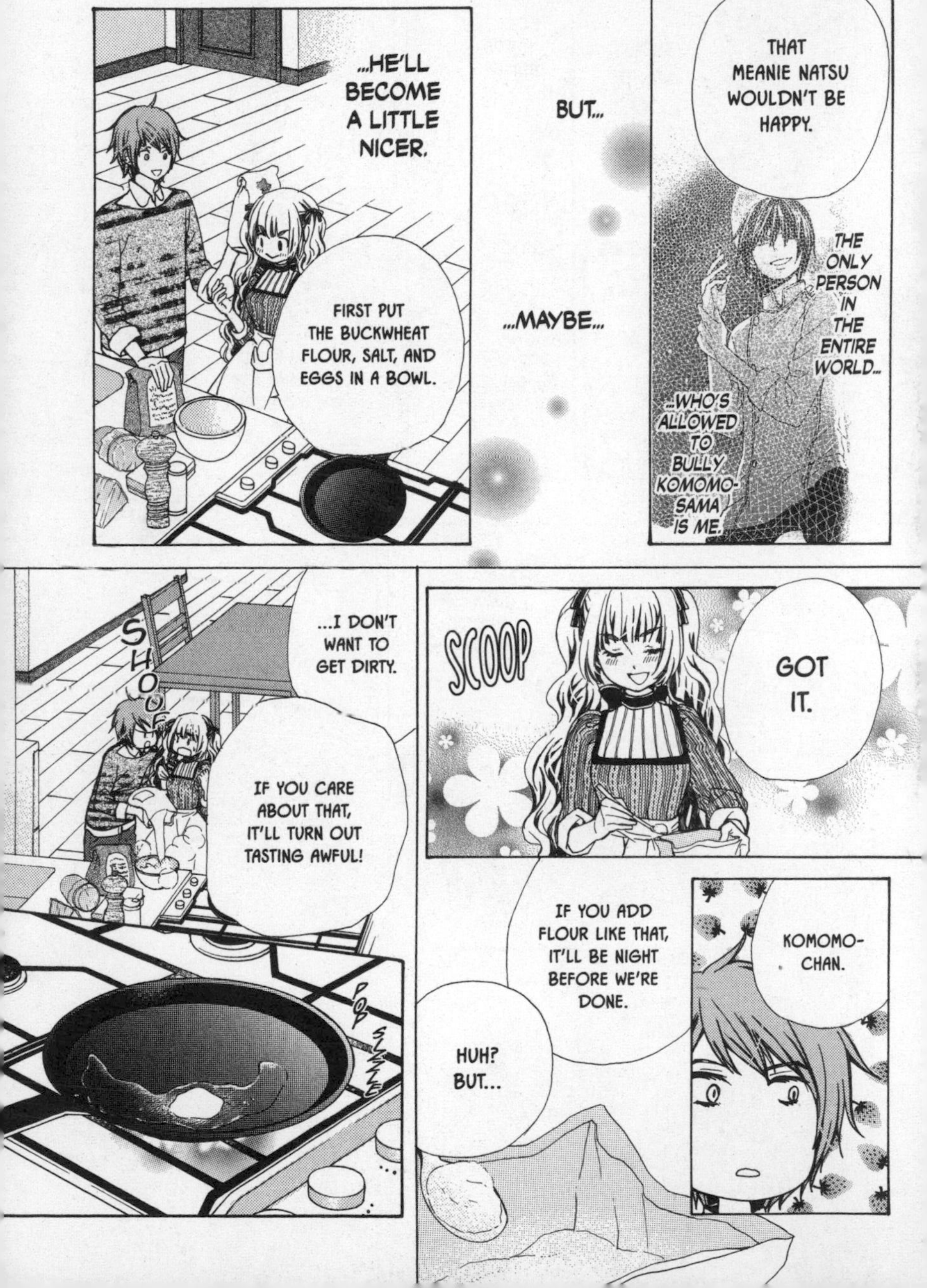
THAT MEANIE NATSU WOULDN'T BE HAPPY.
THE ONLY PERSON IN THE ENTIRE WORLD...
...WHO'S ALLOWED TO BULLY KOMOMO-SAMA IS ME.
BUT...
...MAYBE...
...HE'LL BECOME A LITTLE NICER.
FIRST PUT THE BUCKWHEAT FLOUR, SALT, AND EGGS IN A BOWL.
GOT IT.
SCOOP
KOMOMO-CHAN.
IF YOU ADD FLOUR LIKE THAT, IT'LL BE NIGHT BEFORE WE'RE DONE.
HUH? BUT...
...I DON'T WANT TO GET DIRTY.
SHOOF
IF YOU CARE ABOUT THAT, IT'LL TURN OUT TASTING AWFUL!
POP
SIZZLE
...

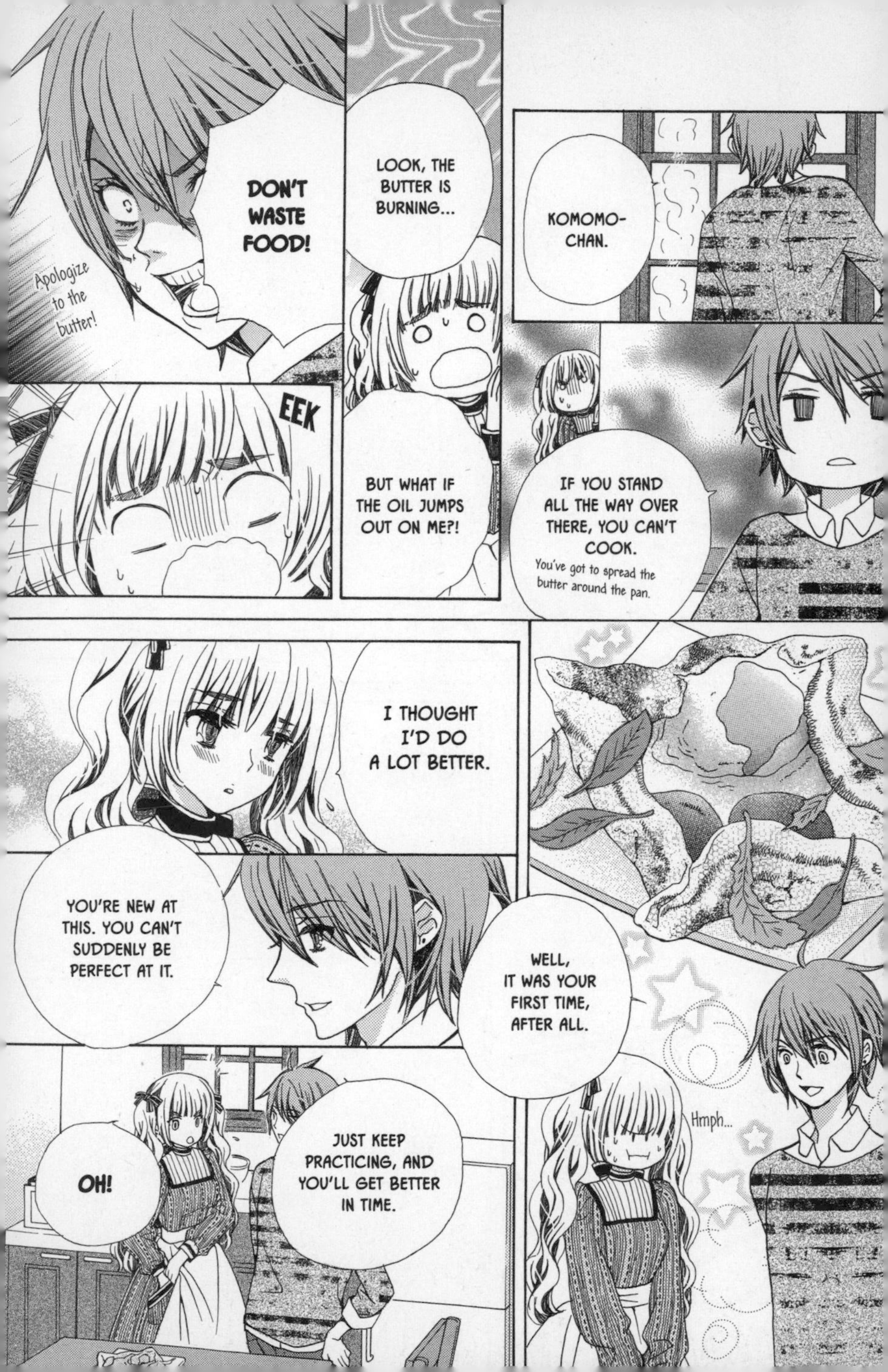
KOMOMO-CHAN.
IF YOU STAND ALL THE WAY OVER THERE, YOU CAN'T COOK.
You've got to spread the butter around the pan.
LOOK, THE BUTTER IS BURNING...
BUT WHAT IF THE OIL JUMPS OUT ON ME?!
DON'T WASTE FOOD!
Apologize to the butter!
EEK
WELL, IT WAS YOUR FIRST TIME, AFTER ALL.
Hmph...
I THOUGHT I'D DO A LOT BETTER.
YOU'RE NEW AT THIS. YOU CAN'T SUDDENLY BE PERFECT AT IT.
JUST KEEP PRACTICING, AND YOU'LL GET BETTER IN TIME.
OH!

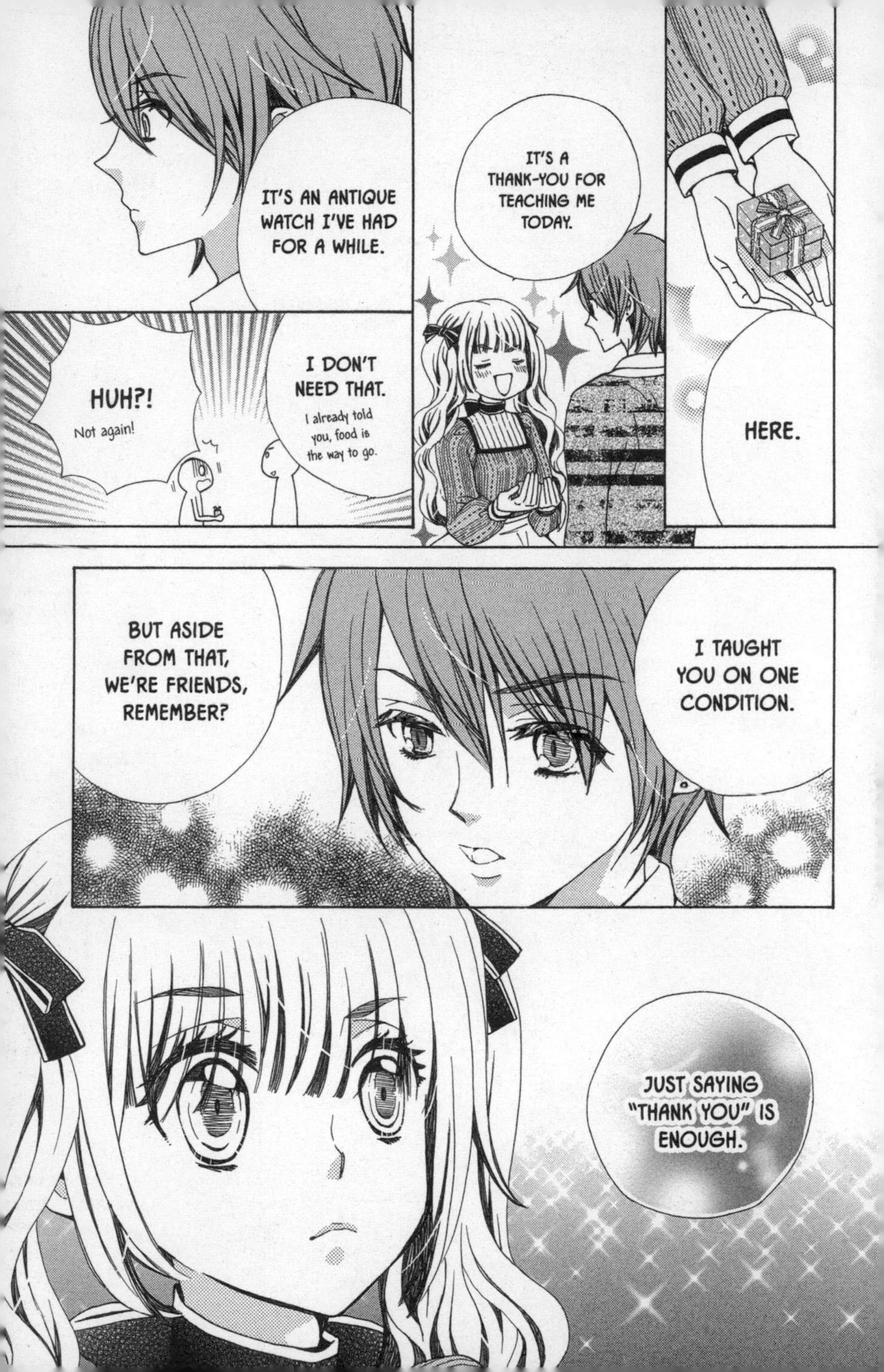
HERE.
IT'S A THANK-YOU FOR TEACHING ME TODAY.
IT'S AN ANTIQUE WATCH I'VE HAD FOR A WHILE.
I DON'T NEED THAT.
I already told you, food is the way to go.
HUH?!
Not again!
I TAUGHT YOU ON ONE CONDITION.
BUT ASIDE FROM THAT, WE'RE FRIENDS, REMEMBER?
JUST SAYING "THANK YOU" IS ENOUGH.

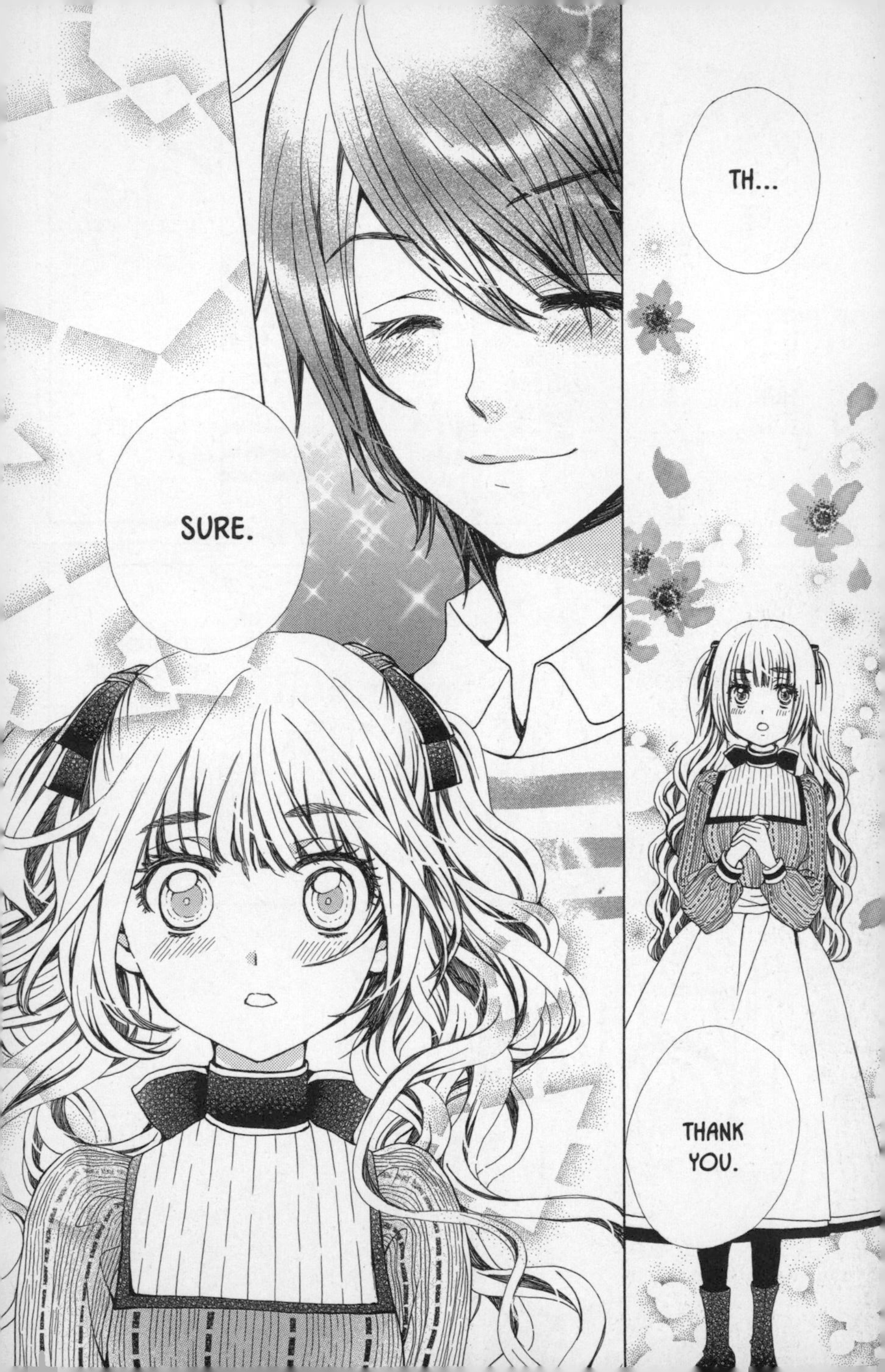
TH...
THANK YOU.
SURE.

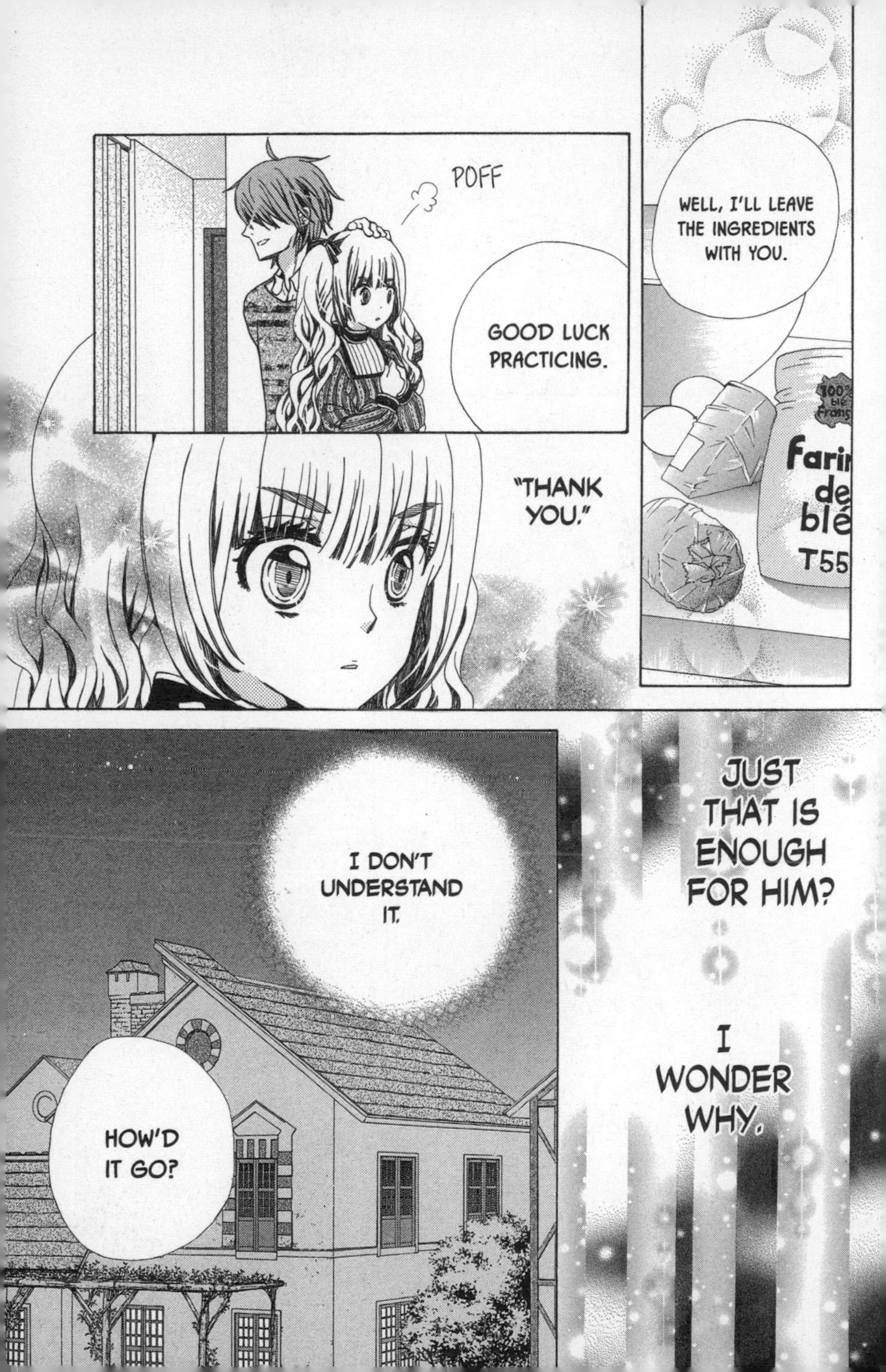
WELL, I'LL LEAVE THE INGREDIENTS WITH YOU.
farin
de
blé
T55
POFF
GOOD LUCK PRACTICING.
"THANK YOU."
JUST THAT IS ENOUGH FOR HIM?
I WONDER WHY.
I DON'T UNDERSTAND IT.
HOW'D IT GO?

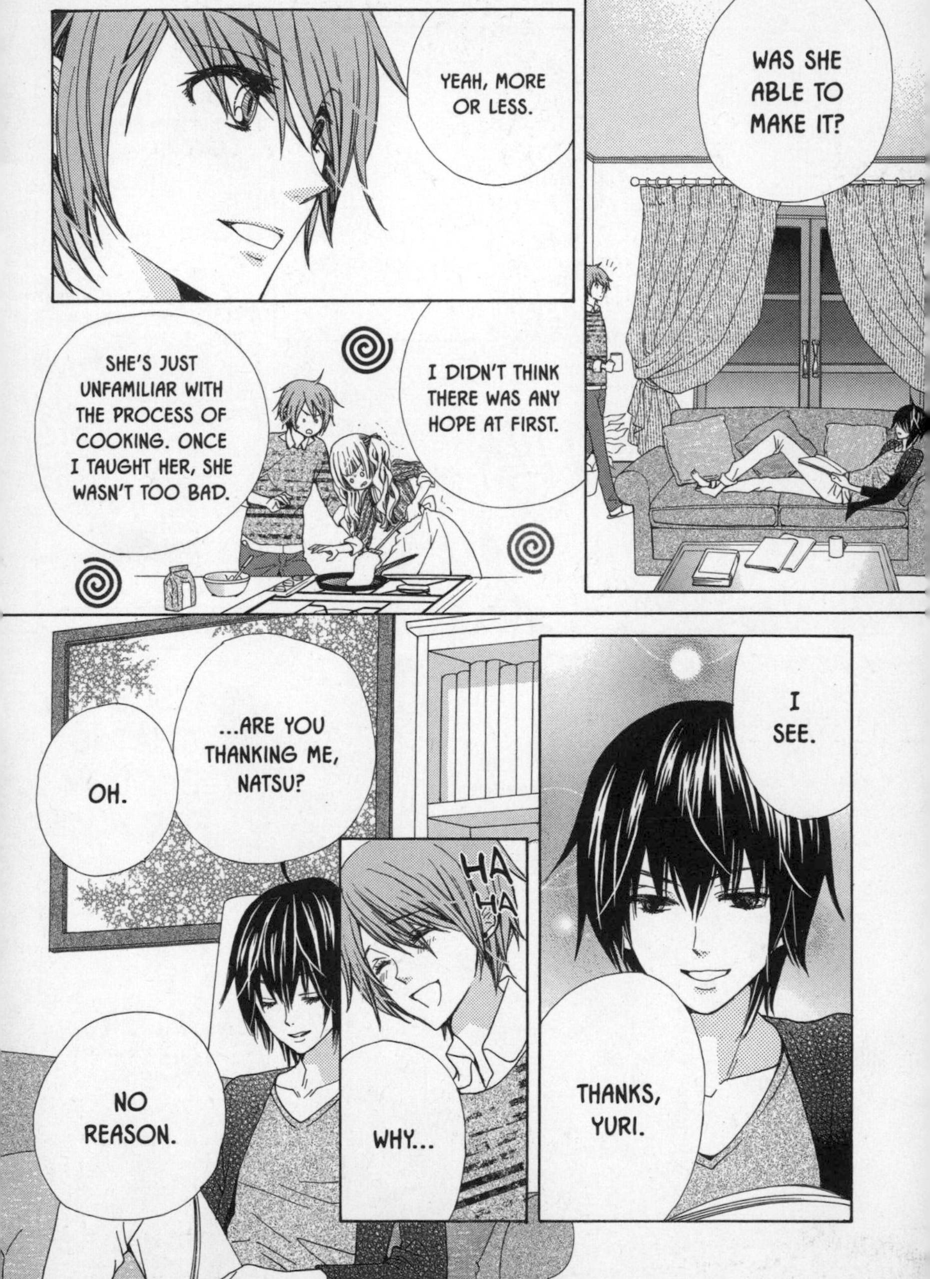
WAS SHE ABLE TO MAKE IT?
YEAH, MORE OR LESS.
I DIDN'T THINK THERE WAS ANY HOPE AT FIRST.
SHE'S JUST UNFAMILIAR WITH THE PROCESS OF COOKING. ONCE I TAUGHT HER, SHE WASN'T TOO BAD.
I SEE.
THANKS, YURI.
...ARE YOU THANKING ME, NATSU?
OH.
HA HA
WHY...
NO REASON.

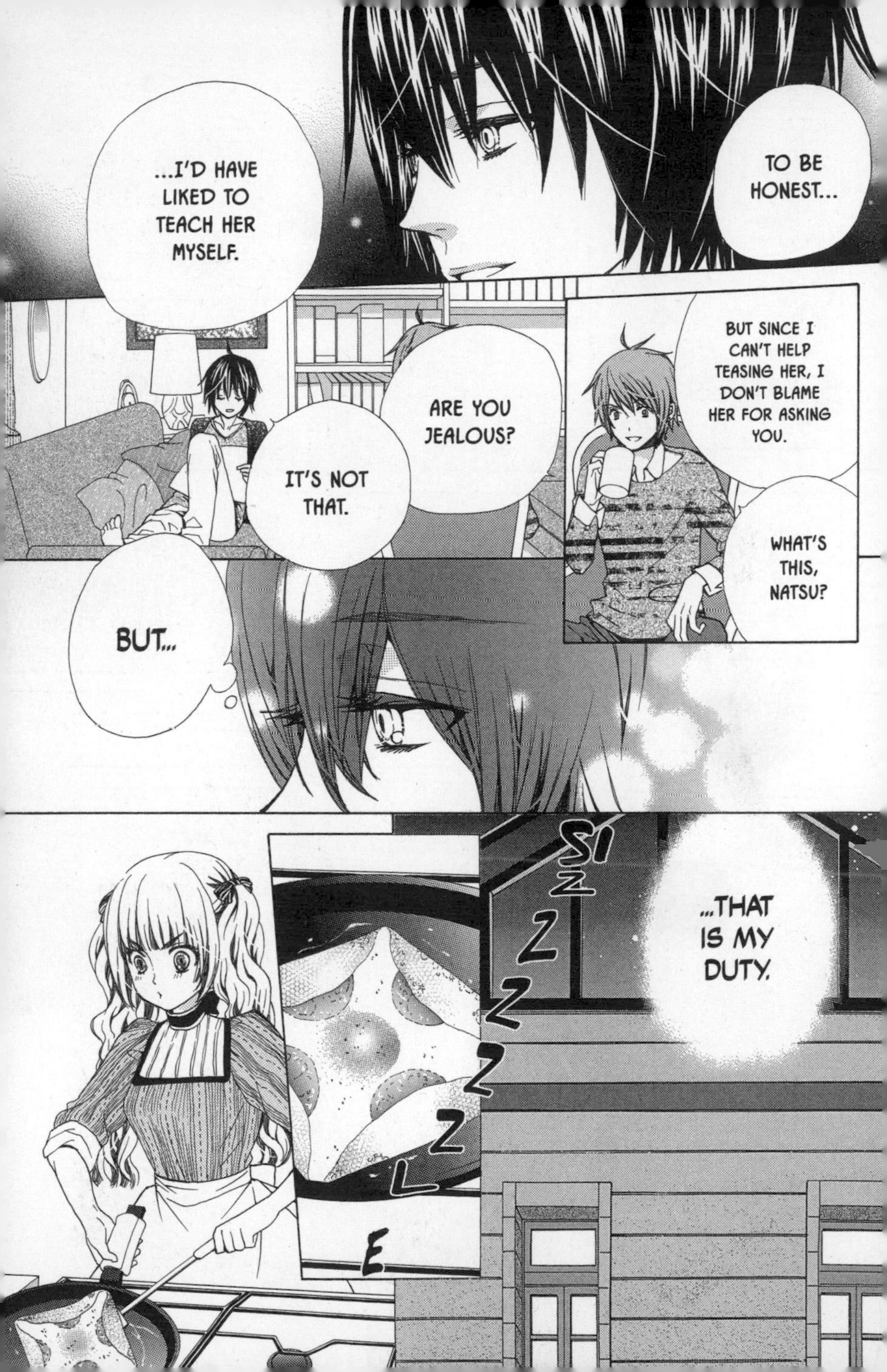
TO BE HONEST...
...I'D HAVE LIKED TO TEACH HER MYSELF.
BUT SINCE I CAN'T HELP TEASING HER, I DON'T BLAME HER FOR ASKING YOU.
WHAT'S THIS, NATSU?
ARE YOU JEALOUS?
IT'S NOT THAT.
BUT...
...THAT IS MY DUTY.
SIZZZZZZLE

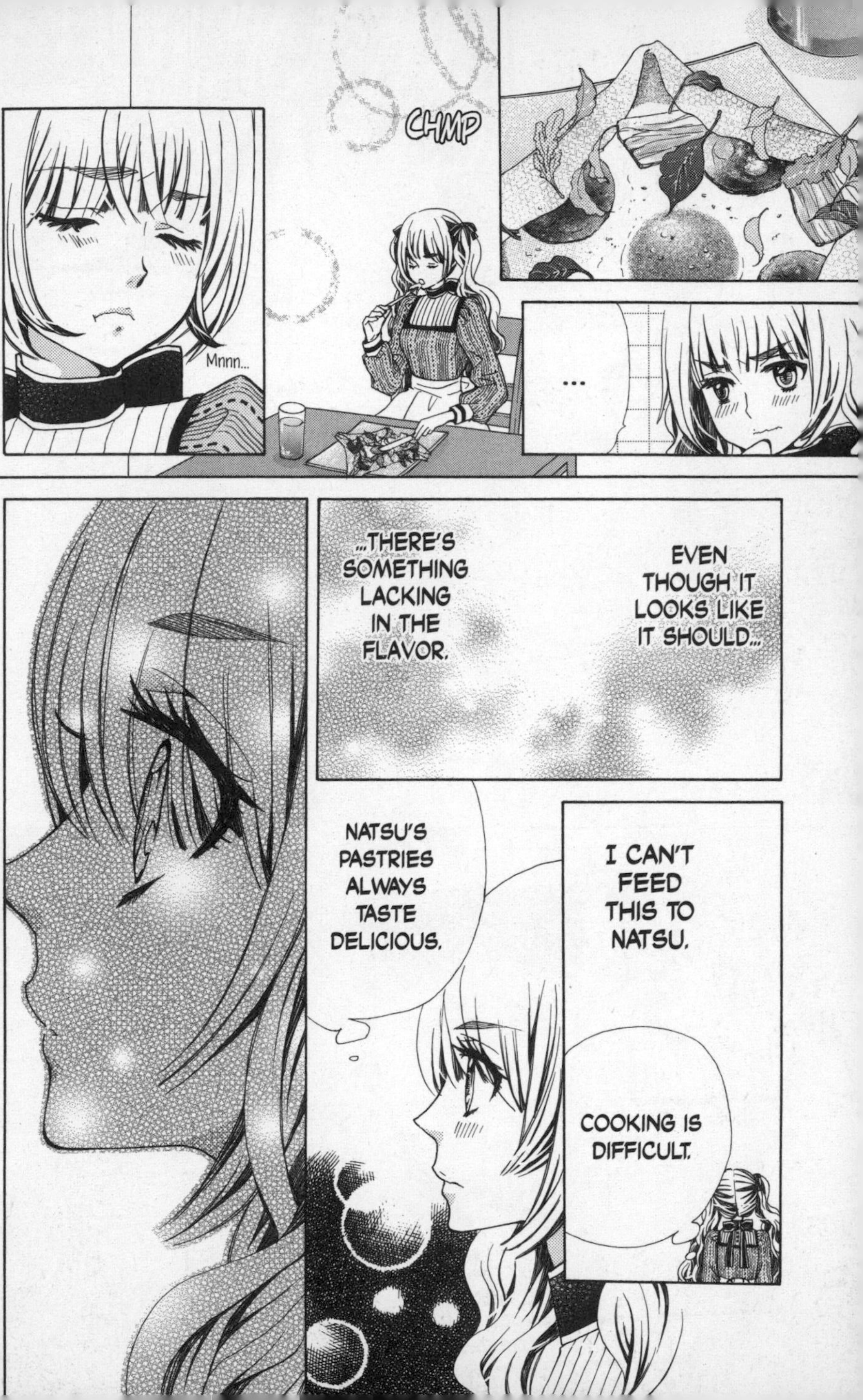
...
CHMP
Mnnn...
EVEN THOUGH IT LOOKS LIKE IT SHOULD...
...THERE'S SOMETHING LACKING IN THE FLAVOR.
I CAN'T FEED THIS TO NATSU.
NATSU'S PASTRIES ALWAYS TASTE DELICIOUS.
COOKING IS DIFFICULT.

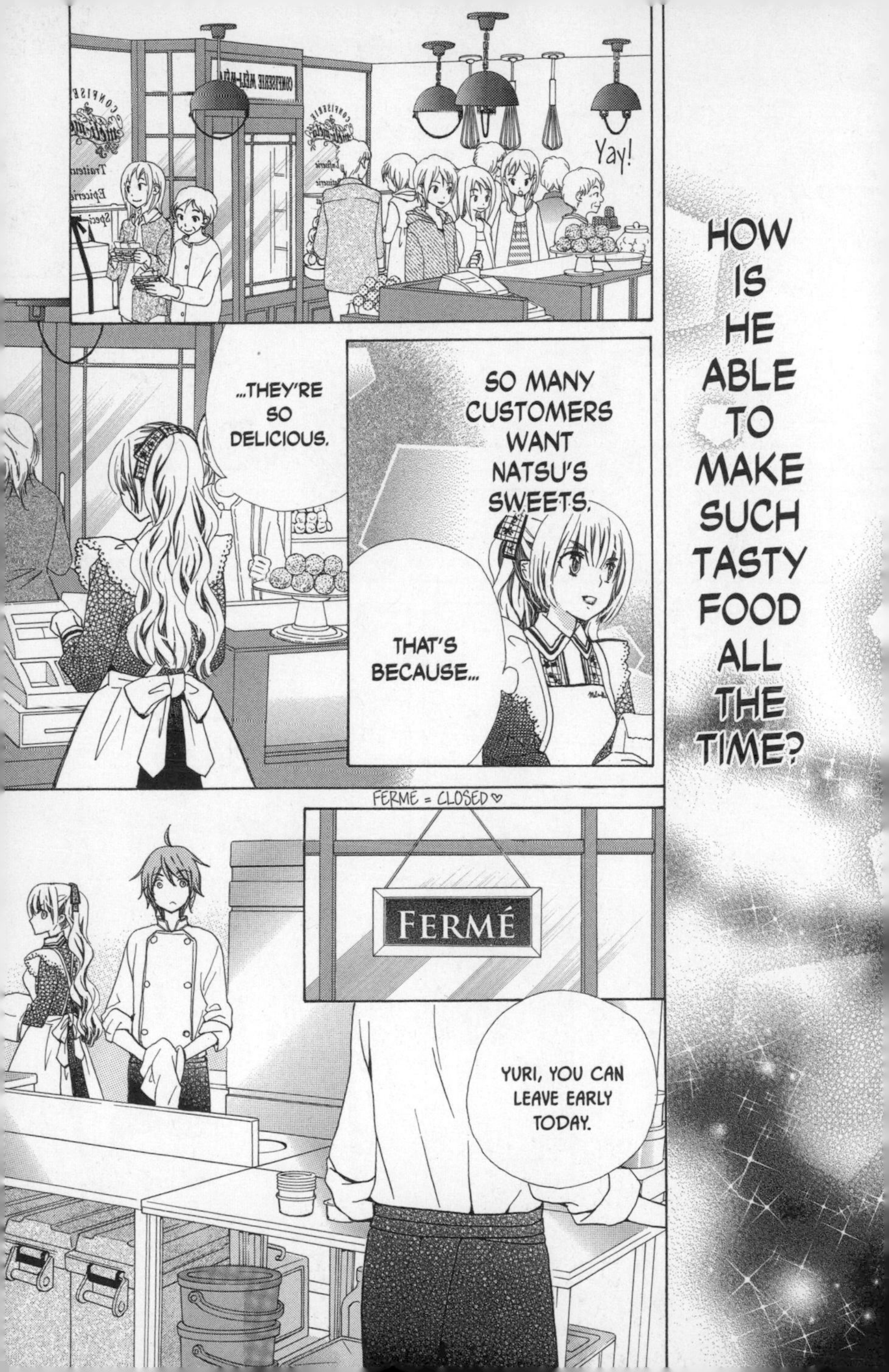
HOW IS HE ABLE TO MAKE SUCH TASTY FOOD ALL THE TIME?
Yay!
SO MANY CUSTOMERS WANT NATSU'S SWEETS.
THAT'S BECAUSE...
...THEY'RE SO DELICIOUS.
FERMÉ = CLOSED♡
FERMÉ
YURI, YOU CAN LEAVE EARLY TODAY.

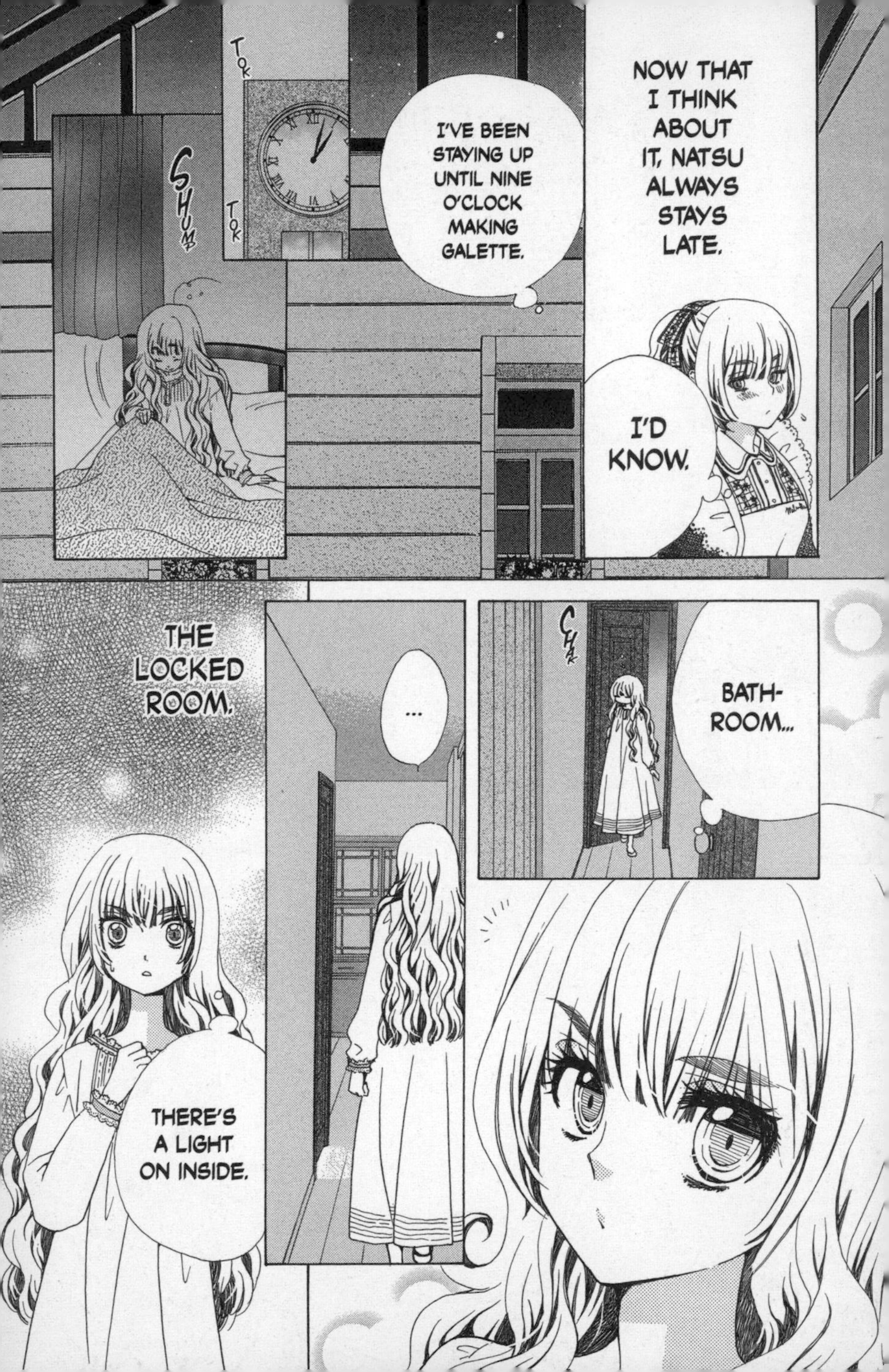
NOW THAT I THINK ABOUT IT, NATSU ALWAYS STAYS LATE.
I'D KNOW.
I'VE BEEN STAYING UP UNTIL NINE O'CLOCK MAKING GALETTE.
TOK
TOK
SHUM
CHAK
BATH-ROOM...
...
THE LOCKED ROOM.
THERE'S A LIGHT ON INSIDE.

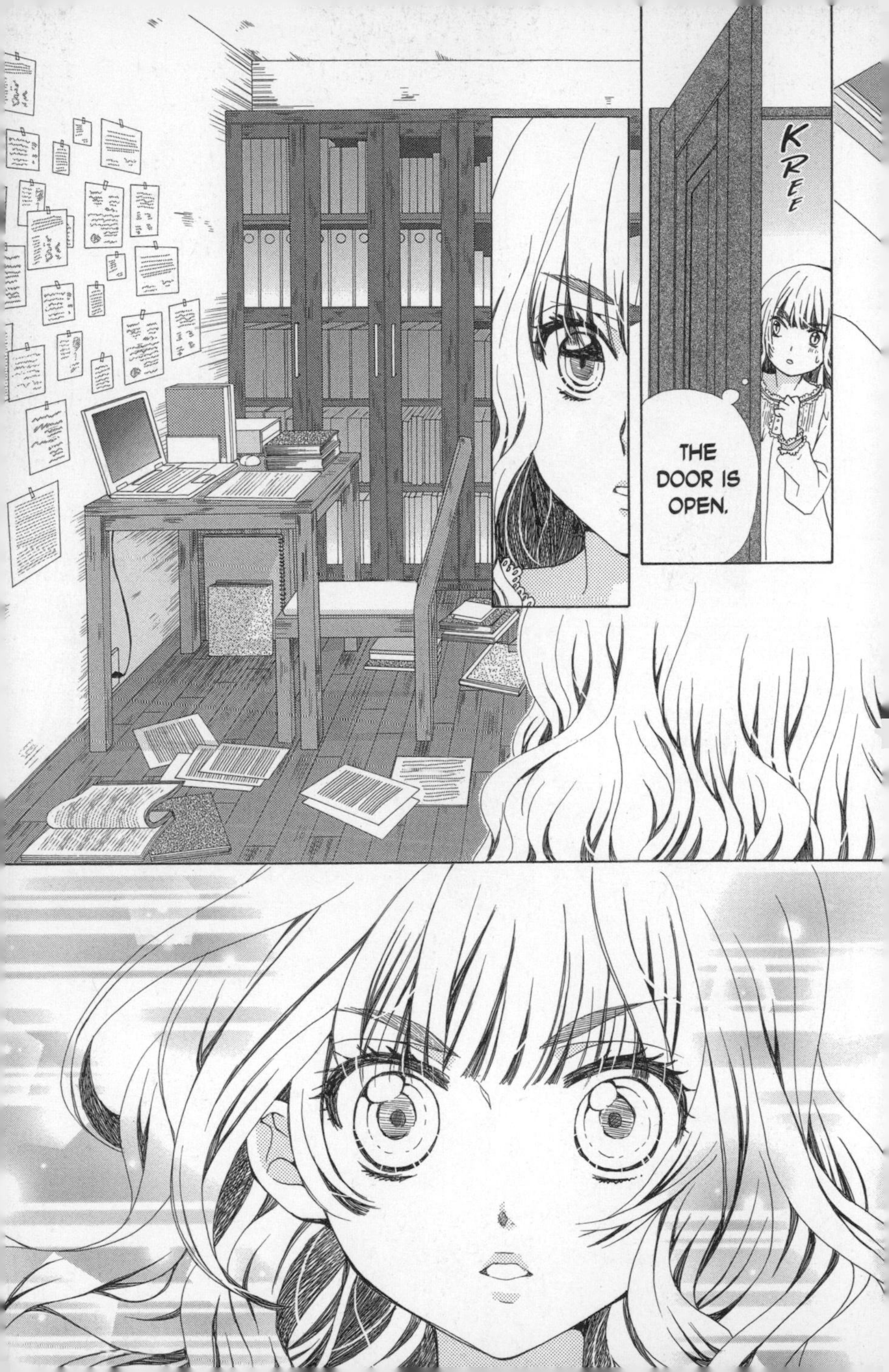
KREE
THE DOOR IS OPEN.

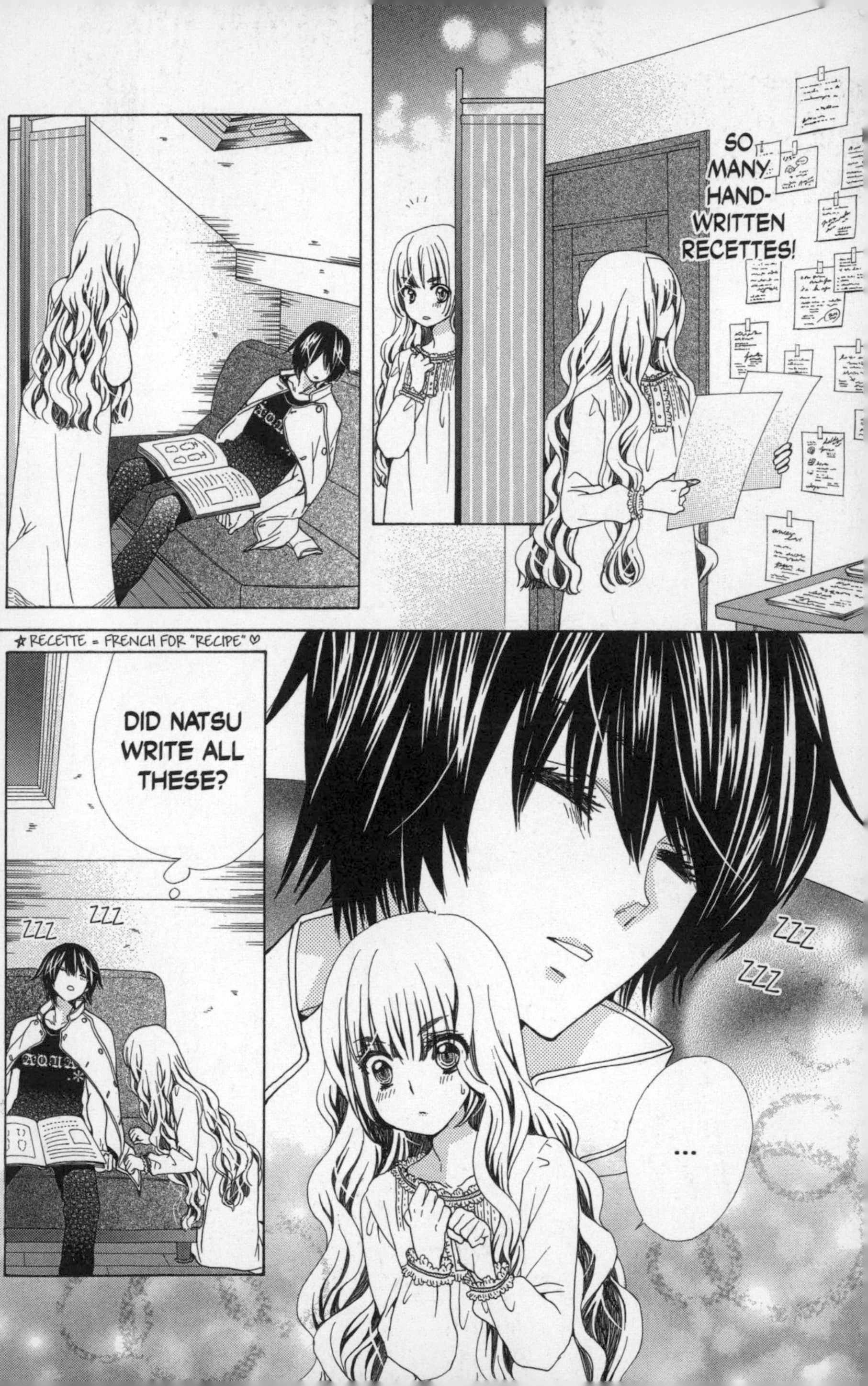
SO MANY HAND-WRITTEN RECETTES!
☆ RECETTE = FRENCH FOR "RECIPE" ♡
ZZZ
ZZZ
...
DID NATSU WRITE ALL THESE?
ZZZ
ZZZ

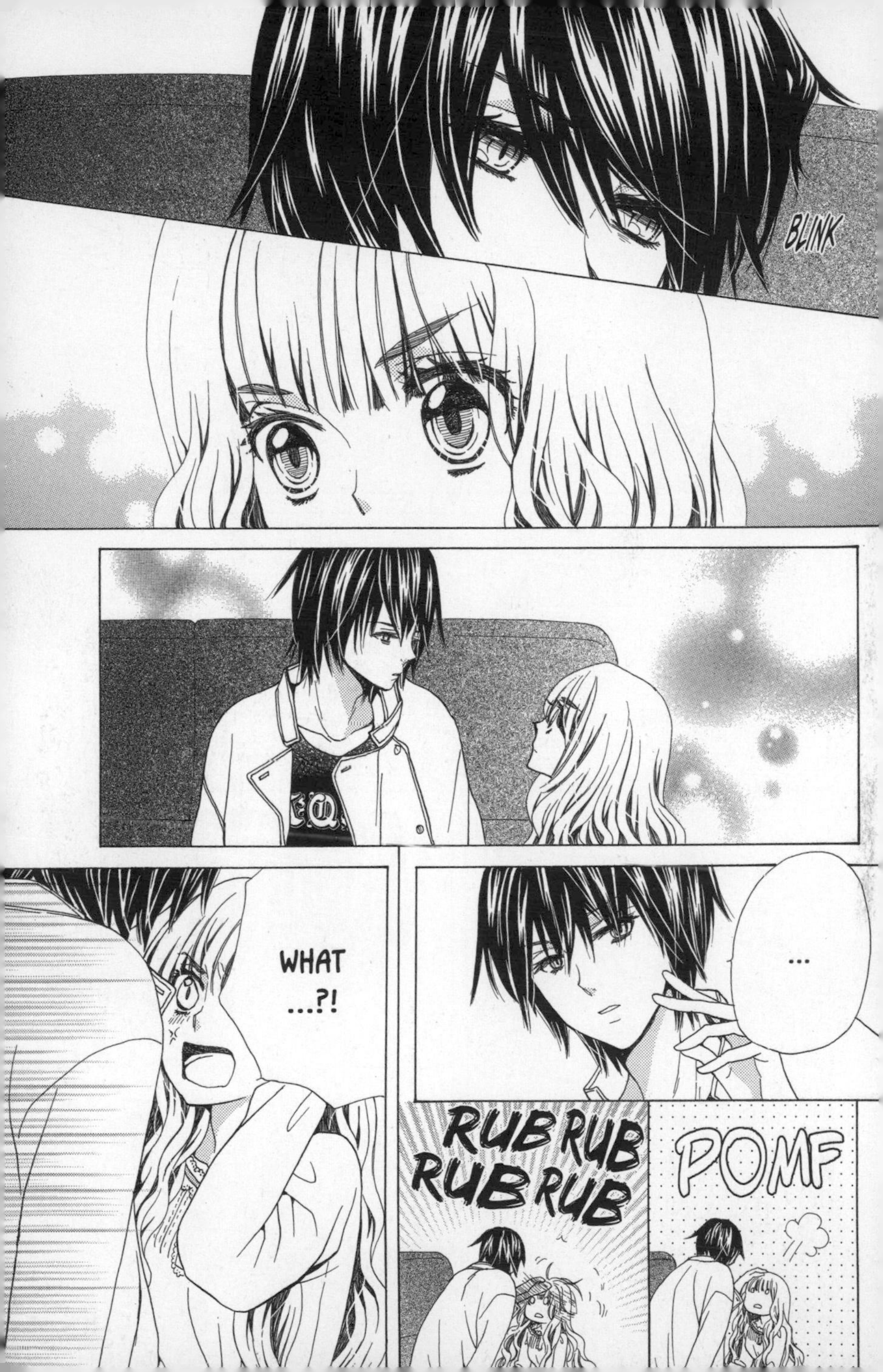
BLINK
...
POMF
RUB RUB
RUB RUB
WHAT
...?!

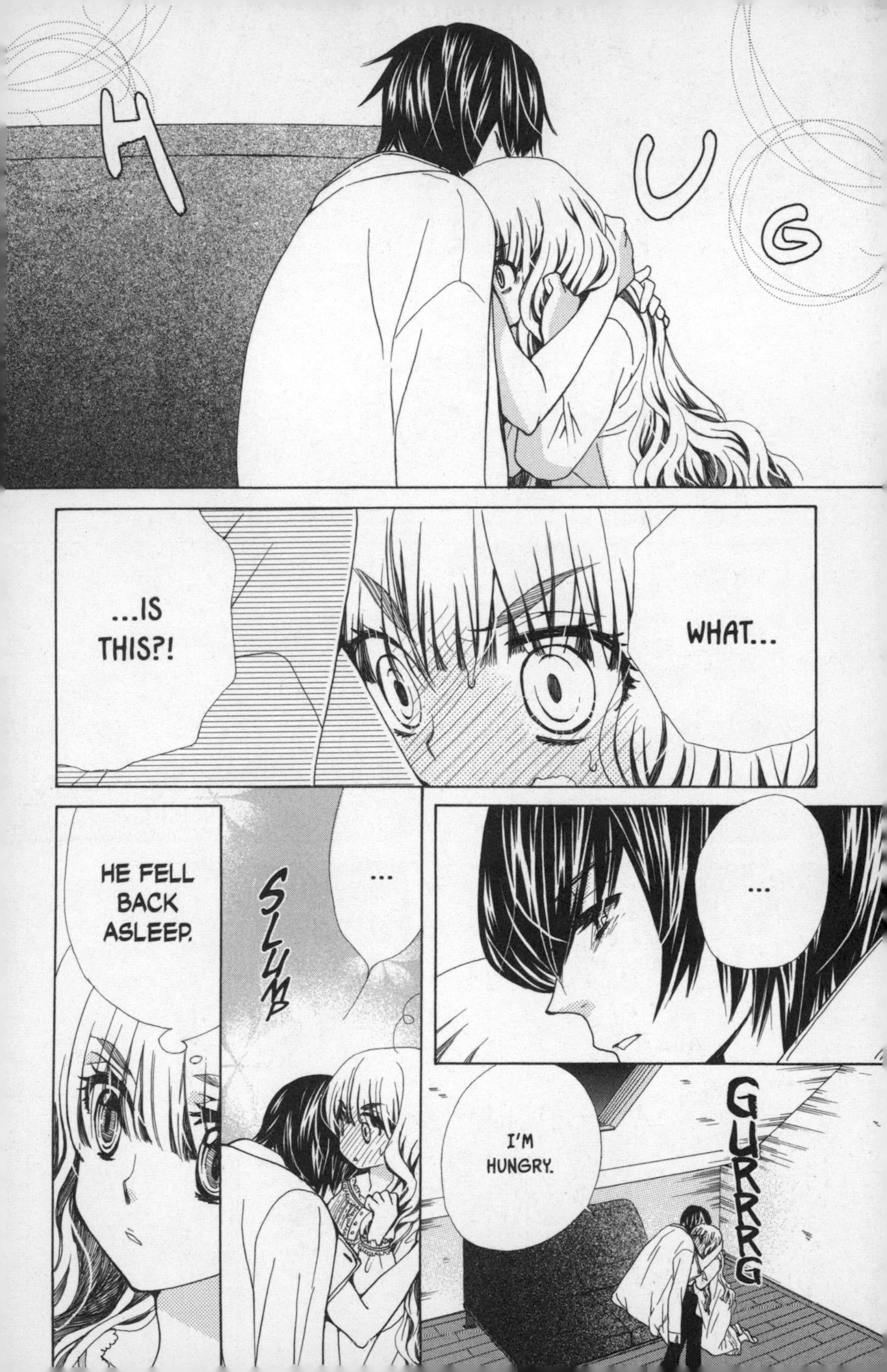
HUG
WHAT...
...IS THIS?!
...
GURRRG
I'M HUNGRY.
...
SLUMP
HE FELL BACK ASLEEP.

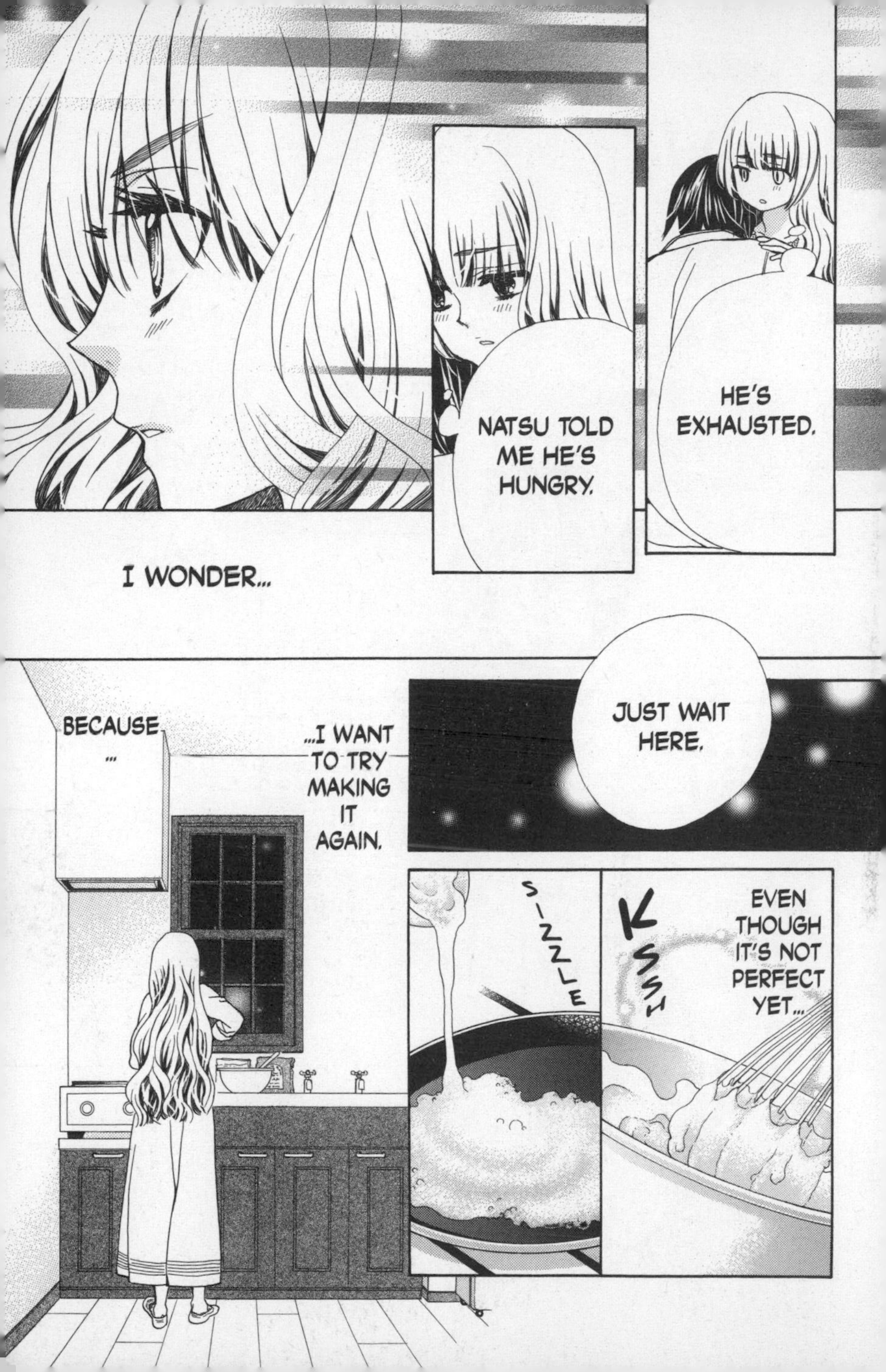
HE'S EXHAUSTED.
NATSU TOLD ME HE'S HUNGRY.
I WONDER...
JUST WAIT HERE.
EVEN THOUGH IT'S NOT PERFECT YET...
SSH
SIZZLE
BECAUSE ...
...I WANT TO TRY MAKING IT AGAIN.

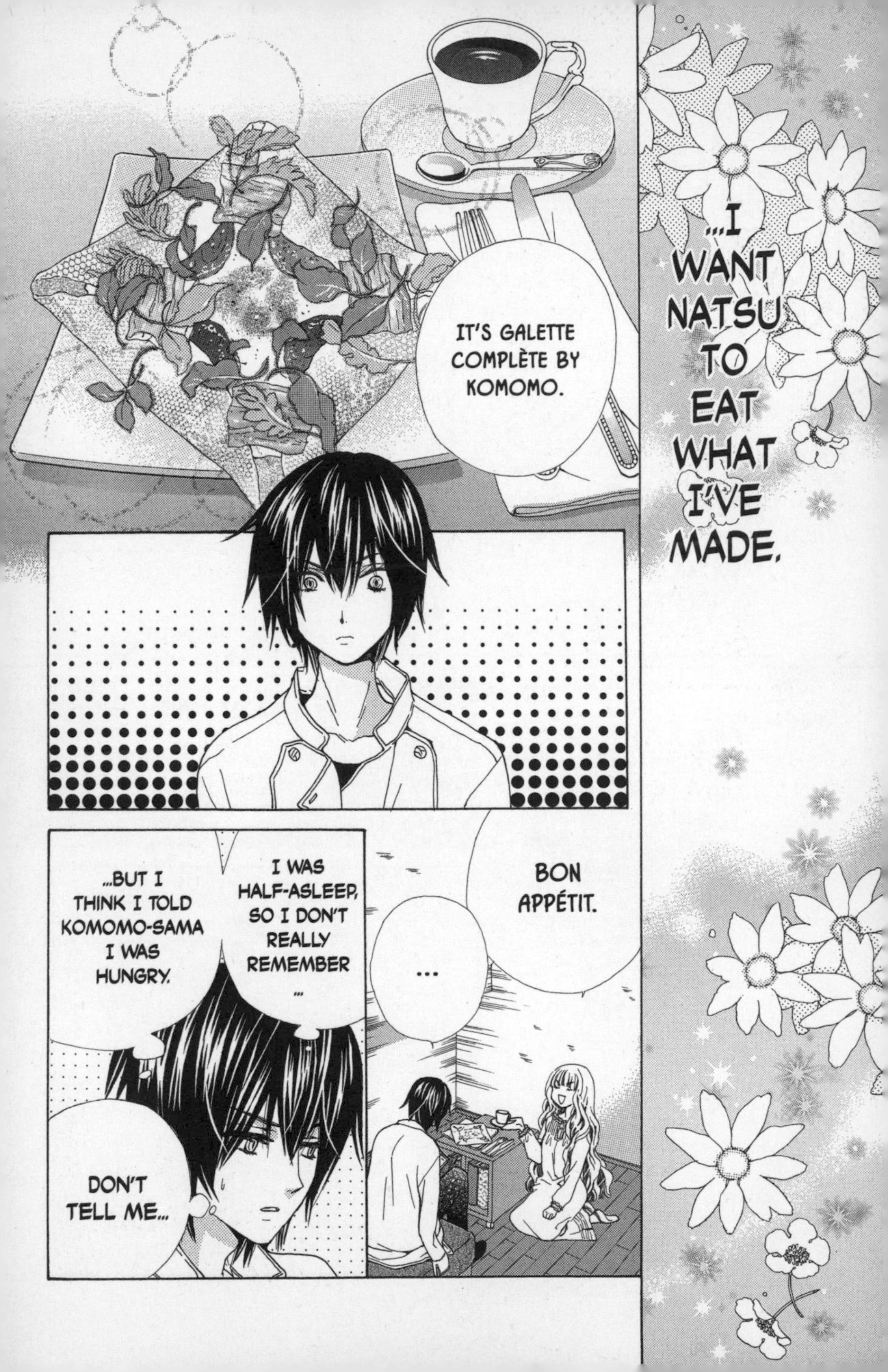
...I WANT NATSU TO EAT WHAT I'VE MADE.
IT'S GALETTE COMPLÈTE BY KOMOMO.
BON APPÉTIT.
...
I WAS HALF-ASLEEP, SO I DON'T REALLY REMEMBER...
...BUT I THINK I TOLD KOMOMO-SAMA I WAS HUNGRY.
DON'T TELL ME...

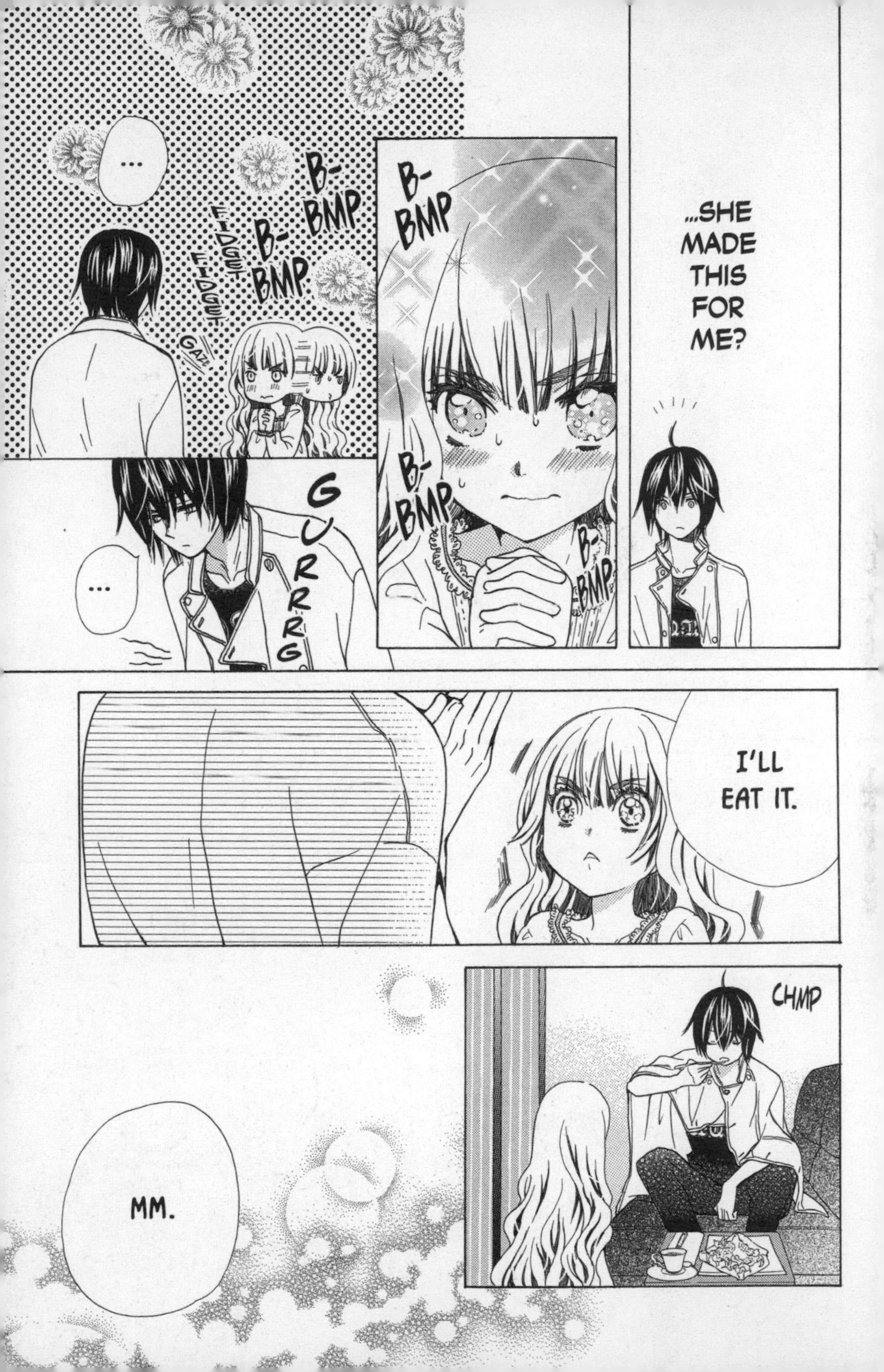
...SHE MADE THIS FOR ME?
B-BMP
B-BMP
B-BMP
...
B-BMP
B-BMP
FIDGET FIDGET
GAZE
...
GURRRRG
I'LL EAT IT.
CHMP
MM.

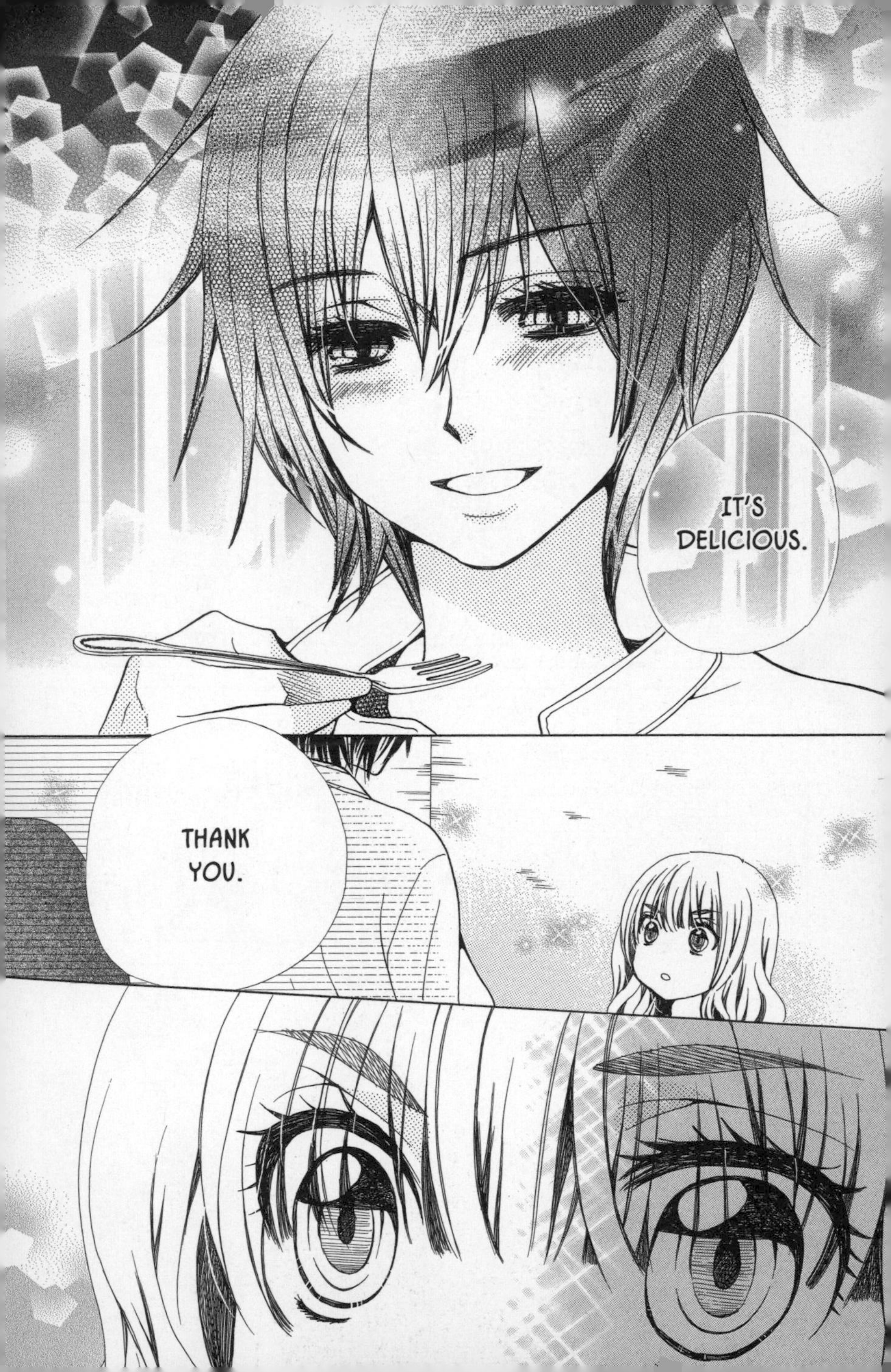
IT'S DELICIOUS.
THANK YOU.

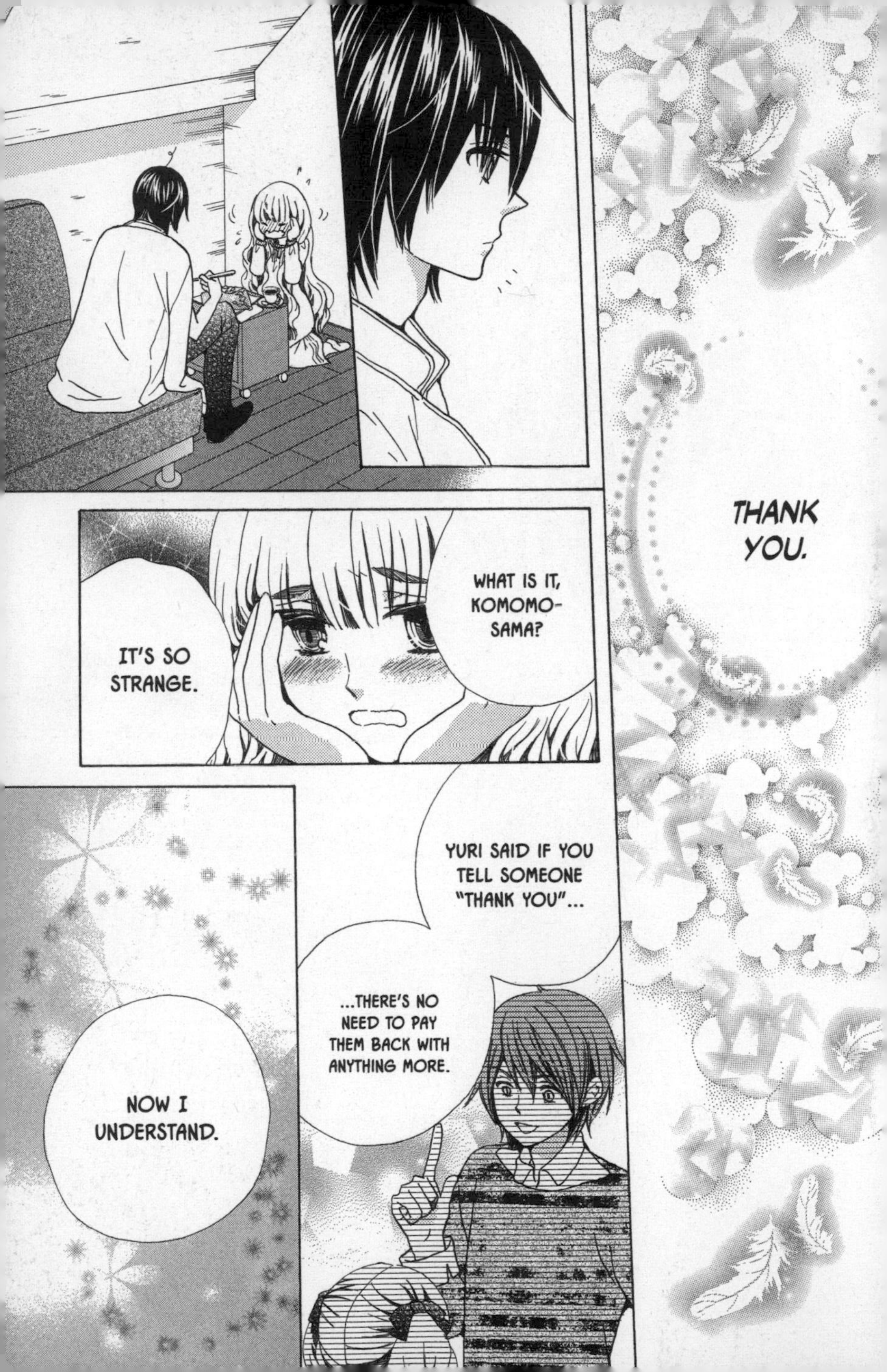
THANK YOU.
WHAT IS IT, KOMOMO-SAMA?
IT'S SO STRANGE.
YURI SAID IF YOU TELL SOMEONE "THANK YOU"...
...THERE'S NO NEED TO PAY THEM BACK WITH ANYTHING MORE.
NOW I UNDERSTAND.

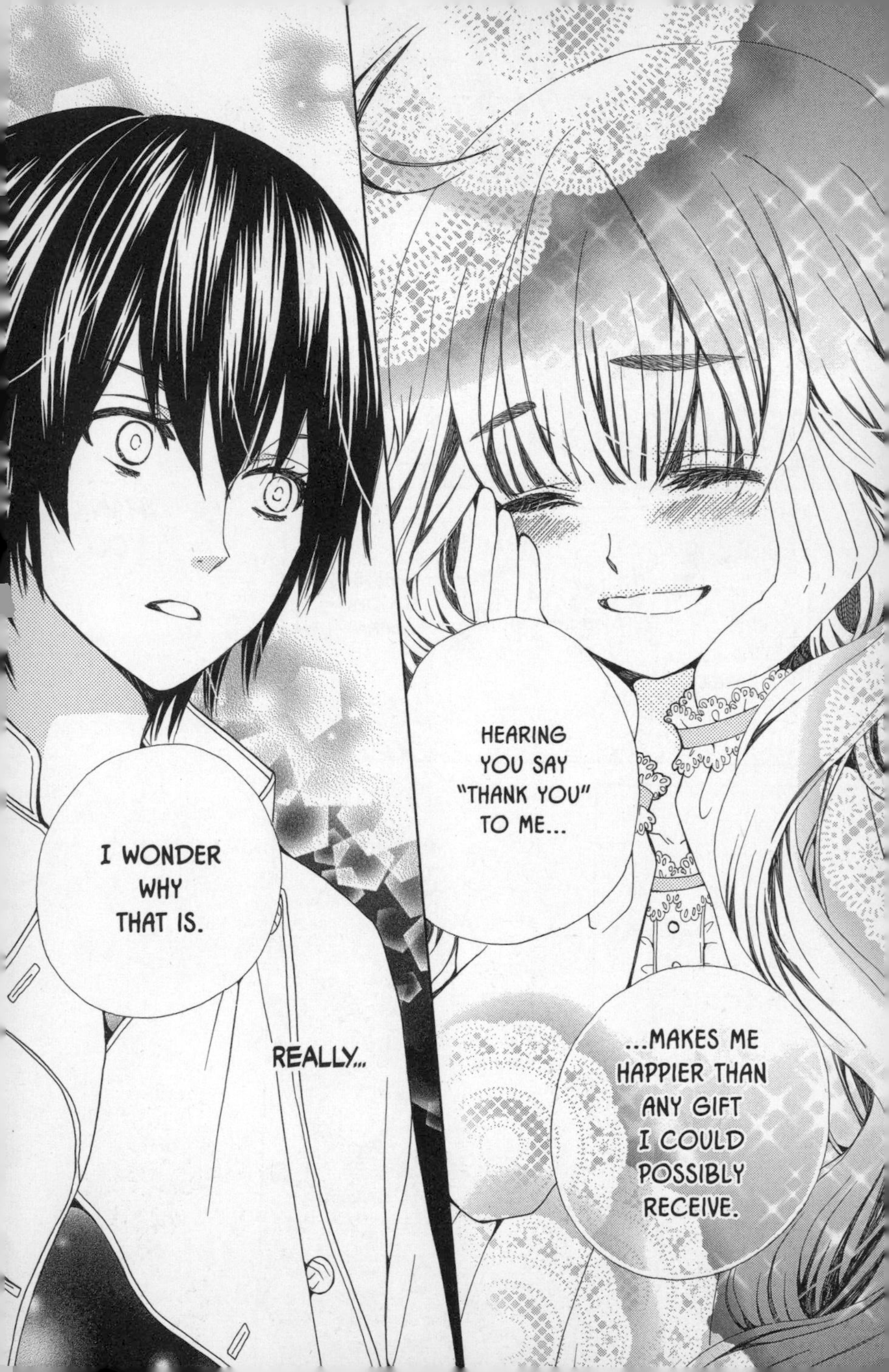
HEARING YOU SAY "THANK YOU" TO ME...
...MAKES ME HAPPIER THAN ANY GIFT I COULD POSSIBLY RECEIVE.
I WONDER WHY THAT IS.
REALLY...

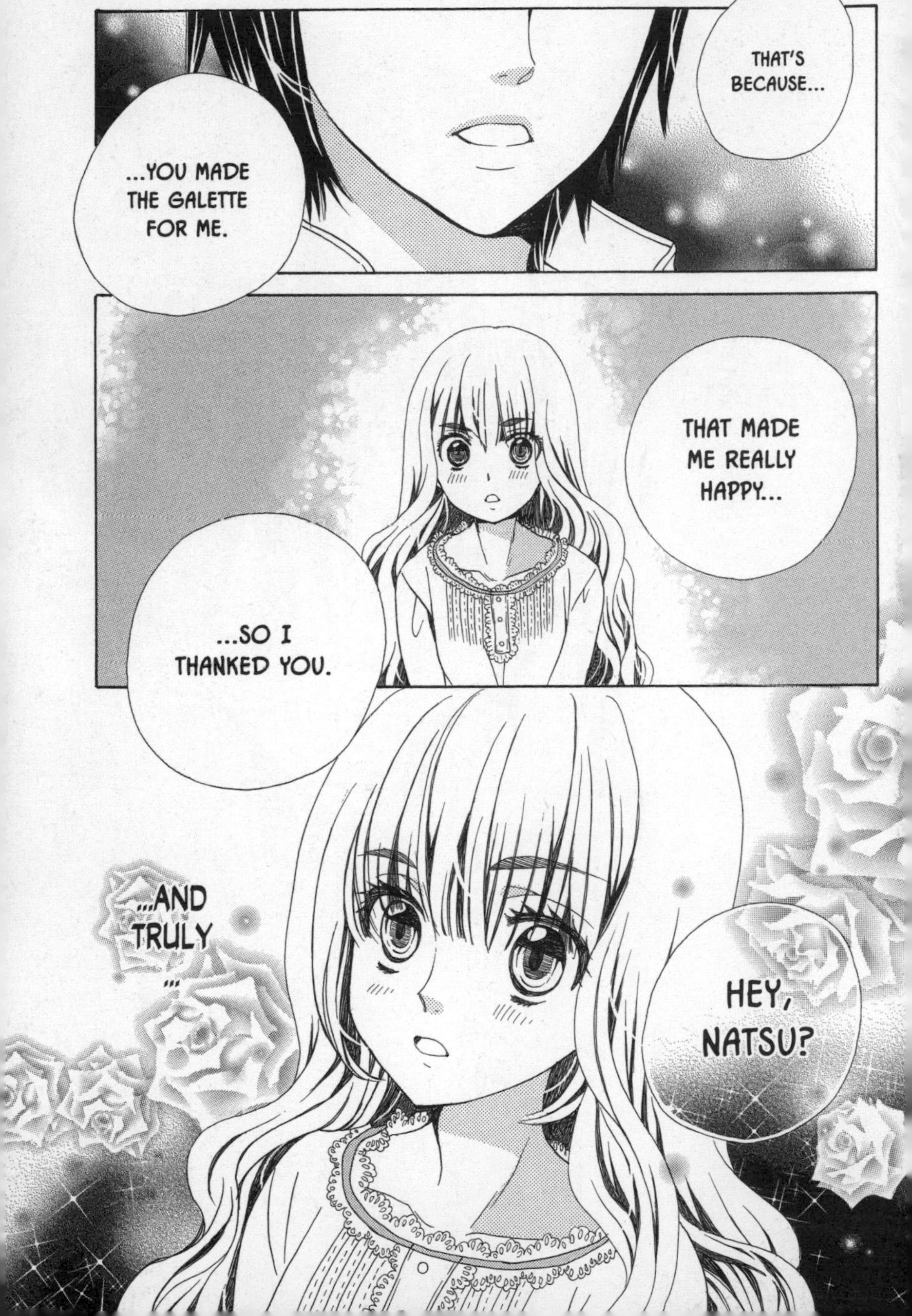
THAT'S BECAUSE...
...YOU MADE THE GALETTE FOR ME.
THAT MADE ME REALLY HAPPY...
...SO I THANKED YOU.
...AND TRULY ...
HEY, NATSU?

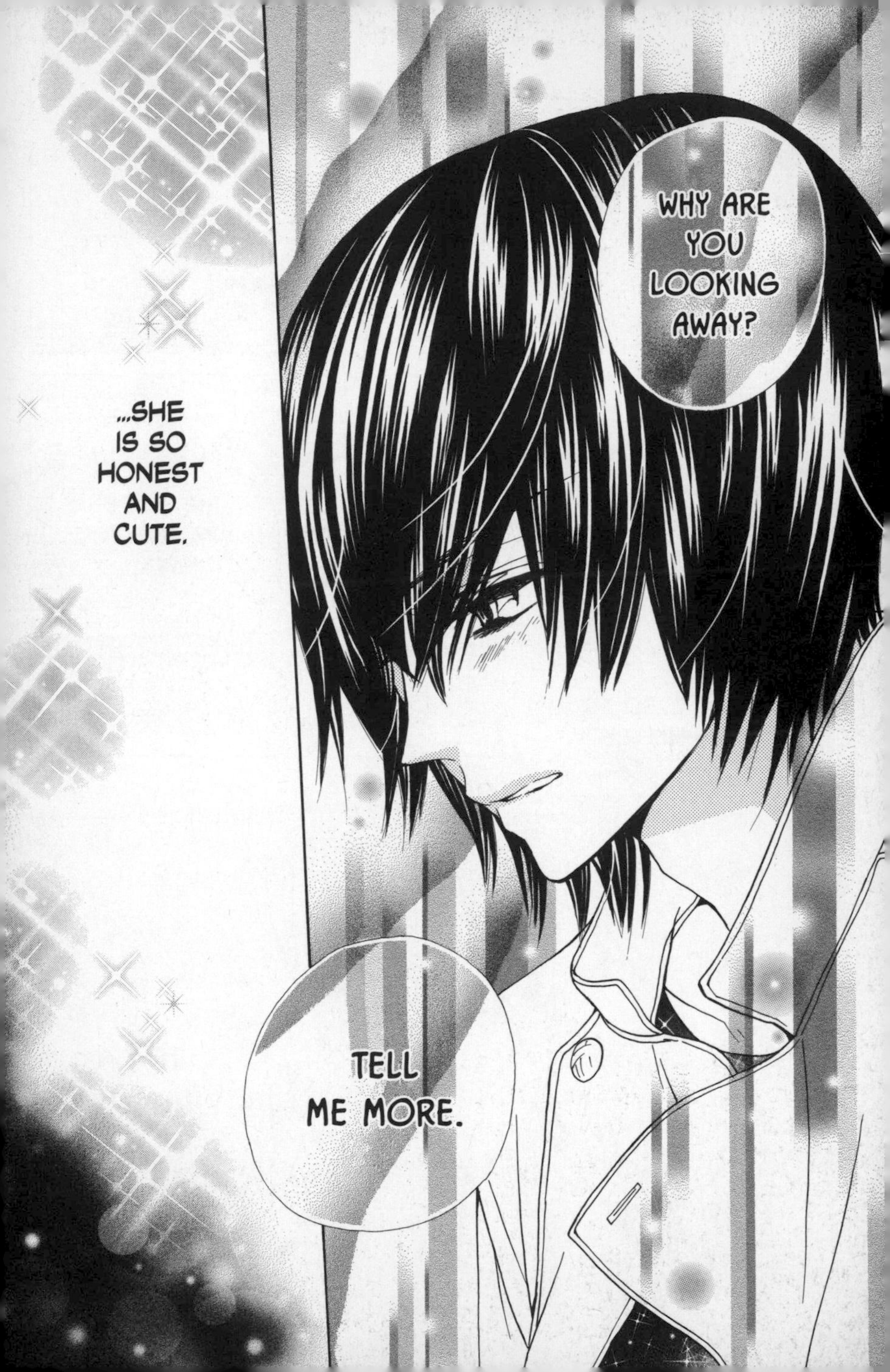
WHY ARE YOU LOOKING AWAY?
TELL ME MORE.
...SHE IS SO HONEST AND CUTE.

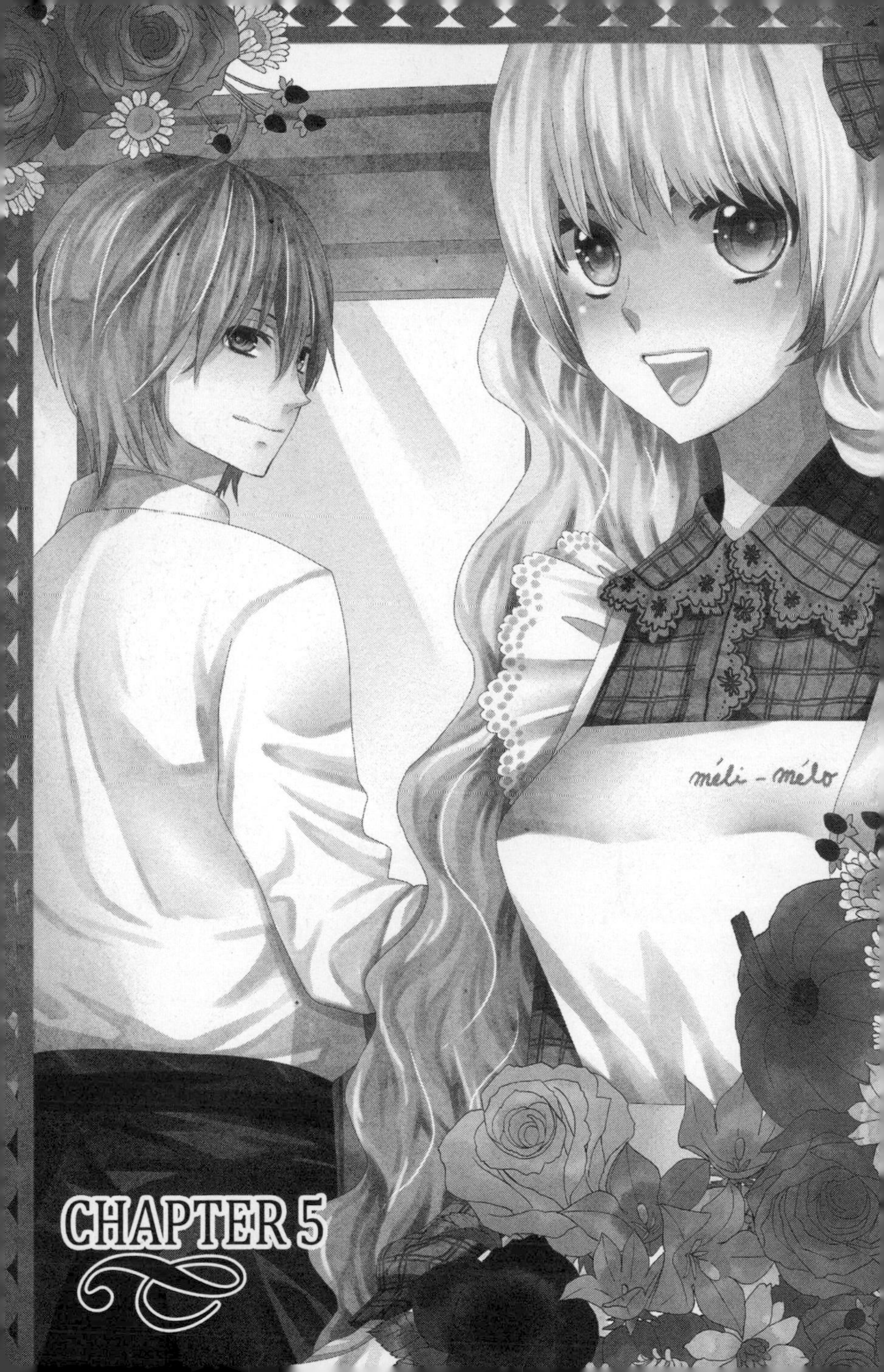
méli-mélo
CHAPTER 5

~ My personal takes on different pastries ~

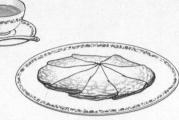

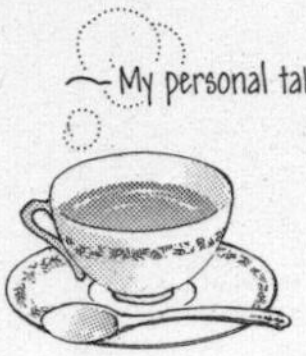

~ crêpes au sucre ~

Also known as "sweet crêpes."

You can wrap them around jam, cream, or anything else you like. I like to sprinkle them with granulated sugar myself. I just love how the soft sweetness of the crepe and crunchy sugar feels on my teeth. Oh, they're also really good with salted caramel too!

~ Succès praliné ~

A delicious pastry that has crunchy meringue and aromatic hazelnut cream. I love when a flavor can be described as "aromatic." Lots of French sweets have nuts, which is why I love them so much. The crunchy and flaky meringue is so good! I love it!!

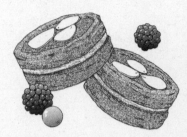

~ Crémet d'Anjou ~

A creamy dish that includes a blend of cream cheese called fromage blanc and whipped cream. It's creamy in every sense of the word and simply traps your taste buds. I like to eat it with a flakey meringue. It has a thick and creamy taste. Try it with jam and fruit too! I personally like to put nuts on mine. This is bound to make you fat!!

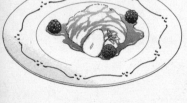

~ Galette complète ~

A "crêpe meal." It's a filling crêpe made by putting cheese, eggs, ham, and other ingredients in a buck-wheat dough. This is a little off-topic, but I've had it before with avocado and fresh arugula with basil sauce. With the salty ham and cheese, it makes for a delicious balance of flavors. I personally loved it, but I know not everyone is crazy about avocado. Ahh! Ahh!

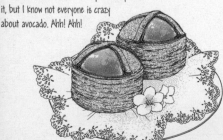

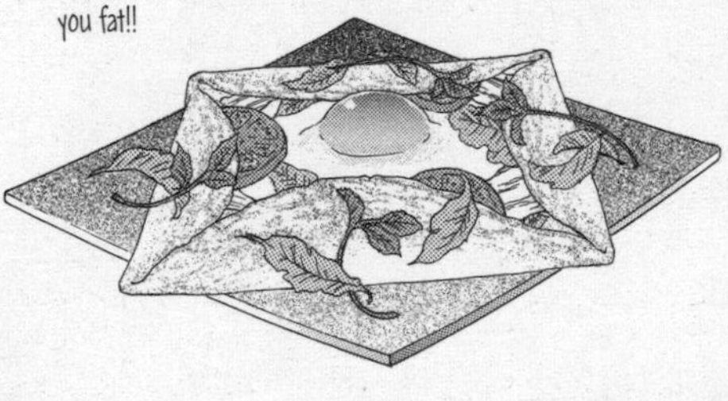

~ Pont-neuf ~

A beautiful little baked pastry with a cross shape on top. It can come with groseille or raspberry jam on top. The pie is made with baked custard cream and choux pastry dough. The ones I've eaten before had apple compote in them. The custard has a gentle sweetness to it and is very good. Apparently, the cross on the top is supposed to look like a bridge called "Pont Neuf" that crosses the Seine river.

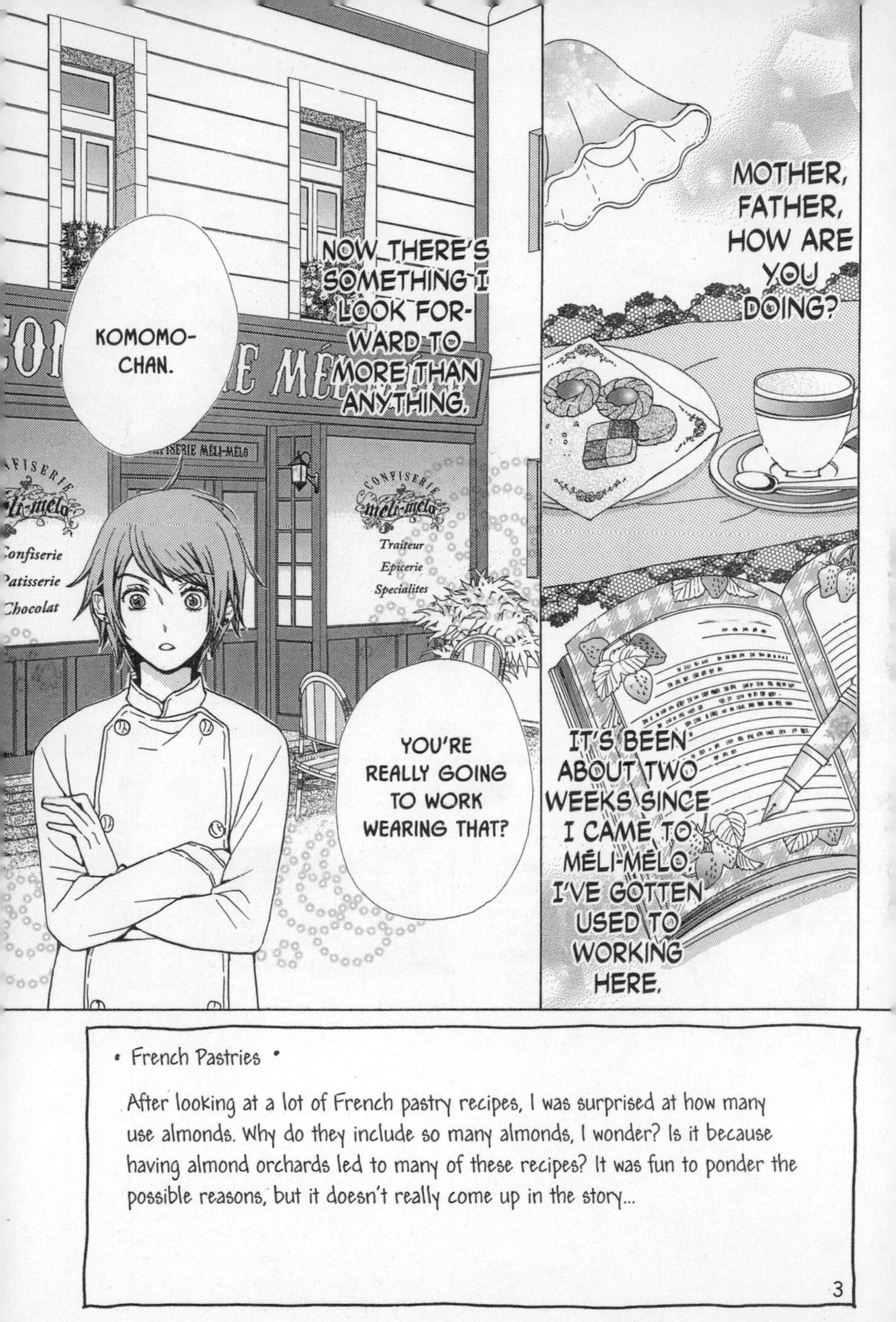
MOTHER, FATHER, HOW ARE YOU DOING?
IT'S BEEN ABOUT TWO WEEKS SINCE I CAME TO MÉLI-MÉLO. I'VE GOTTEN USED TO WORKING HERE.
NOW THERE'S SOMETHING I LOOK FOR-WARD TO MORE THAN ANYTHING.
KOMOMO-CHAN.
CONFISERIE MÉLI-MÉLO
Confiserie méli-mélo
Traiteur
Epicerie
Specialites
Confiserie
Patisserie
Chocolat
YOU'RE REALLY GOING TO WORK WEARING THAT?

• French Pastries •

After looking at a lot of French pastry recipes, I was surprised at how many use almonds. Why do they include so many almonds, I wonder? Is it because having almond orchards led to many of these recipes? It was fun to ponder the possible reasons, but it doesn't really come up in the story...

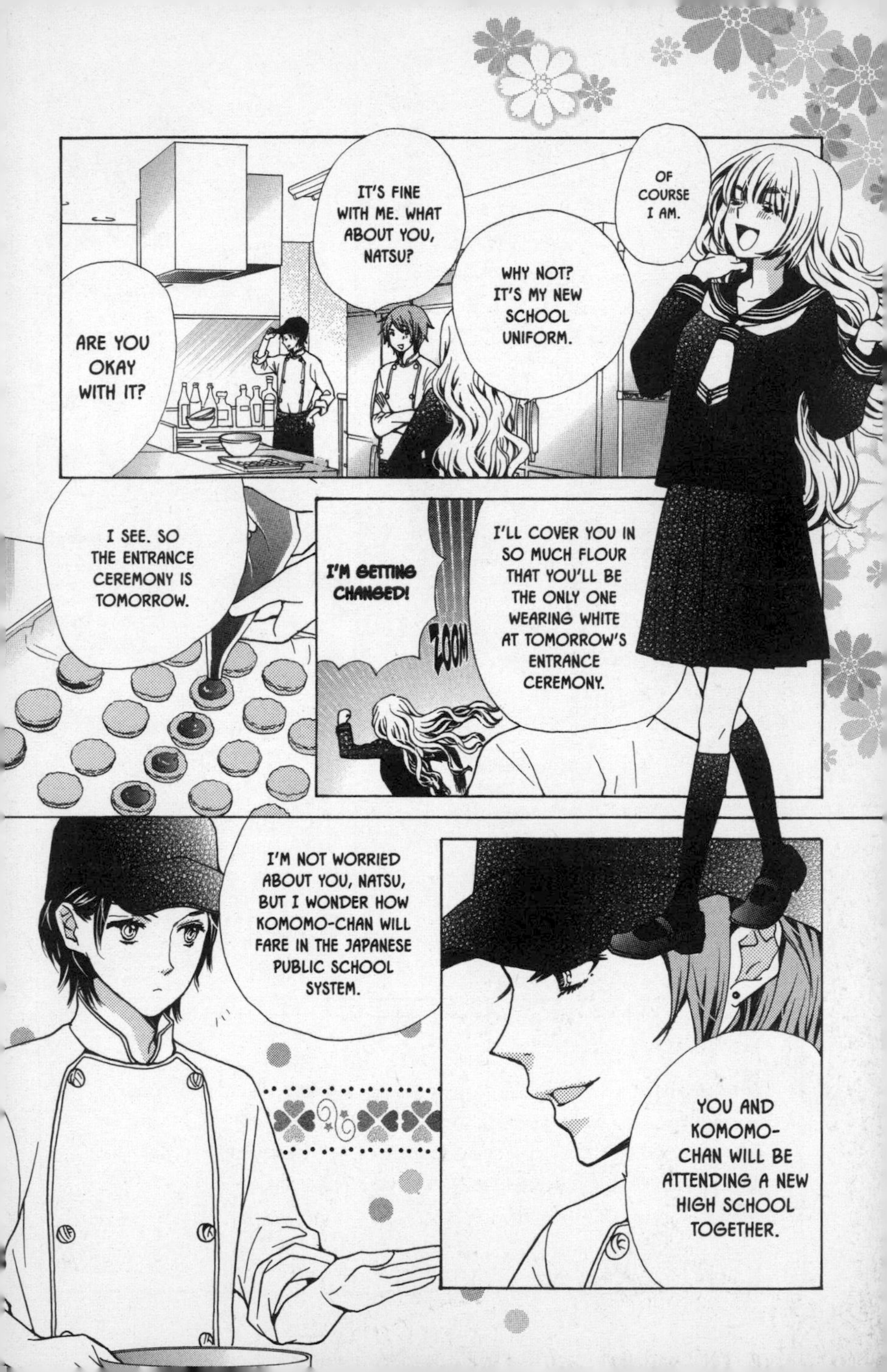
OF COURSE I AM.
WHY NOT? IT'S MY NEW SCHOOL UNIFORM.
IT'S FINE WITH ME. WHAT ABOUT YOU, NATSU?
ARE YOU OKAY WITH IT?
I'LL COVER YOU IN SO MUCH FLOUR THAT YOU'LL BE THE ONLY ONE WEARING WHITE AT TOMORROW'S ENTRANCE CEREMONY.
I'M GETTING CHANGED!
ZOOM
I SEE. SO THE ENTRANCE CEREMONY IS TOMORROW.
YOU AND KOMOMO-CHAN WILL BE ATTENDING A NEW HIGH SCHOOL TOGETHER.
I'M NOT WORRIED ABOUT YOU, NATSU, BUT I WONDER HOW KOMOMO-CHAN WILL FARE IN THE JAPANESE PUBLIC SCHOOL SYSTEM.

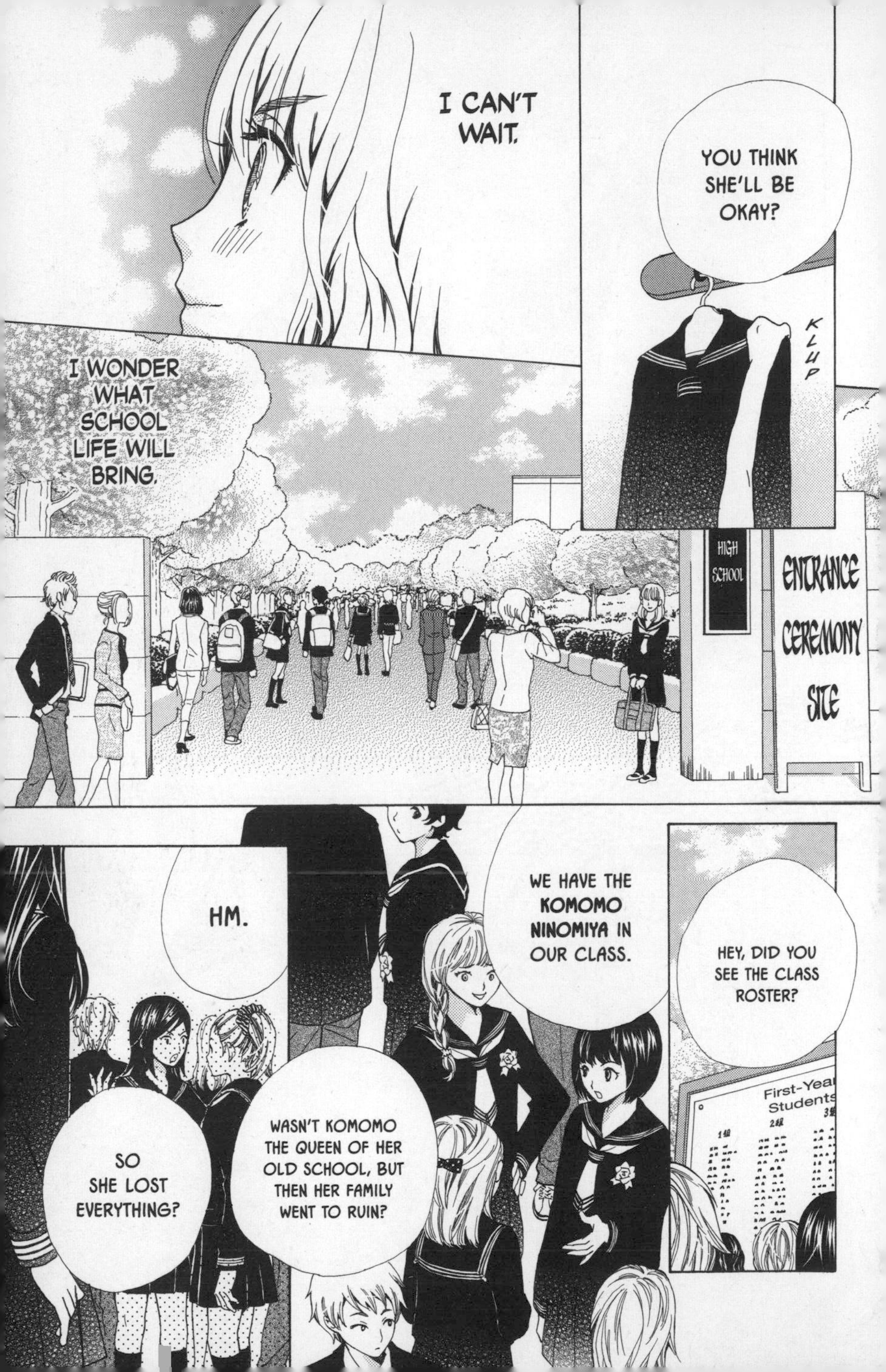
YOU THINK SHE'LL BE OKAY?
KLUP
I CAN'T WAIT.
I WONDER WHAT SCHOOL LIFE WILL BRING.
HIGH SCHOOL
ENTRANCE CEREMONY SITE
HEY, DID YOU SEE THE CLASS ROSTER?
WE HAVE THE KOMOMO NINOMIYA IN OUR CLASS.
HM.
WASN'T KOMOMO THE QUEEN OF HER OLD SCHOOL, BUT THEN HER FAMILY WENT TO RUIN?
SO SHE LOST EVERYTHING?

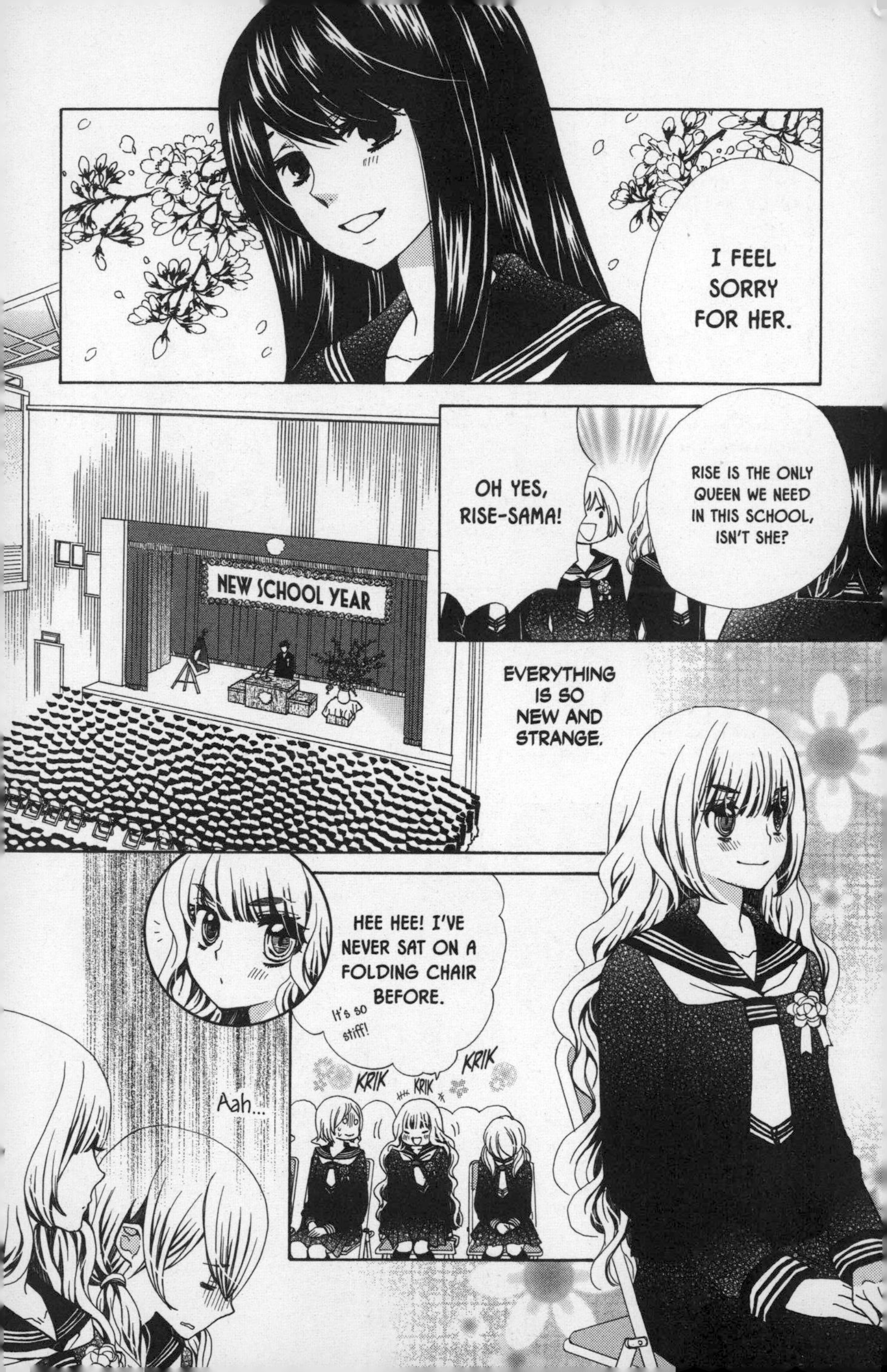
I FEEL SORRY FOR HER.
RISE IS THE ONLY QUEEN WE NEED IN THIS SCHOOL, ISN'T SHE?
OH YES, RISE-SAMA!
NEW SCHOOL YEAR
EVERYTHING IS SO NEW AND STRANGE.
HEE HEE! I'VE NEVER SAT ON A FOLDING CHAIR BEFORE.
It's so stiff!
KRIK
KRIK
KRIK
Aah...

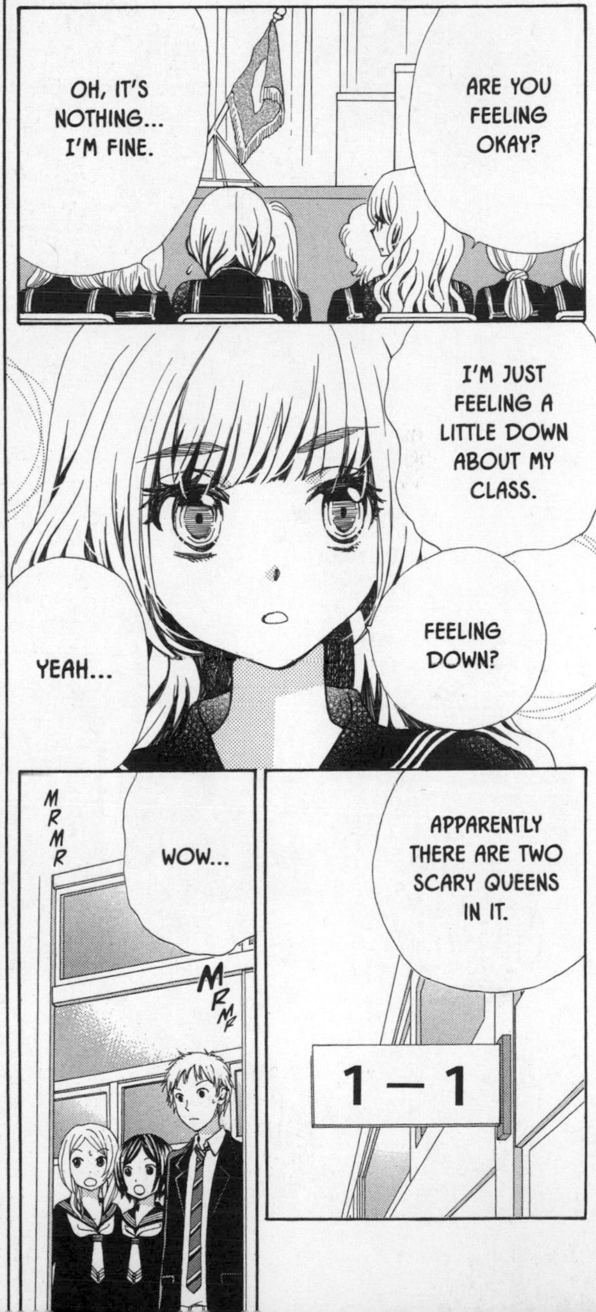
ARE YOU FEELING OKAY?
OH, IT'S NOTHING... I'M FINE.
I'M JUST FEELING A LITTLE DOWN ABOUT MY CLASS.
FEELING DOWN?
YEAH...
APPARENTLY THERE ARE TWO SCARY QUEENS IN IT.
1—1
MRMR
WOW...
MRMR

F

•Various•

This is my last sidebar with you in this volume. Thank you for staying with me so far.

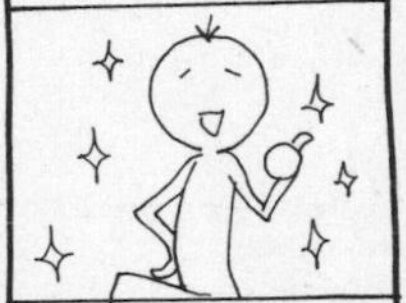

Since a confectionary shop is the stage for this story, I'm indulging myself by eating all kinds of sweets. It makes me so happy.

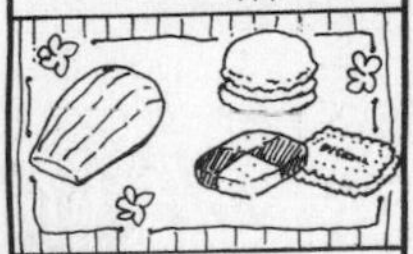

To all of you who read this far, to all my assistants who helped me out, to my editor, to everyone who let me interview them, including the entire crew at Tsujicho Cooking School and Blondir, to my friends, and to my family: Thank you so much!

♥I hope you'll send me your impressions of the story!♥

-Maki Minami

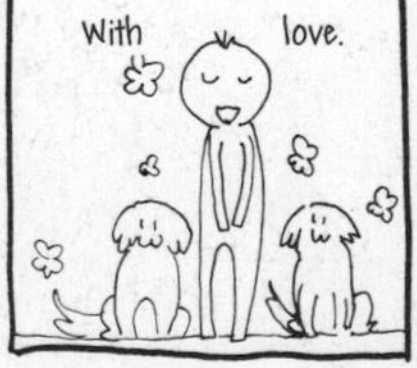
With love.

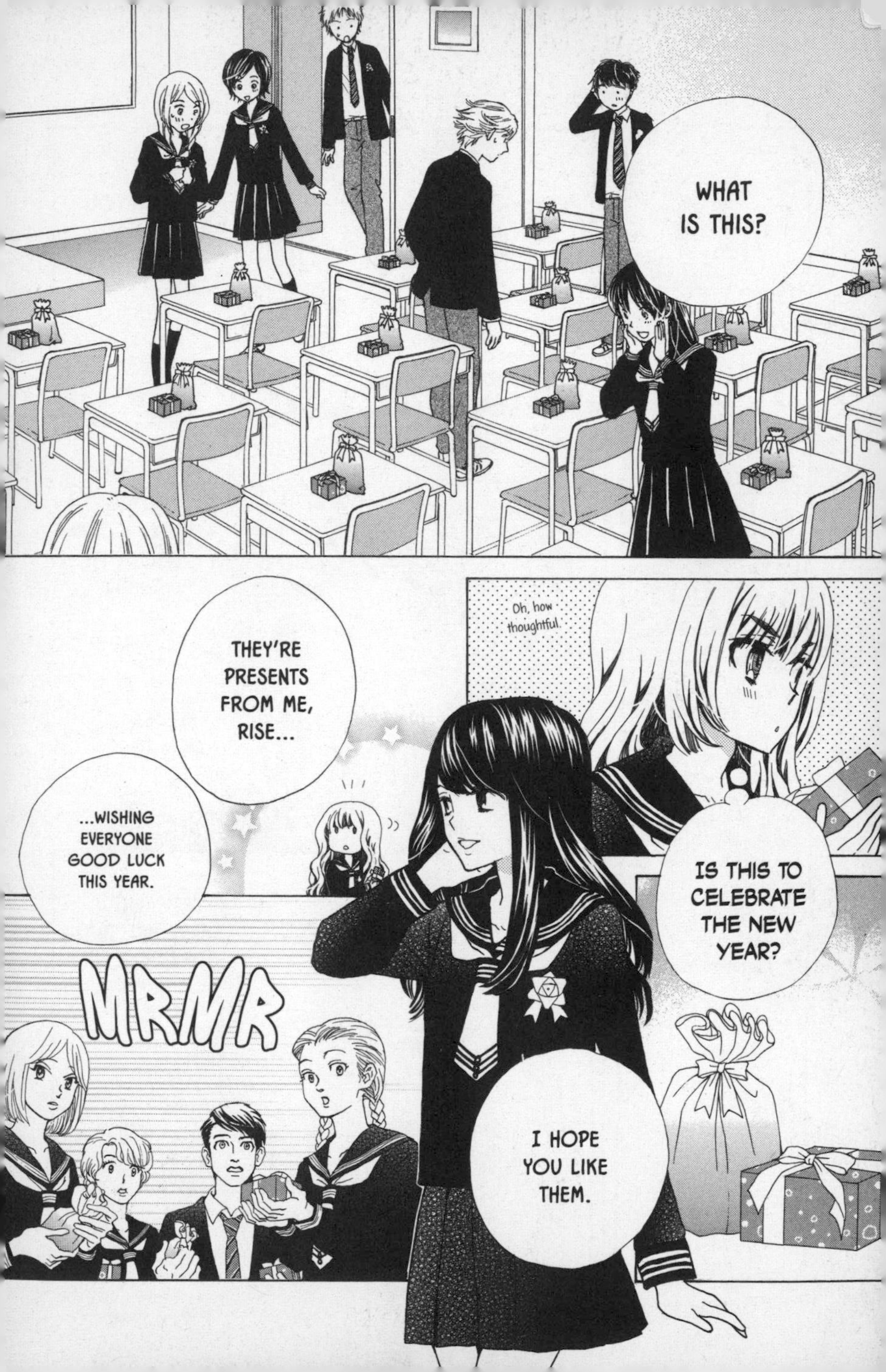
WHAT IS THIS?
Oh, how thoughtful.
IS THIS TO CELEBRATE THE NEW YEAR?
THEY'RE PRESENTS FROM ME, RISE...
...WISHING EVERYONE GOOD LUCK THIS YEAR.
I HOPE YOU LIKE THEM.
MRMR

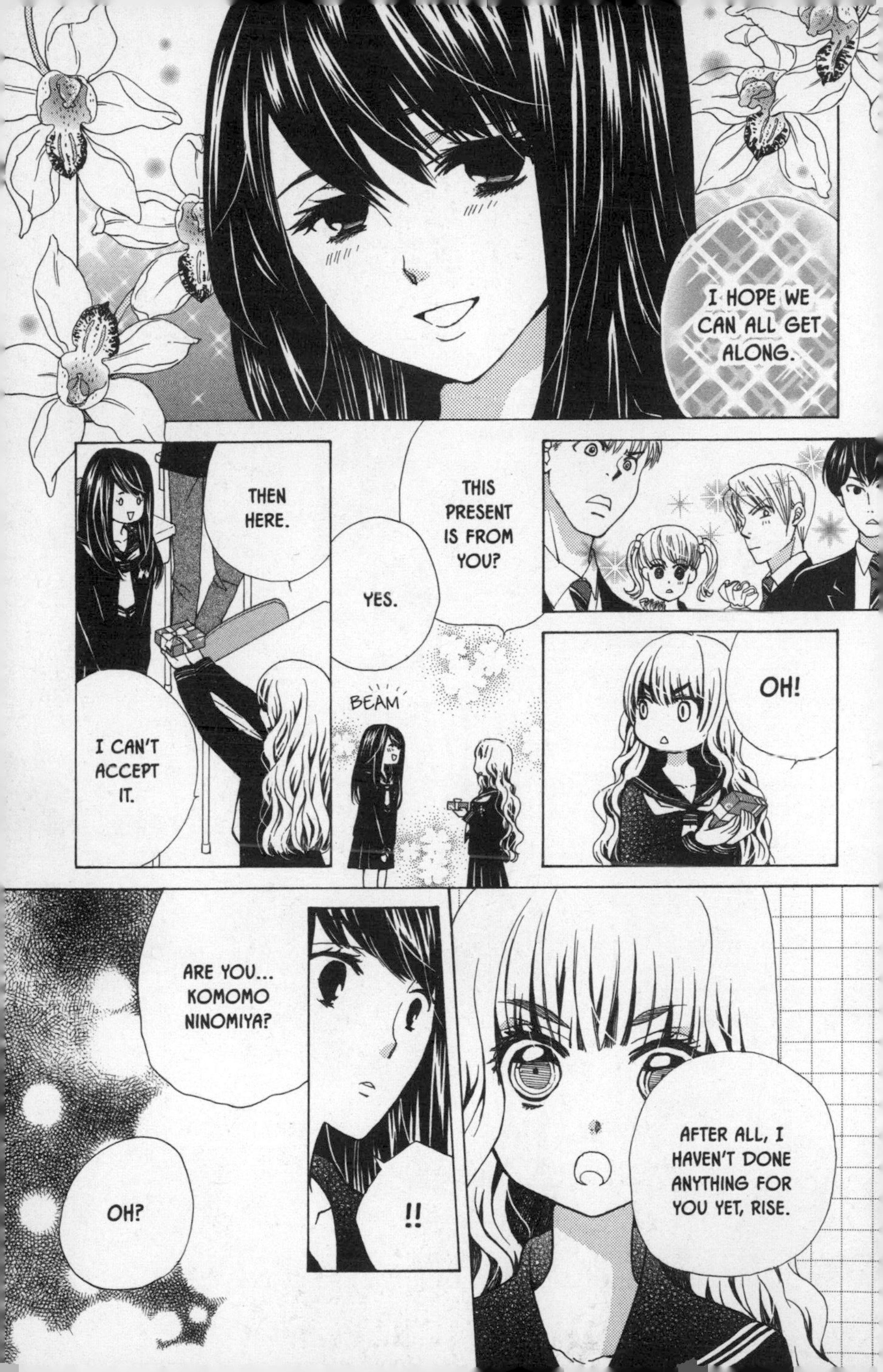
I HOPE WE CAN ALL GET ALONG.
OH!
THIS PRESENT IS FROM YOU?
YES.
BEAM
THEN HERE.
I CAN'T ACCEPT IT.
AFTER ALL, I HAVEN'T DONE ANYTHING FOR YOU YET, RISE.
!!
ARE YOU... KOMOMO NINOMIYA?
OH?

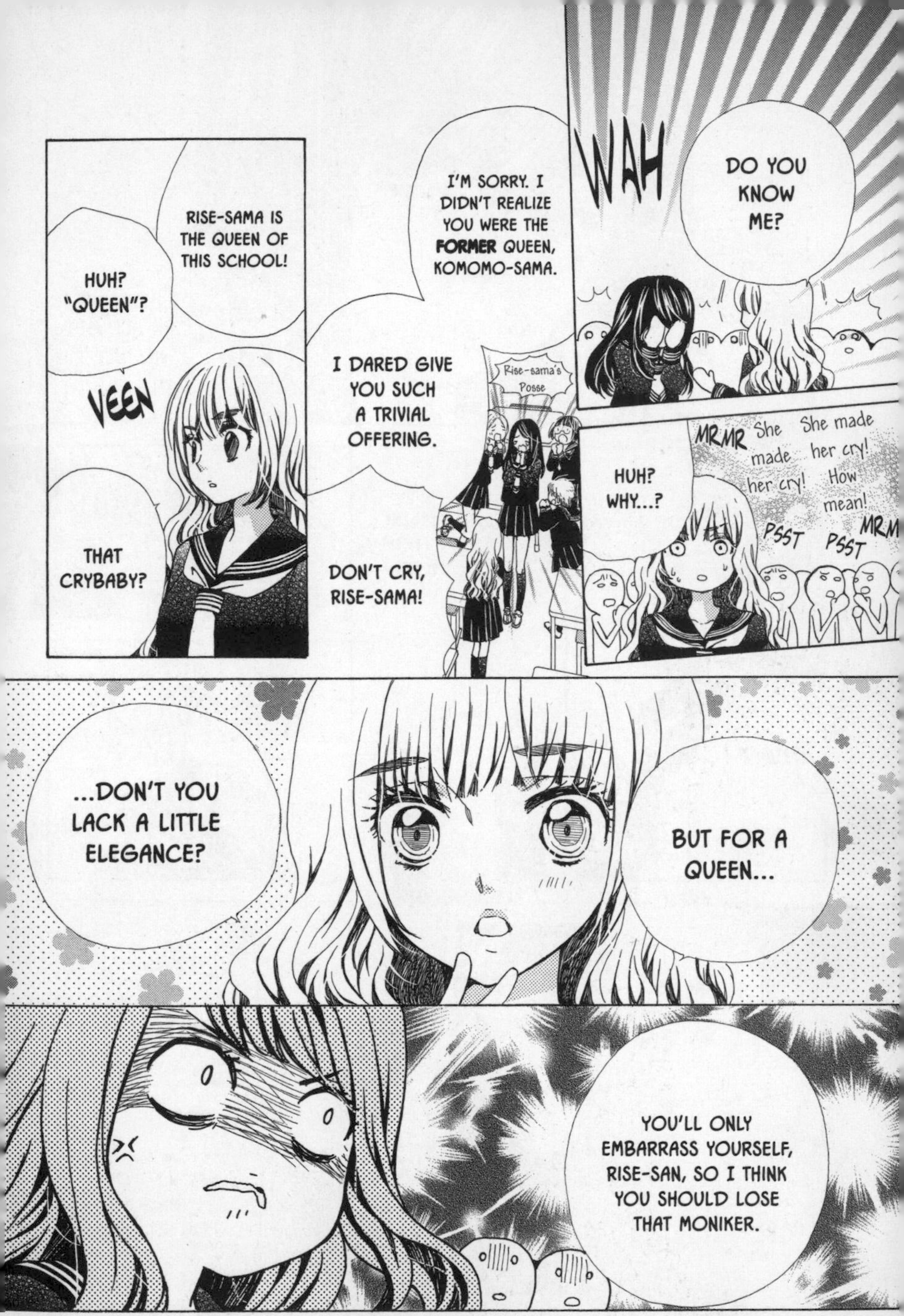
WAH
DO YOU KNOW ME?
MRM
She made her cry! How mean!
She made her cry!
MRMR
HUH? WHY...?
PSST
PSST
I'M SORRY. I DIDN'T REALIZE YOU WERE THE **FORMER** QUEEN, KOMOMO-SAMA.
I DARED GIVE YOU SUCH A TRIVIAL OFFERING.
Rise-sama's Posse
DON'T CRY, RISE-SAMA!
RISE-SAMA IS THE QUEEN OF THIS SCHOOL!
HUH? "QUEEN"?
VEEN
THAT CRYBABY?
BUT FOR A QUEEN...
...DON'T YOU LACK A LITTLE ELEGANCE?
YOU'LL ONLY EMBARRASS YOURSELF, RISE-SAN, SO I THINK YOU SHOULD LOSE THAT MONIKER.

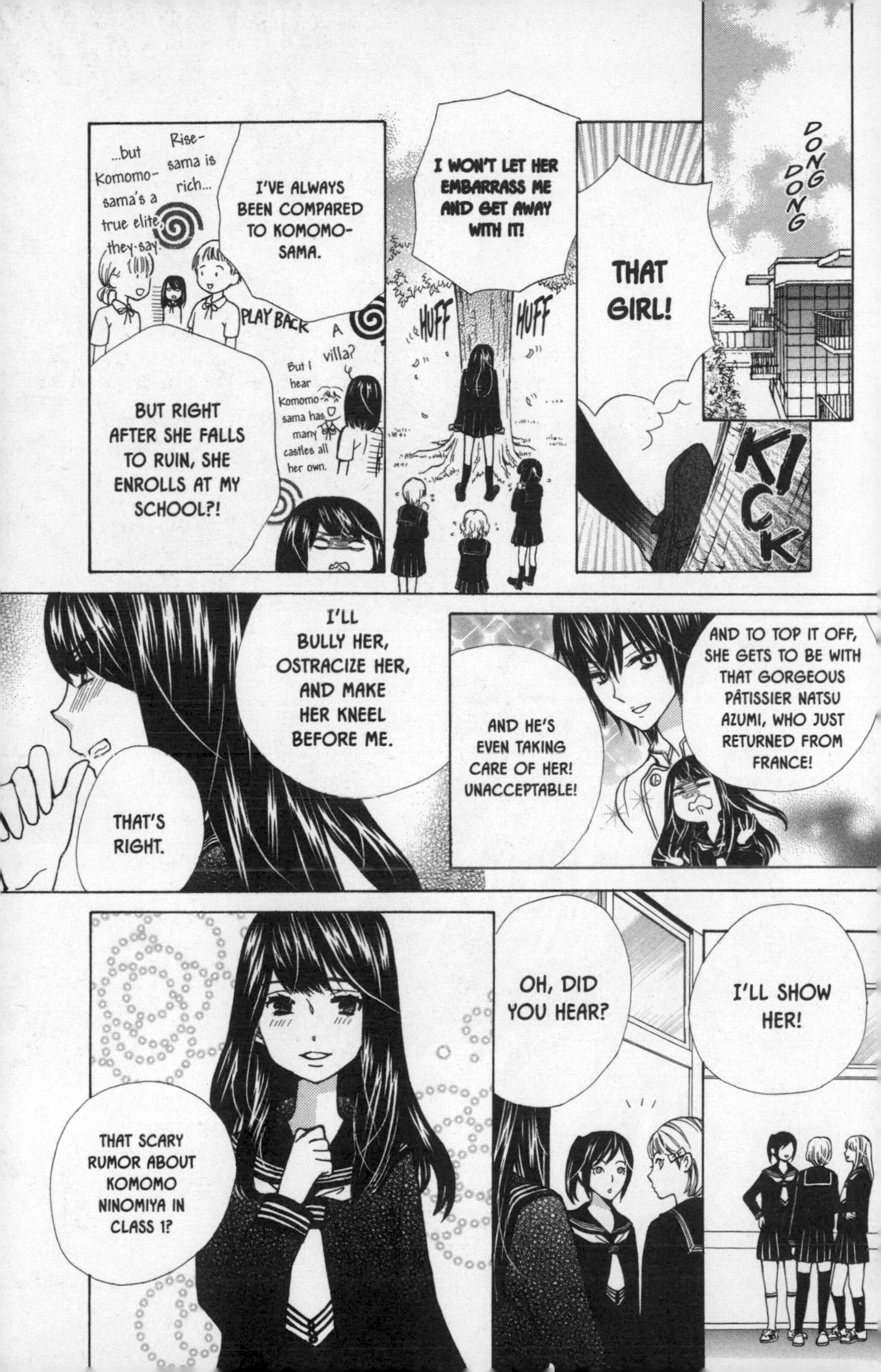
DONG DONG
THAT GIRL!
KICK
I WON'T LET HER EMBARRASS ME AND GET AWAY WITH IT!
HUFF
HUFF
I'VE ALWAYS BEEN COMPARED TO KOMOMO-SAMA.
Rise-sama is rich...
...but Komomo-sama's a true elite, they say.
PLAY BACK
A villa?
But I hear Komomo-sama has many castles all her own.
BUT RIGHT AFTER SHE FALLS TO RUIN, SHE ENROLLS AT MY SCHOOL?!
AND TO TOP IT OFF, SHE GETS TO BE WITH THAT GORGEOUS PÂTISSIER NATSU AZUMI, WHO JUST RETURNED FROM FRANCE!
AND HE'S EVEN TAKING CARE OF HER! UNACCEPTABLE!
I'LL BULLY HER, OSTRACIZE HER, AND MAKE HER KNEEL BEFORE ME.
THAT'S RIGHT.
I'LL SHOW HER!
OH, DID YOU HEAR?
THAT SCARY RUMOR ABOUT KOMOMO NINOMIYA IN CLASS 1?

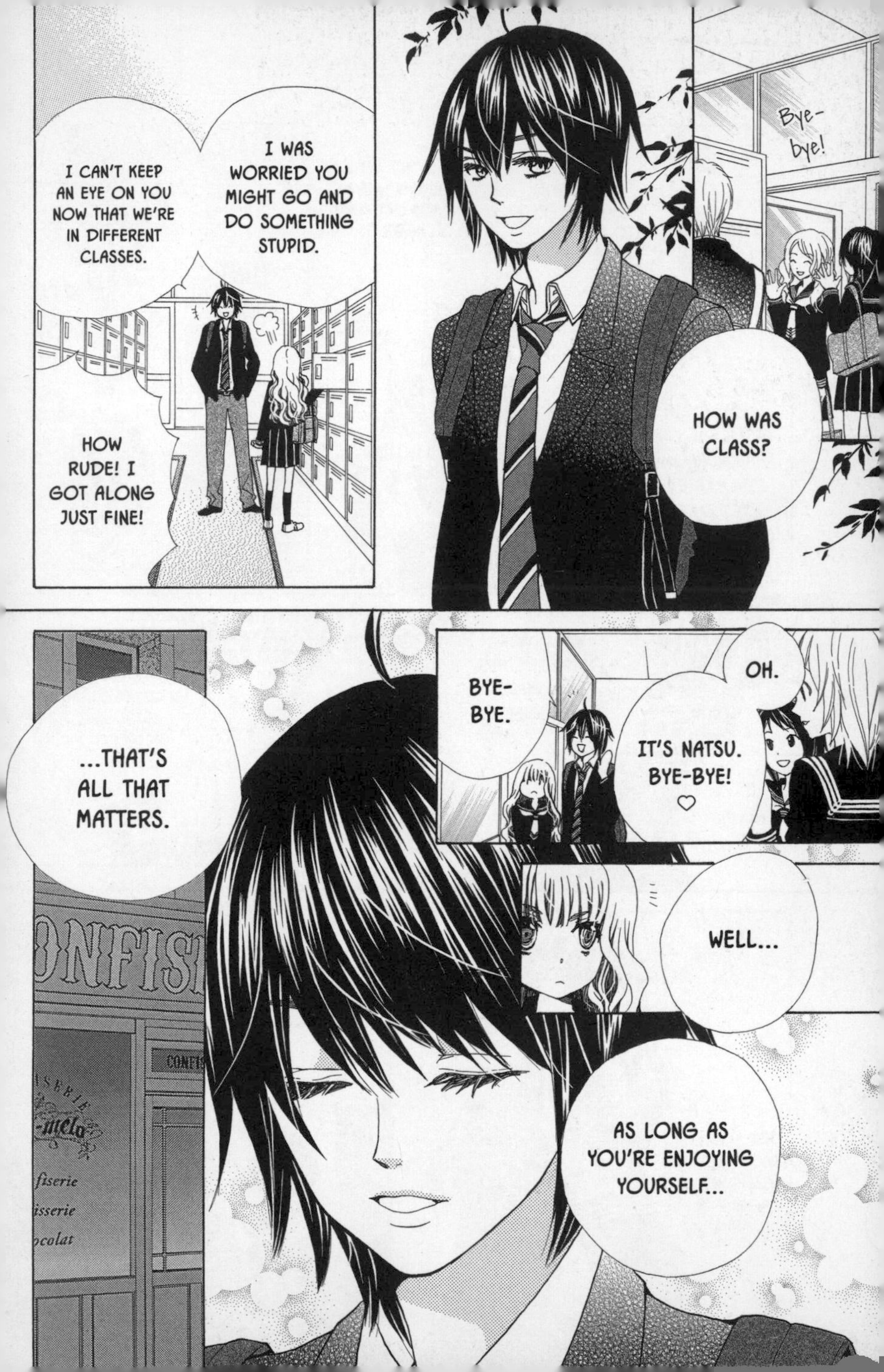
Bye-bye!
HOW WAS CLASS?
I WAS WORRIED YOU MIGHT GO AND DO SOMETHING STUPID.
I CAN'T KEEP AN EYE ON YOU NOW THAT WE'RE IN DIFFERENT CLASSES.
HOW RUDE! I GOT ALONG JUST FINE!
OH.
IT'S NATSU. BYE-BYE! ♡
BYE-BYE.
WELL...
AS LONG AS YOU'RE ENJOYING YOURSELF...
...THAT'S ALL THAT MATTERS.

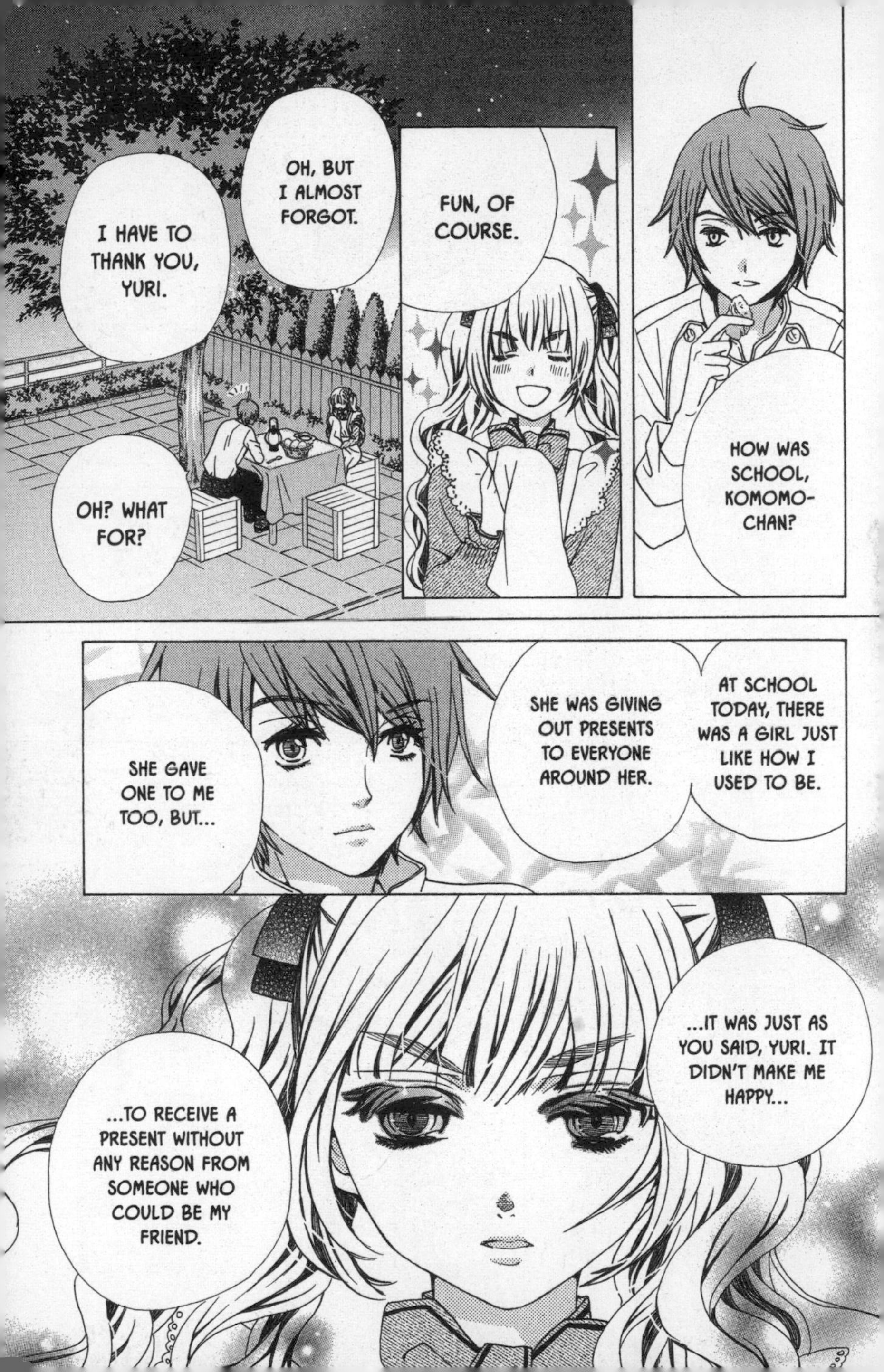
HOW WAS SCHOOL, KOMOMO-CHAN?
FUN, OF COURSE.
OH, BUT I ALMOST FORGOT.
I HAVE TO THANK YOU, YURI.
OH? WHAT FOR?
AT SCHOOL TODAY, THERE WAS A GIRL JUST LIKE HOW I USED TO BE.
SHE WAS GIVING OUT PRESENTS TO EVERYONE AROUND HER.
SHE GAVE ONE TO ME TOO, BUT...
...IT WAS JUST AS YOU SAID, YURI. IT DIDN'T MAKE ME HAPPY...
...TO RECEIVE A PRESENT WITHOUT ANY REASON FROM SOMEONE WHO COULD BE MY FRIEND.

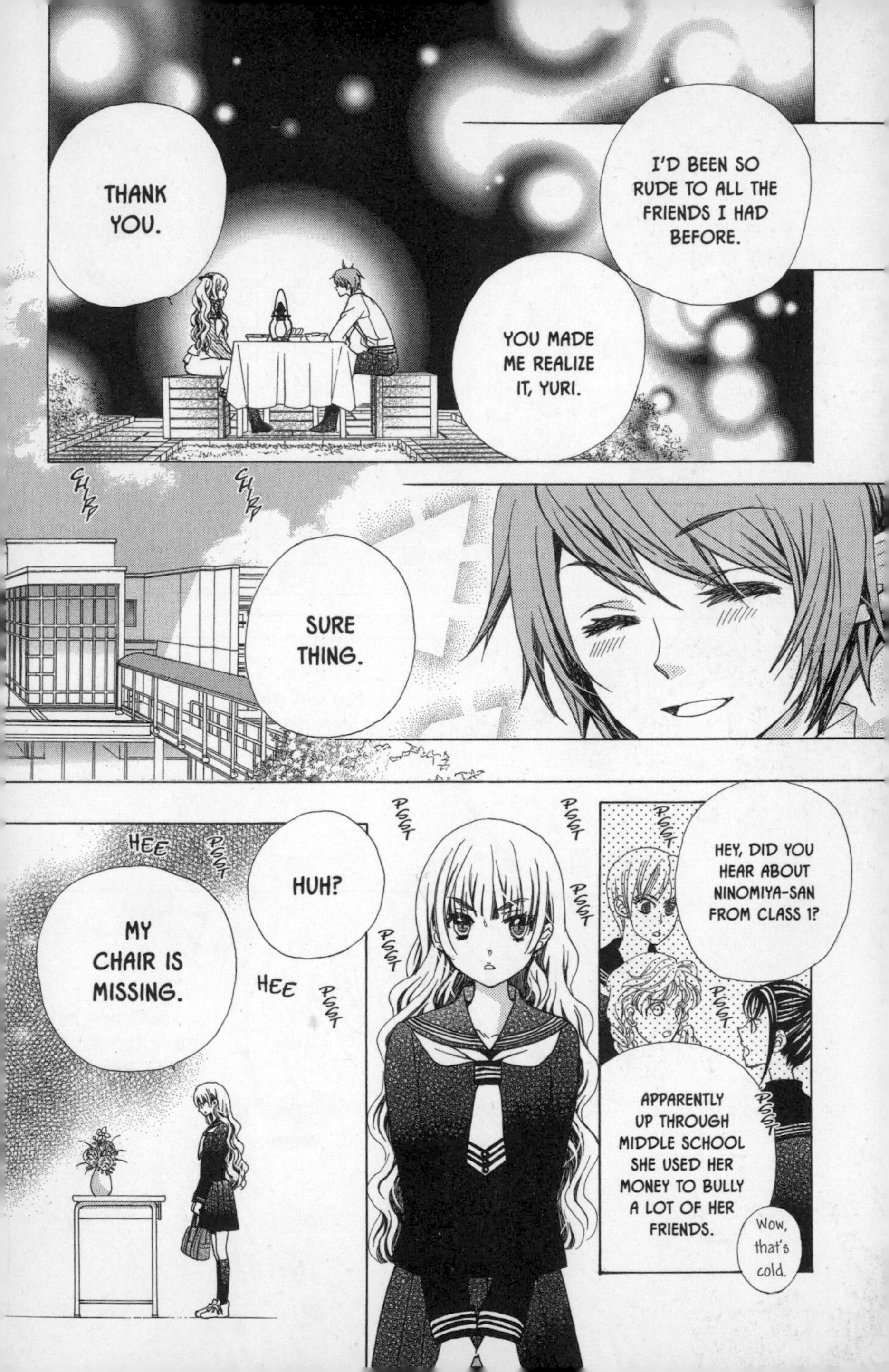

I'D BEEN SO RUDE TO ALL THE FRIENDS I HAD BEFORE.
YOU MADE ME REALIZE IT, YURI.
THANK YOU.
SURE THING.
CHIRP
CHIRP
HEY, DID YOU HEAR ABOUT NINOMIYA-SAN FROM CLASS 1?
APPARENTLY UP THROUGH MIDDLE SCHOOL SHE USED HER MONEY TO BULLY A LOT OF HER FRIENDS.
Wow, that's cold.
HUH?
MY CHAIR IS MISSING.
HEE
HEE

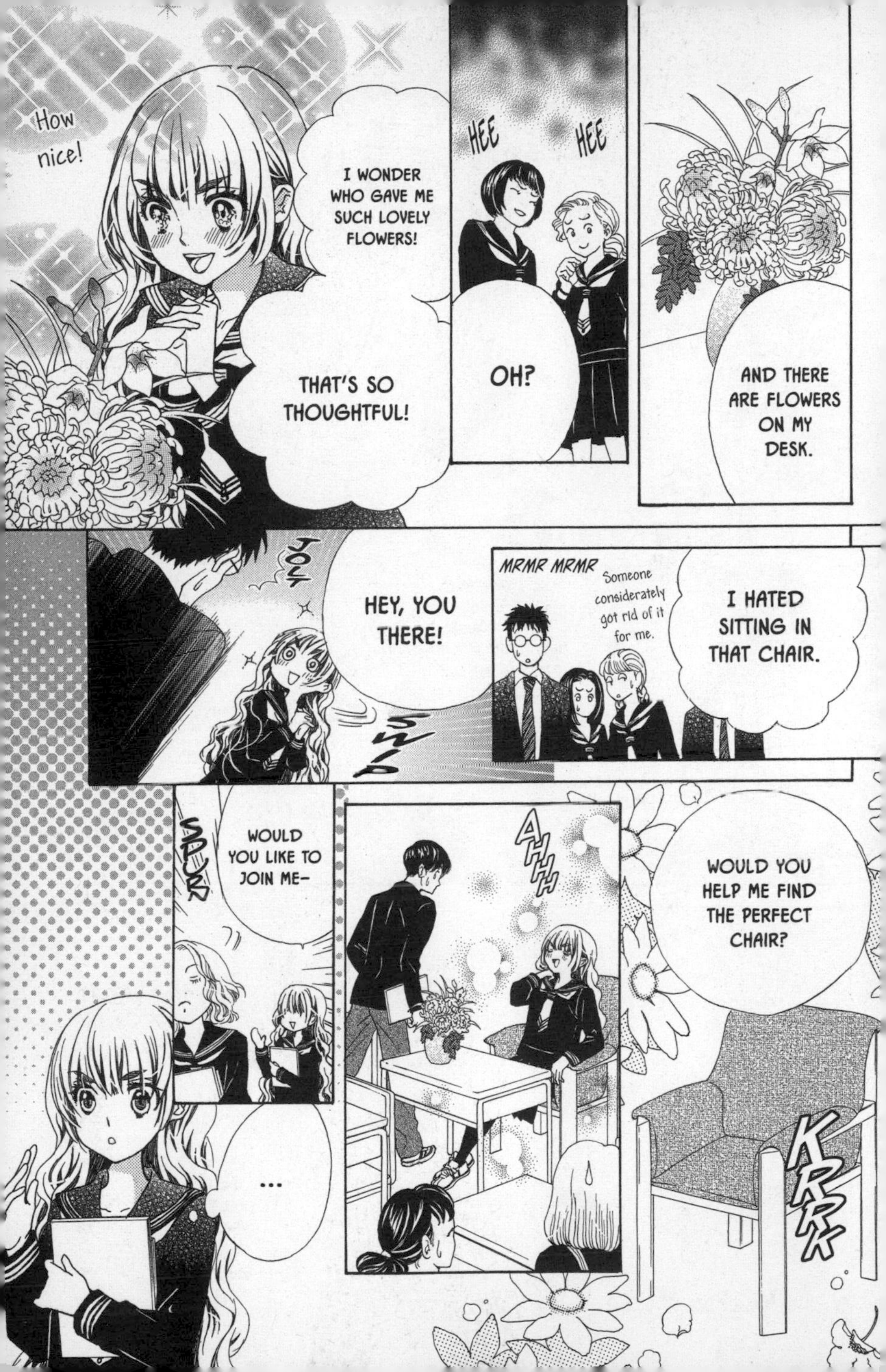
AND THERE ARE FLOWERS ON MY DESK.
HEE
HEE
OH?
I WONDER WHO GAVE ME SUCH LOVELY FLOWERS!
How nice!
THAT'S SO THOUGHTFUL!
I HATED SITTING IN THAT CHAIR.
MRMR MRMR
Someone considerately got rid of it for me.
JOLT
HEY, YOU THERE!
SWIP
WOULD YOU HELP ME FIND THE PERFECT CHAIR?
KRRK
AHHH
SPURN
WOULD YOU LIKE TO JOIN ME–
...

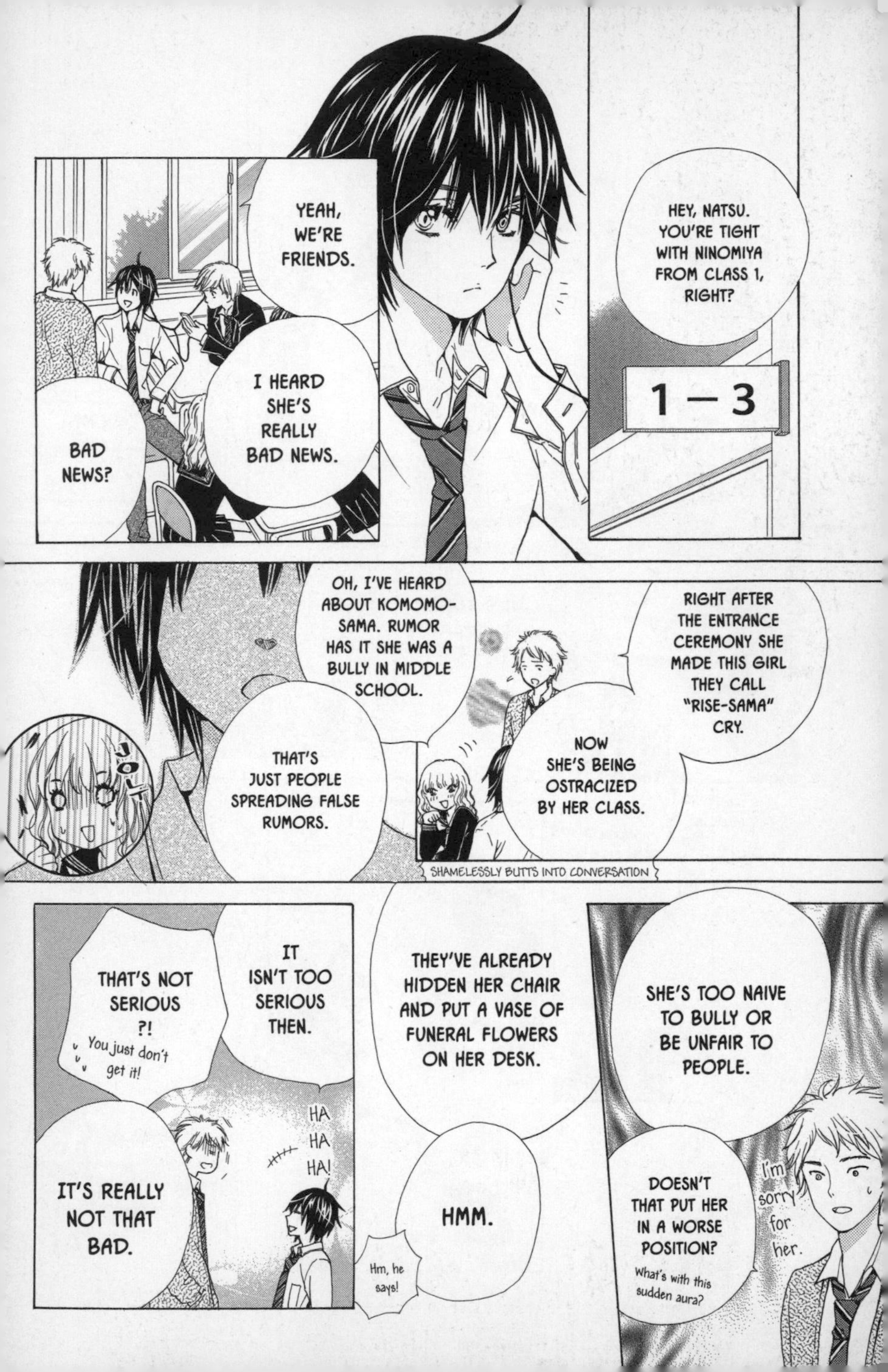
HEY, NATSU. YOU'RE TIGHT WITH NINOMIYA FROM CLASS 1, RIGHT?
1 — 3
YEAH, WE'RE FRIENDS.
I HEARD SHE'S REALLY BAD NEWS.
BAD NEWS?
OH, I'VE HEARD ABOUT KOMOMO-SAMA. RUMOR HAS IT SHE WAS A BULLY IN MIDDLE SCHOOL.
RIGHT AFTER THE ENTRANCE CEREMONY SHE MADE THIS GIRL THEY CALL "RISE-SAMA" CRY.
NOW SHE'S BEING OSTRACIZED BY HER CLASS.
SHAMELESSLY BUTTS INTO CONVERSATION
JOLT
THAT'S JUST PEOPLE SPREADING FALSE RUMORS.
SHE'S TOO NAIVE TO BULLY OR BE UNFAIR TO PEOPLE.
DOESN'T THAT PUT HER IN A WORSE POSITION?
I'm sorry for her.
What's with this sudden aura?
THEY'VE ALREADY HIDDEN HER CHAIR AND PUT A VASE OF FUNERAL FLOWERS ON HER DESK.
HMM.
Hm, he says!
IT ISN'T TOO SERIOUS THEN.
THAT'S NOT SERIOUS?!
You just don't get it!
HA HA HA!
IT'S REALLY NOT THAT BAD.

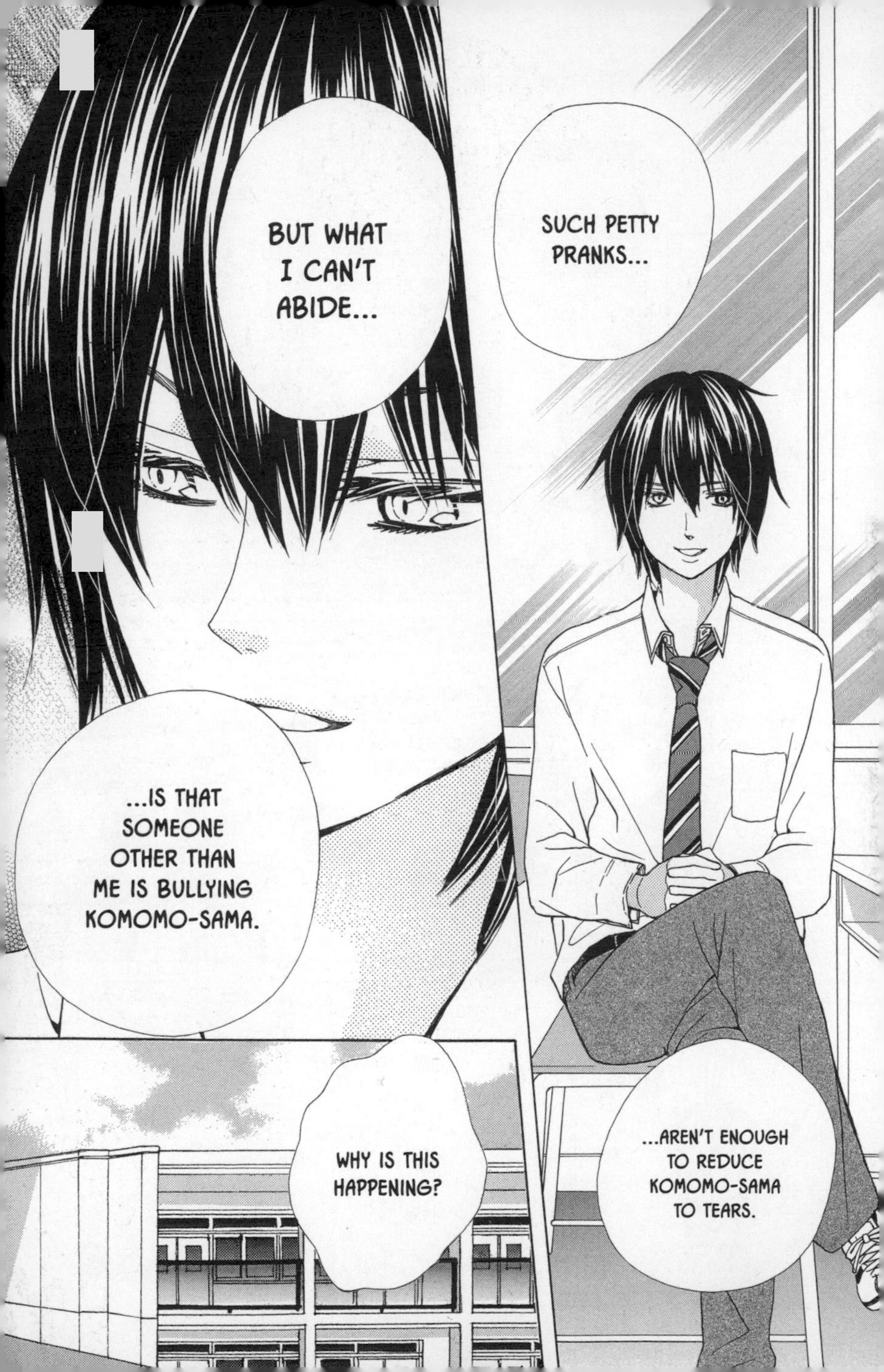
SUCH PETTY PRANKS...
...AREN'T ENOUGH TO REDUCE KOMOMO-SAMA TO TEARS.
BUT WHAT I CAN'T ABIDE...
...IS THAT SOMEONE OTHER THAN ME IS BULLYING KOMOMO-SAMA.
WHY IS THIS HAPPENING?

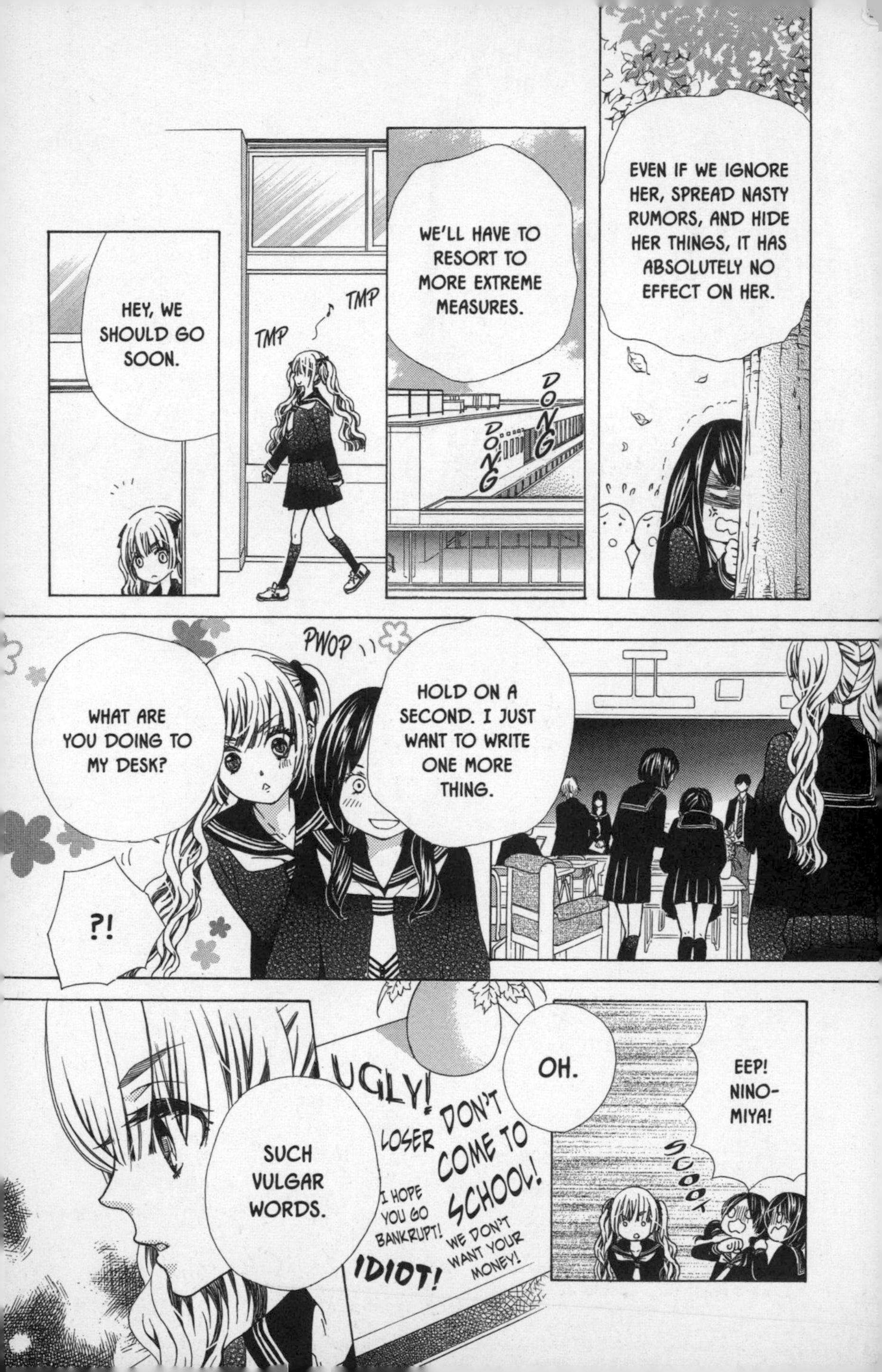
EVEN IF WE IGNORE HER, SPREAD NASTY RUMORS, AND HIDE HER THINGS, IT HAS ABSOLUTELY NO EFFECT ON HER.
WE'LL HAVE TO RESORT TO MORE EXTREME MEASURES.
DONG
DONG
TMP
TMP
HEY, WE SHOULD GO SOON.
PWOP
HOLD ON A SECOND. I JUST WANT TO WRITE ONE MORE THING.
WHAT ARE YOU DOING TO MY DESK?
?!
EEP! NINO-MIYA!
SCOOT
OH.
SUCH VULGAR WORDS.
UGLY!
LOSER
DON'T COME TO SCHOOL!
I HOPE YOU GO BANKRUPT!
WE DON'T WANT YOUR MONEY!
IDIOT!

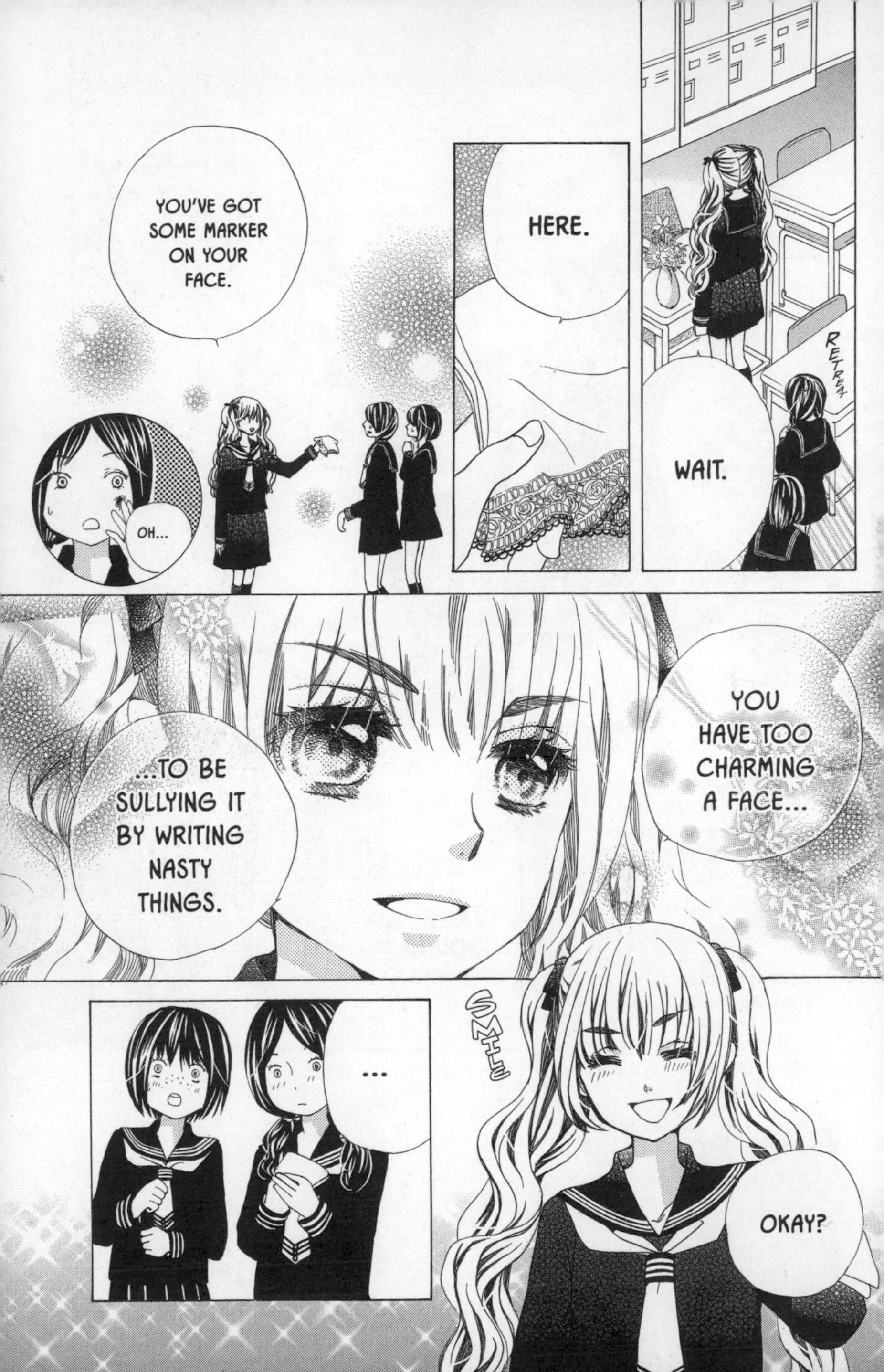
RETREAT
WAIT.
HERE.
YOU'VE GOT SOME MARKER ON YOUR FACE.
OH...
YOU HAVE TOO CHARMING A FACE...
...TO BE SULLYING IT BY WRITING NASTY THINGS.
SMILE
OKAY?
...

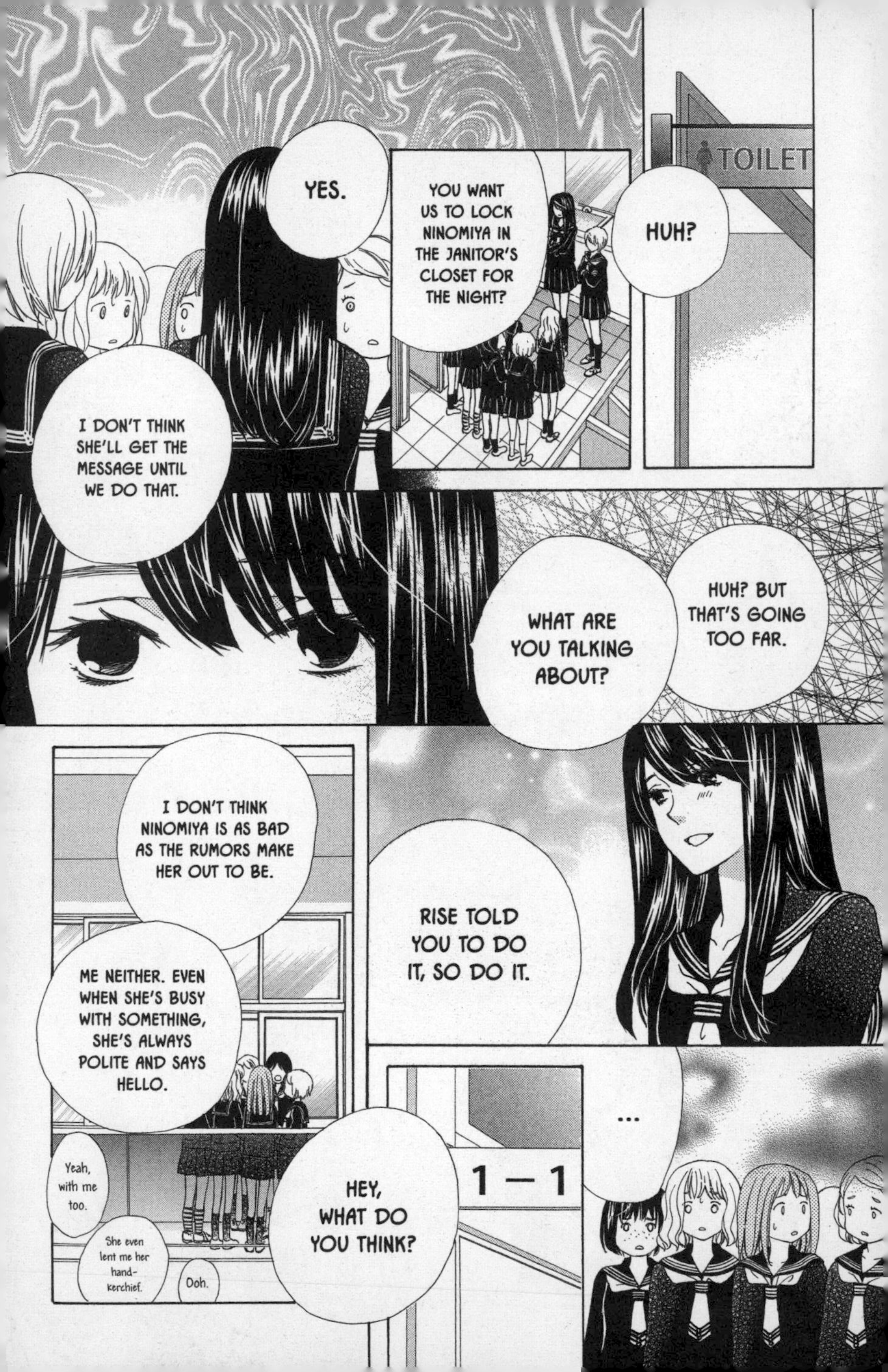
HUH?
YOU WANT US TO LOCK NINOMIYA IN THE JANITOR'S CLOSET FOR THE NIGHT?
TOILET
YES.
I DON'T THINK SHE'LL GET THE MESSAGE UNTIL WE DO THAT.
HUH? BUT THAT'S GOING TOO FAR.
WHAT ARE YOU TALKING ABOUT?
RISE TOLD YOU TO DO IT, SO DO IT.
...
1 — 1
HEY, WHAT DO YOU THINK?
I DON'T THINK NINOMIYA IS AS BAD AS THE RUMORS MAKE HER OUT TO BE.
ME NEITHER. EVEN WHEN SHE'S BUSY WITH SOMETHING, SHE'S ALWAYS POLITE AND SAYS HELLO.
Yeah, with me too.
She even lent me her hand-kerchief.
Ooh.

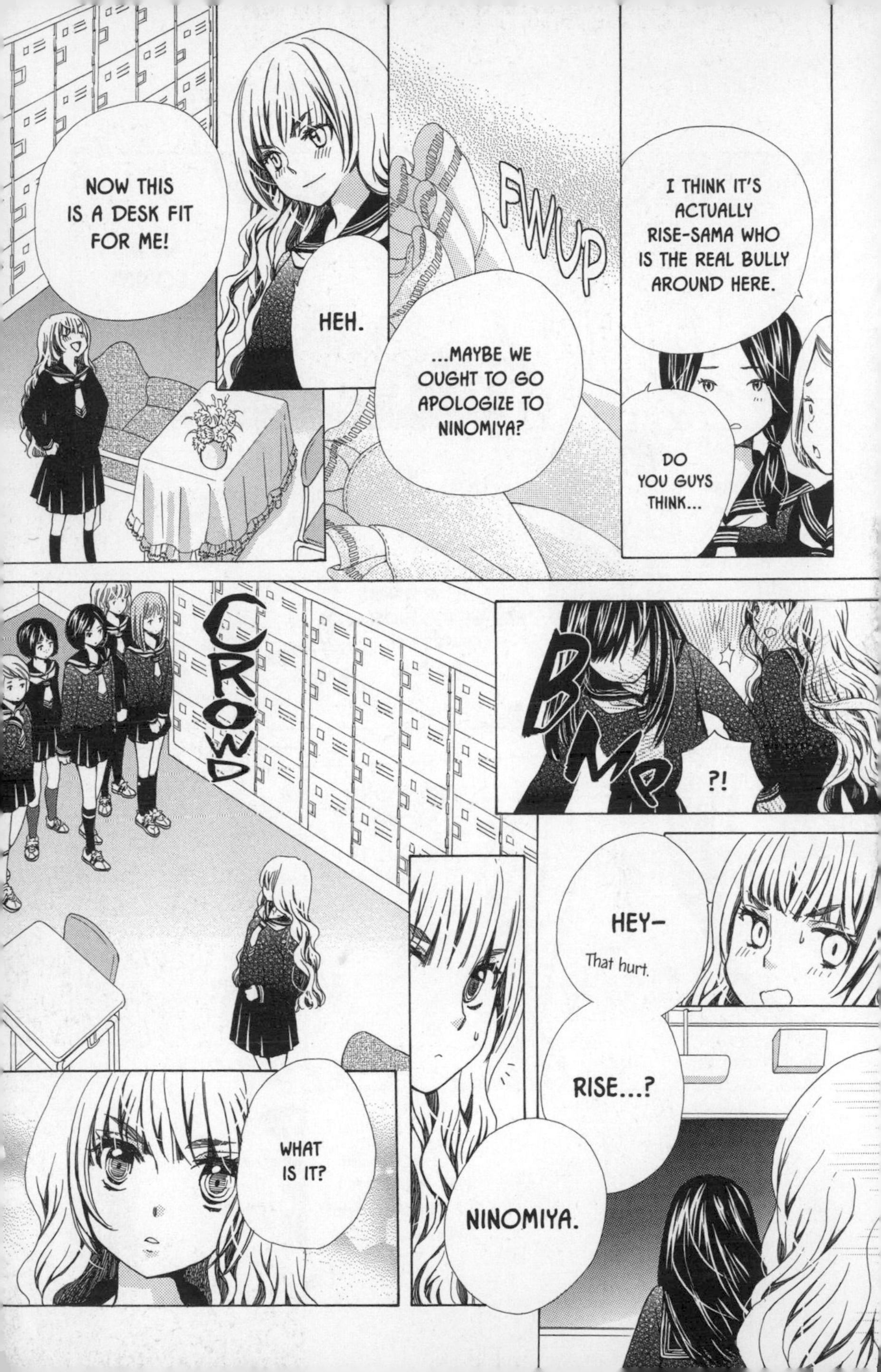

I THINK IT'S ACTUALLY RISE-SAMA WHO IS THE REAL BULLY AROUND HERE.
DO YOU GUYS THINK...
FWUP
...MAYBE WE OUGHT TO GO APOLOGIZE TO NINOMIYA?
NOW THIS IS A DESK FIT FOR ME!
HEH.
BUMP
?!
CROWD
HEY—
That hurt.
RISE...?
NINOMIYA.
WHAT IS IT?

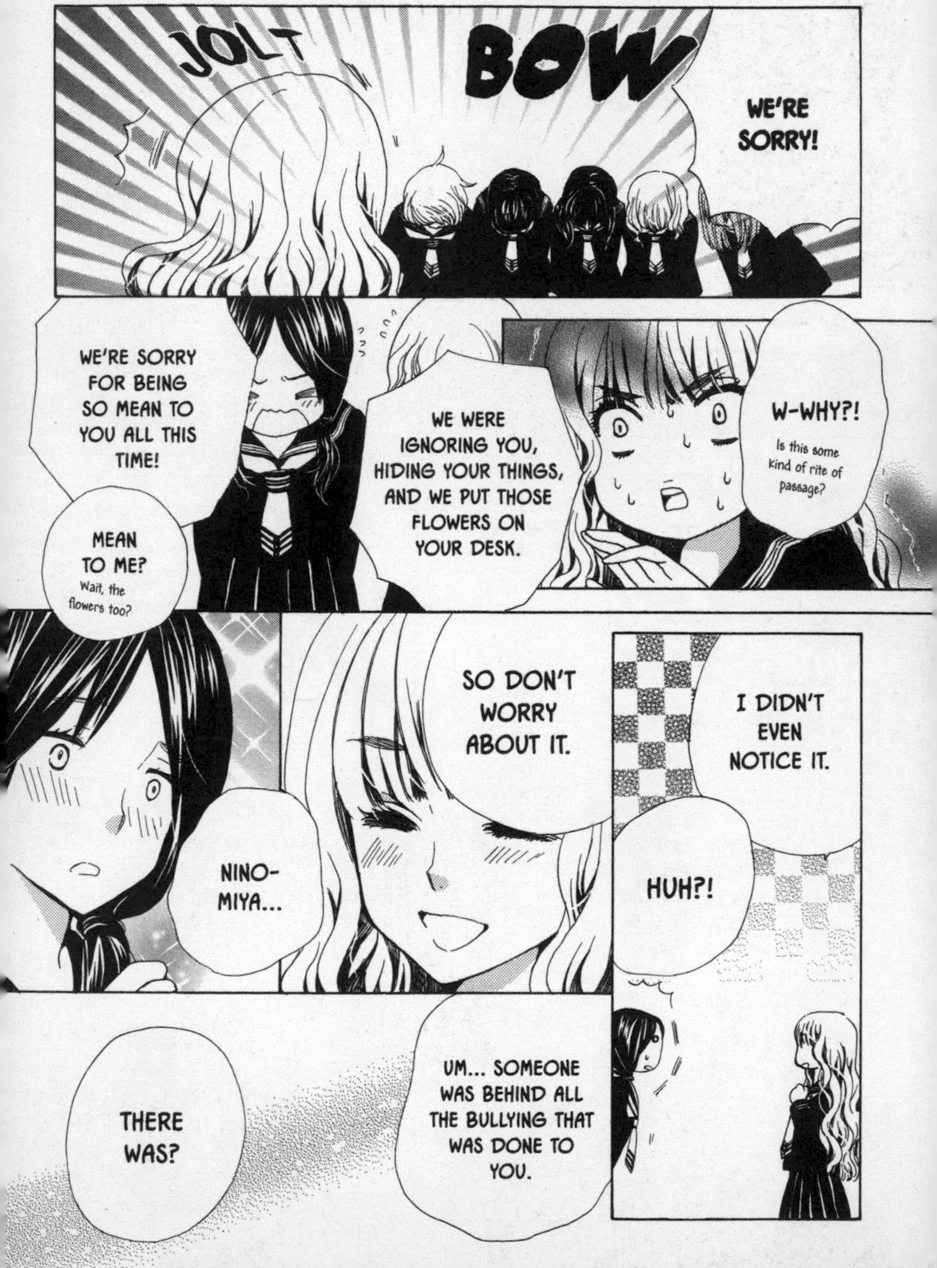
BOW
WE'RE SORRY!
JOLT
W-WHY?!
Is this some kind of rite of passage?
WE WERE IGNORING YOU, HIDING YOUR THINGS, AND WE PUT THOSE FLOWERS ON YOUR DESK.
WE'RE SORRY FOR BEING SO MEAN TO YOU ALL THIS TIME!
MEAN TO ME?
Wait, the flowers too?
I DIDN'T EVEN NOTICE IT.
HUH?!
SO DON'T WORRY ABOUT IT.
NINO-MIYA...
UM... SOMEONE WAS BEHIND ALL THE BULLYING THAT WAS DONE TO YOU.
THERE WAS?

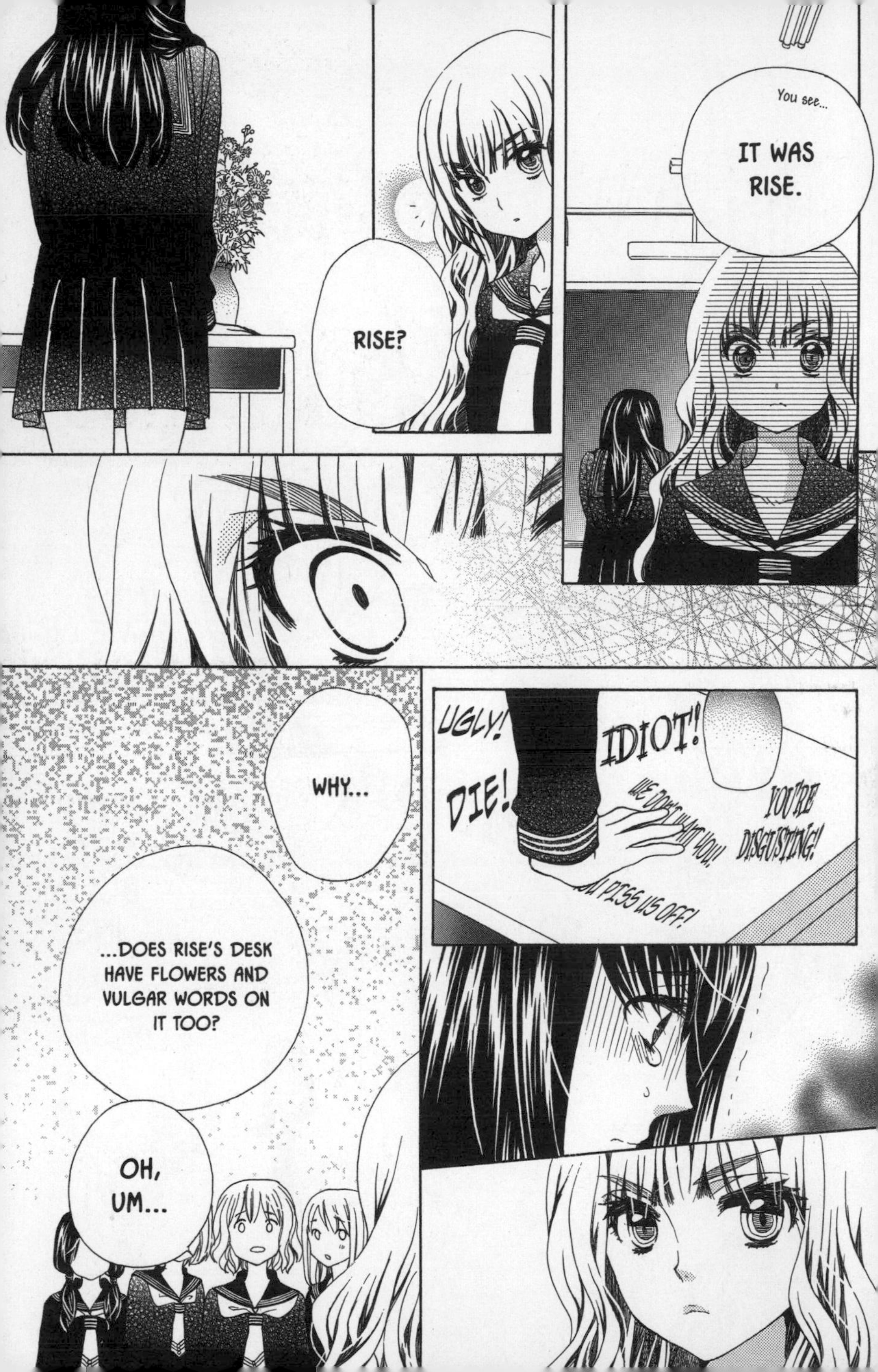
You see...
IT WAS RISE.
RISE?
UGLY!
IDIOT!
DIE!
YOU'RE DISGUSTING!
U PISS US OFF!
WHY...
...DOES RISE'S DESK HAVE FLOWERS AND VULGAR WORDS ON IT TOO?
OH, UM...

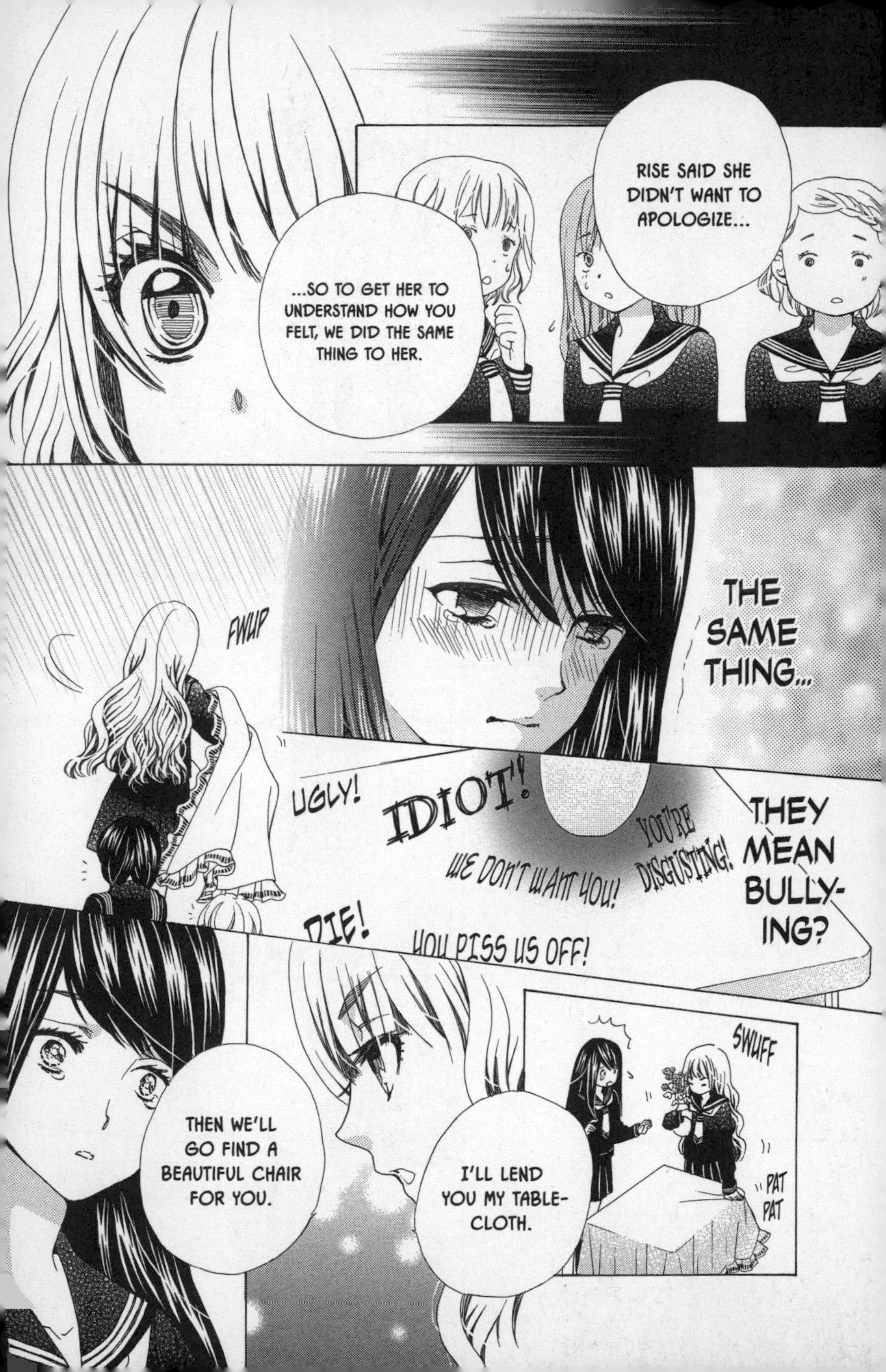
RISE SAID SHE DIDN'T WANT TO APOLOGIZE...
...SO TO GET HER TO UNDERSTAND HOW YOU FELT, WE DID THE SAME THING TO HER.
THE SAME THING...
FWUP
THEY MEAN BULLY-ING?
YOU'RE DISGUSTING!
IDIOT!
UGLY!
WE DON'T WANT YOU!
YOU PISS US OFF!
DIE!
SWUFF
PAT PAT
I'LL LEND YOU MY TABLE-CLOTH.
THEN WE'LL GO FIND A BEAUTIFUL CHAIR FOR YOU.

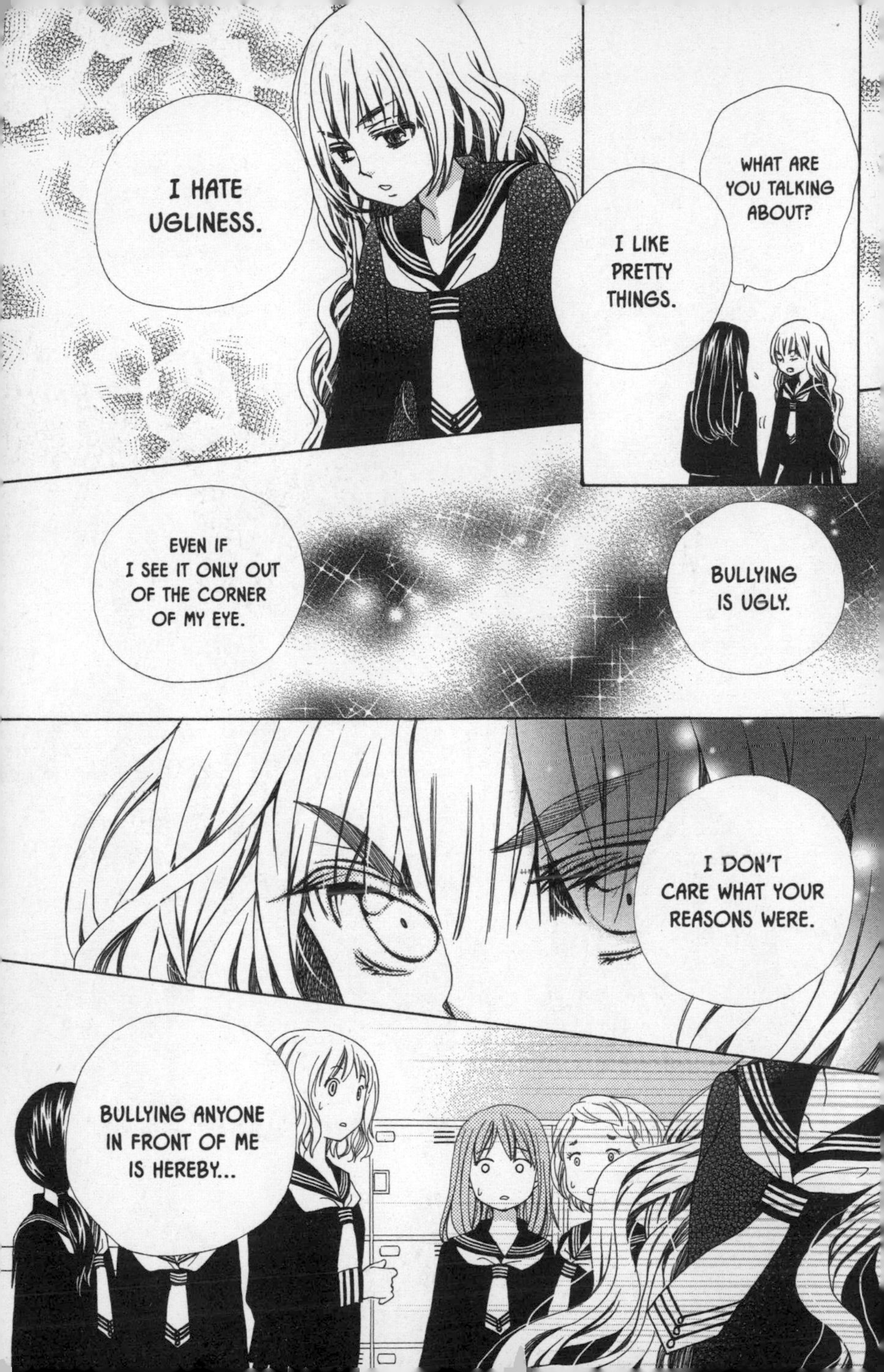
WHAT ARE YOU TALKING ABOUT?
I LIKE PRETTY THINGS.
I HATE UGLINESS.
BULLYING IS UGLY.
EVEN IF I SEE IT ONLY OUT OF THE CORNER OF MY EYE.
I DON'T CARE WHAT YOUR REASONS WERE.
BULLYING ANYONE IN FRONT OF ME IS HEREBY...

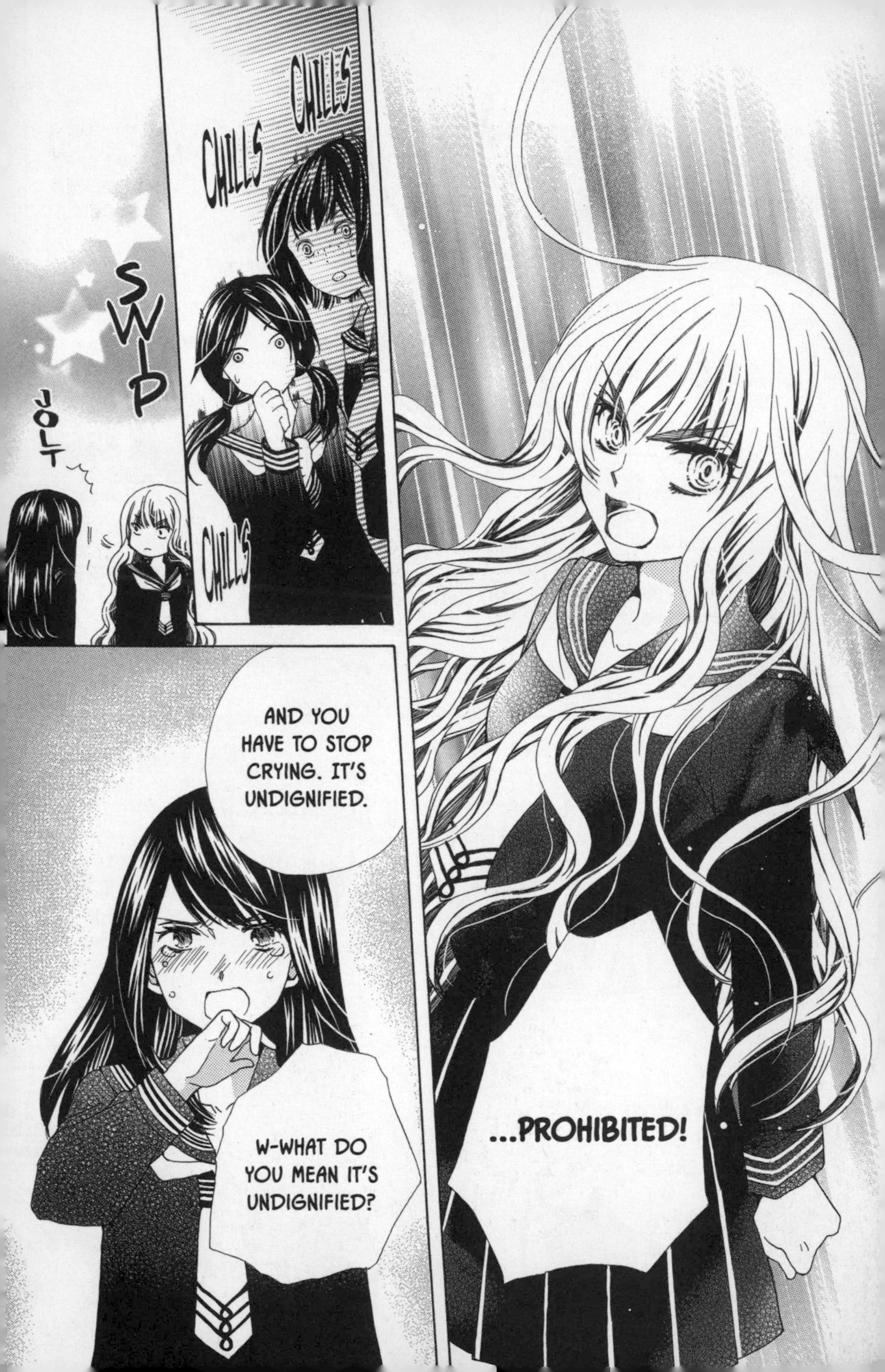
...PROHIBITED!
CHILLS
CHILLS
SWIP
JOLT
CHILLS
AND YOU HAVE TO STOP CRYING. IT'S UNDIGNIFIED.
W-WHAT DO YOU MEAN IT'S UNDIGNIFIED?

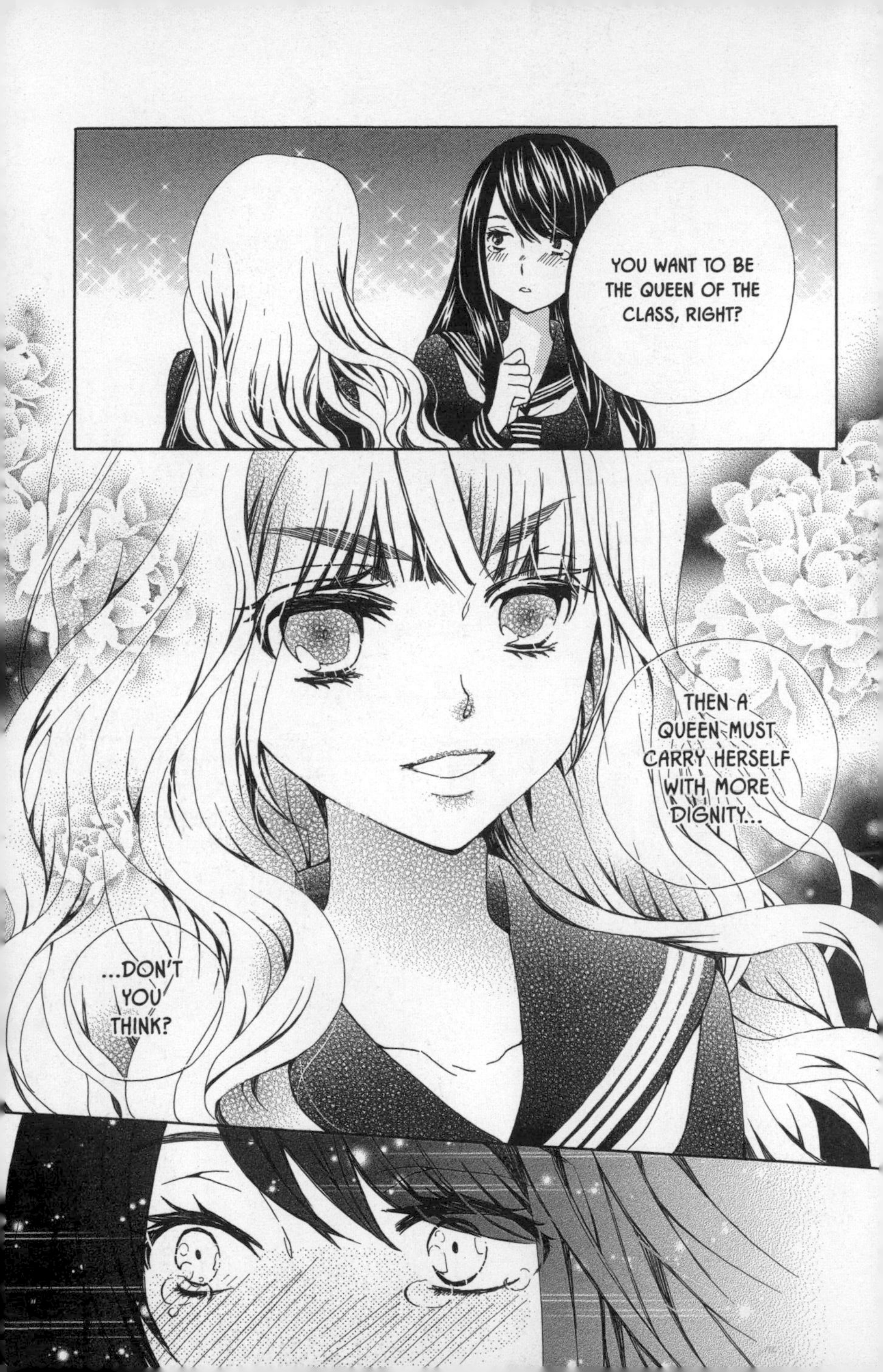
YOU WANT TO BE THE QUEEN OF THE CLASS, RIGHT?
THEN A QUEEN MUST CARRY HERSELF WITH MORE DIGNITY...
...DON'T YOU THINK?

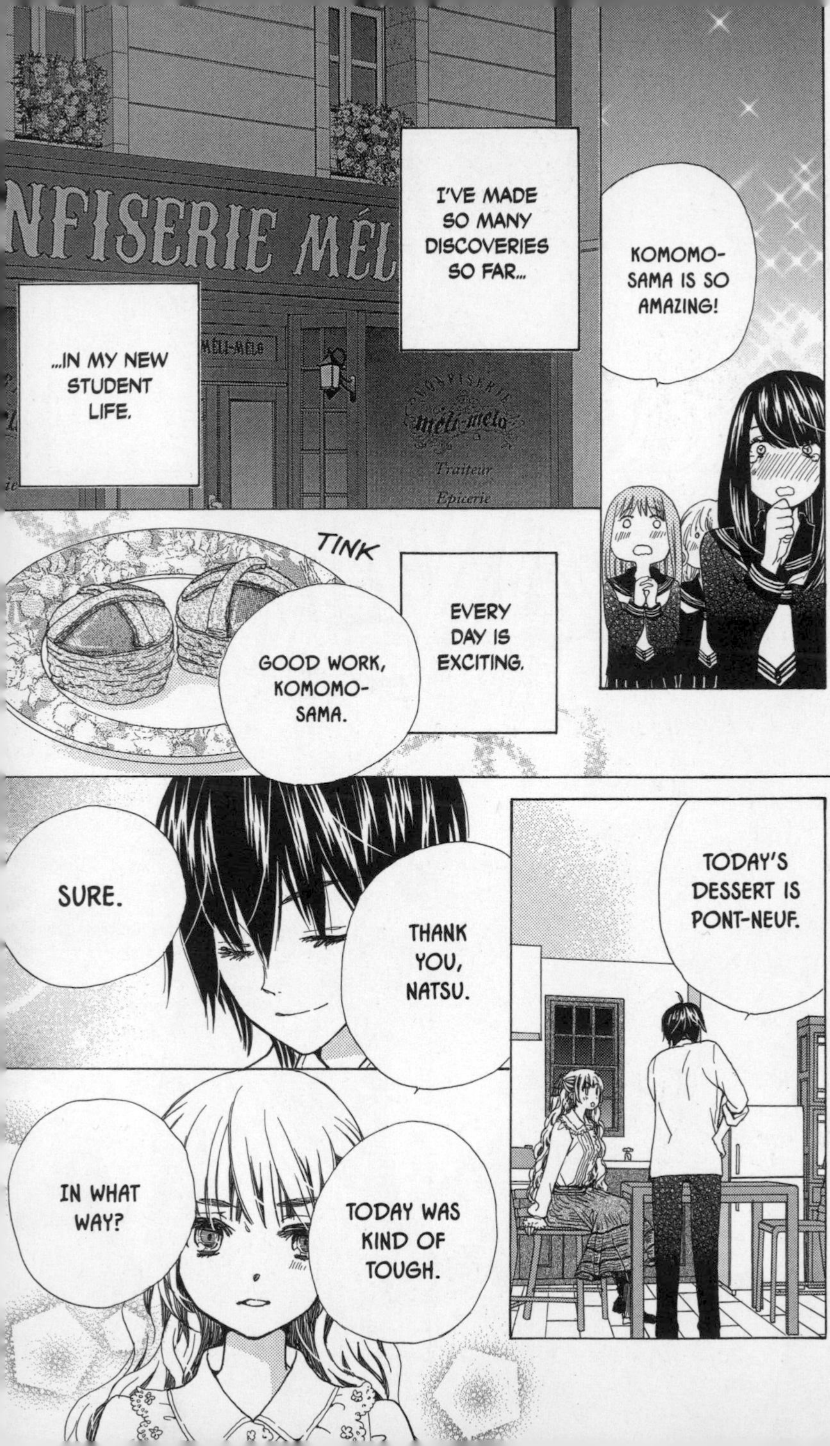
KOMOMO-SAMA IS SO AMAZING!
I'VE MADE SO MANY DISCOVERIES SO FAR...
...IN MY NEW STUDENT LIFE.
NFISERIE MÉL
MÉLI-MÉLO
Traiteur
Epicerie
EVERY DAY IS EXCITING.
TINK
GOOD WORK, KOMOMO-SAMA.
TODAY'S DESSERT IS PONT-NEUF.
THANK YOU, NATSU.
SURE.
TODAY WAS KIND OF TOUGH.
IN WHAT WAY?

*PONT-NEUF = A CUSTARD AND CHOUX PASTRY PIE WITH JAM AND ICING SUGAR CRISS-CROSSED ON TOP.

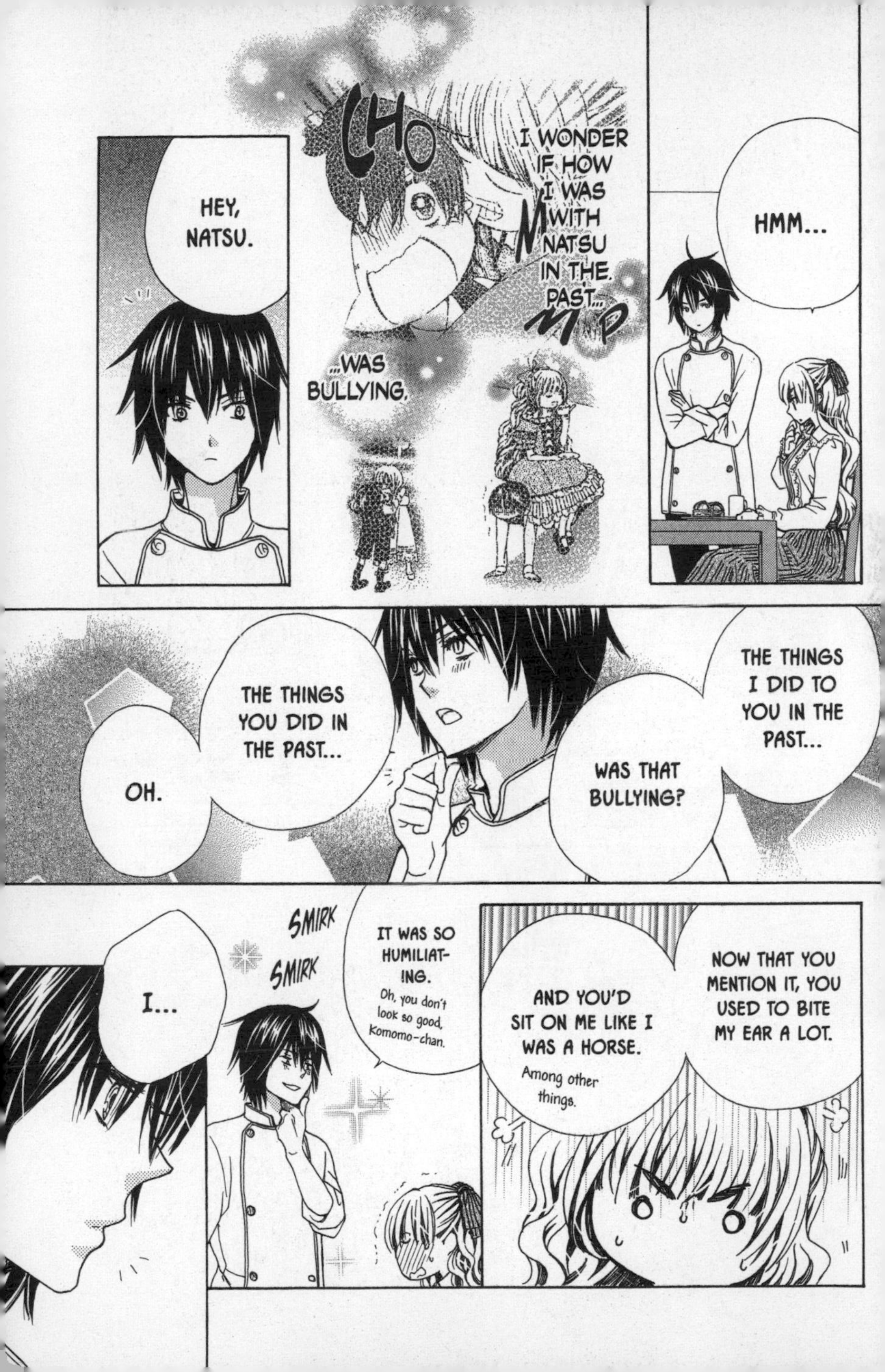
HMM...
I WONDER IF HOW I WAS WITH NATSU IN THE PAST...
CHO
M
M P
...WAS BULLYING.
HEY, NATSU.
THE THINGS I DID TO YOU IN THE PAST...
WAS THAT BULLYING?
THE THINGS YOU DID IN THE PAST...
OH.
NOW THAT YOU MENTION IT, YOU USED TO BITE MY EAR A LOT.
AND YOU'D SIT ON ME LIKE I WAS A HORSE.
Among other things.
IT WAS SO HUMILIAT-ING.
Oh, you don't look so good, Komomo-chan.
SMIRK
SMIRK
I...

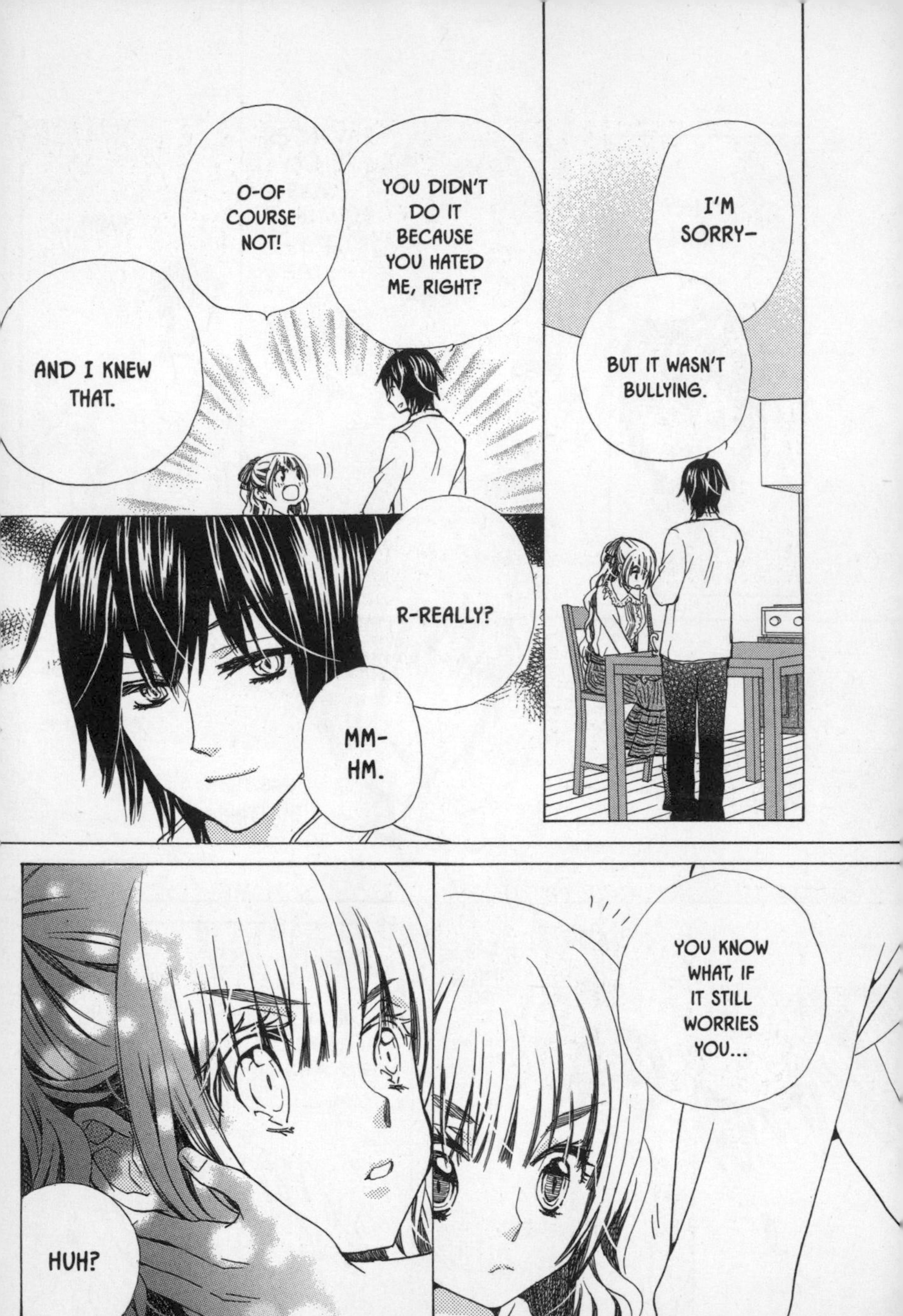
I'M SORRY—
BUT IT WASN'T BULLYING.
YOU DIDN'T DO IT BECAUSE YOU HATED ME, RIGHT?
O-OF COURSE NOT!
AND I KNEW THAT.
R-REALLY?
MM-HM.
YOU KNOW WHAT, IF IT STILL WORRIES YOU...
HUH?

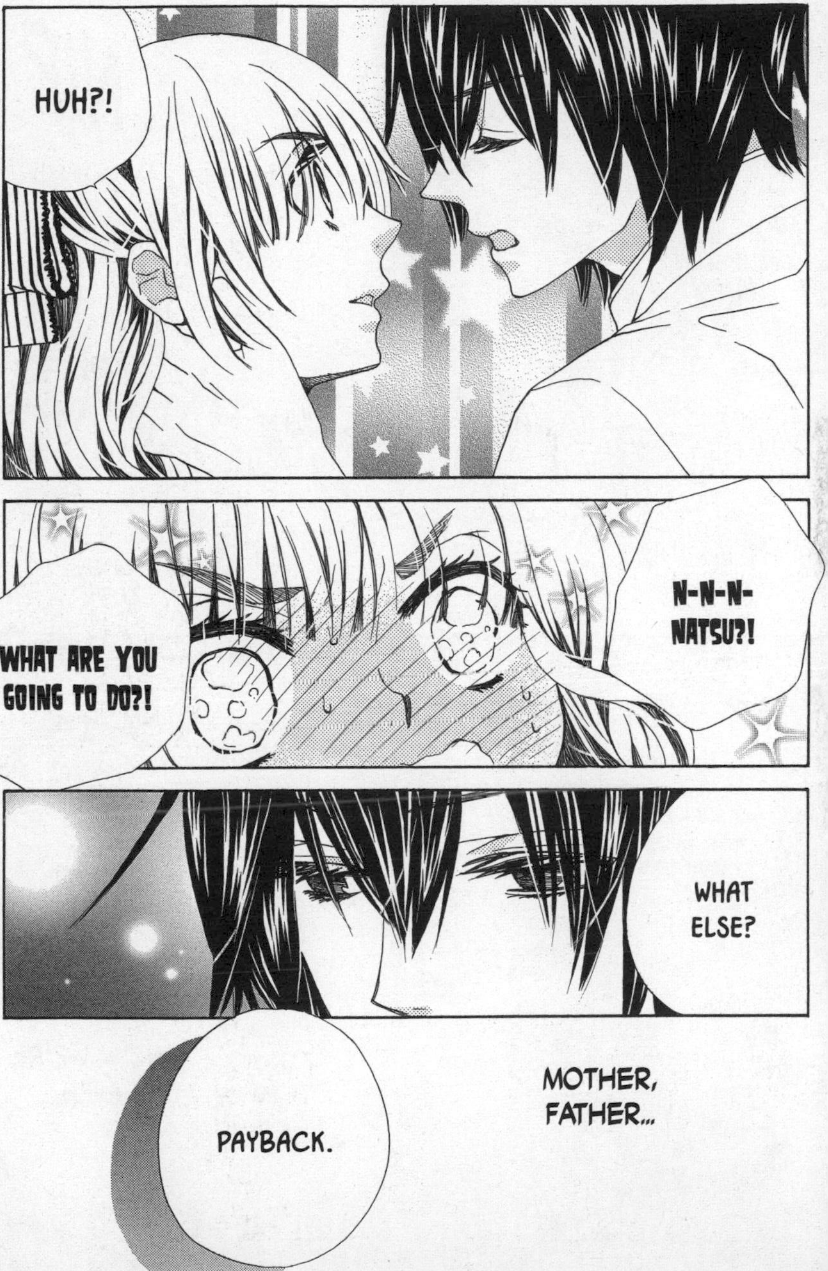
HUH?!
N-N-N-NATSU?!
WHAT ARE YOU GOING TO DO?!
WHAT ELSE?
MOTHER, FATHER...
PAYBACK.

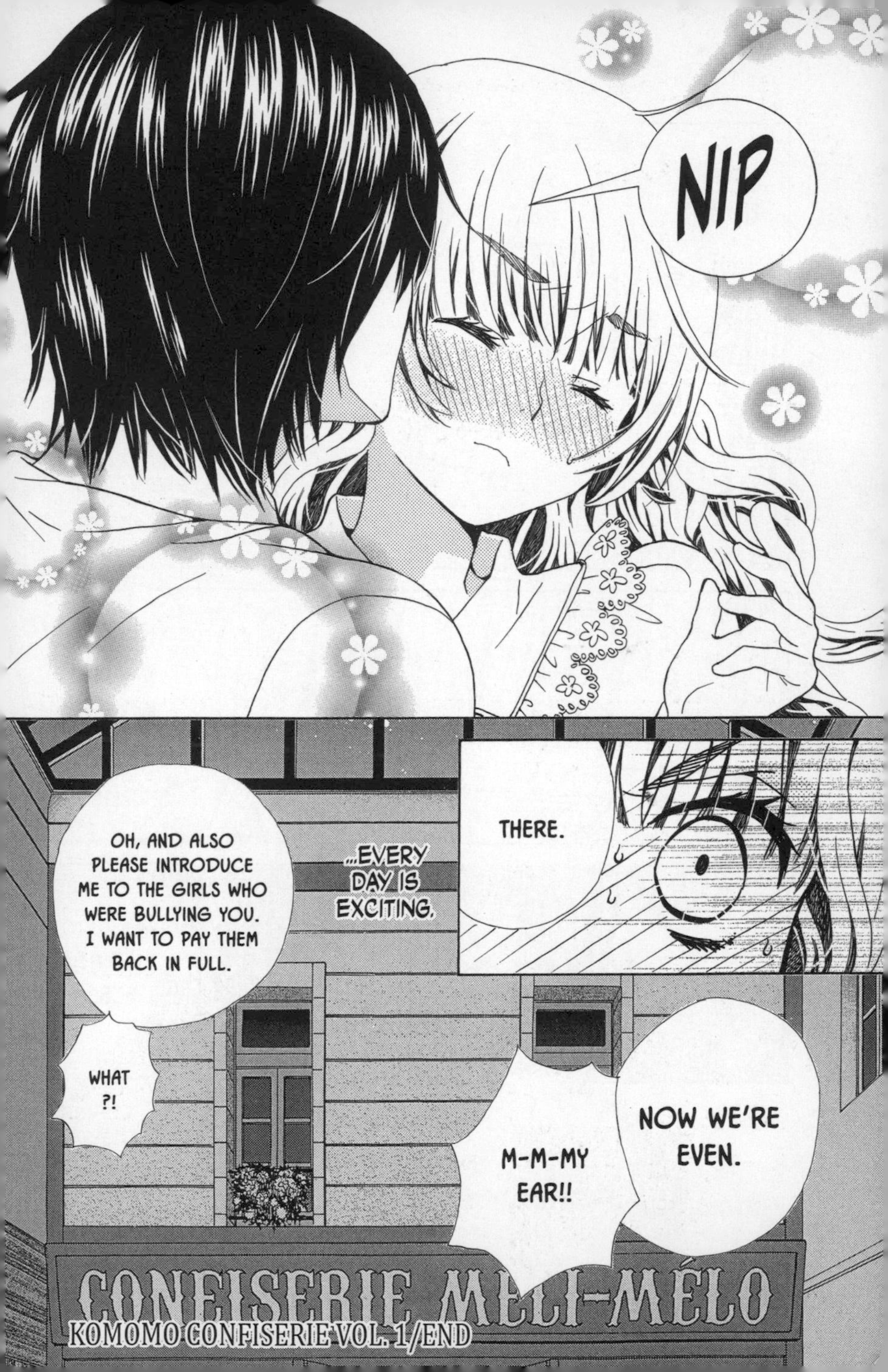
NIP
THERE.
...EVERY DAY IS EXCITING.
OH, AND ALSO PLEASE INTRODUCE ME TO THE GIRLS WHO WERE BULLYING YOU. I WANT TO PAY THEM BACK IN FULL.
NOW WE'RE EVEN.
M-M-MY EAR!!
WHAT ?!
CONFISERIE MÉLI-MÉLO
KOMOMO CONFISERIE VOL. 1/END

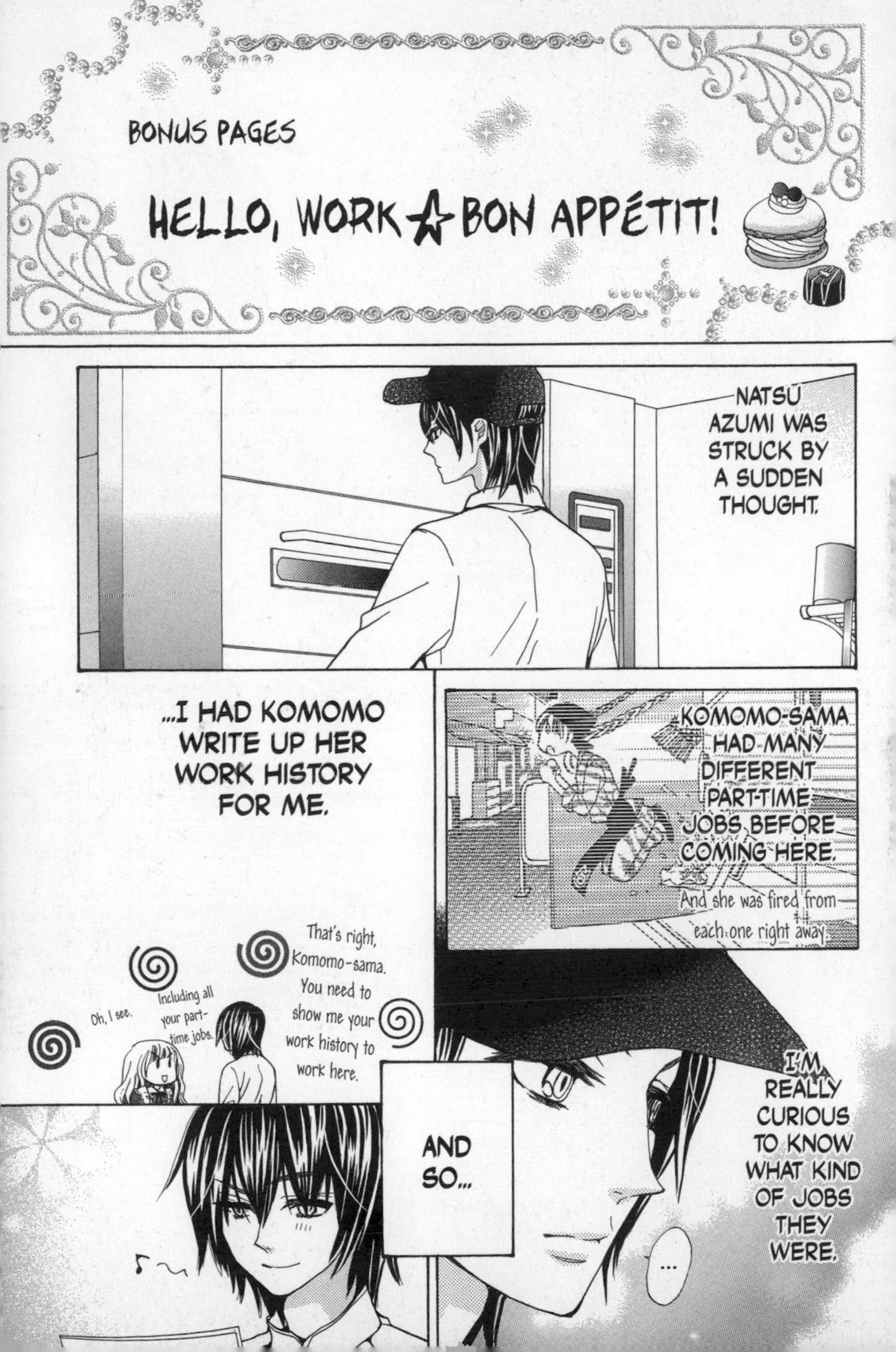
BONUS PAGES
HELLO, WORK ☆ BON APPÉTIT!
NATSU AZUMI WAS STRUCK BY A SUDDEN THOUGHT.
KOMOMO-SAMA HAD MANY DIFFERENT PART-TIME JOBS BEFORE COMING HERE.
And she was fired from each one right away.
I'M REALLY CURIOUS TO KNOW WHAT KIND OF JOBS THEY WERE.
...
AND SO...
...I HAD KOMOMO WRITE UP HER WORK HISTORY FOR ME.
That's right, Komomo-sama. You need to show me your work history to work here.
Including all your part-time jobs.
Oh, I see.

THIS IS KOMOMO-SAMA'S WORK HISTORY.

WORK HISTORY

APRIL 3, 20XX

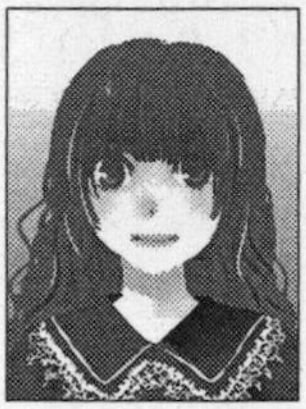

FIRST NAME: KOMOMO

LAST NAME: NINOMIYA

SEPTEMBER 9, 20XX (AGE 15)

GENDER FEMALE

CURRENT ADDRESS: MIKAMO PASSAGE D-7, 3-2-3 CENTRAL MIKAMO, MIKAMO CITY, OO PREFECTURE

PHONE NUMBER: (XAA) 076-0141

CELL PHONE: – –

FAX:

E-MAIL

BILLING ADDRESS

SEE ABOVE

PHONE: –

FAX:( ) –

YEAR	MONTH	EDUCATION/WORK
XX	MAR	GRADUATED FROM PRIVATE SCHOOL (HAKUSENKAN MIDDLE SCHOOL)
〃	MAR 16	MIKAMO BAKERY
〃	SAME DAY	SUPERMARKET, MIKAMO BRANCH
〃	SAME DAY	BICDONALD'S, ACROSS FROM MIKAMO STATION
〃	MAR 17	WHIPPED CREAM LIFE CREPE SHOP, MIKAMO ALTO BRANCH
〃	SAME DAY	MELON KINGDOM JUICE STAND, MIKAMO ALTO BRANCH
〃	MAR 18	CAFE ALPS SANGETSU
〃	MAR 19	KENTUCKY FRIED & ROASTED CHICKEN, MIKAMO STATION SOUTH EXIT
〃	SAME DAY	TACO SPAIN, MIKAMO MAIN STREET
〃	SAME DAY	REAL ESTATE AGENCY, MIKAMO STATION SOUTH EXIT
〃	MAR 20	KYUTARO-KUN TAKOYAKI, MIKAMO ALTO BRANCH
〃	MAR 21	JISABURO STAMINA, ON MIKAMO MAIN STREET
	SAME DAY	SWEET HOUSE FRESH BAKED BREAD SHOP
	MAR 22	FOUQUET PANCAKE HOUSE

〃 SAME DAY KYUSHU DEEP-FRY KYUSHU DANJI, MIKAMO STATION NORTH EXIT

〃 SAME DAY FRUIT PARLOR, MIKAMO ALTO BRANCH

〃 MAR 24TH MERCI RAMEN

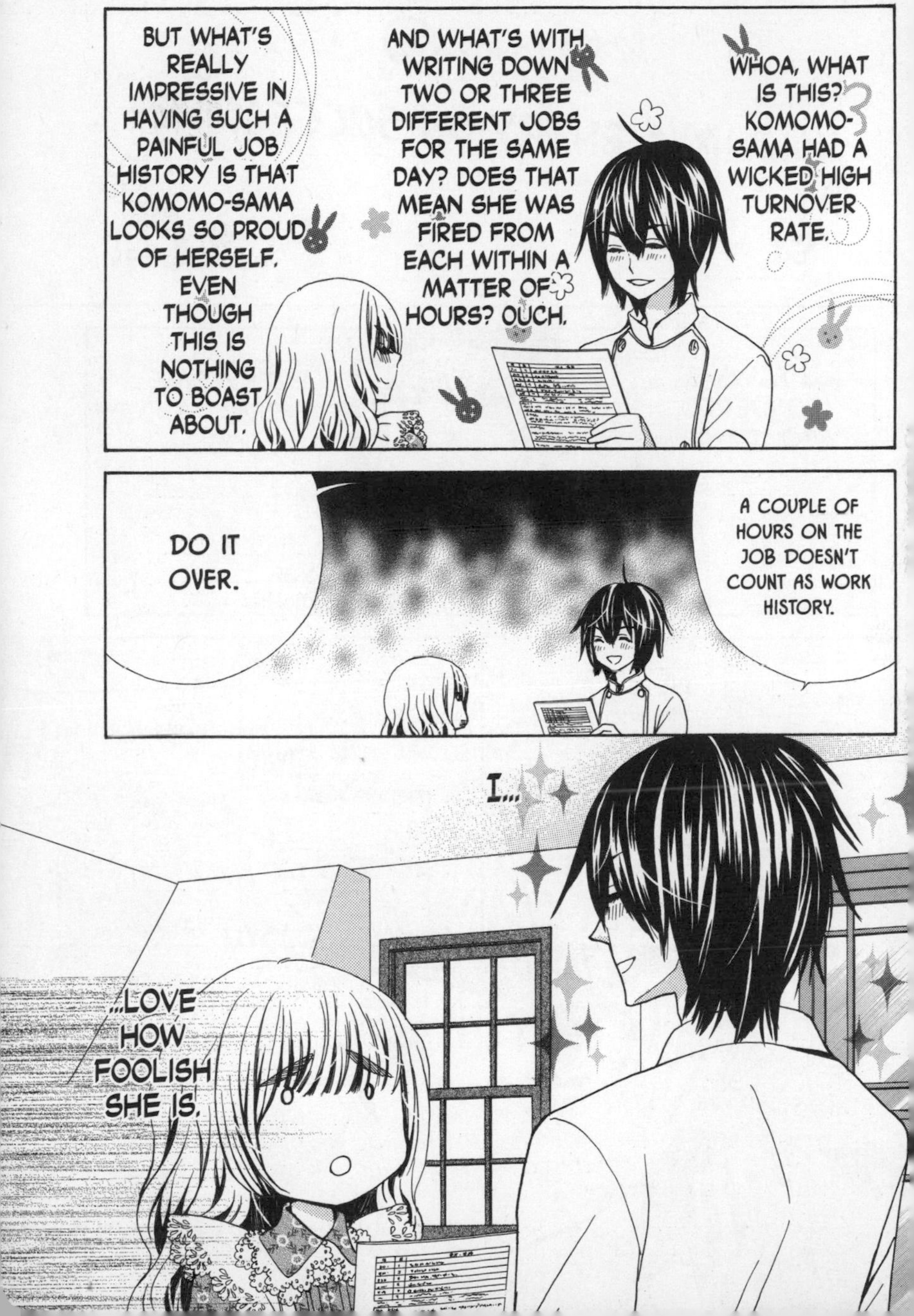
WHOA, WHAT IS THIS? KOMOMO-SAMA HAD A WICKED HIGH TURNOVER RATE.
AND WHAT'S WITH WRITING DOWN TWO OR THREE DIFFERENT JOBS FOR THE SAME DAY? DOES THAT MEAN SHE WAS FIRED FROM EACH WITHIN A MATTER OF HOURS? OUCH.
BUT WHAT'S REALLY IMPRESSIVE IN HAVING SUCH A PAINFUL JOB HISTORY IS THAT KOMOMO-SAMA LOOKS SO PROUD OF HERSELF. EVEN THOUGH THIS IS NOTHING TO BOAST ABOUT.
A COUPLE OF HOURS ON THE JOB DOESN'T COUNT AS WORK HISTORY.
DO IT OVER.
I...
...LOVE HOW FOOLISH SHE IS.

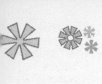

BONUS PAGES ②

KOMOMO'S ENTRY ON SUCCEEDING

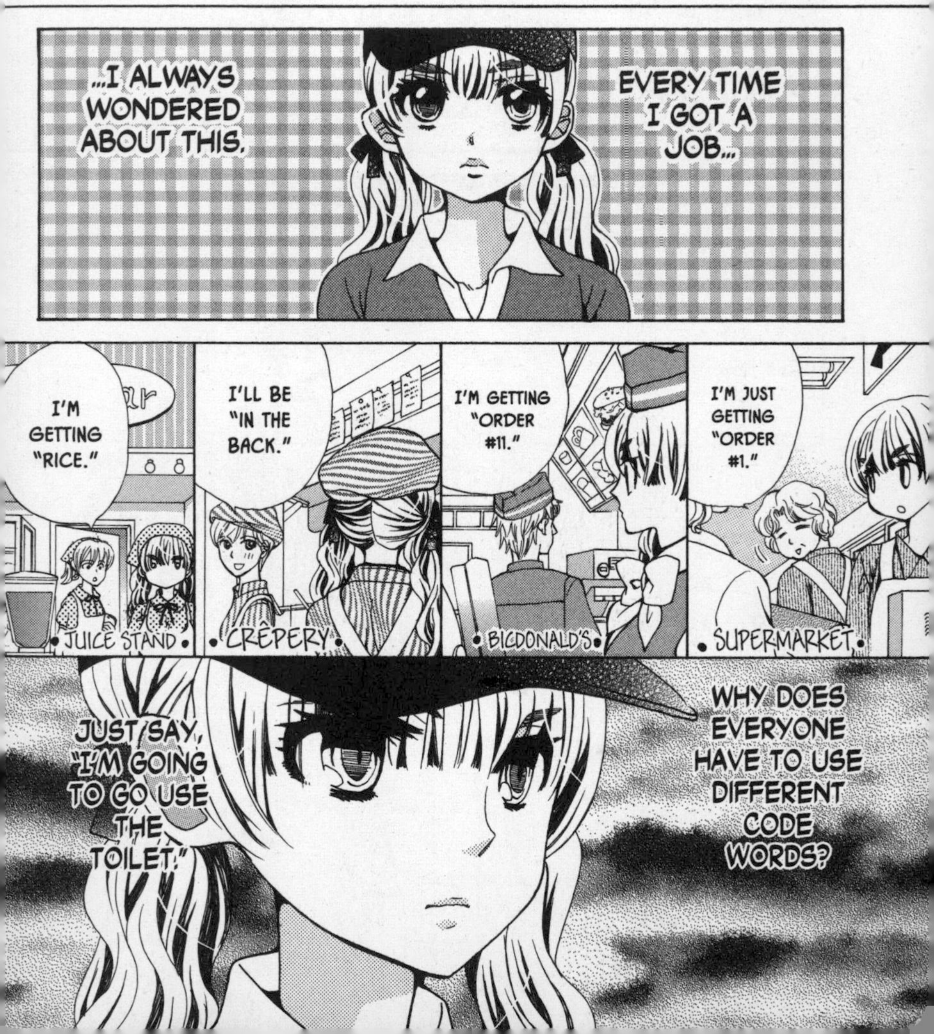
EVERY TIME I GOT A JOB...
...I ALWAYS WONDERED ABOUT THIS.
I'M JUST GETTING "ORDER #1."
SUPERMARKET
I'M GETTING "ORDER #11."
BIGDONALD'S
I'LL BE "IN THE BACK."
CRÊPERY
I'M GETTING "RICE."
JUICE STAND
WHY DOES EVERYONE HAVE TO USE DIFFERENT CODE WORDS?
JUST SAY, "I'M GOING TO GO USE THE TOILET."

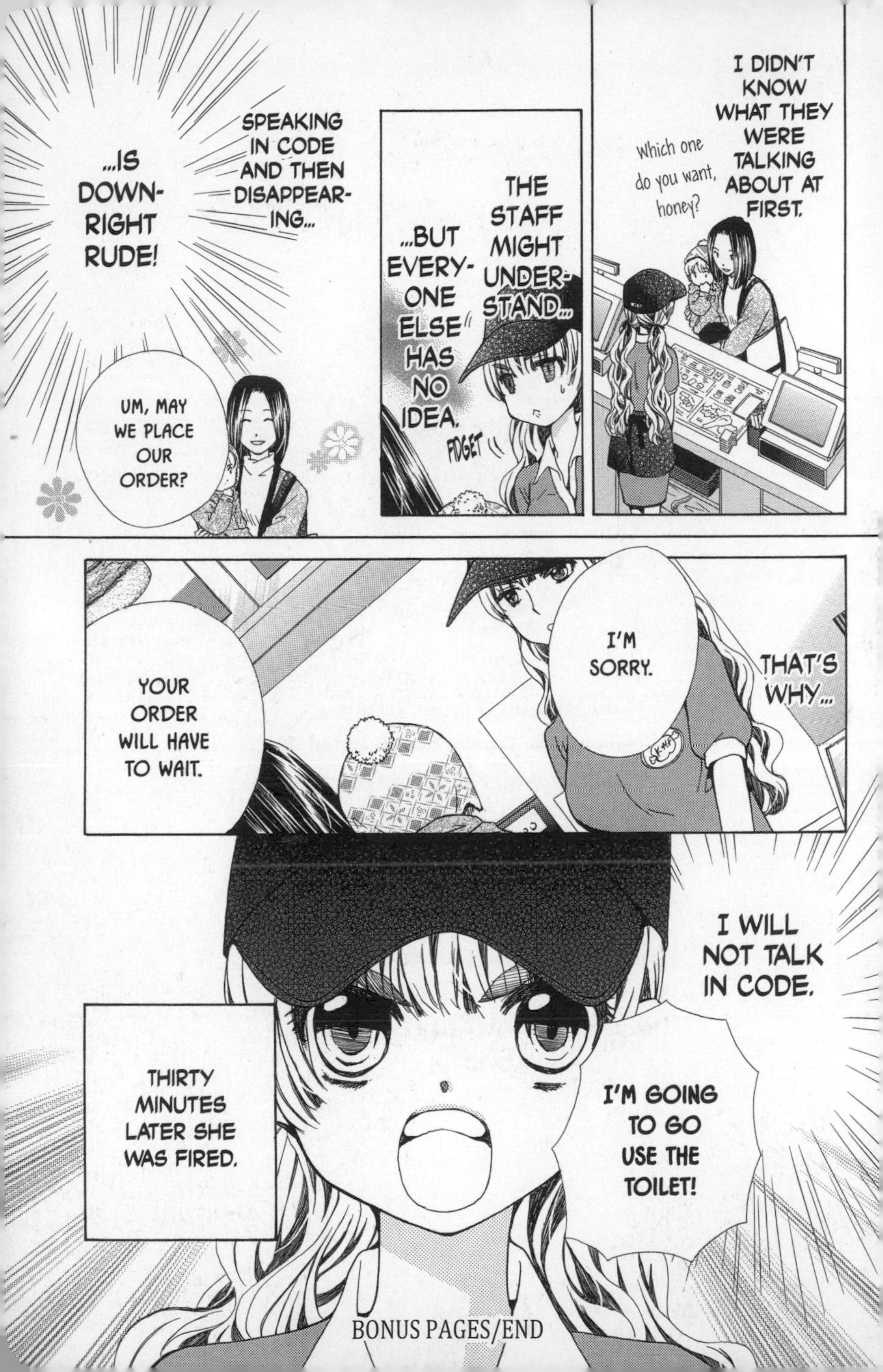

I DIDN'T KNOW WHAT THEY WERE TALKING ABOUT AT FIRST.
Which one do you want, honey?
THE STAFF MIGHT UNDER-STAND...
...BUT EVERY-ONE ELSE HAS NO IDEA.
FIDGET
SPEAKING IN CODE AND THEN DISAPPEAR-ING...
...IS DOWN-RIGHT RUDE!
UM, MAY WE PLACE OUR ORDER?
THAT'S WHY...
I'M SORRY.
YOUR ORDER WILL HAVE TO WAIT.
I WILL NOT TALK IN CODE.
I'M GOING TO GO USE THE TOILET!
THIRTY MINUTES LATER SHE WAS FIRED.
BONUS PAGES/END

MEAT

Maki Minami is from Saitama Prefecture in Japan. She debuted in 2001 with *Kanata no Ao* (Faraway Blue). Her other works include *Kimi wa Girlfriend* (You're My Girlfriend), *Mainichi ga Takaramono* (Every Day Is a Treasure) and *Yuki Atataka* (Warm Winter). *S•A* and *Voice Over!: Seiyu Academy* are published in English by VIZ Media.

Komomo Confiserie
Shojo Beat Edition
Volume 1

STORY AND ART BY
Maki Minami

Supervisor: Tsuji Shizuo Ryori Kyoiku Kenkyujo/Hiromi Kosaka
Special thanks to Tsujicho Group

Translation/Christine Dashiell
Touch-Up Art & Lettering/John Hunt
Design/Yukiko Whitley
Editor/Nancy Thistlethwaite

Komomo Confiserie by Maki Minami
© Maki Minami 2013
All rights reserved.
First published in Japan in 2013 by HAKUSENSHA, Inc., Tokyo.
English language translation rights arranged with HAKUSENSHA, Inc., Tokyo.

Printed in the U.S.A.

Published by VIZ Media, LLC
P.O. Box 77010
San Francisco, CA 94107

10 9 8 7 6 5 4 3 2 1
First printing, September 2015

www.viz.com   www.shojobeat.com

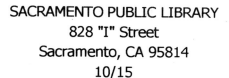
You may be reading the wrong way!

In keeping with the original Japanese comic format, this book reads from right to left, so action, sound effects and word balloons are reversed. This preserves the orientation of the original artwork. Check out the diagram below to get the order of things, and then turn to the other side of the book to get started!

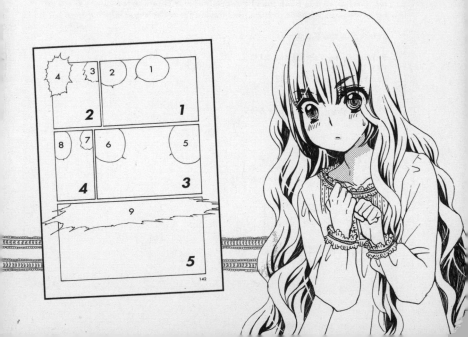